LEVEL 1/LEVEL 2

CREATIVE IMEDIA

J834

Judi Brown, Sarah McAtominey, Kevin Wells

The teaching content of this resource is endorsed by OCR for use with specification Level 1/Level 2 Cambridge National in Creative iMedia (J834).

All references to assessment, including assessment preparation and practice questions of any format/style are the publisher's interpretation of the specification and are not endorsed by OCR.

This resource was designed for use with the version of the specification available at the time of publication. However, as specifications are updated over time, there may be contradictions between the resource and the specification, therefore please use the information on the latest specification and Sample Assessment Materials at all times when ensuring students are fully prepared for their assessments.

Endorsement indicates that a resource is suitable to support delivery of an OCR specification, but it does not mean that the endorsed resource is the only suitable resource to support delivery, or that it is required or necessary to achieve the qualification.

OCR recommends that teachers consider using a range of teaching and learning resources based on their own professional judgement for their students' needs. OCR has not paid for the production of this resource, nor does OCR receive any royalties from its sale. For more information about the endorsement process, please visit the OCR website.

Although every effort has been made to ensure that website addresses are correct at time of going to press, Hodder Education cannot be held responsible for the content of any website mentioned in this book. It is sometimes possible to find a relocated web page by typing in the address of the home page for a website in the URL window of your browser.

Hachette UK's policy is to use papers that are natural, renewable and recyclable products and made from wood grown in well-managed forests and other controlled sources. The logging and manufacturing processes are expected to conform to the environmental regulations of the country of origin.

Orders: please contact Hachette UK Distribution, Hely Hutchinson Centre, Milton Road, Didcot, Oxfordshire, OX11 7HH. Telephone: +44 (0)1235 827827. Email education@hachette.co.uk Lines are open from 9 a.m. to 5 p.m., Monday to Friday. You can also order through our website: www.hoddereducation.co.uk

ISBN: 978 1 3983 5056 4

First published in 2022 by
Hodder Education,
An Hachette UK Company
Carmelite House
50 Victoria Embankment
London EC4Y 0DZ
www.hoddereducation.co.uk

Impression number 10 9 8 7 6 5 4 3 2

Year 2026 2025 2024 2023

Cover photo
Typeset in India
Printed and bound by CPI Group (UK) Ltd, Croydon, CR0 4YY
A catalogue record for this title is available from the British Library.

Contents

Introduction

This book will help you to develop the knowledge, understanding and practical skills you need to complete your Level 1/2 Cambridge National Creative iMedia course. As well as preparing you for your final exam and set assignments, the book will introduce you to the creative digital media sector. You will learn how to design, plan, create and review digital media products to meet client briefs and target audience demands.

Each of the chapters in this book closely follows all the topics required for each unit in the course specification, which you can find on the OCR website. To help with your learning the book covers the key content in detail and includes a range of real-world examples. There are also lots of activities and learning features; you can find out more about these and how to use them on the next page.

Note for teachers: You can find out more about how we have designed the textbook to support you at: www.hoddereducation.co.uk/creative-imedia-teacher-intro.

Mandatory and optional units

The Cambridge National in Creative iMedia qualification is made up of seven different subject units. All students will need to complete Units R093 (Creative iMedia in the media industry) and R094 (Visual identity and digital graphics); these are the mandatory/compulsory units.

In addition, you will complete one of the following optional units:

- R095 Characters and comics
- R096 Animation with audio
- R097 Interactive digital media
- R098 Visual imaging
- R099 Digital games.

Assessment: Examined unit and final set assignments

- Unit R093 is an examined unit where you will sit a one hour 30-minute examination paper, which is set and marked by OCR.
- Units R094 through to R099 are assessed through a series of tasks for a set assignment that you will be given. The assignments are set by OCR each academic year, marked by your tutor and then moderated by OCR.

All the examination questions contain 'command' words. These tell you what you have to do to answer a question or complete the task. You can find definitions of the most common command words on page 2; a full list is available on the OCR website. Always check the command word before starting a task or answering a question. For example, if you describe something when an explanation is required, you will not be able to gain full marks; this is because an explanation requires more detail than a description. There are a range of practice questions in this book in Unit R093 to help you get to grips with the command words.

Once you have learned all the required parts of the moderated units, you will complete an assignment that will be used to assess your knowledge and skills of the subject. It will be set in a vocational context, which means that it will simulate what it would be like to be given a project by a client or employer in a work situation. You will use the OCR set assignment for the assessment. This assignment will include a series of tasks that follows the same process and sequence of the unit, to plan, create and review a creative media product. The assignment practice features in this book in Units R094–R099 will help you get used to working in the relevant media contexts.

Note: The practice questions and accompanying marks and mark schemes included in this resource are an opportunity to practise exam skills, but they do not replicate examination papers and are not endorsed by OCR.

Plagiarism and referencing

Your work for the OCR set assignments in Units R094–R099 must be in your own words. You must not plagiarise. Plagiarism is the submission of another's work as one's own and/or failure to acknowledge the source correctly. Sometimes you might need to use a diagram or include a quotation from someone else or a website. If you do this it is very important that you always provide a reference for any information you use that is not your own work. Quotation marks should be placed around any quoted text. You should put the source reference next to the information used. In addition to referencing the picture, diagram, table or quotation, you should explain in your own words why you have used it, what it tells you, how it relates to your work or summarise what it means.

Providing a reference means that you will include details of the source, which is where you found the information. You should include the full website address (url) and date that you found it or for a textbook, the page number, title, author's name, date it was published and the name of the publisher. For newspaper or magazine articles you should give the date of publication, title of the paper or magazine and the name of the author. When producing your work for the assessment, you should never use any templates or writing frames. You must always decide yourself how to present your information.

How to use this book

This book covers all units for the Cambridge National in Creative iMedia, including the two mandatory units, R093 and R094 as well as the five optional units R095–R099. All of the teaching content for each topic area is covered in the book.

The book is organised into chapters as per the units in the qualification. Each unit is broken down into the topic areas from the specification. Each unit opener will help you to understand what is covered in the unit, the list of topic areas covered, and how you will be assessed, fully matched to the requirements of the specification.

Key features of the book

About this unit
A short introduction to the unit.

Topic areas
A list of the unit's topic areas, so you know exactly what is going to be covered.

Resources for this unit
An overview of the resources, including software and hardware, needed for the unit.

How will I be assessed?
A summary of how the unit will be assessed.

Getting started
Short activities to introduce you to the topic.

Key terms
Definitions of important and useful terms across the qualification.

Case study
A real-life scenario that involves the creative and digital media concepts covered in the unit.

Activity
A short task to help you understand an idea or assessment criteria. These can include group and research tasks.

Test your knowledge
Short questions designed to test your knowledge and understanding.

Synoptic links
Links to other sections of the book so you can see how topics link together.

Practice questions
Summary questions that allow you to apply the knowledge and skills covered in the unit. This feature appears in examined Unit R093 and will help you prepare for the exam. The accompanying mark schemes are available online at www.hoddereducation.co.uk/cambridge-nationals-2022/answers.

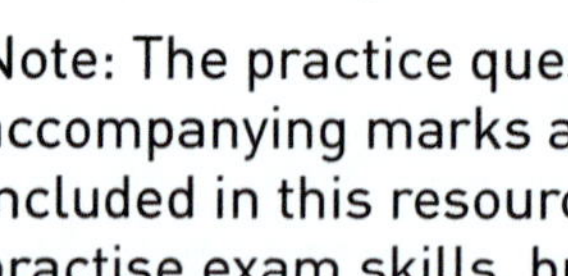

Note: The practice questions and accompanying marks and mark schemes included in this resource are an opportunity to practise exam skills, but they do not replicate examination papers and are not endorsed by OCR.

Assignment practice
A summary activity that will allow you to apply the knowledge and skills covered in this unit. This feature appears in the optional non-examined units and will help you prepare for non-examined assessment.

Unit R093

Creative iMedia in the media industry

About this unit

This unit is a foundation in what makes up the media industry and how Creative iMedia fits into it. You will learn about the job roles and processes required to create a wide range of media products. As part of this, you will find out how to convey meaning, create impact and engage audiences through the use of media codes when planning a product. You will move on to pre-production techniques, media formats and distribution platforms to further develop your knowledge of the media industry.

Topic areas

In this chapter you will learn about:

- the media industry (TA1)
- factors influencing product design (TA2)
- pre-production planning (TA3)
- distribution considerations (TA4).

Resources for this unit

With this being the examined unit, you will not be using computers and software applications in the final assessment, which is a written exam paper. However, you may use a range of these in your learning about the media industry and pre-production techniques prior to taking the exam, which may help you in your answers to the questions.

How will I be assessed?

You will be assessed through a 1 hour 30-minute written exam, which is set and marked by OCR. It will be marked out of 70 and worth 40 per cent of the total when working towards a Certificate in Creative iMedia. There will typically be two sections:

- Section A will have multiple-choice questions and other questions needing a short written response.
- Section B will have a scenario with questions based on it. This will provide a context for the paper and your answers should always relate closely to this. Within this section there will be some longer (extended response) questions.

Exam command words

Many exam questions will use straightforward command words such as choose, label, circle, draw and annotate. The following table shows what some commonly used ones mean.

Table 1.1 Command words

Command word in the question	What it means you should do
Identify	Your answer might select the relevant part or state what it is.
Explain	Your answer must include reasons why, so aim to include the word 'because ...'.
Describe	Your answer must be detailed, using words to express an overall concept, idea or need so that it is clear for the reader/listener.
Discuss	Your answer must give both sides of the argument with some analysis and evaluation.
Outline	Your answer should state the key points with a brief description.

Another word you will see used is 'Purpose'. This may be part of a question. This means what the subject of the question is used for or the reason for its use.

Topic area 1 The media industry

Getting started

In small groups, discuss what media products you see or use as part of everyday life. You can include school, home, hobbies and interests. What do you actively do (for example, read or watch on TV, computer or smartphone) in addition to what is around you (for example, billboards, posters and advertisements)?

1.1 Media industry sectors and products

Sectors of the media industry

This is separated into two different areas. Firstly, there are traditional media sectors that have adapted to use digital technologies and processes. Secondly, there is the evolving area of 'new media' that is only produced in a digital format.

Figure 1.1 Different parts of the media industry

Traditional media

This includes:

- film
- television (TV)
- radio
- print publishing.

Film and television are closely related but they are different sectors of the media industry. You might watch a TV for both films and regular television broadcasting but the production process and hence media sectors are different.

Film making

Films tend to be large media projects that can take months or years to produce. They involve large teams of people and high budgets since they can be very expensive to make.

The film industry is evolving in many ways, both for production, post-production and distribution

> **Key terms**
>
> **CGI** Computer generated imagery.
>
> **SFX** Special effects or sound effects.
>
> **VFX** Visual effects.
>
> **4K/8K** Very high-resolution video formats.
>
> **3D** three-dimensional video (most films are made in 2D).

through the use of **CGI**, **SFX**, **VFX**, **4K**, **8K**, **3D**, surround sound, plus the use of premium streaming services for new releases.

Television (TV)

This covers a wide range of content such as:

- soaps
- TV series
- chat shows
- game shows
- reality TV shows
- cartoons
- outside broadcasts (OB) to include events coverage, sports (for example, football matches) and news location reporting
- documentaries
- news and weather.

The production of these is much shorter and quicker than film making. This might be an episode per week for a TV series or daily broadcasting for news programmes. Reality shows can include live streaming, which adds another challenge to the production.

The television sector is evolving through on-demand, streaming and catch-up services. These services are available using Apps on smart devices or set-top boxes/plug in accessories for use with a regular TV.

Content is also evolving with service providers, such as BBC, ITV, Channel 4, Netflix®, Amazon Prime®, Disney+® and Apple TV®, all producing their own exclusive content and TV series (note that these have the ® symbol to show it is a registered trademark – more on that later). It is likely that many of the technologies used in film making will also appear in the television industry.

Radio

The traditional format for radio broadcasting is on AM or FM frequencies, although this has now become multi-platform distribution through digital technologies. Basic radio programming is typically created in a similar way to traditional broadcast radio, but can now be distributed over the internet, through DAB and catch-up services using smartphones and tablets.

Radio stations still work to schedules and broadcast clocks (which is a term used to define the content and sequence of a programme). Some examples of content for a radio programme or broadcast would be:

- news
- weather
- adverts
- traffic
- talk/music show
- radio play
- sport
- phone-ins.

Radio is evolving through multi-platform distribution methods and on-demand, catch-up services. These services are available using apps on smart devices or through a website. An internet radio is a device that can be connected to a home Wi-Fi network and used to stream high-quality audio via the internet.

Print publishing

This includes:

- newspapers
- magazines
- leaflets
- posters
- brochures
- comics and graphic novels.

Print publishing has evolved through the use of digital technology and printing processes. This includes better printing inks and printer technology (colour laser and ink based), together with production using computer equipment and desktop publishing software.

Figure 1.2 Radio recording and broadcast facilities

Note that print publishing is declining in some areas with more content being made available in a digital format, saving resources and the environment. Newspapers and magazines are examples where the trend is more noticeable. Comics and graphic novels are another product that were traditionally print based but are now frequently published in both digital and print based formats.

Activity

Obtain a newspaper and a magazine. Make a list of the different content that is found in each one. Identify the range of text, images, articles and advertisements. As a class discussion, talk about how some of these may have been created. Would it make any difference if the content was to be distributed in a digital rather than printed format?

New media

This includes any form of digital media. A common distribution method is now the internet. New media sectors include:

- computer games
- **interactive** media
- internet
- digital publishing.

Key term

Interactive Something which allows the user to be involved in the process of watching or listening. This could involve user input such as clicking, typing or speaking to interact with the media.

Computer games

The computer games sector covers both the development of the games and the development of the platform (the hardware) they sit on. These are typically different industries. For example, a digital games developer may not build and sell a dedicated gaming computer for the game to be played on. Some games are online only.

Popular platforms include:

- consoles
- computers
- smartphones
- tablets
- hand-held gaming devices.

Games are categorised by their genre. Some of the main examples would be:

- FPS (first person shooter)
- RPG (role-player games)
- racing
- action/adventure
- quiz.

Computer games are evolving in several ways, through the use of:

- higher **resolution** graphics
- realistic video motion
- online/multiplayer games
- VR (virtual reality).

Interactive media

Any form of media that enables the user to interact with it is part of this sector and includes a broad range of products. For example:

- websites
- information kiosks, for example, for local maps, shopping malls, train timetables, ordering systems in shops
- apps (for use on smartphones and tablets)
- interactive multimedia (used on computer systems, for example, interactive presentations)
- Blu-ray/DVD feature selection menus
- learning resources
- quizzes.

Interactive media is evolving through web technologies, software availability, smart device capabilities and cross **platform** support. A computer game is another form of interactive media but is classified as a different sector.

Internet

As a sector, this covers internet-based media. The internet is a worldwide network or wide area network (WAN). It connects millions of web servers together to make up the World Wide Web. The websites and content that are hosted on the internet becomes the Internet Industry, which is very broad in scope.

Examples of the content found on the internet include:

- websites (for example, to sell products, services, provide information, news, entertainment)
- social media (for example, Facebook, Twitter, Instagram, YouTube) and the work of influencers
- streaming services (for example, for on-demand services such as films, TV series, radio, **podcasts**)
- communication (such as email, VoIP for voice calls, online meetings (for example, Zoom, Microsoft Teams), messaging services (for example, iMessage, Signal, WhatsApp).

Key terms

Resolution A property of an image that states how many dots per inch are present. (Different to the resolution of a story.)

Platform A method for sharing media content.

Podcast A digital audio file made available online. Often created as a series and involving spoken dialogue, interviews and conversation.

The internet is evolving through the range of content and services together with the connection speeds through wired, Wi-Fi and mobile connections.

Digital publishing

This is where the product is only available in a digital format and not physically printed or distributed. As an example, a comic could be published as a PDF file or provided via an app, rather than be physically printed. The distribution of digital formats is typically by the internet, whether by download or through streaming services. The **interface** could be either a website or an app on a smartphone or tablet. Some apps can now work on a computer as well as a smartphone.

Examples of media found in the digital publishing sector include:

- web graphics (for example, buttons, banners and backgrounds)
- animations (for example, animated/moving advertisements, banners or short films as entertainment products)
- eBooks
- podcasts
- video podcasts
- slide shows of images
- tutorials (video)
- blogs and vlogs
- comics and graphic novels
- computer games.

Digital publishing is evolving through a wider range of image, text, audio and video products. This is made possible by wider availability of simple and cheap equipment used to produce content, which is available to home users. Apps are readily available for distribution purposes for both Apple and Android devices. More efficient compression techniques enable a high quality but with a lower file size.

Key term

Interface The system that allows the user to interact with the product.

Activity

What forms of digital publishing content do you enjoy the most? Make a list of the type of content and where you access it. What is it that makes it enjoyable?

Test your knowledge

1 What is the difference between digital publishing and the internet?
2 A film would be produced by the film making sector but what sectors might be involved in the distribution for people to watch it?
3 For the film, what other sectors could be involved for its promotion and advertising?

Synoptic links

Creative iMedia has strong links to the digital publishing sector within the media industry. Further information on products and sectors is in the NEA units as follows:

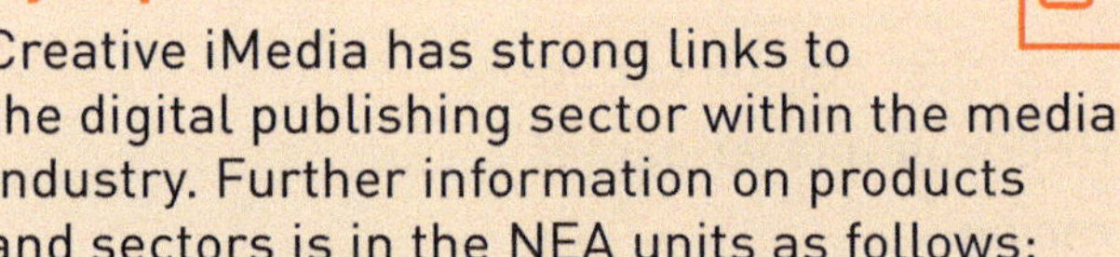

- R094 (mandatory): digital and web graphics, print publishing, digital publishing
- R095 (optional): comics, print publishing, digital publishing
- R096 (optional): animation and audio, digital publishing
- R097 (optional): interactive media, digital publishing, interactive digital media
- R098 (optional): visual imaging, digital publishing, print publishing,
- R099 (optional): digital games, computer games, digital publishing.

Products in the media industry

Both the traditional and new media sectors have a range of typical products. However, that does not mean a specific product is limited to one sector – it could also be used as part of other sectors. Although not a complete list, in Table 1.2 are some examples.

Table 1.2 Products in the primary and secondary sectors

Product	Primary sectors	Secondary sectors
Video	Film, TV	Interactive media, internet/social media
Audio	Radio	Internet/podcasts, digital publishing
Music	Radio	Digital publishing
Animation	Digital publishing	Film
Special effects (SFX, VFX)	Film, TV	Computer games
Digital imaging and graphics	Print publishing, digital publishing	Internet (websites)
Social media platforms/ apps	Internet	
Digital games	Computer games	Internet (online gaming), digital publishing
Comics and graphic novels	Print publishing	Digital publishing
Websites	Interactive media, internet	
Multimedia	interactive media, internet	Digital publishing, computer games
eBooks	Digital publishing	Internet
AR/VR	Interactive media	Computer games

1.2 Job roles in the media industry

As you have learned, the media industry includes many sectors and a wide range of product types and media. The many different job roles within the industry can be categorised in a number of ways, including by:

- sector: for example, job roles in television or digital games creation
- medium or platform: for example, jobs in creating online content or print publishing
- production phase: for example, jobs which are carried out in only the pre-production or post-production phase
- skill type: for example, jobs which are creative and ideas-based or technical and practical
- seniority: for example, junior, mid-weight or senior job roles.

Some people work alone as freelance or independent creatives, meaning they may carry out several job roles at once. They may have to liaise with clients, design, create and review products and control budgets and oversee project time management. Others work as members of a larger team for design studios or companies and have a particular role often with a narrow specialism. The larger the project and production, the more likely that it will involve many people. Each job role within the production is important in its own right, and has its own distinctive responsibilities.

Senior roles

Design studios and companies have a hierarchy of job roles based on experience and expertise. Senior roles involve overseeing projects, taking overall responsibility for style and design decisions and managing teams of people to ensure work is completed on time and within budget. Many senior roles also include liaising with clients to agree a design brief and check that designs meet the client requirements and expectations.

Campaign manager

A campaign manager controls the overall direction of projects in the advertising sector. They will often have marketing experience and will oversee the choice of **assets** during the pre-production phase of advertising campaigns. During production and post-production, the campaign manager will check that the campaign matches the overall style and direction agreed with the client.

Creative director

Creative directors work across a number of sectors and media including motion, video and animation and 2D and 3D design. They are responsible for interpreting the client brief and

Key term

Assets The different images collected that will be used to make the final product.

developing the overall design response and **concept** for a product in the pre-production phase. Creative directors work closely with other team members such as art directors, animators or developers to oversee the production phase. They also ensure the final product meets the client requirements by overseeing the post-production phase. In larger design studios, the creative director may have one or more creative leads. This role is one step lower in the line of seniority and may undertake management of single projects, while the creative director will oversee a number of projects at the same time.

Director

A director leads the creative and technical teams for products such as video, television, animation and live theatre during the production phase. The director may provide creative input to explain how a script or storyboard will be translated into action by suggesting how **dialogue** should be delivered. Technical input is also involved, as the director decides which shot types, camera angles and lighting work best. The director may also contribute to the post-production phase by taking part in the editing process for a product.

Editor

An editor takes completed aspects of a product and compiles them into a 'rough cut', removing unwanted and less successful elements, before generating a final product. Individual elements may be edited separately, for example by video editors, copy editors and sound editors, before the editor receives a rough working version. Some editor roles, for example a web content editor, require expertise in a range of media types including sound, video, images and text.

Production manager

Production managers are often employed in the TV and film sectors. They oversee the business, budgeting and recruitment aspects of television and film during all phases of a production. The role includes monitoring the workplan or production schedule and liaising with producers to check that a project will meet its deadlines and keep within the agreed budget. Production managers are often involved in employing technical crew, organising locations, equipment and resources and arranging permissions and risk assessments. They need to be well organised and able to manage teams of people effectively.

- In larger design studios, leads are also employed as one step below the senior roles. Creative leads, lead animators, design leads and so on will generally take charge of one project at a time and report to the senior role as a sort of deputy.
- Mid-weight job roles fill the gap between junior and senior roles. They generally earn more than juniors and may have some individual areas of responsibility.
- Junior designers, artists, animators and developers will typically carry out basic, small assignments such as preparing assets and writing code to generate items designed by more senior staff.

Creative and technical roles

Some job roles within the media industry are more creative and ideas-based than others which involve practical or technical skills. This is an advantage because it allows people to work to their strengths. For example, some people excel at thinking up wonderful ideas for new digital games or stories which can be turned into film, comics or animation; but they lack the technical skills to produce them. Others love to write code for applications, work in 3D character modelling or use technical and practical skills to bring ideas to reality but prefer to work from designs which are provided for them. Some of the most common creative and technical roles are described in Tables 1.3 and 1.4.

Key terms

Concept An idea for something which has not yet been created.

Dialogue The words spoken by a character, narrator or voiceover artist.

Table 1.3 Creative roles in the media industry

Creative role	Main type/s of products created	Main responsibilities	Main production phase/s
Animator	Animation, film, TV, web, games	Generate moving images based on script/storyboard	Production
Content creator	Websites, applications, podcasts, blogs/vlogs, social media, print-based publishing	Generate posts for online platforms including text, video, static images to promote a brand, company or individual	Production
Copy writer	Print-based publishing, journalism, websites, applications, podcasts, blogs/vlogs, social media posts, advertising campaigns	Write text-based content based on a brief or rough plan to convey a message clearly	Production
Graphic designer	Digital and print graphics, visual branding, adverts, brochures, magazines, product packaging, web pages, comics	Plan and design graphics, create graphics, review graphics with client	Pre-production Production Post-production
Illustrator/ graphic artist	Digital and print graphics, artwork and diagrams for comics, books, product packaging, greetings cards	Generate original artwork by drawing or painting, either by hand or digitally	Production Post-production
Photographer	Photographs, static images digital or print	Capture photographs based on a client's requirements to convey a theme	Production Post-production
Script writer	Plays, TV and radio programmes, podcasts, films, adverts, instructional videos	Write scripts for scenes including action, narration and dialogue	Pre-production
Web designer	Websites, applications, interactive digital products	Design the style, appearance, content, layout and functionality of new websites, redevelop existing websites	Pre-production Post-production

Table 1.4 Technical roles in the media industry

Technical role	Main type/s of products created	Main responsibilities	Main production phase/s
Camera operator	Video, film, TV	Select and operate cameras and equipment to ensure shots and scenes are in focus and captured according to the director's plan, storyboard or script	Production
Games programmer/ games developer	Digital games	Generate computer gameplay and interactions according to a **Game Design Document** (GDD), flowchart or storyboard. Test functionality during and/or after production	Production Post-production
Sound editor	Audio for radio, TV, film, animation, websites, podcasts, interactive digital media	Operate editing software and equipment to trim, cut and edit captured sounds together with **non-diegetic** sound to generate a final audio product according to a script, graphic score or storyboard	Production Post-production
Audio technician	Audio for radio, TV, film, animation, websites, podcasts, interactive digital media	Select and operate recording equipment to ensure speech, **ambient** (**diegetic**) sound, **foley** and non-diegetic sound are captured at a suitable **volume** and clarity for use by the editor according to a script or storyboard	Production
Video editor	Video for TV, film, games, websites, podcasts, interactive digital media	Operate editing software and equipment to trim, cut and edit video footage together with 'B roll' or stock footage to generate a final video product according to a script or storyboard or under the director's supervision	Production Post-production
Web developer	Web pages and websites, applications, interactive digital media products	Use programming and coding languages, software and Content Management Systems to create, test, upload and maintain web pages, websites and web applications based on a web designer's site map, wire frame or UI design	Production Post-production

Key terms

Game Design Document (GDD) A pre-production planning resource outlining all the details of the proposed game.

Non-diegetic Sound that is outside the action captured on film and not heard by characters in a scene. For example, background music, narration and voiceover.

Ambient (diegetic) Sounds which are part of the action and can be heard by the characters in a scene. For example, dialogue and ambient noise.

Foley Named after sound-effects artist Jack Foley. The process of recording everyday sound effects to enhance audio quality and support visual actions.

Volume The output level or loudness of a sound.

Activity

Research job roles by searching creative and media job profiles on

https://nationalcareers.service.gov.uk/

Choose one senior, creative or technical role from the list and make a note of the skills required, the main activities involved and the pay rates.

What qualifications, training or experience are required?

Practice questions

1 An education book publisher is aiming to create additional digital resources for use online. What two sectors would these resources be part of? [2]

2 Complete the following sentence:
A multiplayer online computer game would be a sector of ________ media. [1]

3 Identify three sectors where video could be used:
Film   Interactive media   Print publishing   Radio   Retail   Television [3]

4 A pop music radio station has evolved to use digital technologies.
  a Other than an AM/FM broadcast radio receiver, state two alternative platforms that could be used by an audience to listen to the pop music radio station. [2]
  b Explain one benefit of an alternative platform. [2]

5 A film is being planned and a workplan has been created. State one senior job role which would include using the workplan. [1]

6 State one difference between the roles and responsibilities of a web designer and a web developer. [1]

Topic area 2 Factors influencing product design

Getting started

Think about the different types of media you have seen this week (for example, video, photo animation, posters). Make a note of each item you think of and try to write down the purpose for that media item. For example: 'I saw a billboard for a car brand – the purpose of this was to advertise a new car from this brand.'

2.1 How style, content and layout are linked to the purpose

Purpose

When creating media products there will always be a purpose to the product and this purpose will have a significant impact on all aspects of the design of the product. That is why it is so important to understand the main purpose of a product.

Advertise or promote

This is a large part of the media industry and can use many of the different types of media you looked at in Section 1.1. Advertising is a method of promotion that is used to sell a product or service to viewers, readers or listeners. Advertising banners on websites are one example of using media to advertise.

Educate

Media is used in education all the time to teach skills or provide new knowledge. For example, an animation could be used to demonstrate how to carry out a task or a podcast of a talk with an author could provide knowledge about a book.

Entertain

You are all likely to be familiar with media which is used as a form of entertainment as there are many different types. Examples of media to entertain include comics, films or podcasts.

Inform

This is similar to educate but media which informs can also be used to give instructions or information too. Examples of media which inform are instruction signage or maps.

Influence

It is now common to see media used to influence people, for example, encouraging people to follow a certain movement or point of view. Examples of media to influence could be campaign posters or videos of interviews which could be shared online or on the television.

Activity

Search the internet for three different media items, such as a video or poster. For each one state its purpose and explain your reasoning.

Figure 1.3 Examples of a graphic used to inform and a graphic used to advertise

Table 1.5 How style, content and layout can be influenced by purpose

Influence	Examples
Colour: The purpose of the media will influence the choice of colour that you will use in your media product	• Advertise – using bold colours and text to ensure the message is clear • Inform – for official information media often formal fonts and a simpler, muted colour scheme are used
Conventions of genre: The purpose of the product will indicate the genre and this in turn will influence the design of the product	• Educate – an academic genre will use a more formal and simpler layout and formal language • Entertain – the genre of entertainment media will influence the design of a product, e.g. a horror film poster will have text styles and colour schemes to reflect this genre
Tone: Formal/informal language – purpose influences the tone of language used in the media and whether more formal or informal language is used	• Entertain – when using media to entertain it is likely that the tone will be informal and relaxed as this information is being engaged with at the user's choice. For example, it is unlikely that an important safety announcement would use informal language • Educate – language is likely to be more formal in this use, as information is being presented as factually accurate and important. The age of the audience being educated will also influence this tone
Positioning of elements: Purpose influences the positioning of different elements within the product	• Advertising – in advertisements, the product will be placed in a prominent, often central place or towards the beginning of the video, to ensure the focus is on the correct element. Other elements are not relevant and positioned in less prominent positions • Inform – in media designed to inform, information will be the prominent feature of the product
Style of audio representation: When presenting media using audio, the style of the product will change based on the purpose	• Inform/educate – audio used to educate or inform is likely to have the learning or information content clearly explained, with any other audio elements in the background so as not to distract from the key message • Entertain – when using audio to entertain there are often a collection of sound elements combined for the listener's entertainment and interpretation and no one element needs to stand out
Style of visual representation: Purpose impacts the style of the visual representation used in the product	• Advertise – media used to advertise will often have a visual style which mirrors the house style of the product brand. This can include font colours and the structure of the media product • Inform – graphics used to inform often follow conventions to ensure that the user recognises that form of graphic. Again, this can involve the use of colour, fonts and layout as well as other consistent features such as a consistent use of audio elements

Style, content and layout

All three of these things can all be influenced by purpose and can be adapted to reflect different purposes. Table 1.5 outlines some examples.

2.2 Client requirements and how they are defined

Client requirements

When you take on a project for a client, you will receive a brief from them which outlines the main points of the product you need to make. The brief will include lots of information giving you the details you need to make an effective product. It would be unusual for the client brief to be a concise list of requirements – often you will identify the key information from the brief yourself. Table 1.6 shows some of the items you will need to identify from the brief.

Table 1.6 Things you need to identity from a brief

Type of product	Your client requirements will include details of what it is you need to create, for example a video, animation, comic or poster
Purpose	As we saw in Section 2.1, the purpose is key to the product design. This will also be outlined in the client brief
Audience	The brief will tell you about the audience for the product. This could include details such as the age, gender, interests and location of those the product is aimed at
Client ethos	The client will use the brief to explain their ethos; this is what the client stands for and believes in or represents
Content	The client will give you some ideas about what type of content they are looking for in their product. This could be details of images, videos, audio assets etc.
Genre	The brief should also give an indication of the genre of the product. For example, horror, comedy, mystery
Style/theme	The style and theme of the product can also be indicated in the client brief. This is often linked to the genre of the product
Timescales	Most projects will require the creators to work to a given timescale. This timescale could depend on a number of things, but you will need to plan your project to meet any timescales given to you by the client. This could include timescales for particular parts of the project to be completed

Client brief formats

The brief can come in lots of different formats and one of the skills that you need to be able to use is the ability to collect key information from a brief in any format.

Some work is offered to creators by commission and is likely to be a written outline of the requirements needed for the product. It will be a formal document which the client will create to present to potential creators. Sometimes sharing the brief will be less formal and will be part of a conversation between the clients and the creators. In other projects, this will be a more formal conversation with the client stating their requirements, while at other times this will be more of a negotiation between the client and the creator to craft the brief for the product together.

Figure 1.4 A meeting can be used to negotiate a client brief

Understanding the brief

When you receive a brief, particularly a written brief, one way that you can make sure that you are successful in achieving the requirements is to look closely at the brief and try to pick out key words and important phrases. You can then use these as the starting point for your ideas and to help you make plans for when creating the product. The key elements of the brief are good for providing structure to your product, but sometimes they can also provide **constraints** to your planning and production. Constraints are items that restrict the creativity of your project or the way you might carry it out. Examples of constraints could be items such as the timescale you have to complete your work or the format the client requires your final product to be in.

Key terms

Ethos A set of ideals or characteristics that are followed by a group of people.

Genre A way of describing the theme or style of creative work, for example horror or romance.

Constraints Things that restrict the way a task can be carried out.

Generating ideas from the brief

When you receive a brief from a client and have picked out all the key points, you will then need to think about how you can use these in your ideas generation. We will look more at documents to support ideas generation in Section 3.2.

Activity

In a group of three or four, discuss the different things you could identify from a brief, as outlined in Table 1.6. Ask yourself how these details about the brief and the client could impact on the creation of a product. Prepare your thoughts with some examples to share with the class.

2.3 Audience demographics and segmentation

When you are planning your product one of the key considerations is who the product is aimed at – the target audience. The study of target audience characteristics is called **demographics**. Target audiences can be split into categories using a process called **segmentation**.

Different categories of audience segmentation

- **Age**: In most client requirements there will be an indication of the age of the target audience. This will usually be an age range such as 11–16 or 20–40 years, rather than a specific single age. A target audience of everyone is generally too wide to allow you to make a product which is suitable and accessible to all.
- **Gender**: Traditionally this would be men and women, but you should also consider other identities such as transgender and non-binary, as well as gender neutral approaches.
- **Location**: Sometimes your product requirements will include detail of a location which is relevant to the product, for example if you are making an interactive product for a local attraction. It can also link to a type of location, for example intercity, coastal or rural locations which may need to be considered when planning your product.
- **Occupation**: When looking at your brief you might need to consider the types of jobs that your audience may have.
- **Education**: The educational level of your audience may impact on the type and style of content in your product.
- **Income**: Depending on the purpose of your product you may need to consider the income of your audience. This might include details of the audience's income and how this might influence their way of life.
- **Interests**: The details of your audience's interests may be included in the client brief. There are lots of potential pieces of information that could be included here, for example musical tastes or details of hobbies or pastimes.
- **Lifestyle**: To make a product appeal to a particular audience sometimes you will need to consider details about their lifestyle. This is information about how people live their lives and examples could include things such as a healthy or unhealthy lifestyle or a nomadic or rural lifestyle.

When designing you need to consider these categories and what it might mean for your design. Using this information will enable you to design your product to meet the needs of your specific target audience and to have created a design that they can relate to, which will improve the success of your final product.

It is very easy to get caught up in **stereotypes** when you are looking at audience segmentation, and you need to be mindful of not using audience segmentation in a way that could be offensive or discriminatory.

Key terms

Demographics Study of target audience characteristics.

Segmentation Splitting a target audience into different categories.

Stereotypes An assumption made about people who are part of a particular demographic.

How categories of audience segmentation influence the design and production of media product

Age

Age can influence how you design a product in a number of ways. For example, if you're making a product for a younger target audience it is likely that you will use simpler language to allow the content to be accessible to a younger age range, whose reading skills may not be as advanced. The age of the target audience can also influence the layout and choice of colour schemes for your product. You may design a more complex product with more written content on the screen for an adult audience, whereas a product for a younger audience may rely more on imagery to provide information. You can also consider things such as graphical content – for a younger audience you may take inspiration from cartoons or anime, for an older audience you may use more realistic style imagery or photographs.

Gender

The gender of the target audience may influence the design and content of your product in a number of ways and it may be that you think about how the colour scheme and layout might appeal more to different genders. You need to reflect the demographic of the audience in your product so that they feel that it is designed for them and gender considerations may impact on this. To ensure that your product is accessible to a range of genders you can also look at using gender-neutral language in your product, such as they/their instead of he/his or she/her.

Occupation

When planning and making your product the occupation of the audience may impact the design and content. The occupation of the audience could influence the user's technical ability in terms of how they interact with the product – someone with a more technical occupation may be happy to use more complex interactions in the product. Similarly, with the content of the product depending on the brief, the content will be more or less familiar to your audience and this will mean you need to make the content simpler or more complex depending on how the audience occupation fits with the topics for the content of the product.

Income

If you are provided with details of the target audience's income you will need to consider this in your design work. This is likely to be reflected in the content of your work. You need to ensure that if you are basing your work on a wide income range that you do not create content which alienates certain parts of the audience. For example, when using colour if you are creating a bargain brand you may choose bold stand-out colours such as red and yellow, whereas if you are trying to create a prestige high-quality brand you would probably be using more subtle colour schemes such as black and silver.

Education

The education level of the target audience for the brief can have a significant impact on the choices you make for the content and functionality of your product. You can use the educational level of your audience to justify the complexity of your content and of the interactions. For example, if you are aiming a product at an audience with primary school level education, you would have to make sure that the interaction is clear and not too text based, and when creating the content you need to think about the vocabulary used to make sure that it is understandable.

Interests and lifestyle

The interests and lifestyle of your target audience are most likely to influence the choice of content for your product. If you are trying to engage an audience with particular interests, featuring those interests in your content where it is relevant will increase the appeal of your product. For example, if you were creating a product to advertise an adventure holiday to adventure-loving families, you would expect the content, such as the images, to reflect this audience and their lifestyles. If you were aiming at an audience who were already engaged in an activity you can pitch your product on the assumption that they already have some knowledge, whereas if you were aiming your product at beginners you will need to create information that covers all the basic knowledge they may need.

Location

The location details should influence your design. For example, if you were making a product about a national event you would need to consider how to make it equally relevant to people in a wider range of locations. Similarly, if you were making a product for a specific local audience you would want to link the content to the local area to ensure that it was engaging and relevant. When planning products, things like the location of the audience may be relevant from an accessibility perspective, for example considering the levels of connectivity in a rural area to allow sharing of online content.

Activity

Write a description of a character you know from TV, radio, a book or a game (without using their name), include as much detail you can, at least a paragraph, and try to include information about different categories of audience segmentation.

Swap your description with a partner, annotate their description to label the different categories of audience segmentation you can find in their description. Underneath jot down any they missed.

Take your work back and see if you can add to your description based on any missed categories your partner listed.

Key terms

Primary sources Those from which you obtain information 'first-hand' from an original source and are typically more reliable.

Secondary sources Those where the information is obtained 'second-hand' or where somebody else has already put their own interpretation on the original information. The accuracy of information might need to be checked when using secondary sources.

2.4 Research methods, sources and types of data

Researching a product and its audience

If a media product is to be successful, some form of research will most likely be needed. There are two main areas where this can be done:

1. Before developing the media product (but after some initial ideas).
2. Following a trial release of early versions (for example, a game or multimedia product).

By conducting research before creating the product, a creator or media producer can predict what the target audience response will be like and modify the product so that it has more appeal.

By conducting research on a trial version of a new product you can obtain feedback on its appeal, how well it works and if there are any bugs or errors (especially applicable to a new game). This gives you time to fix and improve the product before it goes on general release.

Research can involve the use of either **primary** or **secondary sources** (see Table 1.7).

The main advantage of primary research is that it is normally more reliable and accurate. First-hand experience is better than information that has been passed on from one person to another. The disadvantage of secondary research is that it can be based on rumour, opinion and hearsay, which are not always reliable.

However, an advantage of secondary research is that it the information gained can be broad and wide ranging. It doesn't have to be limited to a single source and a researcher can look for the same information from multiple sources. This increases the chances of finding accurate information.

Table 1.7 Primary and secondary research

Primary research	Secondary research
Directly from the source, e.g. from an equipment manufacturer, actual audience	Indirectly sourced, e.g. forums, reviews and opinions from users
Autobiography	Biography
Original works	Commentaries
First-hand account	Second-hand account
Diary	History textbook
Interview	Magazines and newspapers
Focus group	Books and journals
Online survey	Internet sites/research
Questionnaires	Television
Video footage	Encyclopaedias
Photo	Report
Relics	Other people's products
Official records	News broadcasts

Research data

There are two types of data that can be gathered when conducting research. These are:

- **qualitative** information. This is where the data is informative about thoughts, ideas and feelings. For example, comments from a focus group might describe how a recent film is a good comedy and why a sequel should be made.
- **quantitative** information. This is based on numbers and statistics. For example, a survey might conclude that 80 per cent of people have a smartphone to play games.

Basically, qualitative research data does not include any numbers or statistical analysis. Both types of research data are useful to media producers. They can give an idea of the potential success and appeal of a product, which is a great advantage when making decisions.

Key terms

Qualitative Research data based on what people think or feel about something.

Quantitative Research data based on numbers and statistical analysis.

The analysis of qualitative or quantitative data can be useful and yet misleading at the same time unless the participants represent a fair cross-section. The people that reply to a questionnaire should be profiled as it is important to know if the data is useful, valid and representative of a larger population. This is where the demographics of the participants should be identified, to check the validity or usefulness of the results. As an example, a focus group might be asked if they think it is important to pay into a pension fund. The responses might be very different if the average age group are teenagers or those in their fifties and sixties.

The analysis of quantitative data is more straightforward since responses to specific questions are just counted. This produces statistical information, which can be shown on graphs, bar charts and so on. The profile of the people who respond is still important if the information is to be useful. Hence a disadvantage of any research can be that it provides the wrong impression, depending on the range of people that reply. For example, a survey on a social media group that asks if people are happy about a specific organisation. Statistically, more people are likely to get involved if they are not happy and have something to say. Having no research data or data that does not accurately reflect the views of the target audience can be a disadvantage to decision making by the media producers.

Activity

You have been asked to research ideas and the target audience for an animated film based on comedy and superheroes. List who and what you could use as both primary and secondary sources of information. You should also state whether these are likely to be quantitative or qualitative sources, with a suitable explanation to support your thinking.

2.5 Media codes used to convey meaning, create impact and/or engage audiences

Media codes

An important part of any media product is the use of media codes and conventions. These are always closely connected so that codes are used in relation to the conventions of a genre or product. You will learn about the concept of codes in this unit and the conventions in your two NEA units.

Technical codes

Technical codes are basically about how the equipment is used in certain ways to create the appropriate content of the media product. Examples include:

- Audio recording techniques: Microphone type and positioning, for example, shotgun mic for directional sound pickup.
- Audio editing techniques: Using diegetic (connected to events that happen such as sound effects) and non-diegetic sounds (background music).
- Camera techniques: Camera shot, angle, direction and speed of movement.
- Lighting techniques (for photography and video): Type, strength and direction.
- Video editing techniques: Jump cut versus fade, pace of scene changes.
- Navigation techniques (IDM): Use of buttons, mouse clicks, interaction.
- Animation: Type of animation and techniques, for example stop motion.
- Games: Configuring interactions, object properties, triggers.

Key terms

Technical codes The use of equipment or techniques in specific ways.

Symbolic codes What something represents.

Written codes The language that is used, whether printed or spoken.

Symbolic codes

Symbolic codes are more about what something represents, symbolises or means. They are generally defined by the action, setting and what happens in the scene. For example:

- Environment/scene setting: Influenced by time of day and the location, for example a quiet position by a stream would represent a different atmosphere to a busy street in a city during rush hour.
- Actor's body language and facial expressions: For example, how a smile or frown conveys different emotions by the actor.
- Colour: Different colours have different meanings, for example red represents danger, blue is cool, green is calm and yellow is happy.
- Mise-en-scene: This covers everything in the frame and where it is placed, including background, props and actors.
- Musical genre, pace, tempo and how the instrument is played: For example, music for an action film would be different to a romantic comedy.

Some symbolic codes such as colour will apply to several different types of product. Examples would be digital graphics, animation, interactive digital media, comics, photographic and video products since all of these are visual. However, colour would not be relevant to audio since we only listen to it.

Written codes

Written codes cover the use of language and how it is written, whether to be printed or spoken by actors in their dialogue, such as:

- text-based information that is included in a graphic
- storytelling in a comic or graphic novel
- narrative and dialogue in a video, film or radio play
- communication of information to the audience or viewer.

Ways that meaning, impact and/or engagement are created

Symbolic codes are used to convey **meaning** and the recognition is generally from the viewer's own life and social experience. Technical codes add techniques to convey the message more effectively and efficiently. When a media product is created using a suitable combination of technical, symbolic and written codes, then the scene or product should have more **impact** and increase the engagement of the audience (assuming they have an interest in the first place).

Note that there can be some crossover between technical and symbolic codes. An example would be a technical code in camera work with a high angle shot (looking down on the subject). This represents dominance or authority as a shot type and therefore has some association with symbolic codes, because of that meaning.

Animations

Animations can be made to appeal and be visually attractive. Character features can be exaggerated to give meaning, for example big (loving) eyes or dark mean facial expressions, applying some elements of symbolic codes. Animating their movement creates impact for the viewer, whether graceful, aggressive, fast or slow. Taking the concept of a symbolic code and moving it through animation techniques can increase its impact.

Audio

Generally, these are technical codes in the equipment and techniques but with some crossover with symbolic meaning and written codes where there is a script. Examples would be:

- Dialogue – what is spoken between people and how it is recorded.
- Music genre, theme, style, volume.
- Silence, which can also be a symbolic code when something is about to happen (the audience might sense something is coming).
- Sound effects, recording techniques being used and part of technical codes.
- Vocal intonation – the way that something is said.
- Storytelling through the use of written codes in a script (both in actor dialogue and the use of voiceovers).

Camera techniques

These are part of the technical codes and include:

- Camera angles: For example, high angle looking downwards, low angle looking upwards.
- Camera shots: For example, long shot (LS), mid shot (MS), close-up (CU), extreme close-up (XCU).
- Camera movement: For example, panning left/right, tilting up/down or walking/moving with the camera (can also use a **track and dolly**).

Lighting

Generally a technical code although it can have specific meanings and work alongside symbolic codes. The main considerations are:

- light intensity/brightness
- number of lights and illumination, such as even or spotlight
- position and placement, especially with spotlight effects
- direction and how this affects shadows.

Note this is closely related to the choice and use of colour.

Key terms

Meaning What is being communicated indirectly.

Impact The effect or influence on the viewer.

Track/dolly When moving the camera position, with the camera attached to a moving dolly that is placed on a fixed track.

Colour

Different colours have different meanings. Depending on what message is to be given, a suitable colour should be chosen. Colour can be applied in different ways, such as background colours and foreground images. It can also be combined with **typography** to add more impact or meaning to the words:

- red: danger, action, passion, love
- orange: energetic
- yellow: happiness, summer
- green: peaceful, calm
- blue: cool, cold
- black: dark, gloomy
- white: purity, cleanliness.

Mise-en-scene

The term 'mise-en-scene' is commonly used in media, especially video scenes. It means 'everything in the scene' and how all elements combine to give the visual effect that is wanted. The placement of props, positioning of people, lighting and the camera shot/angle are key elements. Generally part of the symbolic codes.

Transitions

Transitions are audio or video editing techniques and therefore part of technical codes. They define how the scenes of two video clips are merged together, whether jumping from one to the next or fading in between. A music track could also be faded in or out in a similar way.

Images and graphics

Technical codes would be about the way an image is processed in a software application or how a graphic is constructed using layers. Symbolic codes can then be added in the form of colour and typography in addition to the content of the actual images used.

Key term

Typography The style and arrangement of letters in a particular way to make sure that it can be read and fits the style of the document it is used in.

Typography

This is the use of text and includes:

- font type
- font size
- use of emphasis.

This is about how the use of typography creates impact and engages the audience and so can include:

- use of block capitals
- use of drop capitals
- use of large fonts
- serif versus sans serif fonts
- use of **bold** text
- use of *italics*
- use of specialised fonts
- use of font colour
- how to convey speech characteristics with a text-based language (for example, exclamation marks!)
- shouting versus soft, assertive versus gentle
- use of hard fonts versus soft round edged fonts
- use of special characters such as ***.

Activity

Look at the following examples of typography that have different meanings and impact. Summarise what each represents:

IMPORTANT

Need to know

General information

Interactivity

Technical codes are about the way a user interacts with a product, such as through navigational features, buttons and mouse clicks. Symbolic codes can then be added in the form of colour and typography, in addition to the content of the actual images and graphics used. Forms of technical interactivity include:

- click to select (either with a mouse, touchpad or touchscreen)
- gestures, for example hand movements
- rollover, for example with a cursor
- play/pause/stop, for example for audio, video or animation
- navigate to different pages
- enter text information.

Movement

An important difference between static and moving content is how much impact and engagement is created with the audience. As people, we are automatically drawn to movement as it more readily catches our eye and therefore attention. This characteristic can be used in most forms of media. Some examples include:

- Video: Movement of actors, scene content as well as the camera. Even a simple movement of the camera makes the video more interesting than a steady shot.
- Animation: The concept of animating static objects to create movement.
- Interactive media: Elements of the content that move or change size/shape.
- Games: Movement of the character through a game world.

Since movement attracts the attention of an audience, this is an effective way to increase audience engagement.

How the combination of content and codes/conventions work together to convey meaning, create impact and engagement

Many different techniques and processes are combined together when creating media products. These include the use of technical, symbolic and written codes from this unit together with the conventions that are included in the NEA units. Codes and conventions work side-by-side. For example, a particular technical camera shot may be needed to fit with the conventions of a genre in a video. When all of these are planned and brought together, much stronger media products are produced. These can convey meaning to the audience in storytelling, create an impact in advertisements and engage them in the delivery of entertainment and information.

Activity

Investigate the definitions of technical, symbolic and written codes. You could use the web to search for these in a media context as opposed to more generic definitions. For each type of code, list several examples that will depend on the type of media product that is to be created.

Practice questions

1 Identify three different purposes that could be given for a product. [3]

2 You are creating an advertising flyer. Explain two style, content and layout considerations you would need to think about when creating a plan for the flyer and how the purpose of the product would influence those considerations. [4]

3 You have been asked to create a comic to help teach about odd and even numbers. The target audience for the comic will be children of Years 1 and 2 age (5- to 7-year-olds). The product should be ready to launch in school libraries at the start of the new school year.

  a Select three key points from the brief that you would need to consider when creating the product. [3]

  b You receive the details of the brief in a meeting with the client. What other information might you ask the client for to help you plan the project? [1]

4 Identify three different categories of target audience segmentation. [3]

5 You have been asked to design an advert for KaPaw! Dog Toys, who are launching a range of value toys and accessories to be sold in their town centre outlet stores. Explain two ways in which target audience segmentation may influence your design. [4]

6 A social media group is created for feedback on a new comedy film. Out of 236 responses, 174 said the storyline was true to life. What type of data would this be? [1]

7 Describe how symbolic codes can be used in a television documentary on climate change. [3]

Topic area 3 Pre-production planning

3.1 Work planning

The process of creating a new product can be split in to three main phases or parts:

- pre-production planning
- production
- post-production.

These phases broadly consist of designing, making and checking. A workplan is usually drawn up to enable the finished product to be delivered to the client by an agreed deadline. Workplans are necessary whether a new product is being created by a single individual or a large team of creatives. Workplans cover the pre-production, production and post-production phases.

Pre-production phase

This phase begins with a commission for work. This is where a client approaches a designer to request a product is created. The client will have a list of requirements and maybe some ideas for how the product will look, sound or function. There will also be a means for distributing the product so that the correct target audience can access it.

Before the product can be created, the following will be required:

- Initial ideas will be generated. This could be sketches, words and concepts which will often be discussed and agreed between the client and designer and sometimes a representative of the target audience.
- The final idea will be chosen and planned using a relevant pre-production planning document. (The type of pre-production document or documents will differ depending on the medium, as explained later in this unit.)
- Assets and resources will be planned.
- Any **location**- or product-specific **recces** and **risk assessments** will be carried out.
- Any relevant legislation affecting the choice of assets and resources will need to be considered.

Production phase

This phase involves the creation of the product which has been planned. The product will often go through several versions before the client and designer are happy with it.

During the production phase, products should be **saved** using the 'native' file formats of the editing software whilst the following activities are carried out:

- Assets will be created or obtained and made ready for use.
- Resources will be collected together ready for use.
- Assets will be imported into editing software and the final product will be generated and edited.
- In a real-life vocational context, feedback on the early version/s of the product will be obtained from the client and/or target audience to suggest any required amendments.

- A finished 'master file' version will be saved in the native software. This is retained by the designer for use if the client requests further work or future products at a later date.
- A final copy of the product is **exported** and delivered to the client or distributed using the agreed platform (for example, publishing a website, uploading a video to a streaming service or producing printer-ready files for a print-based product).

Post-production phase

This phase sometimes overlaps with the production phase, especially if early or draft versions of the product are checked and tested before the final product is completed.

Post-production involves some or all of the following, depending on the type of product being created and the medium used:

- Checking whether all the client requirements have been met.
- Checking whether the product will appeal to the right target audience.
- Testing and/or checking whether the final product's technical properties are appropriate for the chosen distribution platform or method.
- Testing whether the product functions correctly and as expected.
- Reviewing whether the product is fit for purpose.
- Working out whether any improvements are needed.
- Working out if any further developments could be made and whether future commissions could be generated out of the final product.

The purpose of workplans

The purpose of the workplan is to ensure the pre-production, production and post-production phases run smoothly. By listing what needs to be done and when it must be done by, the workplan ensures everything is in place and available when required.

Large design teams use workplans to make sure those in the production team are not left waiting with no work to do whilst the pre-production team finish their tasks, and so they know when the post-production team will be brought in to the project. The workplan also makes sure one phase is completed before the next phase is due to start. This is known as **workflow** and can be used to keep the project on track and on time for delivery.

Workplans are helpful even if an entire product is being planned, created and reviewed by one individual. By working out how much time is needed to complete each phase, the individual designer can give the client a realistic deadline for delivery of the product. This is important in a commercial context because there are often financial implications such as penalties for missing deadlines.

Key terms

Location recce Short for reconnaissance. A visit to a location to check its suitability and requirements for producing media.

Risk assessments The process of identifying what risks exist, documenting the results.

Save The process of storing your master file in the image editing software at high resolution in its proprietary format. In Adobe Photoshop, this will be a .PSD file.

Export The process of changing the image properties and saving a file for use by the client in a suitable file format. This should be a format that is not specific to your image editing software. Examples would be JPG, PNG or PDF.

Workflow The order that tasks and activities are completed in, including which activities must be finished before others can begin and which can be completed at the same time as each other. Good workflow means that a project runs smoothly and efficiently without wasting time.

Format of workplans

The simplest workplans are little more than a list of things to be done and an estimation of the time needed to do each thing on the list. This might give you an idea how long in total is needed, but without showing things that can be done concurrently (at the same time) and which things must be finished before something else can start, it is not much help to a design team. So workplans are more often set out using a **Gantt chart** or specific project management software applications. These commonly represent each part of the project with a line or block along a timeline, giving a clear visual indication of any overlapping elements. Workplans can be physical or digital. The advantage of using a digital workplan is that it can be shared online and updated by all members of a project team in real time, even if not all in the same place.

Components of workplans

Workplans include the following components:

- Tasks: These are major parts of a product's generation, for example generating ideas.
- Activities: Tasks are broken down into smaller activities, for example creating a mood board and a mind map to generate ideas.
- Timescales: Each activity is given a notional (rough) idea of the time needed to complete it. This is often shown as a block or line along a timeline. Timescales may be indicated in minutes, hours or even months depending on the product. Taking photographs of a sprint race will be measured in seconds or minutes, whilst generating visual effects for a movie would take months.
- Workflow: Workflow is indicated by showing which tasks and activities can overlap and be done at the same time and which must be finished before something else can begin.
- Milestones: Milestones are points where one phase is completed before another begins. For example, 'The pre-production planning phase must be completed by the end of June because production begins on 1st August'.
- Contingencies: Contingency time is a buffer or allowance of spare time in case activities take longer than expected to complete. If you know the final deadline for delivery of a product is Monday, you would be unwise to plan to finish at midnight on Sunday. You may experience a power cut, a file may become corrupted or a voiceover artist may be unwell and unable to finish recording in time.

  The best organised project managers allow contingency time along the way, for example at each milestone or phase, instead of at the end of the whole project. This is also an advantage when a team of people is working on a product. If the pre-production team experience delays, they will not hold up the production team, and the post-production team will be able to begin work when scheduled if contingency time is allowed at the end of the production phase.

Resources

Resources are made up of:

- Hardware: The physical tools, equipment, computers and so on needed to plan, create or review a product.
- People: These may be creatives, designers, editors and so on, or people featuring in a product such as actors in a video or subjects in a photograph.
- Software: The applications and programmes needed to plan, create and review a product.

Key term

Gantt chart A type of horizontal bar chart used to plan a project schedule (what needs to be done and when). It is a good way to monitor whether a project is within its deadlines, what work has been completed and what is still to be done.

Resources are included in workplans so that all equipment and people are available when required. Expense can be saved if you only employ people and hire equipment for the time they are needed.

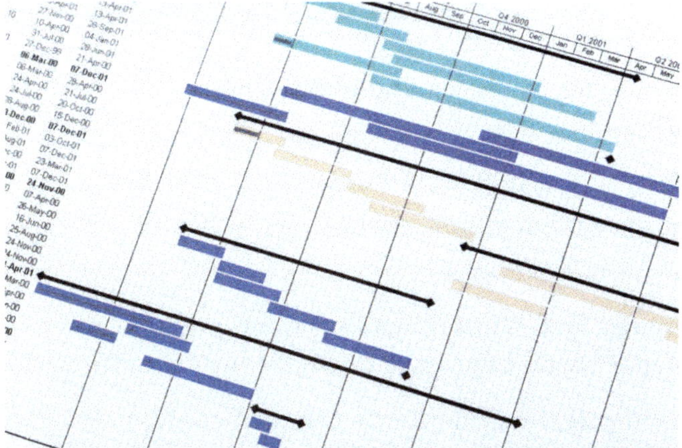

Figure 1.5 A workplan created using a Gantt chart

Activity

Discuss with a partner or as a group:
You are creating a 2-week workplan to organise the production of a music video for an indie band's debut single. After you have allocated time for all the tasks and activities, you have 5 hours of contingency time left over. Where would you put the contingency time in the workplan, and why?

3.2 Documents used to support ideas generation

The early planning process for a new product involves generating many ideas. Some of these will be discounted, whilst others will be chosen for further development and pre-production planning. This process will often include different people such as the client/s, design team and sometimes representatives of the target audience. Two key documents used to generate many ideas quickly at the early stage of a new product are mind maps and mood boards.

Mind maps

A mind map is a diagram which represents key words and ideas as **nodes** branching off a central hub containing the theme or title. Each node can be further described or broken down into **sub-nodes** to give greater detail or range of ideas. Nodes and sub-nodes are joined using **branches** in the form of arrows or lines to show connections or links between the ideas.

Mind maps are used to:

- quickly generate many ideas
- break them down to add detail
- show links between ideas.

Images can sometimes be used on sub-nodes to show examples of ideas. The text on mind maps tends to be brief, providing key words, terms and ideas rather than sentences. Mind maps can be hand drawn with paper and pencil or coloured inks and digitised using a scanner or camera. Mind maps can also be created digitally using Office applications which support autoshapes and desktop publishing tools. Dedicated mind-mapping software can also be used to create and share digital mind maps online and many free or open source examples are available for Android and iOS as well as desktop-based systems.

To be effective, mind maps should be concise rather than wordy. However, their purpose is to show many ideas, so multiple nodes should be shown and ideally sub-nodes should be used to add detail. Ideas must all be linked to the central theme either directly or through a node.

Key terms

Node Main idea leading off from the central title or theme 'hub' in a mind map.

Sub-node More detailed idea linked to the content of a node.

Branch Line or arrow linking the central title, nodes and sub-nodes to show connections.

Branches should not overlap as this can cause confusion. Ideas should all be relevant to the central title or theme. Mind maps are ideal for use by a team of people, since one person may provide a node which sparks ideas for someone else to add sub-nodes.

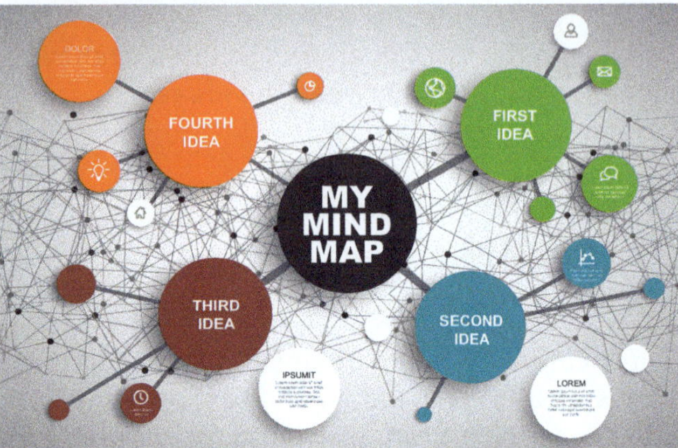

Figure 1.6 A digital mind map

Activity

Create a mind map to help generate ideas for a website to inform the general public about British insects. Include ideas for the site's content and style as well as technical aspects.

Mood boards

A mood board is a very useful initial planning document which is created by designers to share with a design team and with clients at the beginning of a design process. By providing a range of ideas, it is used to help decide the:

- visual 'look'
- design style
- mood/emotional response or 'feel' for a theme or product.

Once these aspects have been finalised, the product can be planned using the appropriate pre-production documents.

Mood boards collect together ideas and examples of what has been done before. This could include similar products, items on a similar theme or examples of designs aimed at a similar audience to that targeted by the client for the new design. Mood boards can be physical or digital and include:

- titles or themes
- colours and colour palettes (combinations of colours)
- text such as key words
- images, pictures and photographs
- shapes
- graphics (digital images)
- annotations and labels
- fonts/typefaces.

There can be differences between physical and digital mood boards as to what they contain:

- Physical mood boards can also contain textiles, materials (such as card or paper types for a print product) and textures and may use post-it notes.
- Digital mood boards can include multimedia such as audio files, video and animated images such as buttons and GIFs.

The layout or arrangement of items on a mood board tends to be random rather than tightly structured, although items may be grouped together, for instance by putting all the typeface suggestions in one area and all the colours and palettes in another. Text can include specific words to be used in the product (such as a brand name) and key words can be used to indicate the kind of mood to be created (for example, 'relax', 'tranquil', 'chill out'). A designer may sometimes create one mood board just to show the style which will appeal to a particular target audience and a separate mood board which brings together many examples of existing products using the same medium or platform.

To be effective, a mood board needs to be suitable for the type of product which is going to be designed. Digital mood boards are more helpful than physical ones when planning multimedia products, because moving images and sound can be included. However, if a print product is the final outcome, then a physical mood board may be preferred. Digital mood boards will be saved using a file format which supports all the various components including sound and moving images. Physical mood boards can also be digitised by scanning or photographing them so that they can be uploaded or sent as email attachments to share with clients or members of the design team.

The more items included on a mood board, the more effective it will be in providing a clear sense of the intended style, look or feel of a product. Depending on the type of product, some items may not be required (for example, materials would not be essential for a mood board for a website). But the main aspects (words, images and colours) should always be included in order for a mood board to be effective.

Activity

Create a mood board to help generate ideas for a visual identity for a new chain of 'Pound' shops. Include examples of existing and previously launched brands. Your mood board could include text, typography, images, colours and slogans.

Figure 1.7 A physical mood board

3.3 Documents used to design and plan media products

Once the initial ideas for a product have been generated and a style and direction have been decided, more detailed pre-production planning documents are created. The type of document will depend on the kind of product being designed and the medium and output format to be used. The most common types of pre-production document are shown in Table 1.8.

Table 1.8 Types of pre-production document

Pre-production document	User	Purpose	When used	Hardware and software
Asset log	Designer, creator of a product	To keep a record of the source and location of assets and any legislation such as permissions for use	Pre-production Production	Table in word processing (*Office*) software
Flowchart	Game designer, game programmer, web designer, UX/UI designer	To show the progression through a product such as a game, a knowledge-based expert system or quiz, or navigation options in an interactive digital media product	Pre-production Production Post-production	Hand drawn or digital using autoshapes in *Office* or graphics software, or a dedicated flowchart tool or application
Script	Actor, voiceover artist, director, camera operator, sound engineer/recorder, foley artist, stage manager, animator, client	To show who speaks when, to provide stage directions for actions and indicate sounds and sound effects, and to indicate locations and the sequence of events and scenes	Pre-production Production	Hand written or typed using word processing software

Pre-production document	User	Purpose	When used	Hardware and software
Storyboard	Designer, client, director, actor, graphic artist/illustrator, animator, client	To show a sequence of events and action over time for a moving image product by including movements and actions, camera shots and angles, dialogue and sounds. To show how scenes progress from one to the next and the order that scenes will appear	Pre-production Production	Hand drawn or created using desktop publishing software or dedicated storyboard applications
Visualisation diagram	Graphic designer, client	To show what a static image product will look like, what it will include, and the design and layout of items such as assets	Pre-production Production Post-production	Hand drawn or created using graphics editing or desktop publishing software
Wire frame layout	Graphic designer, web designer, UX/UI designer, programmer	To show the layout, structure and functionality of a web page or application screen	Pre-production Production	Graphics editing software, desktop publishing software or dedicated UX wire frame applications

Asset logs

Assets can be a range of file types including graphics, sounds, videos, animations and text. Keeping track of where these will come from, whether permission needs to be obtained and where they are stored helps to make a project run smoothly.

An asset log is generally created as a table using word processing software and asset table templates are widely available. The file name, source, properties and permissions for use for each asset are usually recorded in the asset log. If the asset log is stored online, hyperlinks or shortcuts to the individual asset files can also be included. This makes it easy to find each asset when it is required. You should make sure file names in the asset log are updated when using version control, especially if assets are repurposed or altered prior to use in a product.

Flowchart

A flowchart is a diagram which shows the sequence of actions and events when progressing through a product such as a website, interactive digital multimedia product or digital game. Flowcharts are especially useful where the progression is non-linear and depends on user input and interaction. A flowchart consists of shapes representing interactions and decisions of different kinds, connected with lines and directional arrows.

Table 1.9 Example of an asset log

Asset	Properties	Source	Legal Issues	Use
Company logo	160 x 160px PNG 13.4KB	Company image log, client to supply	None – client owns rights	Website header
Product demo video promo	30s long MP4 at 720p 2.8MB	Obtain from company's YouTube channel	Client owns rights but video created by external company	Product page on company website
Music short clip	MP3 30s long	Premiumbeat from Shutterstock	Royalty free, but licence required	Website homepage, cut to 10s long

Loops and procedures are also included in flowcharts where relevant. For example, 'The splash screen is displayed on an application until the user clicks a navigation button to load the home page'.

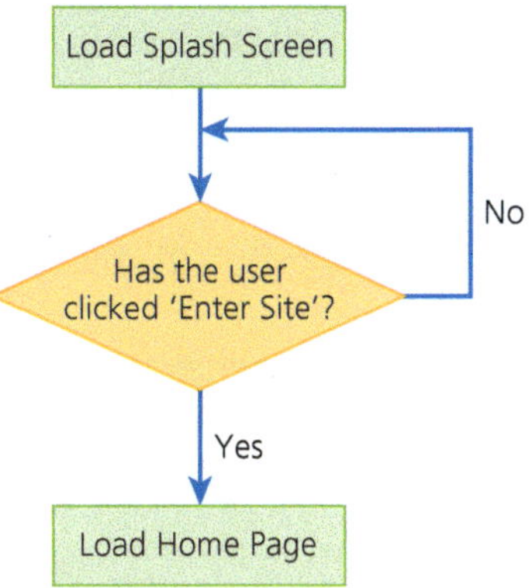

Figure 1.8 Example of a flowchart

Flowcharts are useful in the pre-production phase when designing complicated products such as games with multiple player choices and progression routes. They are used to keep a product on track during the production phase, particularly when inserting navigation links. They are helpful when testing a product's functionality in the post-production phase when the flowchart can be followed like a map and the product's actions can be checked against the expected progression and navigation.

Activity

Figure 1.8 shows a flowchart for an application. Using the information in the flowchart, make a visualisation diagram. You should include annotations to show dimensions, colour scheme, fonts and actions.

Consider the platform for the application – is your splash screen portrait or landscape?

Script

A script is a text-based document which describes the setting, participants, dialogue and action for a scene or series of scenes. It is particularly suited to audio products, but scripts are also used when planning video and animation in addition to a storyboard.

Scripts are used in the planning phase so that locations, equipment and the right people can be ready when the scene is recorded or created. During the production phase, a script tells people what happens and what is said, when and by whom. It also describes how moods and emotions are conveyed using voices, sounds and camera shots and angles. Script layout follows some conventions, for example:

- A description of the time and place where the scene takes place is usually included at the start of a script.
- Scene numbers are included to show the script's place in a larger product.

SCENE SEVEN

EXT. A GARDEN. DAYTIME.

WIDE SHOT

Two large rose bushes make an archway through to the croquet ground. Three gardeners are busily painting the white roses red. ALICE enters. She approaches the gardeners cautiously.

MID SHOT (3 gardeners)

TWO:

(*Protesting angrily*) Oi! Look out Five! Don't go splashing paint over me like that!

FIVE:

(*sulkily*) I couldn't help it. Seven jogged my elbow.

SEVEN:

That's right, Five! Always lay the blame on others!

FIVE:

You'd better not talk! I heard the Queen say yesterday you deserved to be beheaded for bringing the Cook tulip roots instead of onions!

SEVEN:

(*Flinging down his paintbrush*) Well, of all the unjust things – (*He turns to see Alice. TWO, FIVE and SEVEN look round and notice Alice. They bow.*)

CLOSE-UP

ALICE:

(*timidly*) Excuse me, but why you are painting those roses?

Figure 1.9 Example of a script

- Location and camera shots and angles start at the left-hand margin.
- **Stage directions** may be placed within brackets so they stand out from the dialogue (the speech or lines said by actors and voiceover artists).
- The name of the character speaking is indented from the left-hand margin and usually written in capitals.
- Dialogue is also indented from the left-hand margin underneath the name of the character who is speaking.

To be effective, a script must be clearly set out so that each person using it can see which parts relate to their role in a product's creation. For example, the foley artist should know exactly when a sound effect should begin and end. An effective script is also much more than simply a set of words which characters will say. Stage directions should describe how the dialogue is intended to be delivered, so that actors know what mood or emotion they are supposed to put into their voices.

> **Activity**
>
> Figure 1.9 shows a script for a scene from *Alice's Adventures in Wonderland*. Use the information in the script to create a storyboard for a live action film of this scene.
>
> Include technical details such as camera angles, timings, shot types etc. Try to use these technical aspects consistently (i.e. in all panels).

Storyboard

A storyboard is used to plan products with moving visual components such as video, animation and digital game 'cut scenes' and also to show how a sequence of images in a comic strip tells a story over time.

Storyboards indicate key visual elements for a scene, shot or panel using sketches which show what the camera will capture. Annotations are added to indicate camera movements and angles, sounds and timings. The sequence of images is shown using shot or panel numbers so that scenes and shots can be edited together in the correct order. How one shot or panel transitions or changes to the next may also be indicated for moving image products. Arrows are used to show movement of characters and objects and also to indicate camera movements such as **pans**, **tilts** and **zooms**. Speech or dialogue is often separated from the annotations by placing it below the panels or frames of the storyboard.

Figure 1.10 Example of a storyboard

> **Key terms**
>
> **Stage directions** Descriptions of what happens in a scene and how dialogue is said (tone of voice).
>
> **Pan** Camera movement from side to side.
>
> **Tilt** Camera movement up and down.
>
> **Zoom in/out** Camera change to a closer or longer distance shot.

Visualisation diagram

A visualisation diagram is the main pre-production document used when planning a static image or digital graphics product. It is a hand drawn or digital 'rough sketch' showing the layout, content and style of the product. Visualisation diagrams can be used to obtain early client feedback on an approach to a client brief. This allows changes to be made to the design before too much time and money is spent on creating the final product.

In large design studios a visualisation diagram will often be created by a senior designer, but the actual product may be made by a junior graphic artist or illustrator. This means an effective visualisation diagram needs to be detailed enough to be used by someone other than the person who drew it. Annotations are used to specify dimensions, colours and layers or effects. The resolution of particular assets may also be included in the annotations, and any specific typefaces or text sizes required for the product should be clearly labelled. The type or style of any image assets should be specified, so the artist knows whether to use cartoon-style images, drawings or photographs. When creating a digital visualisation diagram, the images chosen are usually representations of the style and type needed, rather than the actual assets for the final product.

Activity

Figure 1.11 shows a visualisation diagram for a flyer. Review the effectiveness of the visualisation diagram.

- Which information is helpful?
- What details or annotations could be added to make this more effective?

Key term

Wire frame A plan using basic lines and shapes to show where items would be placed in a design.

Wire frame layout

A **wire frame** is a diagram which shows the layout and interaction for a web page, application or interactive product screen. Wire frames are usually created after the initial sketching of layouts and ideas has been completed and an overall design style has been chosen. This means they are often the last elements made in the pre-production phase, before the final product is coded, and they may be created by web or UX designers rather than programmers.

Wire frames follow a few conventions:

- They are often hand drawn although free wire frame tools and applications such as Figma and Balsamiq are also available.
- They use placeholders (labelled boxes and simple geometric shapes) to represent the components of a page such as navigation buttons, images and text blocks and are created in black and white.

Figure 1.11 Example of a visualisation diagram

- They can be used to test whether a user interface is **intuitive** – logically set out and easy to use, and also to check that different screens, pages and areas of a product have a consistent layout and design.
- Annotations are used to indicate what each placeholder does, for example an image links to a particular place in the product when it is clicked. This means that the designer of the wire frame does not necessarily have to know how to code the product, making it a useful tool to share between the designer and creator.

Figure 1.12 Example of a wire frame diagram

3.4 The legal issues that affect media

Legal issues relate to both the creation and publication of media products. This includes the permission to take photographs and video plus the permissions and licences to publish any work in a commercial context.

Legal considerations to protect individuals

Privacy and permissions

Privacy affects whether your work to capture photographs and videos becomes intrusive and even then, you may still need permission. These fall into two main categories – people and property. These are covered by releases that are signed by the appropriate people.

- Model releases: This is a document that gives you the right to take photographs and/or video of individuals. An adult over 18 can sign a release for themselves. A parent or guardian must sign a release for anyone under 18.
- Property releases: If on private land you would need a signed property release from the owner(s).

Rights for recording images/taking photographs in public places

You can take photographs and record video from a public place or footpath without needing express permission in most cases. In the UK there are some restrictions such as notable landmarks in London together with any area close to military bases or places of interest that could be terrorist targets.

Permissions for recording images/taking photographs on private property

When on private property you should always check what permissions are needed to take photographs or record any video. This includes shopping malls, private parks and most tourist attractions that have an entrance fee. If visiting somewhere, check their website for any restrictions, especially before committing to using the materials in a commercial context.

Permissions for publishing and commercial use of images and photographs taken

Social media images and video are still covered by copyright. That means you cannot just copy a picture from a social media site and repost it or use it yourself. There are numerous examples where celebrities have posted a picture of themselves taken by someone else on social media, but they hadn't taken the picture and so didn't own the copyright. Land managed by the National Trust is also restricted to personal use only when it comes to photography and video. Commercial use of any photographs or video is not permitted so check on a map where you are, even on open access land.

Key term

Intuitive Something that feels natural and instinctive to the user.

Harassment and invasion of privacy

In the UK there is no law of privacy as such. However, this is covered by the European Convention of Human Rights (ECHR), which applies within the UK. This includes Article 8 which requires a 'right to respect for private and family life, your home and correspondence'. An example where this can occur is with paparazzi photographers and journalists who follow celebrities and notable people around for a good story or picture. This is covered by IPSO (Independent Press Standards Organisation) in the *Editor's Code of Practice*.

Defamation

One of the main issues in a media context is how people are presented to others. Defamation is to damage the good reputation of someone such as by slander or libel. This is an offence under English Law.

- Libel: Where somebody makes a false statement in writing that damages a person's reputation.
- Slander: Where somebody makes a false statement verbally that damages a person's reputation.

Test your knowledge ✔

1 You see a person's post on social media that makes a serious false statement about somebody they don't like, which goes viral. What form of defamation would this be and what might be the consequences?

Data protection

The principles of data protection have been around since the Data Protection Act (1998) with a number of amendments since then. More recently we now have GDPR (General Data Protection Regulations), which has been included in the Data Protection Act 2018 in a post-Brexit UK. For the original data protection there are eight principles as follows:

1. Fairly and lawfully processed.
2. Processed for limited purposes.
3. Adequate, relevant and not excessive.
4. Accurate.
5. Not kept for longer than is necessary.
6. Processed in line with your rights.
7. Secure.
8. Not transferred to other countries without adequate protection.

GDPR came into force in May 2018 and covers seven key principles:

1. Lawfulness, fairness and transparency.
2. Purpose limitation.
3. Data minimisation.
4. Accuracy.
5. Storage limitation.
6. Integrity and confidentiality (security).
7. Accountability.

The concept of data protection is covered by the GDPR but adds accountability under Principle 7. Note that you don't need to know about GDPR for this course specifically, but it has been included here for you to maintain an up-to-date awareness of legislation in this area.

Rights of data subjects in the collection, use and storage of personal data

Not all forms of creative media will include the collection, use and storage of personal data. For example, a digital graphic wouldn't collect any data, although a website may do so through cookies or by a visitor filling in a form. Any data that is collected and stored is then covered by data protection laws as explained above. That means there are limits on what can be stored in addition to a requirement to keep it secure.

If inaccurate information is used, this can lead to claims of defamation by an individual. A media producer must therefore consider the permissions for using any photographs or video, plus any data that is personally identifiable to an individual. Otherwise, the media producer may have to pay compensation or be fined quite heavily, depending on whether it is a data breach or form of defamation.

Key term

Intellectual property Something unique that is created or developed in a person's mind, which can be an idea, story, game, artistic work, symbol or invention. This can be protected for the creative person's own benefit, through copyright, trademarks or patents.

Activity

Investigate the content of the copyright, designs and patents of the government website at **https://www.gov.uk/government/organisations/intellectual-property-office**. Identify whether the types of protection are automatic or whether they have to be based on an application.

Intellectual property rights

Protecting intellectual property (IP)

There are several areas of legislation that are used to protect **intellectual property**. The protections cover:

- copyrighted material
- intellectual property in the form of ideas
- patents
- trademarks that protect a brand or product name.

Table 1.10 Symbols used to protect work, ideas and organisations

Symbol	Meaning
©	Copyright
™	Trademark
®	Registered

Intellectual property (IP) is a piece of work, idea or an invention, which may at some point be protected by copyright, trademark or patent. The purpose of IP protection is to make sure that others do not profit from the work of the original author. Different types of intellectual property are recognised by copyright, trademarks, patents, designs and ideas. Trademarks and patents have to be registered but copyright does not.

Copyright

This is a legal right that allows the owner to distribute, license and profit from its use, which is typically for a limited period of time. In the UK, that usually means 70 years after the author's death. Once the copyright has expired, its status changes to 'Public Domain', which means it can be freely used by anyone. Sometimes the internet is referred to as the public domain as in 'freely accessible to the public' but this is different to having a more formal 'Public Domain' status. The use of this phrase has two meanings and can easily be misunderstood. Note that the copyright owner is not always the original author or creator since copyright can be transferred.

'Royalty free' means that the work can be used without the need to pay royalties in the way of a fee each time. However, the work is still most likely to be copyrighted and an initial one-off fee may be payable. Note that royalty free is different to copyright free.

Regarding the use of assets, the best approach is to assume that any published content is protected by copyright. Some owners of that copyright might decide to make it free for use through some type of licence but that doesn't mean there is no copyright.

'Published' includes:

- all content on the internet
- photographs
- images and graphics
- books and magazines
- music
- films.

To use published content, you must:

- contact the owner
- ask for permission to use it
- be prepared to pay a fee.

You cannot get around copyright by creating your own version of somebody else's work (for example, by tracing around it, photographing it or changing it beyond recognition). Copyright protection is there to prevent other people from benefitting from original work.

Ideas

The concept of copyrighting or protecting an idea is increasingly becoming a bigger issue with the internet. In creative media work, an idea could be a character or story that becomes a key element of a product before it is created. In time, the character or story may be protected by copyright but initially it will be protected by intellectual property rights as an idea. However, when sharing original creative ideas with others, the use of a non-disclosure agreement is good practice.

Patents

This is not usually an issue for creative media work since it is generally applied to product inventions. However, it is still part of the same legislation in the UK – the Copyright, Designs and Patents Act together with the Intellectual Property Act. Examples of inventions can be a smartphone's innovative features or display technology, so is typically a physical item of hardware. Creative media products tend to be protected by copyright.

Trademarks

These are used to identify an organisation or product and their use is protected by law. The general rule is that these should not be displayed in a graphic, web page, comic, animation, game or video without permission from the trademark holder. Logos are a good example, but trademarks can cover any form of **visual identity** and are often used to protect specific product names.

Using copyrighted materials

With any intellectual property that is protected, permissions will be needed to publish this, whether for personal or commercial use. Personal use would include social media.

Creative commons licence(s)

Creative Commons (CC) is a licence agreement the creator chooses that lets you use that person's copyrighted resources. There are different types of CC licence:

- CC BY: You can use however you want as long as you quote the source.
- CC BY NC: You can use only for non-commercial purposes so you cannot profit from its use but must still quote the source.

Other licences and considerations include:

- GFDL – Share alike licence used by Wikipedia and others.

Fair dealing

Some limited use of copyrighted material is possible in certain situations. Within the UK, this is referred to as fair dealing ('fair use' is the term used in the USA). These exceptions for a limited amount of material includes research, private study, education, criticism and news reporting. An additional area for limited use is that of parody, caricature or pastiche. This is where someone such as a comedian may imitate an existing literary work, character or piece of art but with exaggerated features.

Permissions, fees and licences

These are the options available for using any work that is protected by some form of IP. Permissions must be obtained before they are reproduced in the public domain, especially for commercial uses. There are several ways to do this:

- Obtain written permission from the owner.
- Pay a fee to the owner or agent.
- License the use of the protected work, through a document that defines the terms of use.

Permissions should always be obtained in writing and with a document signed by the actual copyright owner, not somebody else who thinks it will be fine. The alternative to a written permission could be in the form of a more general licence. Media producers, whether a

Key term

Visual identity A combination of elements that are unique to a business, organisation or product, which can be recognised within the market.

freelance individual or a large organisation, must check that they have the correct licences and permissions to use any material. Otherwise, they may have to pay substantial compensation for the unauthorised use.

Watermarks and symbols

A simple way to watermark work is to add a copyright symbol, whether across the middle or somewhere else in a graphic or picture. Some stock libraries include this on the previews to show that it is protected and not yet licensed for use. A watermark might be semi-transparent, so it is possible to see what the image looks like in full.

Figure 1.13 Image with a copyright symbol as a watermark

Test your knowledge

2 Explain the difference between copyright free and royalty free.

3 You have an outdoor project to complete at a public place. What planning documents and considerations do you need to consider?

Regulation, certification, and classification

Organisations responsible for regulation

The main two UK organisations for regulatory purposes are the **ASA** and **Ofcom**.

Key terms

ASA Advertising Standards Authority.

Ofcom UK Regulator for communications services.

Sourcing Locating items such as assets for your work, which you did not create.

ASA (Advertising Standards Authority)

ASA's role is to ensure that advertising by the UK media meets the advertising rules. These rules are set by CAP (Committee of Advertising Practice) using a set of Advertising Codes. Their website is: **www.asa.org.uk**.

Ofcom (The Office of Communications)

Ofcom's role is to monitor the content and delivery of TV, radio, internet/broadband connections, telephone and mobile services plus postal services. Their website is: **www.ofcom.org.uk**.

In terms of permissions, the Ofcom website states: 'We welcome links to Ofcom's website, and there is no need to ask our permission first'. This is an example of the type of information that you should be looking for when **sourcing** content from the web.

Activity

Research the Ofcom website. Find one of the regular bulletins that are released for decisions about complaints made against TV, radio and on-demand broadcasting.

Media producers must ensure they comply with the rules for both regulatory organisations. This is to make sure that people are not exposed to unsuitable or offensive content given their age and demographics. Both organisations can enforce decisions but only Ofcom can issue fines. However, the ASA can refer serious cases to Trading Standards for potential prosecution.

Classification systems and certifications

Different countries have laws on what is allowed to be seen and shown.

- Certification: The process of informing the audience broadly on the suitability of content. It is an important consideration when thinking about the target audience.
- Censorship: When artists/filmmakers are not allowed to show their complete work. Factors that affect the classification according to age ratings include:
  - violence
  - strong language
  - scenes of a sexual nature.

Certification and classification are covered differently depending on the type of media product. The two types that you should know about cover films and computer games.

BBFC

BBFC (British Board of Film Classification) certifications cover films. Ratings are U, PG, 12, 12A, 15 and 18. The numbers refer to advisory ages for the film to be viewed.

- U: Universal, suitable for all ages.
- PG: Stands for parental guidance. Suitable for general viewing although parents are advised that some content may not always be appropriate for very young children.
- 12/12A: Suitable for those people aged 12 or over (12A is used for cinema releases).
- 15: Suitable for people aged 15 or over.
- 18: Suitable for adults aged 18 or over.

If a film is given a 15 rating, the producer may edit some scenes out so that a version is available with a 12/12A rating, depending on who they are targeting as the main audience.

PEGI

PEGI (Pan European Game Information) certifications cover computer games. Ratings are 3, 7, 12, 16 and 18. The numbers refer to advisory age ratings for the game to be played because of the type of content.

- 3: Suitable for all ages.
- 7: Suitable for people aged 7 or older, with only very mild violence in the gameplay.
- 12: Suitable for people aged 12 or older, with moderate violence.
- 16: Suitable for people aged 16 or over, where the graphic content can be more realistic in terms of violence, bad language and forms of illegal activity.
- 18: Suitable for adults aged 18 or over, with more graphic detail and behaviour.

In addition to the age ratings, PEGI also provide content descriptors that identify the type of the content that resulted in a higher age rating. For games developers, an awareness of the PEGI rating system and hence age imitations is always considered. This is to make sure the visual content of the game is suitable for the target audience that they have in mind.

Health and safety

Health and safety risks and hazards in all phases of production

As you have learned, production phases cover pre-production, production and post-production. The **hazards** and **risks** vary depending on the tasks being done. For example, pre-production and post-production might include some computer work whereas production could be at an outside location or in a studio. It might be necessary to produce a risk assessment for one or more stages of producing a creative media product.

Actions to mitigate health and safety risks and hazards

There are several stages that should be completed to mitigate, or reduce, the risks and hazards of media production. It is the media producer's responsibility to ensure safe working. This applies to any media organisation and also a freelance individual who must ensure their own safety.

Key terms

Hazard Something that could result in injury or harm to people or equipment.

Risk The chance that the hazard will actually cause injury or harm.

Risk assessments

This is the first stage that identifies if there are any risks and hazards to health and safety. A good approach would be to produce one of these for every media project and store it with the project files. The risks will vary depending on what activities you need to complete and whether any recording of material will be done outside, for example. This would normally be completed at the same time as a location recce. The process of completing a risk assessment is as follows:

- Identify the hazards and dangers.
- Decide who might be harmed and how.
- Evaluate the risks and decide on precautions to be taken.
- Record your findings and implement them.
- Review your assessment and update if necessary through the project.

Purpose of a risk assessment

This is to identify what hazards exist in the place of work and what risks are involved.

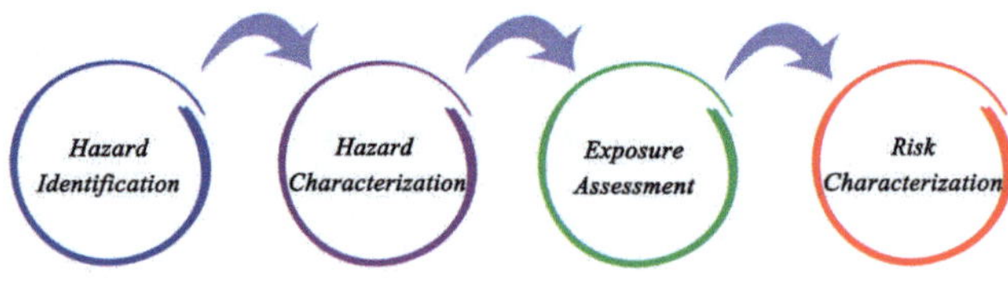

Figure 1.14 Risk assessment processes

Common risks and hazards found in media production

These include:

- electric cables (for example, on the floor – a trip hazard)
- electrical power (possible electric shock)
- computer working (repetitive strain injury (RSI))
- working at heights (for example, while holding a camera)
- moving heavy equipment (possible strain).

> **Key term**
>
> **Safe working practices** A way of working safely when a risk or hazard has been identified.

Risk assessments can be completed using a standard form or template. These must be stored for compliance reasons and as a record if issues did occur. If things were to go wrong and somebody was injured, the risk assessment shows that you and the organisation did everything in your power to prevent the incident. Even if working as a freelance media producer independently, you should still complete risk assessments for your creative projects.

Safe working practices

These follow on from the risk assessments. Having identified a risk, many of these can be reduced through a defined safe way of working. Some basic ones cover the following:

- Procedures for using computers:
  - chair height (adjustment)
  - seating position (posture)
  - distance from screen to eyes
  - comfortable position for keyboard and mouse.
- Procedures for working at heights or hazardous environments for filming and photography:
  - using safety barriers
  - wearing PPE (personal protective equipment).
- Procedures for working with electricity:
  - cable safety on the ground (for example, using tape)
  - location choices.
- Procedures for working with heavy equipment:
  - lifting (limits on weight)
  - moving (for example, use of trolleys and wheels)
  - setting up.

Location recces

Media projects typically use recces for outside locations, for example, for filming, sound recording or photography. 'Recce' is an abbreviation for reconnaissance, which is where somebody goes to visit a specific location before production starts. Within the media industry, a form is commonly used that has a series of questions and considerations.

Purpose of a recce

The main purpose of a recce is to check access, see what is there, identify best positions and assess environmental considerations.

Content of a recce

Generally a recce will include:

- location – how to get there
- access and car parking
- lighting, for example natural, artificial, direction
- availability of power for lights or charging batteries
- health and safety requirements, for example identify need for a risk assessment
- environmental considerations, for example background noise, people
- any potential issues that may arise
- a confirmation that the location is suitable for what needs to be done.

Location Recce

Completed by: ______________________ **Date:** __________

Location	Used for	Potential issues	Actions required

Figure 1.15 Example of a basic recce form

Practice questions

1 a Label parts A–D of the following workplan: [4]

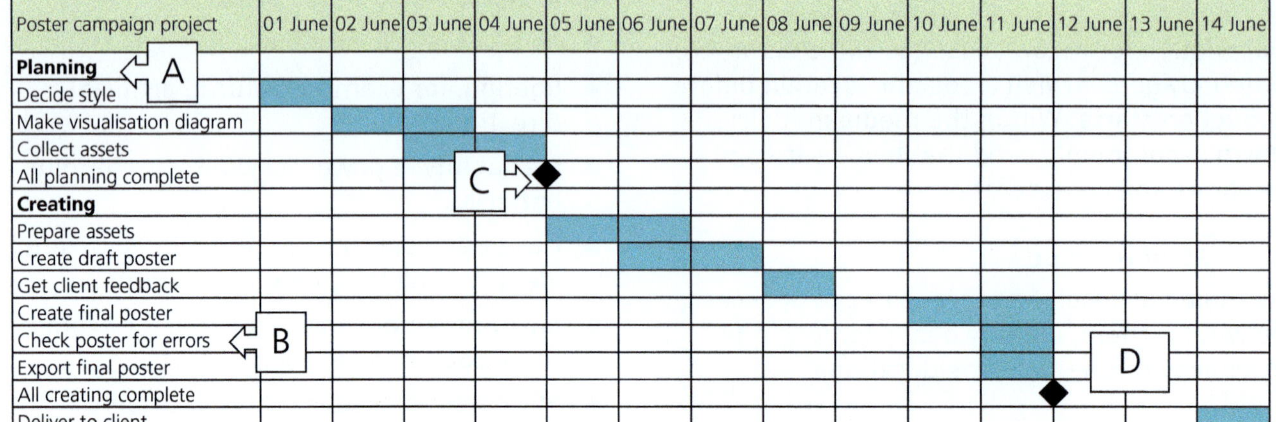

Poster campaign project	01 June	02 June	03 June	04 June	05 June	06 June	07 June	08 June	09 June	10 June	11 June	12 June	13 June	14 June
Planning														
Decide style														
Make visualisation diagram														
Collect assets														
All planning complete														
Creating														
Prepare assets														
Create draft poster														
Get client feedback														
Create final poster														
Check poster for errors														
Export final poster														
All creating complete														
Deliver to client														

b State two things which can be done concurrently, according to this plan. [2]

c When is the final deadline for delivery of the product? [1]

2 A radio interview broadcast in the early evening becomes an argument and the guest becomes offensive. Who should be contacted for you to make a formal complaint? [1]

3 You find a video clip about your favourite band on a social media platform and want to repost it to a different social media group. Explain why this is not allowed. [2]

Topic area 4 Distribution considerations

4.1 Distribution platforms and media to reach audiences

When your product is complete you will need to think about how you distribute the product to reach the audience. There are three main categories of platform or media you can use to do this:

- online
- physical platforms
- physical media.

When considering the distribution platform for your product, it is important to consider the features of the different platforms available as well as any potential advantages or restrictions to the properties of the product that may come from this choice. This could include things such as the size and properties of the final product file but also the file type of the final product. File formats need to be considered to ensure that the file used is compatible with the device or platform it will be distributed on. The details from your brief will give you information about your product that will help you to select the correct file format to meet the needs of the scenario.

Table 1.11 Online distribution

	Characteristics	Advantages	Disadvantages
Apps	An app such as one found on a smartphone or tablet can be used to distribute products such as digital graphics, animations, games or videos. In the case of a video, animation or game, the product may form the content of the app	Apps allow the product to be distributed on a range of different devices so it will be accessible to a wider range of users. Allows the user to access interactive content	If distributing using an app you may need to consider how your content will respond to the range of different devices the content could be viewed on. You would also need to think about what devices the app was compatible with and whether this would restrict the distribution to the audience
Multimedia	Some specific types of products can be distributed using the internet but not on a website. Examples include online games and streaming services	Enables multiplayer or multiuser environments for games and audio/video on-demand	Can use a lot of bandwidth and slow other services that use the same connection
Web	Your product could be distributed via a website hosted on the internet. Most forms of product could be distributed in this form, though it works particularly well for multimedia products	A product distributed on the web will be available to a wide audience as it is not hosted on a specific device or app and is easily searchable by a range of users. The web can host a range of content from videos or animations to graphics	When distributing on the web you need to consider the bandwidth requirements of your product. If there is a lot of content that makes the product a large file type, this can make viewing online a challenge if the file needs to be uploaded or downloaded. You will not have control of the device the web content is viewed on so this may cause challenges to ensure all content is accessible

Table 1.12 Physical platforms

	Characteristics	Advantages	Disadvantages
Computer	A computer usually operates with a screen, keyboard and mouse as standard and can be used with other input and output devices such as joysticks and speakers	Useful for interactive products which need the use of input and output devices for interactive features. Sounds and moving image content are easily accessible on this device. You can access a range of content from videos or animations to graphics on a computer	When using this distribution platform, you need to be in the same physical location as the device to access the content. It is not uncommon for people to not own a computer; this may restrict who you are able to distribute the product to
Interactive TV	This allows the user to view the content on the screen but also to interact with any content which requires input from the user	This allows you to access interactive products which need the use of input and output devices to make use of interactive features. Sounds and moving image content would be easily accessible on this device	When using this distribution platform, you need to be in the same physical location as the device to access the content. Properties of the TV may impact on the quality of the product, for example it may be restricted by the size and resolution of the screen
Kiosks	Kiosks are static units which allow the user to view the content on a screen. The user will usually access any interactive content using a touchscreen. They are usually located in public places such as shopping centres or museums	The large size of the screens on kiosks makes it easy for users to view the content of the product. When a touchscreen is used it can provide a user-friendly form of interaction	When using this distribution platform, you need to be in the same physical location as the device to access the content. Due to the public nature of most kiosks it is not always easy to allow users to access audio content. Interaction on kiosks is often limited to the touchscreen content

	Characteristics	Advantages	Disadvantages
Mobile devices	Mobile devices include phones and tablets which are portable computers. They often use a touchscreen as both an input and output device	Mobile devices can be used to distribute a range of different products, including multimedia and interactive products. They enable the product to be distributed to a wide audience and a large number of people have access to mobile devices	The screen size of mobile devices is often relatively small so some content may be difficult to view. Some interaction would potentially be more challenging due to relying on a touchscreen rather than other peripherals such as a mouse. Mobile devices generally get their connectivity wirelessly so file size and the quality of the connection may impact on access to any web-based products

Table 1.13 Physical media

	Characteristics	Advantages	Disadvantages
CD/DVD	In this format your product would be distributed on a disc, which would be provided to the user	As the user is not uploading or downloading the content of the disc, the file size of the product is less of a concern. The content of the CD or DVD is usually protected from editing, so the content would be distributed as the creator intended. CD/DVDs are relatively cheap for large-scale distribution	This distribution method relies on the user having access to a CD/DVD player or drive to allow them to access the content. As physical items, these discs are often not very robust and can be damaged or scratched, making the content inaccessible. Discs need to be created and distributed individually, this has an impact on time and cost per unit distributed
Memory stick	This involves saving files onto a portable storage device called a memory stick or USB/ flash drive	Storing the product on a memory stick allows a digital version of the product to be stored, moved and shared easily. As the user is not uploading or downloading the content, the file size of the product is less of a concern, though most memory sticks have a limited capacity before the purchase price becomes very expensive	The product will only be accessible on devices which have a USB port. This will mean that a number of devices, such as mobile phones will not be able to directly access products that are distributed this way. Content needs to be added to a memory stick and the devices distributed, individually. This has an impact on time and cost per unit distributed
Paper based	This involves sharing content in a printed form, for example printing and distributing a poster or comic	This allows you to reach users who do not access content on a digital device. It also allows the creator to control exactly what the audience receives as it will be distributed in static final format to the audience	This distribution method will not be suitable for the distribution of multimedia or interactive products

Activity

Using your knowledge of distribution platforms and the information in section 4.1, create a short multiple-choice quiz that could be used to test the knowledge of others in your class. Don't forget to create a document with the answers.

4.2 Properties and formats of media files

File formats for final media products

The production stage is where the media product is actually created, using the pre-production documents as a guide. The file formats for the media products will be determined by the type of media product, intended platform, distribution method and client requirements.

Different file formats are used in the following categories:

- images and graphics
- audio or sound
- moving images or video
- animation.

Image files

Properties of digital static image files

The main properties of digital static image files are the **pixel dimensions** and resolution.

Pixel dimensions

This is the combination of how many pixels wide by how many pixels high. For example, 3000 pixels wide x 2000 pixels high; this is 6 million pixels in total or 6Mp.

Figure 1.16 Pixel dimensions of an image

DPI/PPI resolution

A property of an image that states how many 'dots per inch' (**DPI**) to use. Printing requires typically 300dpi whereas convention for web use is 72dpi. This property is also referred to as **PPI** or pixels per inch and for the purposes of this qualification, either term can be used.

Good quality prints can be achieved using 200–300dpi but the resolution should not be less than 150dpi.

- An image with 300 pixels in width could be printed at 1 inch, or 2 inches maximum.
- An image with 3000 pixels in width could be printed at 10 inches, 20 inches maximum.

Low quality print products such as newsprint can be around 150dpi but full colour magazines and high-quality printing should be 300dpi. If considering web or multimedia display use then the pixel dimensions and file size are actually more important than the DPI resolution. Keep in mind that a standard display monitor is around full HD resolution, which is 1920 x 1080 pixels. Therefore, an image on a website does not need to be any larger than this unless offering the ability to zoom in, which is not a typical requirement. Larger pixel dimension files and file sizes only increase the page load time, so if not needed they should be avoided.

Test your knowledge

1 Draw the following table and work out the print sizes and pixel dimensions. (You can convert 1 inch to 2.54 cm.)

Image pixel dimensions	Print size (inches)	Print size (cm)
600 x 300		
3600 x 2400		
1500 x 1200		

Static image file formats

There are two different types of image file – raster/bitmap and vector.

Key terms

Pixel The smallest part of a digital image, each with a unique colour.

Pixel dimensions The number of pixels in an image, specified in terms of both width and height

DPI Dots per inch (where a print product needs typically 300 and a web graphic 72).

PPI Pixels per inch (technically the correct way to state the resolution of a digital graphic but otherwise the same as DPI).

Raster/bitmap file types

Bitmap or raster images are based on pixels and are produced by digital cameras or scanners. They are the most common type of file for any graphic that includes pictures. These pixels contain colour information as a mixture of red, green and blue. There is a limit to how far they can be enlarged or viewed at high magnification, because the image will become 'pixelated', that is, the eye can begin to see the individual pixel shape, colour and position.

Vector file types

The second type of digital graphic is called a vector graphic. This is independent of resolution and maintains crisp edges when resized. These do not use pixels and the edges are very smooth even when resized, without any loss of graphical quality. This is because they are based on mathematical formulas that represent curves and lines. Vector graphics are typically made up of shapes and text that are drawn using the shape, pen or text tools in image editing software.

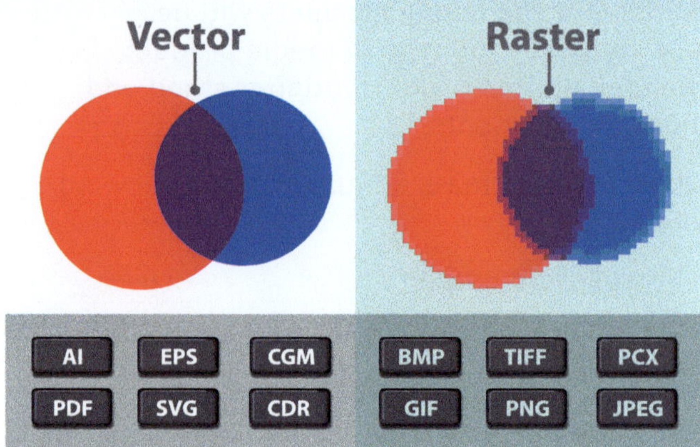

Figure 1.17 Comparison of bitmap and vector graphics at high resolution

File formats

The most important image file formats are shown in Table 1.14. Note that many of these refer to compression, which is explained later in this unit.

Table 1.14 File formats

Format	Properties	Limitations
JPG	This is the most common image file format, used in digital cameras and universally supported by web browsers. It gives a range of options for the amount of lossy compression to reduce the file size, but at the expense of image quality	Image quality can be poor with higher compression settings
PNG	Portable Network Graphics are an alternative to JPG but with the benefit of supporting transparency. Intended as a replacement for GIF images without any licensing restrictions for web use	Not as widely supported (or popular) as JPG
GIF	This has a very limited range of 256 different colours, so is more suitable for clip art graphics and logos than photographs but does support animation and transparency. File sizes are small	Limited range of colours and has licensing restrictions since the format is protected by copyright
TIFF	Tagged Image File Format is now less popular, partly due to its very large file size. However, still sometimes used in print and desktop publishing applications because of its very high quality with no loss of detail	Very large file sizes, which restricts transfer and distribution
PDF	The Adobe Portable Document Format is a widely used format for images, manuals, desktop publishing and other documents combining text and images. Note that is not an image file format that can be edited – only exported for proofing and/or print use	Cannot be edited directly – must use the original file format before being exported
PSD	Adobe Photoshop Document – this is the generic format used by Adobe in its graphics software. Constructed of layers for complex editing	Requires specialist software to open and view the files. Not suitable for web use directly
AI	Adobe Illustrator document, with extensive support for vector-based illustrations, logos and artwork	Requires specialist software to open and view the files. Not suitable for web use directly

Format	Properties	Limitations
SVG	Scalable vector graphics file format, which can be used across different vector graphic editing software applications	Not as widely supported as JPG and file sizes can be quite large
BMP	Bitmap file format developed by Microsoft. Usually uncompressed and supporting a range of different colour depths	An older file format that is less popular. Not suitable for web use directly
HEIC	Used by smartphones for high quality photographic images. You can often choose these in your smartphone camera settings	Requires specialist software to open and view the files. Not suitable for web use directly

Newer file formats but with limited support in web browsers at the time of writing are shown in Table 1.15.

Table 1.15 Newer file formats

JXR, WDP or HDP	JPG XR: A file format used by Windows Media for high-quality photo images with good tonal range. Expected to be replaced with the HDP file format
WEBP	Developed by Google. Uses both lossy and lossless compression. Intended to create files smaller than JPG but with a higher quality

Choosing an image file format

There are two considerations depending on if you are:

- creating or editing an image file
- exporting an image file for use by a client.

So, if creating the image (or graphic), then saving the file in a proprietary or **native file format** for the software would be the most appropriate. This should always be created at the highest resolution that is likely to be needed.

When that process is complete, the next step is to export the image file in a format that will be suitable for your client or consumer. That is more likely to be a generic format instead of the native format for your image editing software.

Compressed and uncompressed file formats

The term compression has different meanings. For the purposes of file formats for the final products, compression is the process of using compressed file types to reduce the file size. There are two types.

Lossless

This is where no information is discarded or thrown away when saving the file. It retains all of the original information and quality, but file sizes are higher. For example, using an A4 image, 3508 x 2480 pixels:

- 8-bit uncompressed TIFF file = 25MB
- 8-bit TIFF file, compressed using lossless lzw = 19MB.

Lossy

This discards some of the original information in order to reduce the size of the file. This is useful for web use or to minimise the required storage capacity but at the expense of quality. A smaller file is faster to upload, download and share online. The amount of information discarded varies depending on what algorithm or settings are used. For example, JPG files typically have quality settings from 0 through to 12, with 12 being the highest quality and therefore a much larger file size.

Using the example of the A4 page at 300dpi, approximate file sizes are:

- JPG low quality (0) = 800kB
- JPG file medium quality (6) = 1.8MB
- JPG file high quality (12) = 8MB.

Key term

Native file format The file format that the software saves into automatically.

Activity

Create a table that includes the following different types or uses of image-based assets. Alongside each one in the second column, decide whether these would best be stored as bitmap/raster or vector image file types.

- Photograph
- Logo
- Clip art
- Digital graphic (combining images and text)
- Artistic illustration

Audio files

The properties of digital audio files

The quality of an audio file depends on the sample rate and bit depth. The higher the sample rate and bit depth, the closer the digital sound will be to the original analogue sound's wave form.

Sample rate

In simple terms, the higher the sample rate, the more often data is 'sampled' or captured per second and the better the quality of the captured sound will be. The most common audio sample rate used for consumer audio and CD quality sound is 44.1kHz, whilst audio used in video is usually sampled at 48kHz.

Bit depth

The greater the bit depth, the wider the range of sound frequencies or amplitude can be captured each time a sound is sampled. Common bit depths include 16-bit, 24-bit and 32-bit. 16-bit is suitable for most consumer audio purposes, and many audio software applications record at 16-bit as a default setting.

A number of different audio file formats are available and it is important to choose the most appropriate format based on the file's intended use and purpose.

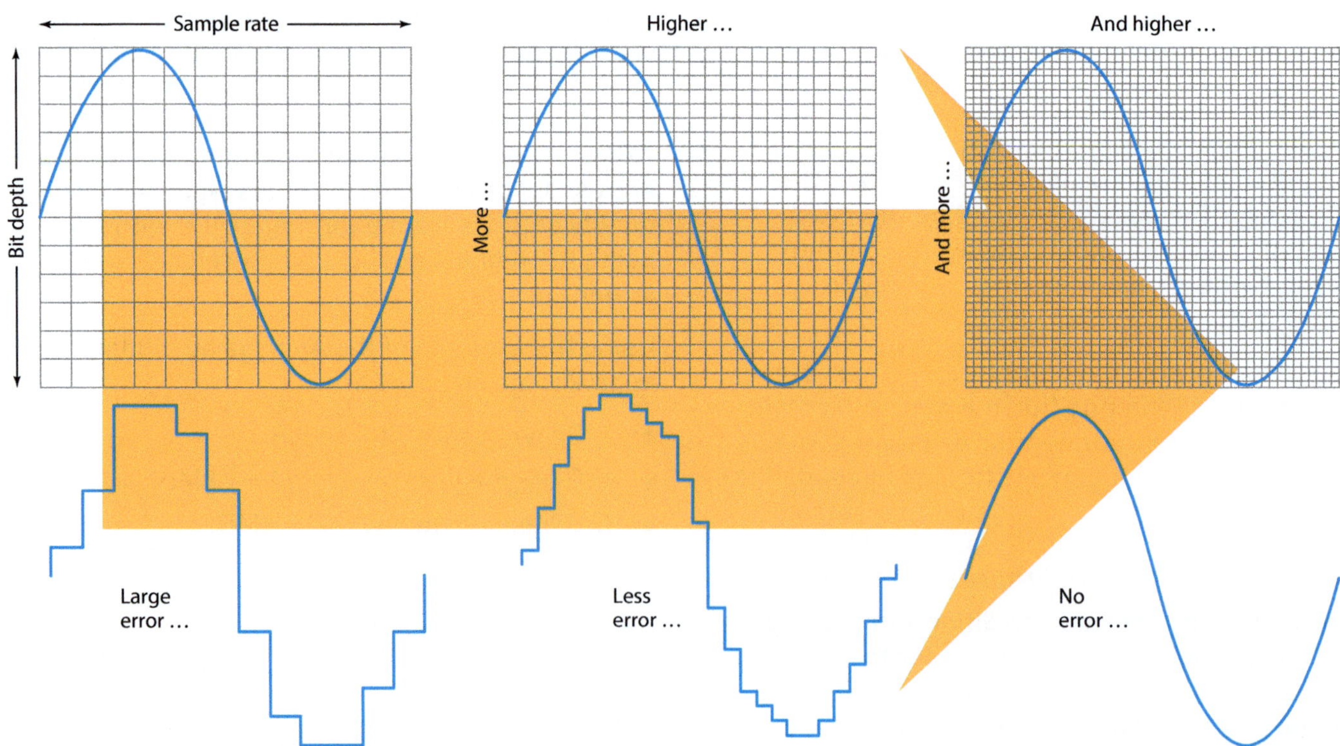

Figure 1.18 The effects of increasing bit depth and sample rate in audio files

Audio file formats

Uncompressed audio file formats

This includes WAV and AIFF file formats. These tend to be large, taking up lots of storage space, proving difficult to transfer via email and slowing down streaming, uploading and downloading. Saving using uncompressed formats is important if the audio file is not yet finished and requires further editing. Audio editing software such as Audacity saves projects in an uncompressed, lossless quality file format.

Compressed audio file formats

These include MP3, AAC, Ogg Vorbis and WMA file formats. These take up less storage space than uncompressed files, making them a popular choice for uploading, downloading and streaming. They may use either lossy or lossless compression to remove sounds which are beyond the hearing range of most humans, with the result that the decrease in quality is not noticeable. Compressed audio formats are best used when an audio file no longer needs to be edited, so they tend to be a good choice for exporting final products.

Activity

Create a mind map to record information about audio file formats. Include details of each file format's size and compression, and try to include examples of where each file format would be used.

Moving image files

The properties of moving image files

The main properties of digital moving image files are the resolution and frame rate.

Resolution (SD, HD, UHD, 4K, 8K)

The resolution for moving image files is to some extent decided by the platform that it will be viewed on. The main examples of this include:

- SD: Standard Definition; 720 x 480 pixels.
- HD: High Definition; 1920x1080 pixels.
- UHD: Ultra High Definition, four times the resolution of HD at 3840 x 2160 pixels.
- 4K: Cinematic quality UHD, which is 4096 x 2160 pixels.
- 8K: A newer video resolution that has four times more pixels than 4K; 7680 x 4320.

Very little video is recorded in SD these days, unless limited by storage capacity in the camera and only for small display use. HD or 4K would be the most popular, depending on the intended use.

Activity

Start to draw out a mind map with nodes for the different resolutions of moving image files. For each resolution, list where it could be used and using what sort of display. Examples would be TV and different forms of interactive media but try to expand on this. You can add to this mind map as you work through the unit.

Frame rate

This is the number of video frames per second that are recorded. In the UK, the standard frame rate has been 25fps, based on 50Hz mains. Very similar to this is 30fps which is a popular standard for modern digital cameras. If wanting to use slow motion effects and still see clean video footage, then 50 or 60fps would be a better choice. This gives more frames to work with in the video editing.

The quality of the video will depend on three main factors:

- Frame rate: Using 25/30fps is fine for standard speed video but should be increased if wanting to use slow motion effects in the video post-production.
- Video resolution: Chosen as SD, HD, 4K and so on. These are found in the digital camera menu, along with the frame rate.
- File format: Also affects the quality of the footage due to the level of compression (which is used to reduce the file size).

Moving image files formats for video and animation

The most important image file formats are shown in Table 1.16. In general, these can be used for video and animation.

Table 1.16 Moving image files formats

File format	Properties	Limitations
MPG	Video file format with lossy compression provides smaller file sizes for faster loading	Compression can lower the video quality
MP4	A multimedia/video compression standard that enables high-quality video over low-bandwidth connections	Very few, although high levels of compression can reduce video quality
MOV	Widely used for video files from digital cameras, providing good quality. Originally developed for use with Apple QuickTime	Not as widely supported as MP4
AVI	Uncompressed video file format for high quality. Often used when editing video before exporting in other formats	File sizes are very large and can be a challenge for some computers and editing software. Not all devices can play .avi files unless they have the right **codec** installed
GIF	Limited colour support but useful for short animations that are supported by web browsers	Quality, resolution and colour

The choice of video file format will depend on where it is to be used. In general, this is chosen when exporting a video file from the video editing software along with the resolution (for example, HD or 4K). If streaming over the internet, 4K files will be very large and high-speed broadband will be needed. Otherwise, HD is a good compromise between quality and file size.

Uncompressed and compressed video files

Most exported video is a significantly compressed format of some sort, as shown in the previous table of moving image file formats. The exception is .avi which is an uncompressed (or minimal compression) video, although the file sizes are very large.

Test your knowledge

2 You have a video camera that is capable of 4K video recording as well as HD. You have a client that wants to view your video footage on a HD monitor for a project but may want to re-use the video later for other uses.
What resolution would you select on the camera and why?

File compression

When saving files, you may wish to use file compression. This reduces the size of the data file whilst keeping most or all of the data.

Reasons for using file compression include:

- files taking up less storage space
- having smaller file sizes for sending as attachments using email
- files being quicker to upload and download
- more stable when streaming files with low bandwidth
- files use less data when browsing, making them less likely to use up mobile data limits
- the loss of file quality is usually undetectable to the user.

Key term

Codec (coder-decoder) A software routine used to initially compress and then extract audio and/or video content

There are two main types of compression: lossy and lossless, which you have started to look at earlier in this section. Lossy compression removes some of the original file information permanently. In image files, this can involve averaging out slightly different shades of colour. In music it can be removing very high or low frequencies which are not easily detectable to the human ear and video compression can remove some of both image and audio information. With lossless compression, the data is removed but retained and can be restored to its original state if required.

The most common (lossy) compressed file formats include:

- images: JPG
- video: MP4
- audio: MP3.

The intended use and purpose of the file should be considered when choosing a compression type and file format. If the original quality file is required, you should choose lossless compression. If the lost data does not matter and small file size is vital, then lossy compression would be a better choice.

Table 1.17 Lossy and lossless compression

Compression type	Advantages	Disadvantages
Lossy	• Smaller compressed file sizes • Variable compression rates can be set by the user • Loss of quality is usually not noticeable	• Each time a file is saved using lossy compression the quality becomes poorer • Lost data cannot be restored
Lossless	• All data is retained so that the original file can be restored	• File sizes are usually larger than possible with lossy compression methods

Practice questions

1 You have been asked to create an animation to teach children about the countryside code. Which distribution method would you choose and why? [3]

2 A design company have created a large-scale print poster for a film that is about to be released. They want to share this with the film company for their approval before they have them printed. Why would sharing this product via the web not be the best approach? [2]

3 a You see a butterfly hovering in the garden and want to record a video of its movement. What frame rate would you choose? [1]

b Explain one reason for using this frame rate. [2]

4 Give one file format which is suitable for emailing an image to a client. [1]

5 A photographer has been editing and saving photographs. They open an image called 'park_v6.jpg' and discover that it is very pixelated. Explain why this might this have happened. [2]

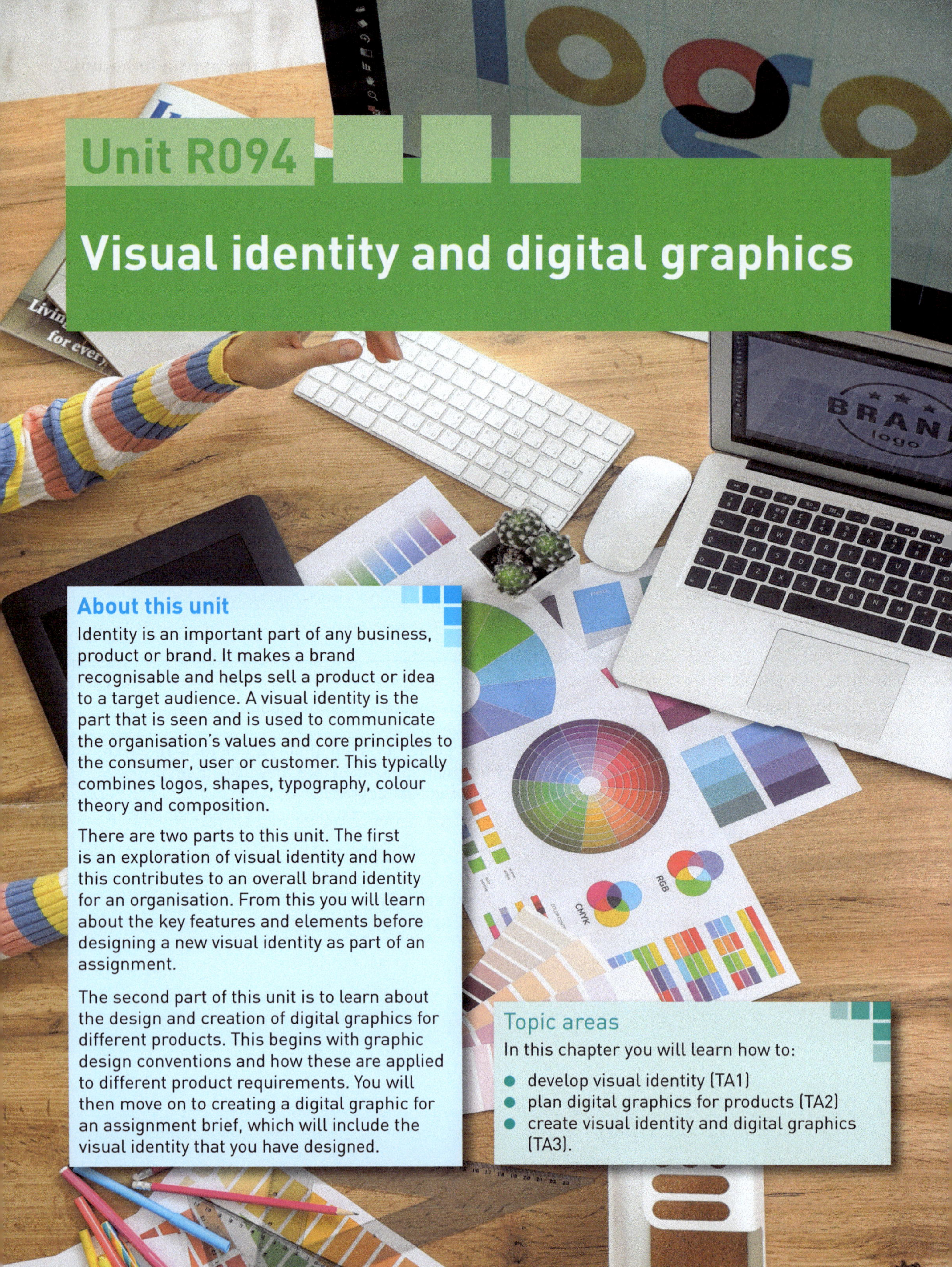

Unit R094

Visual identity and digital graphics

About this unit

Identity is an important part of any business, product or brand. It makes a brand recognisable and helps sell a product or idea to a target audience. A visual identity is the part that is seen and is used to communicate the organisation's values and core principles to the consumer, user or customer. This typically combines logos, shapes, typography, colour theory and composition.

There are two parts to this unit. The first is an exploration of visual identity and how this contributes to an overall brand identity for an organisation. From this you will learn about the key features and elements before designing a new visual identity as part of an assignment.

The second part of this unit is to learn about the design and creation of digital graphics for different products. This begins with graphic design conventions and how these are applied to different product requirements. You will then move on to creating a digital graphic for an assignment brief, which will include the visual identity that you have designed.

Topic areas

In this chapter you will learn how to:

- develop visual identity (TA1)
- plan digital graphics for products (TA2)
- create visual identity and digital graphics (TA3).

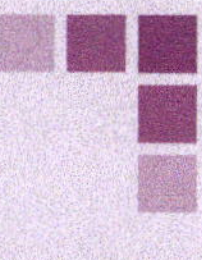

Resources for this unit

Image editing software is required such as Adobe Photoshop, Illustrator, Affinity Photo, Designer, Corel Paint Shop Pro, Pixelmator, Photopea or Gimp. Note that desktop publishing software is not generally considered to be a good alternative to image editing software for this media focused unit.

How will I be assessed?

You will complete an assignment that is set by OCR. This will be completed independently by yourself, without using any additional resources or teacher assistance to help you. The assignment will have a scenario or client brief that defines what you will need to create. Your evidence will then be marked by your teacher using the OCR marking criteria, which will then be externally checked/moderated by OCR to confirm your achievement.

Topic area 1 Develop visual identity

Getting started

Think about what brands you like to be associated with. Is it for a range of clothing, a smartphone or a music band? Make a list of why you like them and use a web search to find out what their visual identity is.

1.1 Purpose, elements and design of a visual identity

Purpose of visual identity

There are four main areas linked to the purpose of a visual identity. These are:

- recognition/familiarity
- establish a brand
- develop brand loyalty
- visual communication with audiences/ consumers.

Recognition/familiarity

Once a visual identity is established, it should also be maintained. This enables it to be recognised by its target audience and become familiar to them. If the audience has decided it likes the brand and wants to be associated with it, then they are more likely to respond to advertisements for new products.

Establish a brand

Most organisations have some form of visual identity, which is part of the overall brand identity. The purpose of this is to establish the brand or business in the market so that it becomes a familiar name. To achieve this, the visual identity must be consistent with the brand values in its style and colour.

Develop brand loyalty

Some people will have purchased an item once, decide they like it, see a visual identity that meets their perception of the business – and buy more when a new product advertisement comes out. Fashion clothing is an example here. By including the visual identity on a TV or page advertisement, a reader is more likely to look at what the product is than just skip across to the next page or advert. In the mid to long term, people can become loyal to a brand.

Visual communication with audiences/ consumers

The visual identity is what is seen. Hence it becomes a way to communicate with its audience and consumers. With any form of communication, the message should be clear. In order to communicate the right message about the brand and its values, the impact of the visual identity should have a good mix of features and component elements so that it is successful and fit for purpose.

Component features of visual identity

The component features are the different pieces that make up the overall identity. There are three main parts:

1. Name: This is the name of the organisation. It might be a manufacturer or brand name. Sometimes this can be a text field alongside other features and in other visual identities, it can be the main logo for the organisation.
2. Logo: This is usually some form of digital graphic. It might have some text embedded with it but not always. It is often the most recognisable part or feature of a visual identity.
3. Slogan or strap line: A visual identity can be more than just a logo. A common approach is to have a strap line or slogan as a text field alongside the logo. As time progresses, an organisation might keep the logo but change the slogan for different marketing promotions.

The features of the visual identity will have a strong connection to the purpose, aims and position in the market for the organisation. This has a significant influence on their design style, content and layout.

Synoptic link

Further information on how style, content and layout are linked to the purpose is found in R093, Section 2.1.

Activity

Find some examples of existing visual identities in different areas of brand positioning. You could choose supermarkets, airline operators or fashion clothing manufacturers. Create a mood board with a range of these for comparison.

Elements of visual identity

Elements are the technical content of the visual identity. These are how a visual identity is constructed from a designer's viewpoint. There are four areas to consider in terms of the different elements:

- graphics
- typography
- colour palette
- layout.

For example, you might compare the bright colours and simplicity of the McDonald's logo against the more complex and detailed Starbucks logo. If the four elements are considered carefully, the resulting visual identity can stimulate some level of emotional response in the audience – as a minimum, it engages them and gains their interest.

Graphics

This includes the use of any shapes, symbols and design graphics. A shape might be a square, rectangle, circle or oval. A symbol might be a single letter in a specialised font, a letter from a different alphabet (for example, Greek, Arabic, Chinese or Japanese) or potentially an ancient symbol representing some form of belief, philosophy or value. Care should be taken with any choice of symbol to make sure it does not offend any race or ethnic group – thorough research may be needed.

Typography

In this section, the use of typography is only related to creating a visual identity. So this needs to be short and snappy, with a style that is easily readable. The font type and size are fundamental aspects of this. These choices will say a lot about the brand or organisation well before the words are actually read.

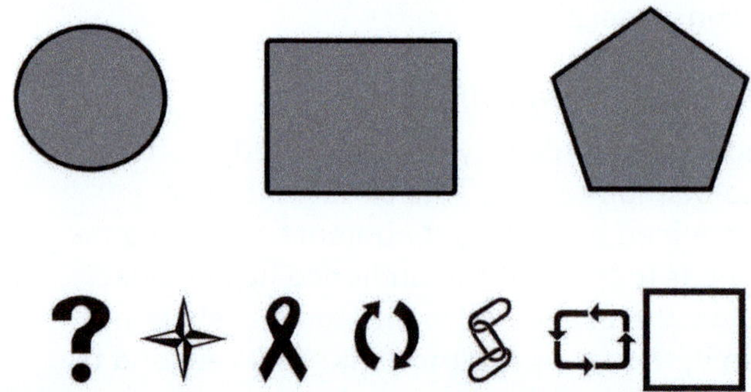

Figure 2.1 Basic symbols that could be used as part of a visual identity

Colour palette and meaning

The meaning of colours is included in this unit in Section 2.1 when designing a digital graphic. However, for the purposes of a visual identity, it is not just the choice of colour but also how it is used and whether colours are combined. Colour options would be:

- basic colours – solid red, green, blue or yellow (collectively known as RGB)
- complex colours – a blend of colour hues to create something more unique.

A colour palette that combines one or two of the basic colours of red, green, blue or yellow could create a quite simple visual identity. This type of identity might be suitable for a young or budget-oriented audience but could be less attractive for higher end adults. Having said that, some high-end identities are also clean and minimalist in their style. In general, simplistic identities would hold some appeal and representation to a particular audience group but that needs to be by careful choice, not accident.

Figure 2.2 A simple logo used as part of a visual identity with the three primary colours

Layout/complexity

The final stage is how the choice of graphics, typography and colour are combined in the layout of the visual identity. Options are for this to be simple or complex, depending on who and what the target market and audience will be.

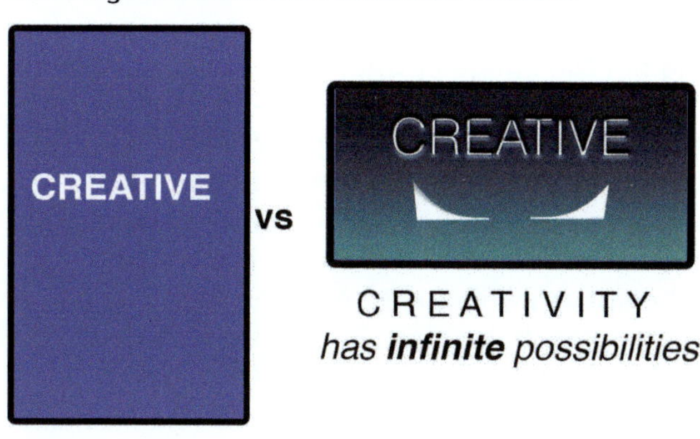

Figure 2.3 Different visual identity layouts – simple vs complex

Visual identity design style

The design style of a visual identity will be decided by a number of different factors. An established organisation will have already defined their business and what image they are wanting to present to their target market. The main three factors are:

- business type
- brand values
- brand positioning.

The combination of the elements should be suitable for the nature of the business, what it stands for and where it fits into the market. The visual identity, as the part of the overall brand identity that people see, must be consistent with the overall business. Otherwise, it would be unsuitable; giving the wrong impression and so not fit for purpose.

Business type

The nature or type of business can be very different. Just a few examples include clothing, supermarkets, snack foods, luxury goods, hi-tech, and health and fitness. Each of these would have different requirements for a visual identity so that it gives the right impression to the target audience.

Brand values

In deciding on a suitable visual identity, it is important to understand what the business stands for. Ethical brand values with a sensitivity for the environment might have a different emphasis to the needs of a budget clothing line. Of course, how the business operates is one thing but the image of what they present to their target audience can be different – that's the way of the world. Marketing objectives might be different to their operational ways of working, but the values are in the public eye. Hence the visual identity should be consistent with how the business wants to be seen and who they are targeting for their sales. As examples, brands that are aiming to include their commitment to the environment may include symbols representing trees, ocean waves, animals or endangered species.

Brand positioning

Related to the brand values is where the business wants to position their products in the market. This is affected by the product quality, as well as the wealth and lifestyle of their target audience. There are three main categories to consider:

- economy
- mid-range
- high-end.

What is suitable for an economy brand or range of goods isn't likely to be very successful at the higher end of the luxury goods market. Expectations are different and the people within the target audience must be inspired to look at the products or be happy to be associated with the business.

Synoptic links

Further information on media codes used to convey meaning, create impact and engage audiences is found in R093, Section 2.5.

Further information on audience demographics and segmentation is found in R093, Section 2.3.

Activity

Using the examples of visual identities from the previous activity, identify the component features and elements for each one. Consider whether there is just a logo or if it includes other components. Summarise how they combine graphic elements with typography and colour. Decide what the identity suggests as their brand positioning. (Don't just rely on what you already know about them – try to analyse what the visual identity is suggesting.)

Topic area 2 Plan digital graphics for products

Getting started

In a small group, collect a range of existing graphic design products to look at. These should include film posters, DVD covers, magazine front covers, packaging and advertisements for products. List their purpose together with who the target audience is. Think about the content of the graphics and reasons why they could appeal to a target audience.

2.1 Graphic design and conventions

Concepts of graphic design

Application of visual identity

Many graphic design products are linked to an organisation, whether the purpose is for promotion, information or entertainment. Any digital graphic that they produce is generally associated with the organisation. That is achieved by including a recognisable logo or some form of visual identity.

In addition to a visual identity, or sometimes part of it, is the organisation's house style. This can be their colour schemes, choices of text fonts and overall layout styles. Some might be modern and minimalist whereas others might be more complex. All of these aspects are chosen for a reason and become easily recognised by the intended audience. The combination of the visual identity and a house style starts to contribute to their brand identity, which is about how the brand is perceived by the audience/consumers. A consistent approach is needed to maintain their customers – unless they are looking to rebrand themselves, which should not be done too often.

Activity

Investigate a range of digital graphics including product packaging, books and magazine advertisements. Look for the use of a logo or visual identity. Identify where it is positioned and summarise the placement of all the content in the graphic.

Alignment

This relates to how the different elements of a graphic design are aligned, whether horizontally or vertically. For example, all the text on this page has the same left-hand margin and the paragraphs start in the same vertical line. Images and feature boxes also have a consistent alignment to match the text. This is important to make the page easy to read.

Alignment options include:

- left
- right
- centred
- indented.

In general, you should aim to have some sort of alignment in your digital graphic. You can plan this later when you know what needs to be included but before you actually start to create it in your image editing software.

Typography

Typography appears as a topic in several places within this unit in addition to R093, but the context is different each time. Here, the emphasis is on how to communicate a clear message. That means using suitable text fonts at a font size that is appropriate for the size of the digital graphic. For example, a handwriting script in a small size will be difficult to read compared to a standard font such as Arial or Helvetica. Using all capital letters is generally more difficult to read and isn't the best choice in most cases.

Different features on a digital graphic can use different font sizes and sometimes different colours. The front cover of a newspaper or magazine are good examples here. These tend to have large font sizes for headlines and smaller font sizes for further information. A website page is similar in the different heading styles. The font styles may be consistent, but the sizes vary depending on how much attention is drawn to it. For example, in a similar way to this book, there will be section headings in bold and a larger size font followed by paragraphs of information in a smaller, regular font.

Synoptic link

The concepts of typography are covered in R093, Section 2.5.

Use of colour and colour systems

Use of colour

Colours can stimulate different moods in the viewer. Some colours can be warm or cool and others can be neutral. There are some typical associations of colour with certain moods and feelings such as:

- reds, orange and yellow are bright, energetic and warming
- blues, greens and purple can be settled and cooling
- neutrals can be used for a larger area, with a colour then highlighted to attract the viewer's attention and give a more targeted message.

The genre or theme of the product will also affect the choice of colours. So, if it is for a film aimed at very young children then bright colours such as blues, pinks and yellow may work but these wouldn't be suitable for a darker crime or thriller theme. An action and adventure poster will probably use the bright energetic colours somewhere, to again convey that sense of mood to the viewer and target audience.

Synoptic link

Further information on media codes used to convey meaning, create impact and engage audiences is found in R093, Section 2.5.

Colour systems

These include Pantone and NCS, which are a way of defining specific colours. This means the same colour can be reproduced in different mediums and formats, while maintaining a consistent house style.

Pantone are influencers and work with colour trends such as in fashion and home furnishings. They decide on a colour (occasionally two) of the year around December for the following year, which conveys a certain meaning that is appropriate for the year ahead. This usually looks at the past year and provides inspiration and forecasting for the next year. Examples would be the use of grey and yellow (two colours) for resilience and hope in 2021, or a shade of green symbolising new beginnings in 2017. Some digital graphic products will also use these colour schemes, especially in advertising. NCS is the Natural Colour System, which enables the exact same colour to be produced on a range of different product surfaces and materials, whether fabric, paint or cardboard packaging.

Use of white space

This is any area within the final graphic that is blank. It does not necessarily mean that it is 'white' as a colour but could be any plain colour. It helps to separate out the different elements.

Layout conventions for different graphics products and purposes

Layout conventions are about the composition of a digital graphic and the placement of the different elements. Some considerations are:

- positioning of the main object or subject so that there is a focus point for the viewer
- using lines and perspective to draw the viewer's attention to the main focus point
- use of balance and alignment – are all the elements symmetrical or does one element stand out?
- use of suitable typeface or font – a science fiction theme probably wouldn't work with an antique style font.

The content, style and conventions are related to the genre of the final work. It means that the overall style should be consistent with what an audience expects, so antique fonts and sepia toned images work for historical pieces whereas futuristic or digital style fonts and images of alien worlds can be used with science fiction.

The range of content used on a digital graphic can be summarised as:

- titles and mastheads
- headlines and copy
- image content
- additional information.

Titles and mastheads tend to be positioned near the top. Examples include newspapers, magazines and product packaging labels. Headlines are the short statements intended to attract the attention of the reader. Below that would be the copy or the main body text. This would be in a smaller font size.

Image content can be distributed almost anywhere, depending on what the graphic is. For example, an advertisement may have a full-size background image with areas of white space for the main headlines/titles, together with an area near the bottom for any additional information such as terms and conditions or contact links.

The characteristics and possible content of some typical products are shown in Table 2.1.

Table 2.1 Characteristics and content for digital graphic products

Examples of digital graphic products	Characteristics and possible content
Advertisements	• Identify a product • Manufacturer • Where to purchase • Price (not always) • The small print
CD/DVD/Blu-ray covers (for music and films)	• State a title on the front cover • Lead actor names • BBFC age rating • Logos for format and sound quality, e.g. DVD, Dolby
Games (box cover)	• Title of the game • Name of games developer • Compatible platform • PEGI rating
Leaflets	• Information • Contact details (address and telephone)

Magazine/book covers	• Title name
	• Book:
	  • Author
	  • Plot summary
	  • Price
	• Magazine:
	  • Features
	  • Bar code
	  • Price

Multimedia products (including website pages)	• Information text • Images and graphics • Navigation buttons and features • Location maps
Packaging	• Product name • Ingredients list • Nutritional information • Images and logos
Posters	• Information • Images, graphics and logos • Contact details • Dates

Synoptic link

Further information on how the style, content and layout are linked to the purpose is found in R093, Section 2.1.

2.2 Properties and use of assets and digital graphics

Technical properties of images and graphics

Synoptic link

An important part of understanding digital graphics is the image properties (pixel dimensions and dpi resolution).
More information on these can be found in R093, Section 4.2.1.

There are two main types of digital graphic which have very different characteristics. These are:

- bitmap/raster
- vector.

Synoptic link

More information on bitmap and raster file formats can be found in R093, Section 4.2.1.

Bitmap/raster images

These are made up from individual pixels, each pixel having a specific colour. The number of pixels determines how large it can be, whether in print or display formats. Bitmap/raster images are always produced by digital cameras.

Colour depth

This is a term associated with bitmap file formats and expressed in the number of bits, or bit depth.

- The lowest of these would be a GIF file, which only supports 256 colours in total. This is generally unsuitable for a photographic image but sufficient for clip art.

- JPG files support three colours (red, green and blue) with 8 bits each. That gives 65,536 different unique colours.
- TIFF files can be saved with 8 bit or 16 bits per colour but not all image editing software can edit 16-bit colour depth. This gives the greatest number of different colours although they cannot be accurately reproduced in a print medium.

Colour mode

In image editing software such as Adobe Photoshop, the main colour modes would be RGB or CMYK, with an additional option of grayscale if including a black/white image. Sometimes this is confused with the colour profile and when opening some images in Adobe Photoshop, it will want to convert the profile to match the working space. Examples would be sRGB, Adobe RGB (1998) or ProPhoto RGB (plus others). Note these are colour profile options, not colour modes or colour spaces for the purposes of digital graphics and image editing (which is a different concept to the colour space selected in the menu of a digital camera when taking photographs).

Compression settings

These relate to file format, for example JPG or TIFF, and potentially what quality settings have been chosen. The purpose of compression is to reduce the file size, but this can be either lossy or lossless compression. JPG files are a good example of lossy compression and offer different quality settings which affect the final file size. In general, lossy compression means lower quality and a smaller file size. This is generally in a range of 0 to 12, where 0 is the lowest quality/ highest compression and 12 is the highest quality, lowest compression.

Scalability

In addition to resolution, colour depth and compression settings, one extra consideration is the scalability. If the bitmap file is to be enlarged or resampled to higher pixel dimensions, the quality will be lower. If detail is not recorded at the outset, it cannot be created by resampling and resizing. This can result in the graphic becoming pixelated, whereby the edges are no longer clean and clear.

Transparency

This is a useful feature for creating assets, logos and graphics for a visual identity. It means that the image content is on a transparent background and not a solid colour. Without this, placing a logo on an existing background image would mean that the logo is seen on a rectangle of solid colour.

Vector graphic properties

These are defined by mathematical formulas using lines and curves instead of individual pixels. They are used quite differently to bitmap/ raster-based images. Vector images are always created using a software application.

Compatibility

Not all image editing software has support for creating and editing vector-based images. Adobe Illustrator is designed for use with this type of graphic. If using Adobe Photoshop, both bitmap and vector-based layers can be combined. When adding shapes and text onto a graphic, these will be created as a vector layer.

File size

These tend to be quite small even though a vector-based image can be printed at very large sizes. This is because of the way that the shapes and lines are defined.

Scalability

This is the main strength of a vector-based graphic file. When printing at very large sizes there is no loss of quality and there is no pixelation.

Software support

Check whether your image editing software can create or use vector-based files. However, vector graphics can be converted to raster images for further editing or use within a bitmap editing application.

Activity

Create a mind map to highlight the differences between bitmap/raster and vector images. Include how these are made up and the main properties that affect their potential use.

Table 2.2 Licences and permissions

Source	Expected licence/permissions requirements
Client images	The client should already hold the copyright or a licence to use any images in their promotional materials. If images are supplied by the client, this should still be checked
Logos	The client's own logo should be free to use although you would normally check any guidelines, e.g. sizes and position, which are their house style Third-party logos (those from another organisation) would need permission to use
Internet	When looking for images online, you can use search engine filters for image size, type and licence conditions, e.g. free for commercial use. In general, any images found on social media feeds should not be re-used since somebody will own the copyright and it might be difficult to find out who that is
Photographs	If you have taken the photographs, then you own the copyright, so you can licence their use for a client project. Other photographs will need permission from the original photographer or copyright owner
Stock library	Image stock libraries will have a page that states the terms and conditions of use. This will usually specify the fees for use, possibly at different sizes and distribution methods. The two types are rights managed and royalty free. Royalty free means a one-off fee is still payable, it just means that images are free from ongoing royalties

Synoptic link

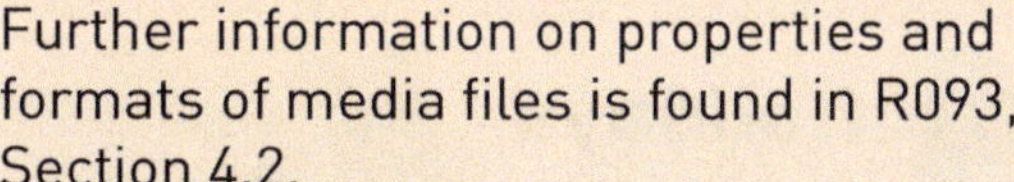

Further information on properties and formats of media files is found in R093, Section 4.2.

Licences and permissions

In a work situation, licences and permissions are needed for any assets that are to be used in digital graphics (see Table 2.2). You can use an asset table to log information requirements along with documentary evidence of any licences and permissions that have been obtained.

Synoptic link

Further information on the legal issues that affect media is found in R093, Section 3.4.

Activity

Create an asset table with selected image assets from three sources: (a) stock library, (b) own photograph, (c) client image (your teacher can act as your client). Identify who owns the copyright in each case and what will be needed for it to be used, for example licence or a specific fee. You will need to research the stock library pages for this information.

Test your knowledge

1 A magazine advertisement includes a photograph, text and a logo. What sort of file format would it need to be saved in?

2.3 Techniques to plan visual identity and digital graphics

Pre-production and planning documentation used to generate ideas and concepts for visual identity and digital graphics

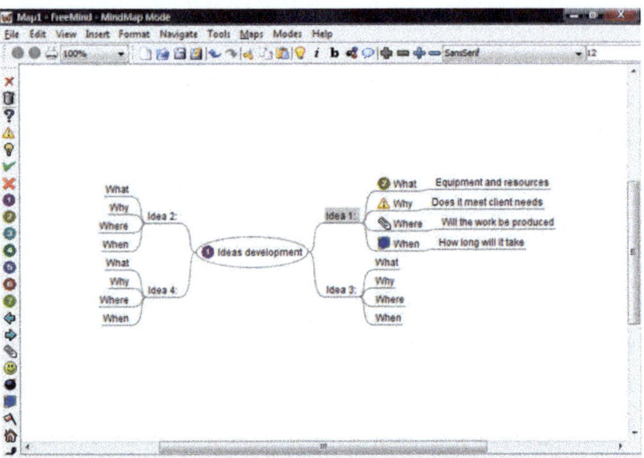

Figure 2.4 Using a mind map to outline what is needed

When planning, you need to consider the requirements for:

- a visual identity that matches the brand values
- a digital graphic that meets the needs of a client.

Pre-production and planning documents are needed for this purpose. The most useful are:

- mood boards to give examples of key points, themes and possible styles
- mind maps to record a range of thoughts and ideas
- concept sketches for a range of different ideas (these can be used for both the visual identity and the digital graphic)
- visualisation diagram for a chosen digital graphic idea.

Synoptic links

Further information on how the style, content and layout are linked to purpose is found in R093, Section 2.1.

Further information on client requirements and how they are defined is found in R093, Section 2.2.

Mood board

A mood board is a collection of sample materials, existing products and related items that represents the style of a new product that could be created. It can be either a physical mood board with randomly placed pictures, samples and ideas or a digital mood board with electronic images, documents, sounds and video.

A physical mood board could be produced on a noticeboard or large piece of paper/card using pictures, text, colours and samples that are fixed to it. Alternatively, a digital mood board can be created in any software application that supports multiple images, graphics, sounds, video, text and other content. The content can be sourced from the web, client libraries or scanned documents. Ideally this should be on a single page or slide within the software although a looping slide show is also a possibility if there is a lot of different material content.

A mood board does not show what a new graphic product could look like but can include examples of what other people and organisations have created that are based on a similar theme or requirement.

Figure 2.5 Example of a mood board for a digital graphic

Purpose of a mood board:

- To assist the generation of ideas by collecting a wide range of material that will give a 'feel' for what is needed.
- To stimulate creativity and innovative approaches.

Where mood boards are used:

- For any creative media project as a starting point.
- A place to collect samples, materials and a range of relevant content.
- As a constant reminder of possible styles.
- To share thoughts, ideas and styles among a creative team.

Content of a mood board:

- Images: From anything that is relevant or related, such as existing similar products, photographs, logos, screenshots from films, website pages, advertisements and posters.
- Colours: Especially those that fit the brief and audience or have been successfully used before in a similar product.
- Text: With key words, fonts and styles.
- Other materials: For example, textures and fabrics.
- Digital mood board: Potentially sounds and video clips.

Activity

In a small group, put together a mood board based on social media. Add examples of different types of social media and the primary type of content, for example text, images or video.

You can then produce a mind map for the users and purposes of the different forms of social media. Users can be categorised using your learning from R093. The purposes can have different branches on the mind map such as information, promotion or entertainment with examples for each.

Mind map

A mind map or spider diagram is a way of recording and organising thoughts and ideas in a structured format. It is based around a central theme (or node) and has branches off for the different aspects using sub-nodes. There should be a logical flow and process when following any of the branches that are based on related aspects of the project.

Mind maps can be created as hand drawn diagrams or in a variety of digital formats.

- Hand drawn diagrams: For these, you would use a large sheet of paper and draw the central node with the main theme or subject in the middle of the page. You can then add branches in different directions with an expansion of the thoughts and ideas.
- Digital formats: Digital mind maps can be created in an Office application such as Word or PowerPoint, or in image editing applications such as Photoshop. There are also a number of dedicated mind map software applications, both online versions and open-source software that you can download and install.

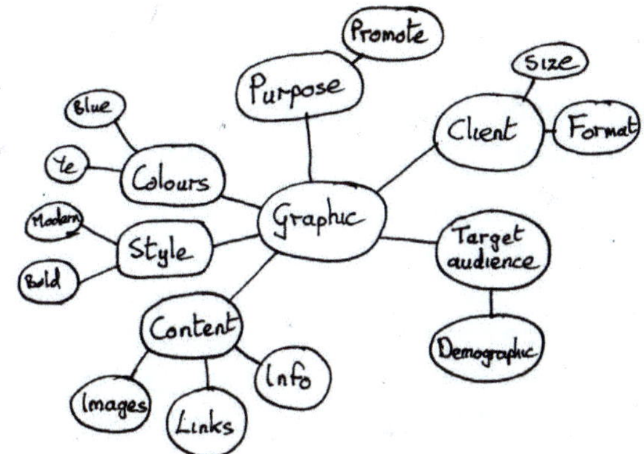

Figure 2.6 Example of the content for a mind map for a digital graphic

Purpose of mind maps/spider diagrams:

- To quickly record thoughts and ideas in a structured way.
- To develop and show links between different thoughts, aspects and processes of a project.
- To help the generation of ideas.

Where mind maps/spider diagrams are used:

- With any project to show the range of ideas.
- To show the connections and links between different parts of the project.
- To illustrate all aspects of a project so that the range of activities needed for a workplan can be included.

Content of mind maps/spider diagrams:

- Central node: With the main theme.
- Sub-nodes: With interconnecting lines or branches for the different parts.
- Text: At each sub-node for key points, ideas, activities, requirements and so on.
- Images: These can also be used on sub-nodes.

> **Synoptic link**
> Further information on documents used to support ideas generation is found in R093, Section 3.2.

Concept sketch

These are very rough and simple diagrams with ideas of what something could look like. They are not as complex, detailed or as thorough as a visualisation diagram (see next section).

Following on from a mind map, you can explore the look and feel of different ideas using concept sketches. These are best produced with a few different ideas on the same page, each of which could be developed further if it works. The design of a visual identity is a great use of concept sketches, so that you can decide visually which are the best ideas.

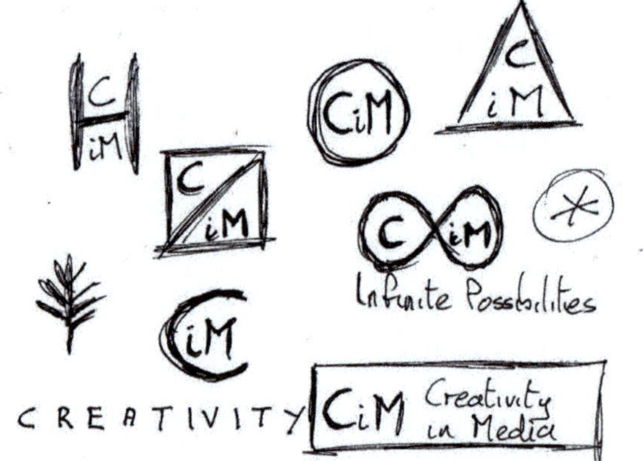

Figure 2.7 A range of concept sketches for a new visual identity

A good approach is to have several ideas as concept sketches, then pick one and develop it further with a more detailed visualisation diagram.

Visualisation diagram

This is a draft layout to show what the final digital graphic (or other static media product) is intended to look like. These are often hand drawn but good art skills are not essential – it is the layout and content that is being illustrated. A good visualisation diagram is one that could be given to somebody else such as a graphic designer, on the basis that there is enough information for them to create what you have in mind. One important use for a visualisation diagram is to present it to the client before you spend a lot of time actually creating the digital graphic.

Visualisation diagrams can be created as hand drawn diagrams or in a variety of digital formats.

- Hand drawn diagrams: Using a sheet of paper, outline the correct shape for the intended graphic as a starting point. Add the content in the position that you intend. Annotate the diagram with comments on assets, colours and typography (fonts and sizes), although these might not be necessary if you use colour and fonts effectively in a more artistic visualisation.

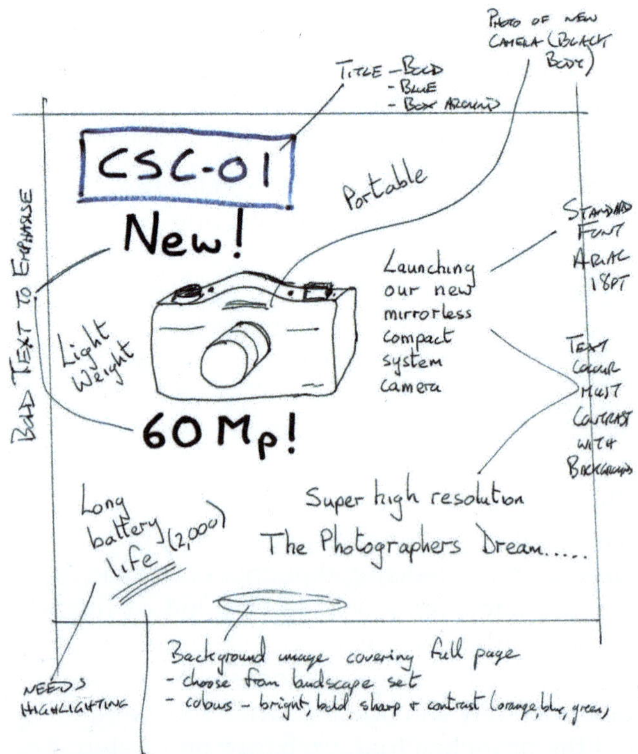

Figure 2.8 Example of a visualisation diagram for a digital graphic

- Digital formats: You can use a range of image editing or Office-based software for this purpose. Keep in mind that this should be a true visualisation or representation of what you will create and not just a wire frame diagram that would be more suitable for a web page or multimedia product. In general, wire frame diagrams can show position and placement but not give an overall feel or impact for your client.

Purpose of a visualisation diagram:

- To plan the layout of a static or still media product.
- To show a client how a finished media product might look.
- To provide a graphic designer with enough information to create what you have in mind.

Where a visualisation diagram is used:

- For any static media image project.
- In a proposal to a client.
- Within a production team to show what the intended product will look like.

Examples include:

- CD/DVD/Blu-ray cover
- Poster, for example for a film, event or advertisement.
- Game scene or display screen, for example for the game environment or game menus.
- Comic book page layout.
- Web page/multimedia page layout.
- Magazine front cover.
- Print based advertisement, for example a magazine, newspaper or poster.

Content of a visualisation diagram:

- Images/graphics: Showing their size and position.
- Visual identity: Of the client or organisation that it relates to.
- Colours (and colour schemes): To make it more eye catching.
- Text: Showing position and style, for example the name of the product or service being promoted.
- Fonts: To be used, which can enhance the appeal and interest.
- Annotations: To provide more detail where needed, such as sizes or colours

Synoptic links

Further information on media codes used to convey meaning, create impact and engage audiences is found in R093, Section 2.5.

Further information on documents used to design and plan media products is found in R093, Section 3.3.

Further information on the legal issues that affect media is found in R093, Section 3.4.

The expectations, needs and requirements of the target audience must always be considered so that the digital graphic will be successful. This is helped by categorising the target audience before thinking about their needs.

Synoptic link

Further information on audience demographics and segmentation is found in R093, Section 2.3.

Activity

In a small group, use a large sheet of paper to sketch out a visualisation diagram for the following scenario:

'A client wants some ideas for the front cover layout of a new magazine which is based around social media. The content will cover different age groups and what forms of social media they use together with the benefits and risks. The cover can have some text, but the client also wants you to consider what image assets would be suitable to attract the audience. Annotations should be added to explain your reasoning.'

Make sure you all contribute some ideas to the visualisation diagram.

Topic area 3 Create visual identity and digital graphics

Getting started

Find a DVD or Blu-ray film case. Look at the content on the front and back covers – making a list of the different content including images, text, logos and symbols.

- What is on the front cover?
- What is on the back cover?
- What is on the box spine?

3.1 Tools and techniques used to create digital graphics

The basic processes and concepts of creating digital graphics are the same whichever software is being used. An example of a standard workflow would be something like:

1. Obtain and store the image assets in a working folder.
2. Open the image assets and check the image quality.
3. Adjust brightness/contrast or levels.
4. Adjust/correct colours.
5. Complete any additional editing that is needed.
6. Save the assets with a descriptive filename in a high-quality format.
7. Create a new file for the final digital graphic to the required print dimension.
8. Import and combine the image assets, using editing tools and techniques as needed.
9. Save the final graphics with the high-resolution pixel dimensions and dpi resolution required.
10. Resize the digital graphic for web or multimedia use as required by the brief. Save this version as a separate file without overwriting your high-resolution master file.

Software tools and techniques used to create digital graphics

Image/canvas size

The first step in creating an asset or graphic is to set up a new image file. The important part here is to make sure the image properties meet what is needed by the client brief (or your own criteria if creating an asset). So, if you are creating an A4 poster for print purposes, it will need to be the following:

- print dimensions: 297 mm × 210 mm or 11.69" × 8.27"
- resolution for print: 300dpi.

Therefore, the pixel dimensions for A4 will need to be 3508 × 2480 based on 25.4 mm per inch. You might need to check what units your image editing software is using to confirm this. It will be either imperial (inches) or metric (millimetres and centimetres). A quick conversion of 300dpi is 118 pixels/cm. If you are creating an asset at this stage, you will need to think about what print size the asset will be, and this will inform your choice of pixel dimensions. Table 2.3 provides examples of products that need specific image properties.

Table 2.3 Products that need specific image properties

Product	Print dimensions (size)	Pixel dimensions
Magazine advert (approx. quarter page)	4" wide × 5.25" high or 101.6 × 133 mm (varies by magazine)	1200 × 1575
Magazine front cover	Typ. 8 3/8" × 10 7/8" high or 213 × 276 mm (varies by magazine)	2512 × 3262
Blu-ray (front cover only)	126 mm wide × 148 mm high	1488 × 1748

Many image editing software applications will have pre-defined templates for popular sizes. However, you should practise creating image documents to your own specific sizes.

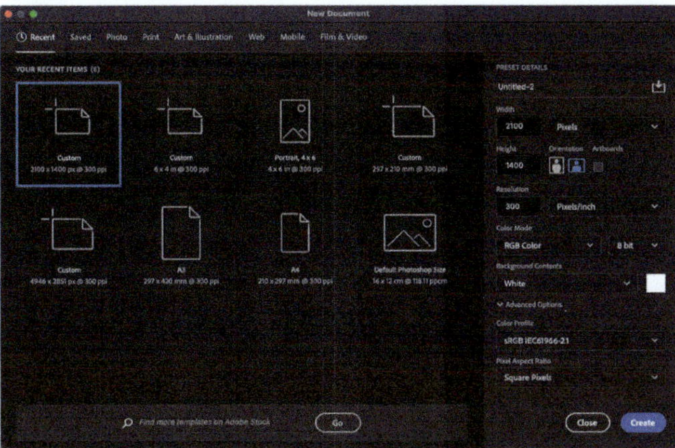

Figure 2.9 Setting up the size and resolution for a new image document

Canvas size

This can be larger than the image size. An example would be a canvas size of A4 with a digital graphic that is slightly smaller, let's say around 10" × 8" (or 250 mm × 200 mm). This will have a white border around the image and an example of what it will print like at 100 per cent scaling using A4 paper. Commercial printing generally recommends a bleed area but that is outside the scope of this qualification.

Another use for increasing the canvas size is to produce a larger graphic. For example, you could create an image document for just the front cover of a magazine and then increase the canvas size on the left to add the back cover. This effectively creates a single graphic that combines both covers for print purposes.

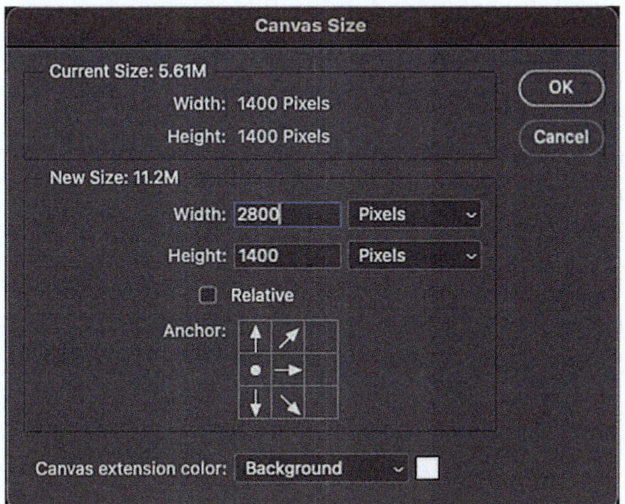

Figure 2.10 Increasing the canvas size by 100 per cent, extending it sideways

Layout tools

These tools are designed to assist the graphic designer in the positioning and correct placement of the different elements. There are three different layout tools to know about:

- Grids: Using these places a square grid over the entire graphic. It is not printed but just for display purposes in the software when positioning the different assets. The grid can be configured in dimensions (inches or cm) or in percentage terms, which is useful as 50 per cent will be halfway.
- Guides: These allow you to position a display line at a specific place on the graphic. If creating a spine for a book or DVD/Blu-ray cover, the width of the spine can be set so that you know where the fold will be. Guides are not printed and only for display use in the software.
- Rulers: These are shown for both horizontal and vertical distances at the top and side of the graphic. This can be useful to check the finished print size in addition to the placement of assets and their respective dimensions.

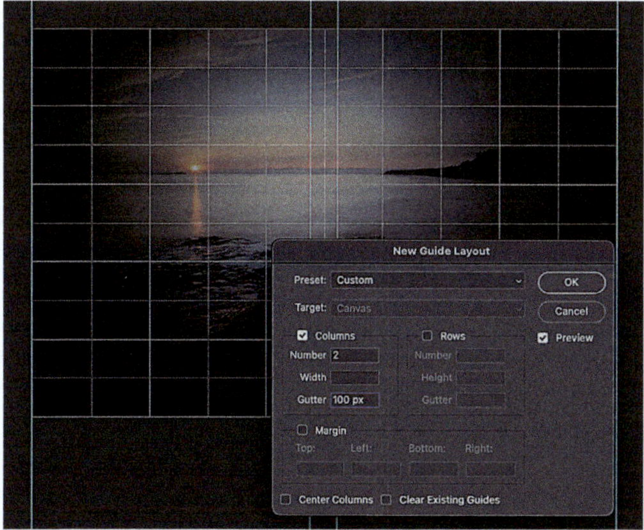

Figure 2.11 A digital graphic being created with assistance of grids, guides and rulers

Activity

Create a new graphic document for use as the cover of a pocket-sized book. The front will be 120 mm wide × 170 mm high. The spine will be 10 mm. As a single graphic to cover front, back and spine, that means the image properties should be 250 mm wide × 170 mm high. Choose 300dpi for use as a print product. You should be able to create new documents in either metric or imperial units (mm or inches) so these can be converted if necessary using 1 inch = 25.4 mm.

Add a guide in the software to show where the spine will be or set up the grid using 10 mm gaps. You will need to show the ruler to see where the spine should be positioned. Save this image document for further use.

Drawing and painting tools

These can be used to create assets and parts of the final graphic.

- Shapes: These are created as vector-based graphics and so they are scalable for any size or resolution. There is also a library of shapes built into most software. The process is to first select a suitable shape and then use the computer mouse or trackpad to draw it at the required size. The colour can be changed and the shape resized or rotated.
- Fill: This tool fills a selected area with a chosen colour. The steps are:
  - define the area using a selection tool
  - select the colour to fill the area
  - click inside the selection area.
- Gradient: This is best created on a new layer to allow editing and further modification. A gradient will consist of two defined colours, which are foreground and background. Changing the foreground colour to transparent can be one of the most useful types of gradient since this creates a very natural blending effect.
- Pencil: The pencil tool allows you to draw thin lines or change the colour of individual pixels, which is similar to a very narrow brush.
- Brush: The brush can be used with quick masks and for freehand painting or filling in shapes. There are different sizes but always larger than the pencil.
- Eraser: This is used to permanently erase parts of an image that is not wanted. It is best used with a small eraser in detail areas. Larger areas are best removed using selection tools, such as when erasing a background. Some software applications have a magic eraser, which attempts to automatically erase the parts that may not be wanted.

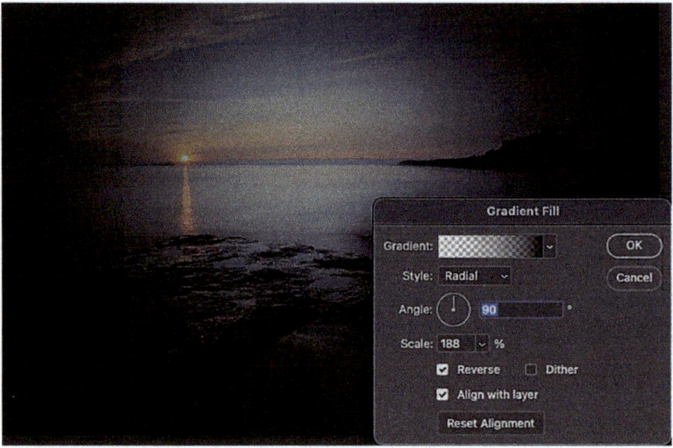

Figure 2.12 Applying a gradient effect to a sky

Adjustments to brightness, contrast and colour

Many image assets will benefit from minor adjustments to the overall brightness and contrast and colour balance since these can be adapted for different uses.

You can use either the brightness/contrast adjustment sliders or 'Levels' adjustment histogram in Adobe Photoshop, which is a more advanced way to achieve a similar result.

Adjustments using brightness/contrast sliders

The sliders are a basic tool that allow you to make manual changes visually on the screen. Move the sliders to the left or right until the best-looking result is achieved.

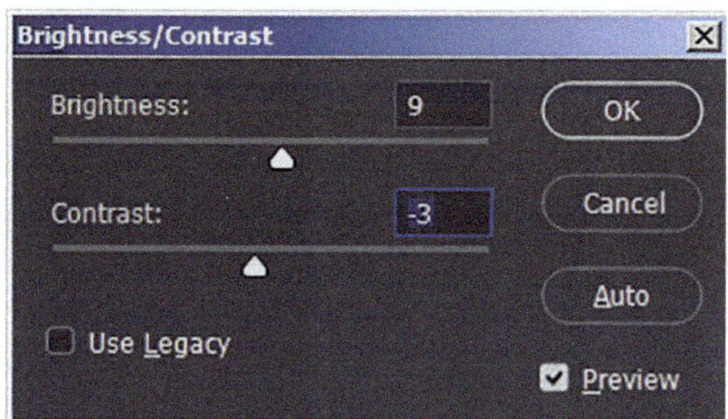

Figure 2.13 Using the brightness/contrast sliders in Adobe Photoshop

Adjustments using Levels

An alternative standard tool is to use the 'Auto Levels' function in Adobe Photoshop, which attempts to automatically decide the optimum settings. This doesn't always work well so you might have to adjust the levels manually.

Adjusting brightness and contrast will make sure that the full tonal range is used in the image, which means the darkest (shadow) areas are a true black and the brightest (highlight) areas are true white. Without this optimisation, an image can look either 'washed out' or very dark.

The benefit of making adjustments using the Auto Levels is that it displays a histogram of how the image is made up in terms of the brightest and darkest points together with everything in between. The darker levels are shown at the left-hand side and brighter levels at the right-hand side.

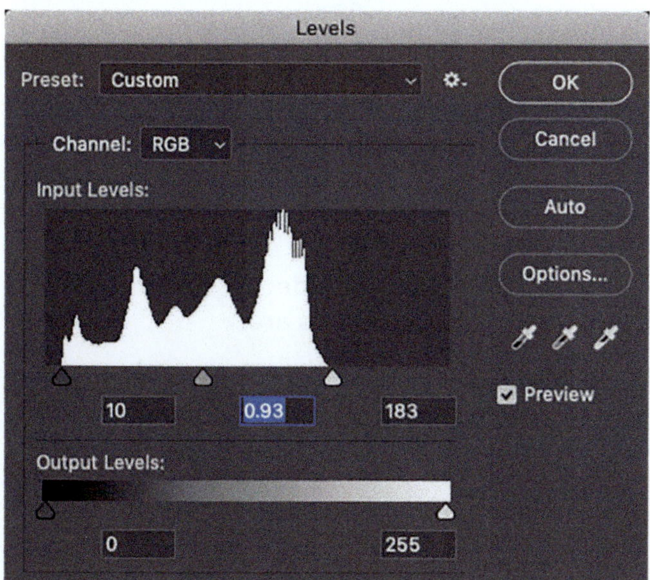

Figure 2.14 Adjusting the Levels in Adobe Photoshop

In the histogram example in Figure 2.14, most of the pixels can be seen to be in the mid-tone range, which is the central section. There are some highlights that tail off to the right-hand side but very little in the shadow detail on the left-hand side. In general, an underexposed image will have most of the pixels to the left (the dark side) and an over exposed image will have most of the pixels to the right. Flat images may have most of the pixels in the central section whereas contrasty images may have many pixels at both ends.

When using the Auto Levels adjustment, note the optimum positions for the black and white point sliders in Figure 2.14 as shown.

An Adobe Photoshop shortcut key to use the levels adjustment is ←CTRL→ and 'L'.

To make adjustments for the levels, do the following:

- Move the black point slider inwards from the left until it is at a point where the black shading on the histogram just begins.
- Move the white point slider from the right-hand side to where the histogram just ends.
- Move the mid-point (gamma slider) to a position that makes the image look the best in terms of the overall brightness and contrast on the screen.

Adjustments using Curves

This is a versatile tool that means you can brighten and darken an image together with adding contrast and adjusting the colours. It offers a wider range of adjustments compared to Levels.

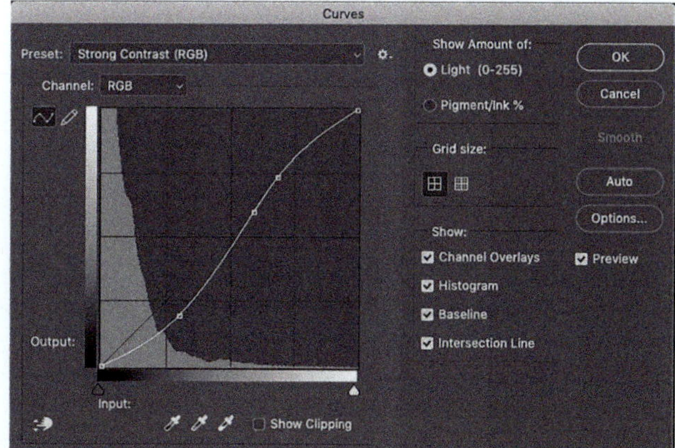

Figure 2.15 Applying a standard 'S' shape Curves adjustment in Adobe Photoshop

Using a Curves adjustment, the input and output levels are shown on a graph, initially as a straight line. You can modify the image by changing the shape of the line. As an example, you can increase the contrast by changing the shape of the curve to look like an 'S', whereas, to decrease the contrast it would be an 'inverted S' shape. Changes are made by clicking on the line to create a point, which can then be moved and repositioned.

Adjustments to colour

In Adobe Photoshop there are a number of options for adjusting the colour balance. Some of these are:

- Image menu → auto colour
- Image menu → adjustments – hue/saturation
- Image menu → adjustments – colour balance.

The auto colour option may not work well with every type of image depending on what range of colours is included. The hue and saturation are a set of sliders similar to the brightness and contrast. They enable you to change overall colour tone and colour saturation.

- Hue: This changes the overall colour. Best used with minor changes otherwise it can become very unreal.
- Saturation: This is the amount or intensity of colour. Increasing it makes a more vivid, bold image whereas reducing it makes it more washed out. Reducing this to zero converts the image to monochrome or black and white.

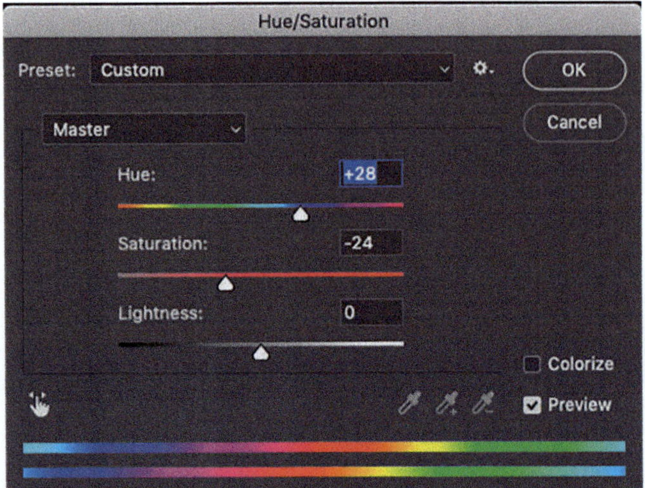

Figure 2.16 Colour adjustment using hue and saturation

Use of selections

Selection tools allow you to define parts of the image so that you can make changes to those parts without affecting the remainder of the image. Another way to use selections is to copy and paste selected parts of an image onto other layers or different image files so that you can assemble a complex digital graphic. When using selections, an active selection area appears with a flashing dotted line around it, sometimes referred to as 'marching ants'.

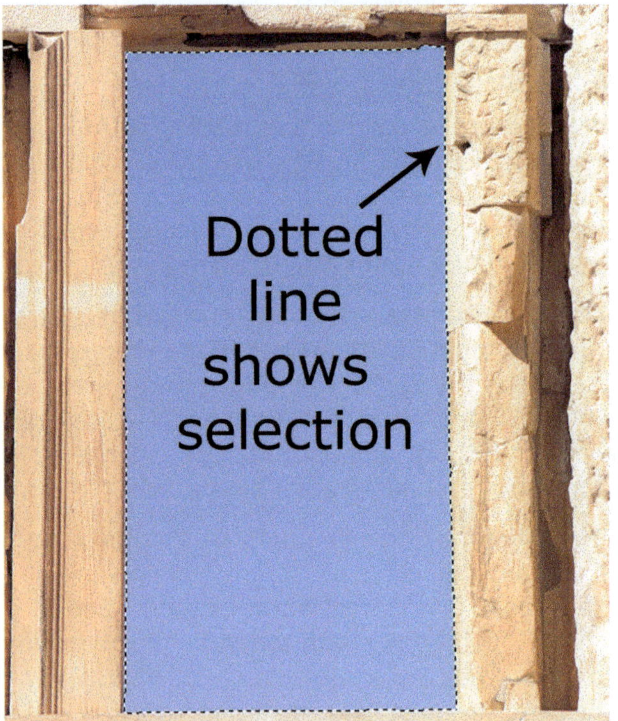

Figure 2.17 Using selection tools on a shape

Selections are generally made through one of the following options:

- shape
- colour
- edge contrast.

The best tool to use is decided by what needs to be selected. The main ones are:

- Marquee: This uses either rectangular or elliptical shapes for regular-shaped outlines in the image. On older versions of Photoshop, you could hold down the keyboard 'shift' key at the same time to draw a perfect square or circle. On later versions, this has changed to be the opposite. Hence the shift key is now only used when you want to create shapes that are not square, such as a rectangle or oval.

- Lasso: There are three different types of lasso tool:
  - The freehand lasso tool works like a pencil on the screen.
  - The polygonal tool draws straight lines between mouse click points.
  - The magnetic lasso tool attempts to trace the outline of an object by automatically recognising the edges.
- Magic wand: This selection tool uses colour to recognise which pixels are to be selected. The options bar has a checkbox to control whether these are either contiguous (all joined together) or non-contiguous (anywhere within a colour tolerance). This can be a very quick way to select large areas that are the same (or very similar) colour.

Later versions of Adobe Photoshop and some other image editing software have smart tools for selections. These attempt to automatically select what is the object.

- New/add/subtract/intersect (found on the options toolbar): Having created an initial selection, you can add extra areas or remove them using one of these modes. They are available with all selection tools.

Use of layers and layer styles

The Layers palette shows how an image is constructed – a new digital graphic will have just a single background layer. Each additional layer can be thought of as a sheet of glass which is transparent in the parts that are shown as a checkerboard pattern. You should always imagine that you are looking down on these layers from above (the top of the layer stack). This is because the top layer is seen first and you will be able to see through all the transparent areas to anything that is underneath.

Individual layers can be added, turned off for editing, renamed or moved. Contents can also be changed and a skilful use of layers is a great way to create complex digital graphics.

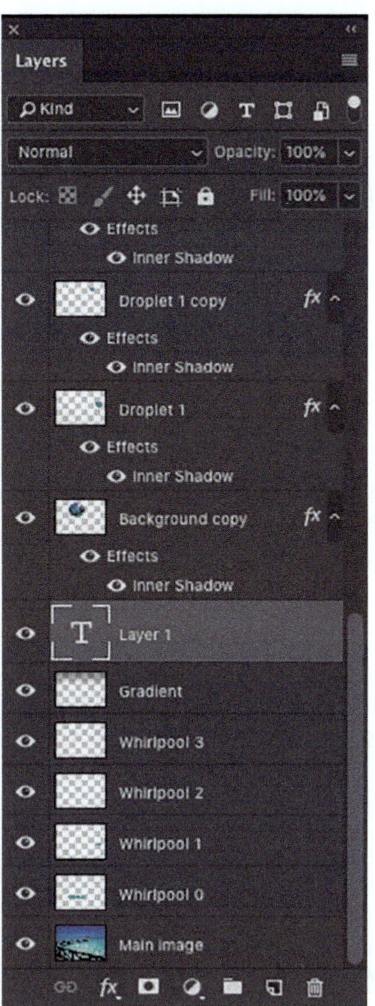

Figure 2.18 A complex layer stack

The tools for working with layers are found at the bottom of the Layers panel. Here you can create different types of layer as well as duplicate or delete them.

- Create a layer: When you first open a single image, there will be one layer in the stack. This is typically named 'background'. By clicking on the new layer icon, a blank layer is created. If you copy an asset from a different image document and paste it onto your digital graphic, it will appear as a new layer.
- Duplicate a layer: This enables you to make an exact copy of a layer so you can work on that without affecting the original. This is referred to as non-destructive editing. Drag an existing layer down and drop it on the new layer icon. This way, if the edit goes wrong then you still have the original layer to start again.

- Delete a layer: Sometimes you can experiment with different techniques on a different layer. If the outcome doesn't work or if you want to try again, you should clean up the layer stack by deleting any layers that are not needed. This is identified as the rubbish bin icon.
- Merge layers: When constructing a graphic from multiple parts, sometimes it is worthwhile to merge selected layers. An example would be where several layers are used that have a different shape, all of which are combined to create an object. However, be careful with merging layers since this cannot be undone and can limit the possibilities for further editing of different elements.
- Rename layers: When creating new layers, they will be named something like layer 1, layer 2 or copy 1, copy 2. With a large layer stack this isn't very helpful in being able to know what element or content is on what layer. A way around this is to double click the layer in the stack and type a more descriptive name, such as 'client logo', 'person' or 'background'.
- Change opacity: The default for all layers is that the opacity is 100 per cent, which means that a solid colour has no transparency and blocks anything that is on a layer below it. However, the opacity for any layer can be adjusted between 0 per cent and 100 per cent. Using something like 50 per cent makes the layer semi-transparent. That can be used as a feature of the graphic with a misty or ghost-like appearance. It can also be useful as a temporary measure when editing edges to make selections to blend two or more layers.

Most image editing software options have the ability to work with layers. This is a core skill in creating graphics since each asset, text and image are all placed on separate layers. That means they can be edited independently from the rest of the graphic content.

Layer styles

These are typically used on text, shapes and sometimes objects that have been cut out and placed on a new layer.

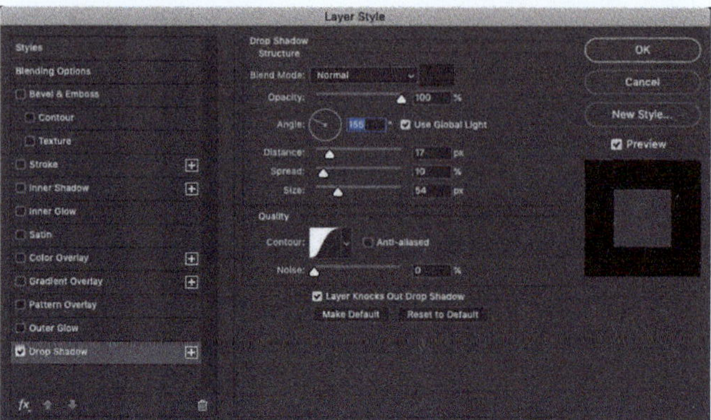

Figure 2.19 Adding a drop shadow layer style to text

The most common styles are a drop shadow plus bevel and emboss. You can experiment with the settings such as light direction and depth. The bevel and emboss adds a three-dimensional effect, which can also be enhanced with a texture.

Retouching

The purpose of the clone stamp is to duplicate parts of the image from one section into a different section. This is a very useful tool that can be used to remove unwanted details from an image, although practice is needed to build up your skill level.

How to use the clone tool:

1. Click on the icon in the toolbox once to select it.
2. If needed, select the brush style from the 'options' bar, although the soft-edged default brush works well on most images.
3. Set the required brush size (use the left and right square brackets [ ] to decrease and increase size).
4. Move the mouse onto the image and position it close to the feature that you want to remove, then press and hold down the 'Alt' key so that the mouse cursor changes to a 'target' icon.
5. Single click with the left mouse button, then release the 'Alt' key.
6. Carefully move the mouse across the image onto the part to be removed, remembering where you have just clicked for the clone source point.
7. Click and hold down the left mouse button so that a cross hair and a circle are shown as mouse cursors. The tool works by copying

the colour information from the cross hair (source) and pasting it into the circle (destination).

8 Repeat as necessary.

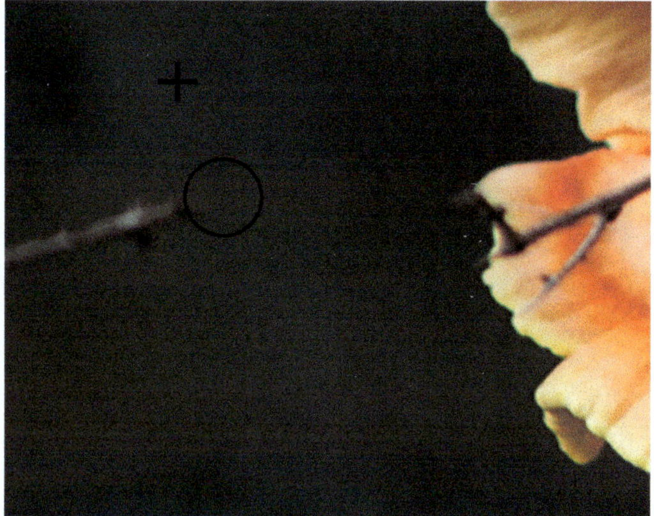

Figure 2.20 Using the cloning tool to remove unwanted objects

Adobe Photoshop has both healing and patch tools. You can use the healing brushes to remove small blemishes and spots by blending the colours and textures. Having selected a suitable tool size that is typically slightly larger than the blemish, you then just click on it with the mouse. The patch tool is a large area healing brush and is used by first drawing a shape with the mouse. This area can be used as the 'source' or 'destination' for the blending.

As part of retouching, some additional tools can be useful. The pencil and brush tools can also be used for fine details. Their use is explained earlier in the unit. Other tools include:

- Blur tool: The blur tool is the opposite of sharpening and effectively blurs the area under the cursor. Used for softening edges.
- Sharpen tool: This does the opposite of blurring but is a fairly subtle effect.
- Smudge tool: This is a good way to 'push' colours around using the mouse. Think of an oil painting when the oils are still wet – you could push the colours around with a finger.
- Stroke tool: This can be used to create a solid line around the edge of a selection. The thickness of the edge can be set in the tool options.
- Fill tool: This can be used to fill a defined area with a specific colour. Typically used with selection tools to create coloured shapes.
- Dodge tool: The name of this tool comes from a darkroom technique whereby the light is restricted from reaching the photographic paper. This makes the image lighter.
- Burn tool: The name of this tool also comes from the darkroom and is the opposite to the dodge tool, so makes it darker.
- Sponge tool: This is used to change the colour saturation of selected parts of the image. You can change the mode between saturate and desaturate to increase or decrease the colour intensity.
- Colour swatches: Adobe Photoshop and other image editing software have swatches, which is a selection of colours for use. In Photoshop, this is a separate panel. You can select a library set, add and remove colours to this. If working with a house style for a client, you can pre-load the standard colours into the swatch panel. This makes it quicker to select and use with the different tools.
- Colour picker: On the main toolbar there is a colour picker tool. This samples the colour at any point in the graphic and loads it ready for use with another tool. One example of its use is to fill a background with a colour that already exists in the graphic.

Transformation techniques

This technique allows you to modify the shape or perspective of an image. For example, it can be used to straighten the vertical angles that are seen when photographing tall buildings from low down. Having selected the entire image, you can use the transform menu options or use Ctrl and 'T' (or Command and 'T' on a Mac) and click on any of the corners to freely adjust the individual points.

Figure 2.21 Adding text to a graphic

Typography

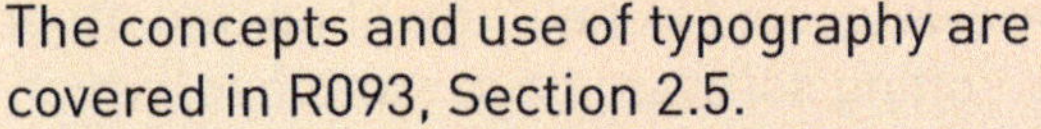

Synoptic link

The concepts and use of typography are covered in R093, Section 2.5.

In this unit, we are now using the tools of the software to add text (or type) to the graphic, which is the application of typography. Most digital graphics will include some sort of text in the form of a title or information.

Adding text or type

Select the type or text tool from the toolbar. Click on the graphic where you want to start and enter the text using the keyboard. You can set up the font, size and colour first or change them later once the text has been placed. It is not unusual to have to change the font size so that it is a suitable size when viewing the graphic.

- Font style: Try to be consistent and not have multiple fonts in the same graphic.
- Font size: This should be large enough so that the viewer finds it easy to read.

In addition to colour, text effects can be used so the text can be transformed or curved. However, this can make it more difficult to read. Keep the audience in mind when choosing colour and any effects.

Filters and effects

There is a large range of filters and effects available in Adobe Photoshop and in some alternative image editing software. A few of the more popular examples would be:

- Stylise: This allows you to modify the visual style, such as changing from a photograph to a water colour or oil-based painting. This is often used to create images for comics and graphic novels.
- Blur: It isn't likely that you would blur an entire image, but this can be useful on a background. The idea here is to leave the subject clean and sharp, while making the background quite blurred so it is not distracting to the viewer. A good option here is to use the gaussian blur option in Adobe Photoshop, but other blurring tools may be available. Motion blur is another effect to consider, to simulate movement.
- Sharpen: This can improve an image, but it can't work miracles. If an image is blurred, pixelated or out of focus, then sharpening isn't going to make it much better. However, minor improvements can be made, such as to the edges or using the unsharp mask in Adobe Photoshop. Typical settings would be around 100–150 per cent and a radius of 1–2 depending on what the image is.

Depending on the software, an effect in the digital graphic can be created in different ways. Some applications will have specific effects in a menu and others will need to be produced by applying a range of tools and techniques. Some examples include:

- Monochrome: Converting an image or perhaps just a background to monochrome can be achieved in several ways. These include changing the colour saturation to zero, desaturating, grayscale mode or a specific black and white adjustment. This is one way to add impact to the subject of a graphic so that its colour stands out from the black and white tones that are behind it.
- Colour toning: The adjustments menu will have various options to modify the colour balance, colour mixing and/or replace colours. You should have an idea in mind based on your planning if attempting to modify the colour to something very different. Otherwise, colour toning can be used to enhance the colours for more impact.
- Vignette: This term means that the image will have darker areas around the edges, especially in the corners. It is a way to produce a more dramatic graphic and emphasise the subject or content that is in the centre of the frame. In Adobe Photoshop, this can be created using an oval marquee selection tool, feathering the edges and filling with a dark colour or changing the levels/curves.

Figure 2.22 Using a monochrome background and vignette in a digital graphic

Filter effects can be applied to individual assets, such as background images or smaller image assets that have been placed on top of the background image. Try not to rely too much on filters though, since it is easy to ruin a graphic that is basically sound.

Activity

Using your pocket-book cover from the previous activity, add the following content to the front cover (you can change the title and images but check with your teacher):

- Background colour: Blue
- Add title text in white: Pocket guide to London
- Add a layer style to the title text for a drop shadow
- Add two small images of London, side by side at the bottom of the front cover
- Make any adjustments to the size, shape or brightness/contrast as needed.

Test your knowledge

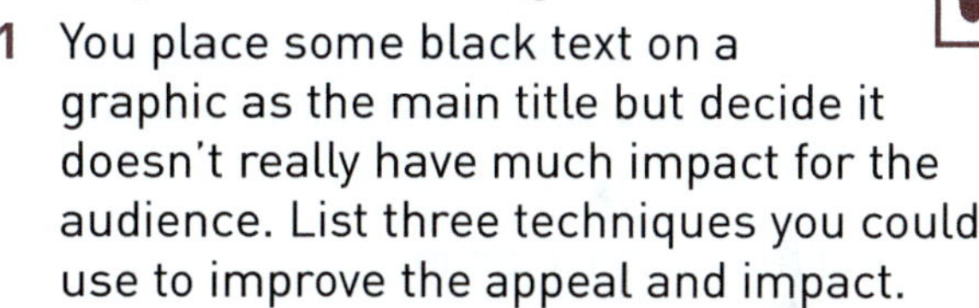

1 You place some black text on a graphic as the main title but decide it doesn't really have much impact for the audience. List three techniques you could use to improve the appeal and impact.

3.2 Technical skills to source, create and prepare assets for use within digital graphics

Source assets for use in digital graphics

The range of assets that could be used within a digital graphic are:

- images
- photographs
- scanned images
- graphics and symbols
- client logos and visual identity.

Table 2.4 Example asset table and main information needed

Image ref	Properties	Source	Legal issues	Potential use

Whatever source these image assets are obtained from, it is good practice to store them all in a working asset folder. Depending on your computer and operating system, you may need to copy these from a download folder into your working folder.

Sources for images and graphics can include:

- Internet: A web search can locate a wide range of images subject to restrictions. Type in a description of the image needed and select image results.
- Stock libraries: Most of these have a website to browse and purchase images.
- Client: For their own logos, visual identity and some potential images.
- Photographers: You may be able to commission work from photographers directly.
- Printed materials: These will need to be scanned at an appropriate resolution to be suitable for use.

When using the internet, an image search is likely to display many pages of results. One of the limitations is usually the image size in terms of pixel dimensions and dpi resolution. If an image is used on a web page, it only needs to be 72dpi and no larger than the display monitor. Unfortunately, if wanting to use the image in a print product that will not be enough as print resolution typically needs to be 300dpi. An advanced search on images can be used so that only images larger than a specific size are shown in the results. This is a better option to ensure the image assets are technically compatible with what you want to do. Always check the pixel dimensions and divide these by 300 to determine how large they could be (in inches) as part of a print-based product.

The second limitation is the permission for use. Most of the content on the web is protected by copyright and you may need permission from the owner to use it. If working in the media industry, you will need to know how to obtain copyright clearance and permissions, so make sure you are able to do this. Always check and record information on copyright and permissions. You can use an asset table for this. The main fields needed are shown in Table 2.4.

The column information includes:

- Image reference: Descriptive name or thumbnail picture.
- Properties: The properties of the asset.
- Source: Where the asset is from (use a URL but not 'Google images').
- Legal issues: Is it copyrighted, trademarked or royalty free and how would you obtain permission for its use?
- Potential use: This should be your own thoughts on how and where you could use the image in the digital graphic.

This qualification is set in a commercial context so you will need to consider the use of all the image assets as if they are to be published in the media industry. There are some allowances to use copyrighted material for educational use, but it is the commercial context that needs to be covered.

Synoptic link

For more information on copyright and permissions, refer to R093, Section 3.4.

Activity

Use the web to search for images of London and 'London logo'. Select image results in the search options. Use the search tools to change the size, colour and usage rights. Download your chosen images but make sure you make notes of the size and usage at the same time.

Create assets for use in digital graphics

If you are creating assets, the range of tools and techniques covered throughout this unit may be useful. Many can also be used when creating the final graphic.

There are two methods used to create assets:

1. Editing sourced assets to create a **derivative** asset.
2. Creating assets using drawing tools.

When planning your final graphic, you may have identified the need for some specific assets that will need to be created. For example, a logo, symbol or other graphic that would be part of the finished design. This may have to be drawn digitally in an image editing software application or created from other assets that act as a starting point. When creating assets using drawing tools, many software options will have the ability to store these as a vector-based file. If modifying an existing image asset from the web, this will most likely be a bitmap or raster-based file. The differences in these two types were covered earlier in this unit, in Section 2.2.

Whether the image assets were sourced, or you intend to create them, at this point you will need to use the image editing software. A good approach is to collect together all of the assets into one folder, including the visual identity that you created for the client, copy text and a range of images that will be used for both the background and foreground graphics. It is important to manage your assets using appropriate file names and folders.

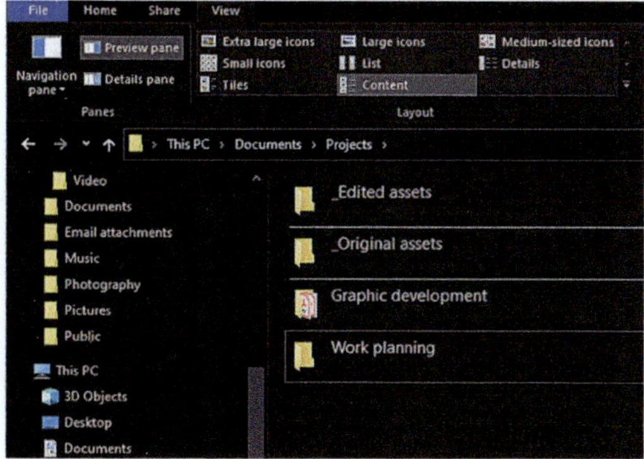

Figure 2.23 Organising folders for sourced, edited and created assets

The following tools and techniques can be used when creating your image-based assets. However, some can also be used when creating the final graphic, so they are not exclusively for creating assets. Another use is when creating a derivative asset that is based on a sourced or downloaded asset. This is where you modify a sourced asset and create a new one of your own (although in terms of copyright, you only own your changes and not the original image such that the derivative is not exclusively yours).

Removing a background

You might want to remove a background from an asset so that it can be placed onto a different image. By deleting a background, it becomes transparent so you can effectively see through to what is underneath when using layers. A transparent area is usually shown as a checkboard pattern. You can use the selection tools and possibly the eraser to do this, as explained earlier in this unit.

Figure 2.24 Deleting a background to make it transparent

Key term

Derivative Based on another source such as the work of another artist or designer or a product which already exists.

Figure 2.25 Cropping an image to be a square layout

Cropping an image

Reasons for the image not being straight could be either a scanned image that was not square on the scanner or a photo from a digital camera where the horizon is not straight across the frame. If wanting to use only part of an image as an asset in a graphic, you may want to crop this from the full picture. Another reason for cropping is to obtain the size and shape that you need.

To crop and straighten an image in the same process:

1. Select the 'Crop' tool from the Toolbox. If wanting a specific size, this can be entered in the option bar fields as shown. In Figure 2.25, we have chosen 150 mm width, 100 mm height and 300dpi.
2. Draw a box around the area that is approximately how you want your composition to look.
3. Adjust the position of the corners and edges as needed. Everything that is outside this crop window will be removed when you complete the crop command.
4. To rotate the crop window, position the mouse cursor just outside a corner of the box so that a 'rotate' icon is displayed for the mouse cursor. You can then freely rotate the box left or right as needed.
5. Press 'Enter' to perform the final crop or click on the tick mark in the Options bar.

Activity

Earlier in this chapter, Figure 2.2 shows a basic visual identity. Use your image editing software to create your own version of this.

Start with a square image document, 600 pixels wide and high at 300dpi.

Add the three colours using fill and drawing tools.

Add the text at the bottom of the logo.

Save the logo with a suitable filename and file format, keeping the layers intact.

Test your knowledge

2. If creating an asset with a transparent background, what file format would you save it in?

Modify images and other assets to ensure the technical compatibility for use within print graphics

Ensuring the technical compatibility of assets

The technical properties of an image asset include the pixel dimensions and dpi resolution. Since you will be creating a print product to begin with, you will need to be using assets that can be printed with 300dpi at the intended size. Therefore, if you have sourced an image from the web at 300 pixels wide, it would only be suitable for viewing if printed at 1 inch (25 mm) width. However, it is possible to edit image assets and crop or resize them to make sure they are technically compatible. To an extent, resampling techniques can be used to increase the resolution, but the quality and sharpness may not be very good.

Figure 2.26 Resampling an asset for use

Activity

Find some low-resolution images from the internet that are less than 300 pixels in width or height and 72dpi.

1. Open the image asset in your image editing software.
2. Check the image properties to view the pixel dimensions and resolution.
3. Check the box for resample image. Change the resolution to 300dpi so that it will be suitable for print use. Enter 600 pixels in the pixel dimensions field so that it will be 2 inches.
4. Click on OK – when the box closes you may notice the display changes with the new resolution.
5. Work through several different images, resizing to larger sizes so that they are technically compatible for use in a print product.
6. Make notes of the 'before' and 'after' pixel dimensions and resolutions.

If you do resample an asset, it is a good idea to check if the image quality will be good enough for what you need so that you are not wasting your time. The best way to review the image quality is to use the zoom control to view the asset at 100 per cent magnification. Look closely to see whether it is blurred, fuzzy or out of focus on the important subject areas. If the image quality is poor, close the file and find something else.

Store assets for use

There are two main factors to consider when storing assets for use. These are:

- Storage location: So that the assets can be easily located and identified.
- Asset properties: So that the image size, resolution and file format is suitable.

Once you have downloaded any images and assets from the internet, these will most likely be stored in your computer 'download' folder. The next step is to copy these across into a working asset folder for creating your digital graphic.

Saving images and graphics

This is where you can save your edited image and graphical assets in an appropriate folder. This could be your computer hard disk, network drive or suitable cloud-based storage medium. It is a good idea to save a full-size high-resolution image as your master file since it is easy to make this smaller later on (but not so easy to make something larger that is a high enough quality). Keep in mind that once pixels or image quality are discarded, they cannot be recovered. If any assets are vector-based files, you may be able to import them directly into your graphic or alternatively they can be converted to a bitmap file format. The process to convert the vector file is straightforward in Adobe Photoshop – from the Layer menu, click on 'Rasterize'.

Synoptic link

Review the file formats for images in R093, Section 4.2.1 before deciding what format to use. In particular, look at the support for the full range of colours and transparency.

Activity

On your computer system, prepare a set of folders for a new project.

Choose a project name, for example practice graphic.

Add sub folders for original assets, visual identity, edited assets and final graphics.

Copy any relevant assets into the appropriate folders (this can include the logo that you created earlier).

Change the file format where necessary, for example, from JPG to PSD or PNG if you will want to use it with a transparent background.

3.3 Techniques to save and export visual identity and digital graphics

Save and export

Saving your work in visual identity and digital graphics has two important stages. This is to make sure you have a master file to work with and your client has a suitable file that they can view and use.

When exporting a version of your work, you should consider the file format and the image properties to make sure it will be fit for purpose by the client. The image properties include both the overall pixel dimensions and the dpi resolution, which are a fundamentally important part of the unit.

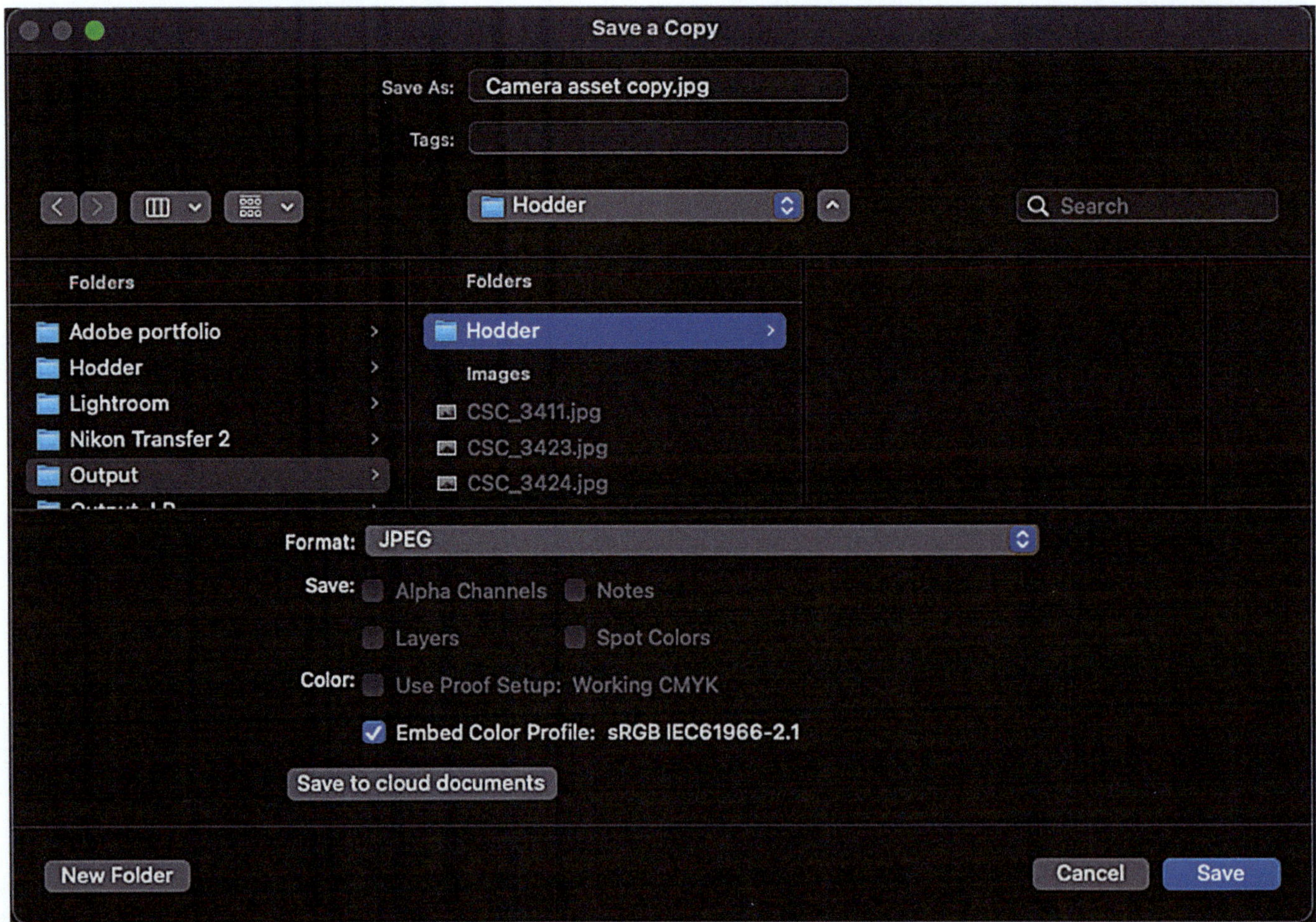

Figure 2.27 Saving an asset for use (File menu – Save as...)

- Print use: Pixel dimensions to be based on print size using 300dpi. To calculate the pixel dimensions, multiply the print size (in inches) by 300. If you need to convert mm to inches, use 25.4 mm = 1 inch.
- Web or multimedia use: Pixel dimensions to be based on a conventional dpi resolution of 72 but the total pixel dimensions are more important to make sure the graphic fits the web page or display and can be downloaded quickly. Unlike print products, there are no calculations as such for this – the pixel dimensions and dpi should be specified in the client requirements but double check the height and width are the right way around.

The choice of file naming is also important. Make sure that you use different names for the print version and web/display version. This should be identifiable in the filename and not just the file extension.

Activity

Use a practice graphic that you have created, for example the pocket-book cover from earlier in this chapter.

Store your graphic in the native file format (i.e. the standard format) for the software. This could be PSD for Photoshop/Photopea or XCF for Gimp.

Export a copy for general use on a different computer system as a high-quality JPG (typically 10–12 on the quality scale that is between 1 and 12).

Change the image properties to make the graphic 800 pixels high (but make sure you maintain the same aspect ratio, otherwise it will be squashed or stretched).

Export the smaller graphic with a different filename (you could add low-res or web on the end).

Close the graphic – without saving (this is important to make sure you don't overwrite your high resolution graphic with the resized web version).

Synoptic links

The choice of file format and image properties depends on how the digital graphics are to be used and distributed. More information can be found in R093, Sections 4.1 and 4.2.

Case study

The visual identity of Starbucks has been iconic for many years. It started with a two tailed mermaid or a siren inside a circle. The original colour was brown although this evolved into green over the years. The siren is now a recognised part of their visual identity.

1. Investigate the rebranding of the logo since its original design in 1971.
2. What was the connection between the siren character and coffee?
3. Why did the company change from brown to green as the colour for the logo?

Assignment practice

You have been asked by an agency to submit a graphic poster to advertise yourself as a graphic designer. The poster should show something about yourself in the images chosen, such as your favourite subjects, hobbies or interests.

Your poster should include a logo with your own initials and other unique identifier to create your own visual identity.

The poster should be created and saved for print use at 10″ × 8″. A second copy for use on the agency website should also be exported, which is 800 pixels wide.

Unit R095

Characters and comics

About this unit

In the creative media industry there are a huge variety of technical and creative job roles involving character creation and comic design. This unit will enable you to identify core conventions of both character and comic creation and understand the basics of planning, designing, creating and reviewing characters and comics.

This unit is all about creating characters and using those characters to create a comic which will tell a story. You will learn how to design and create effective and engaging characters which will engage your target audience. You will also learn how to use comic conventions to design and create comics which tell a story.

Topic areas

In this chapter you will learn how to:

- plan characters and comics (TA1)
- create characters and comics (TA2)
- review characters and comics (TA3).

Resources for this unit

Hardware/equipment: Alongside standard computer hardware, you could use the following if they were available to you – digital cameras, scanner, stylus, graphics tablet, modelling materials.

Software: Graphics creation and photo editing applications, such as Adobe Photoshop, Illustrator, Fireworks, Serif DrawPlus, PhotoPlus, Affinity, Pixelmator, GIMP.
You will also need software to create your comic which could be comic specific such as Comic Life, Pixton and Comic, iStudio or more generic software e.g. Microsoft Publisher.

How will I be assessed?

You will complete an assignment that is set by OCR. This will be completed independently by yourself, without using any additional resources or teacher assistance to help you. The assignment will have a scenario or client brief that defines what you will need to create. You will work through a series of tasks that cover the three topic areas to plan, create and review a character and comic. Your evidence will then be marked by your teacher using the OCR marking criteria, which will then be externally checked/moderated by OCR to confirm your achievement.

Topic area 1 Plan characters and comics

Getting started

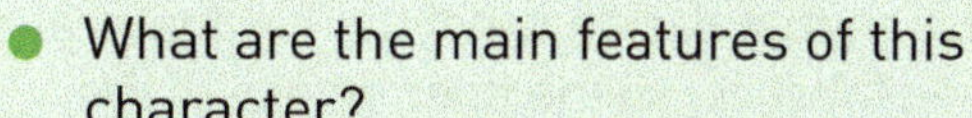

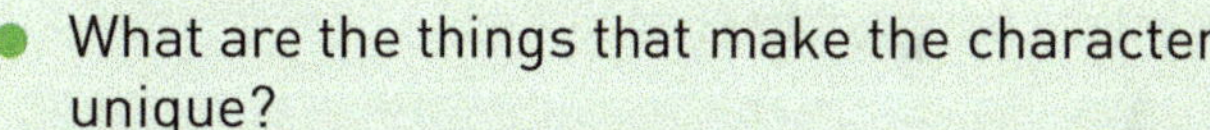

Think of a famous character from a children's film, book or television programme. Draw a sketch of this character. Now think about this character and answer the following questions.

- What are the main features of this character?
- What are the things that make the character unique?
- Why do you think the audience engages with this character?

1.1 Character features and conventions

Types of characters

Characters can be represented in a range of different styles. When deciding on a style there are a number of things to consider, such as target audience and the purpose of the character.

Cartoons

Characters designed to appeal to a young target audience often use bold colours and cartoon styling such as bold outlines and strong detail, usually with limited fine detail, so that they are eye catching and friendly. Characters designed for an older audience may vary more in their appearance and the style may be more dependent on the character's purpose. For example, characters used in infographics are often simplified to show the key points of the graphic, such as using an image of a penguin to show facts about it in the zoo. Characters are also used to display information, as in an infographic, and are often used to complement text when delivering information or a story.

Figure 3.1 Characters designed to engage a younger audience

Doodles and photorealistic

Doodle style characters are used in comic books or as illustrations in fictional books. These types of characters may have the appearance of being created quickly and simply to illustrate a point. But these characters are carefully thought out and designed to create this illusion for the reader. This style of character design has been in use for a very long time.

In contrast, photorealistic character design is a recent addition to the design style of characters. Photorealistic characters are created using computer software and are generally 3D character designs. This style is often used for human character design, such as in video games, but can be used for other types of characters too.

Geometric and minimalist/simplification

Geometric and minimalist/simplification styles are where shapes and silhouettes are combined to form characters. Characters created in a simplified form may, for example, not include facial features or the finer detail that would complicate the design and detract from the purpose of the characters. The detail of the animal design is not the key feature here, that is the statistics, so the finer details of the characters have not been included.

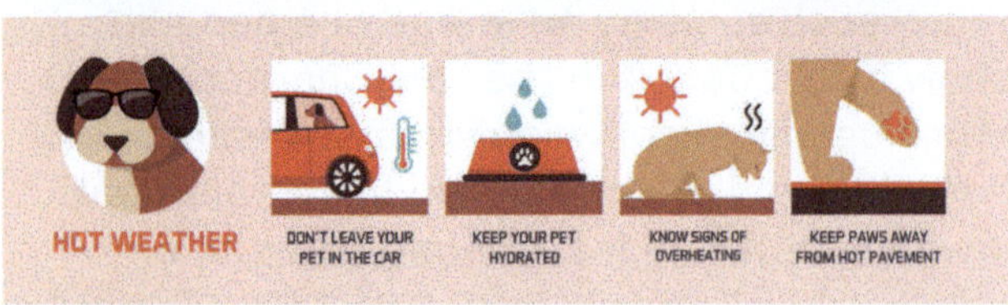

Figure 3.2 Characters can be used to display information using minimalist character design

Features of characters

Colour

Colour is significant for character design. There are particular colours which an audience will identity with different genres, emotions and character traits. Some examples of colour use for character design are shown in Table 3.1.

Table 3.1 Colour use for character design

Colour	Impact
Red	Love, anger, passion
Orange	Energy, happiness, warmth
Yellow	Happiness, hope, energy
Green	Nature, growth, fresh
Blue	Calm, sad, nature, cold
Purple	Royalty, wealth, richness
Black/grey	Mystery, evil, formal

The other colour-based convention used in character design is the assignment of primary and secondary colours. The hero or **protagonist** in a story is generally designed using mainly primary colours, whereas the villain or **antagonist** will usually be designed to incorporate secondary colours. This is a way of subtly indicating the character's position in a story to the reader.

Proportion

It is also possible to create a different style of character by using changes in proportion. This is generally used to either highlight a feature of a particular character or as a general design style for all the characters in a comic. For example, in some comic series all the characters can be see with disproportionately large heads compared to the rest of their bodies. Similarly, in fairytale style stories, the witch characters are often depicted with disproportionally large pointy noses.

Key terms

Protagonist One of the main characters in a story, often the hero.

Antagonist One of the main characters in a story, often the villain.

Activity

Create this table in word processing software and then use your own research to complete it.

Type of character	Example	What audience and purpose do you think suits this type of character?
Cartoon		
Doodle		
Photorealistic		
Geometric shapes		
Minimalist/simplification		

Figure 3.3 Minimalist character design

Key terms

Trope A generalisation of how a character with a particular trait might look.

Anthropomorphism Applying human physical and non-physical characteristics to non-human items such as inanimate objects or animals.

Characteristics and conventions

Character tropes

Simply put, character **tropes** are a generalisation of how a character with a particular trait might look. For example, the 'villain' character in a story may be a large imposing character, dressed in dark colours with strong features. Or the 'hero' characters may wear capes. Character tropes are often used in character design and can allow a character and its place in the story to be easily recognisable to the user. The downside of character tropes is that if overused they can make a character seem a little less authentic and more generic.

Physical characteristics

The physical characteristics of many characters are represented by a signature look or outfit. For example, Superman's blue suit and red cape, with the S icon on his chest or Tintin's quiff hairstyle and signature clothing style are both instantly recognisable.

Comic characters often have exaggerated physical characteristics, such as facial features, hair styles or even outfits. The characters' physical appearance is consistently used throughout the comic and other strips within the series. This consistency allows readers to easily identify the core characters throughout the storylines. Sometimes this look can reflect the characters' personality, such as the use of darker colours in the outfits and design of more sinister characters. Other times it will link more to the overall theme of the comic as an indication of the genre of the story.

Anthropomorphism is very common and well-used in character design. It involves giving an object or non-human being human characteristics. There are many examples of this, such as talking animals or animal characters walking on two legs or wearing clothes like a human. This can also be seen in the design of facial characteristics, where the character is given a more humanised face than the character would have in real life, allowing them to express human emotions more easily. A more extreme version of anthropomorphism is when inanimate objects are given human-like characteristics and in effect come to life. For example, a walking, talking teapot, with arms and legs and a face that is not dissimilar to a human face.

Manga characters have their own distinctive and easily identifiable physical characteristics. For example:

- they are usually drawn with very large eyes, which are used to show the character's feelings
- the mouth and nose are often small
- they have distinctive hairstyles in a range of colours
- they often appear youthful and have a childlike appearance.

Figure 3.4 Examples of Manga facial characteristics

Two comic creators are Charles Schulz and Georges Hergé, who create the American comic *Peanuts* and the Belgian comic *Tintin* respectively. Their character design was much simpler in form than later comics such as Marvel or DC but is distinctive for its hand drawn appearance. The characters were not always as detailed as more modern comic characters. In terms of facial features they are quite simplistic, but as comics which were aimed at a broad audience and have stood the test of time in terms of storytelling and popularity they are none the less very successful designs.

Non-physical characteristics

Superhero characters typically have exaggerated strengths and weaknesses, which are often emphasised in the storyline of the comic strip. They are usually the link between the hero and the villain that go back to the origin of how they came to be adversaries in the character backstory.

As with other fictional media, to draw the user into the story, characters in comic strips often have characteristics that the reader can relate to, whether this is a personality trait, skill, a fear or an insecurity.

Many of the non-physical characteristics seen in superhero comic characters are linked to the superpowers of the hero or villain. For example, mind reading, telepathy, x-ray vision. Some will demonstrate more conventional characteristics such as high intellect and technical ability, as in the character of Tony Stark (*Iron Man*).

Some comic makers create characters which have non-physical characteristics that are woven into their backstory and appear throughout the storylines. For example, DC and Marvel comics both focus on superheroes but with a different approach. DC comics base their characters and storylines on superhuman heroes, such as Superman or Wonder Woman. These characters are often portrayed as the hero saving the human race from disaster. In contrast, Marvel create more 'everyman' characters, with normal people gaining powers or abilities which allow them to become superheroes. For example, Peter Parker and his alter ego Spiderman or the Hulk and his alter ego Bruce Banner. These characters are often more flawed, with storylines tending to depict their weaknesses as well as their strengths. They are often overcoming issues within their own life as well as defeating the villain of the story.

Not all comic book characters are superheroes; the non-physical characteristics will often link to the genre of the comic strip. For example, in a horror comic strip you would expect characters to reflect scary characteristics such as dishonesty and deviousness. Children's comic book characters will have more simplistic characteristics such as happiness, sadness or humour. As there are now such a wide range of comic book genres there are opportunities to create a huge range of both physical and non-physical characteristics for comic characters.

Facial characteristics

Facial characteristics are an important tool for designers in using characters to tell a story or give information. When using characters in static graphics such as comics, rather than dynamic graphics such as animation, the facial expression and characteristics of the character's face have a very important part to play. They can set the scene by showing the tone of the interaction or dialogue. For example, in some scenes there may not be any dialogue between characters or there may only be one character in the scene, but the facial expression of the character shown can indicate what is happening in the scene.

Facial characteristics in character design can often demonstrate a range of different design elements to show emotion. This is often linked to the features of the face and using the position and size of these features can indicate a lot to the reader.

Eyebrows

The placement and design of a character's eyebrows can add a lot of expression to the face, for example:

- harsh eyebrow lines which point downwards towards the nose can be used to express anger (as in Figure 3.5)
- raised or arched eyebrows can show disbelief or surprise
- eyebrows pointing down towards the edge of the face indicate sadness.

Eyes

The size and position of eyes can be used in a similar way to convey the emotion of the characters. The shape of the eye will actually often mirror the shape of the eyebrow to show a particular emotion. For example, to show sadness, eyes are often wide with a slight narrowing at the outside edge, with the eyebrows pointing down towards the edge of the face.

Figure 3.5 Example of character facial expression setting the tone for the scene without words

Mouth

The shape and positioning of the character's mouth can be used as a tool to show emotion or to complement the tone of the dialogue. Sometimes the mouth is shown open simply to allow the reader to see who is speaking, but often the shape of the mouth conveys much more than this. A wide-mouthed smile with the teeth showing is often a sign of happiness or pleasure, while showing the mouth as a straight horizontal line with no lips or teeth can indicate that a character is cross or frustrated, for example.

Techniques

Characters' features are often exaggerated or drawn out of proportion deliberately to help the designer to create a character that appeals to the target audience and that reflects some of the tropes you looked at earlier. Often characters that are designed for a younger target audience have exaggerated or over simplified features to make them appear friendly and their tone easier to read. For more mature audiences, you tend to find that the character design is a little more realistic and the features created are more in proportion with the character as a whole. For example, Mrs Potts the talking teapot from Disney's *Beauty and the Beast* is clearly designed for a younger audience whereas a character such as Wolverine from the Marvel comic books is targeted at a much older audience and so is designed in a much more realistic way.

Activity

Find images of two cartoon-style characters. Label each one to show how colour has been used to indicate physical and non-physical characteristics of the character.

Synoptic links

You can find further information about this topic in Unit R093, Sections 2.1 and 2.5.

1.2 Conventions of comics

Conventions for storytelling in comics

Panel layout and story flow

Comic strips have very clear characteristics in terms of layout and **story flow**, which is unlike many other illustrated storytelling methods. Western-style comic strips conventionally display their artwork in a sequence of boxes, which are read left to right across the page. These boxes are known as **panels**. Comic book pages typically have six to nine panels arranged in a variety of layouts.

In Manga comic strips, the story flow is different. The story flows across the panels from the right to the left. This also applies to the speech and thoughts bubbles, which are also read from right to left. Figure 3.6 demonstrates the story flow in a Manga comic strip.

When creating a story flow, the use of panel layouts to make sure your audience know where the story is set is important. The first panel is called an establishing shot and allows the reader to know where the story is taking place before the story moves on to the action in later panels. The following panel layouts are all important in ensuring the reader can follow the story flow of your comic.

Splash pages

One layout tool which can be used to help establish the scene is called a splash page. This is where the whole page of a comic is made up of one panel. Using one panel shows the context and geographical location of the story in one single image. Splash pages are sometimes combined with the title and other front page details. They can also be used for scenes:

- with lots of action, such as a fight scene, where the creator wants to show lots of different things going on at the same time
- where one character or image is a **focal point** and so surrounded by a vast amount of space, such as a figure standing in an empty warehouse.

Spread pages are another tool used in a similar way. A spread page is in effect an extended splash page, where the scale of the panel and its imagery is increased to cover two whole pages in a comic. This can be done in two ways:

- by using the centre pages of the comic as a double page spread
- by creating a fold-out page from a single page in order to create the same effect.

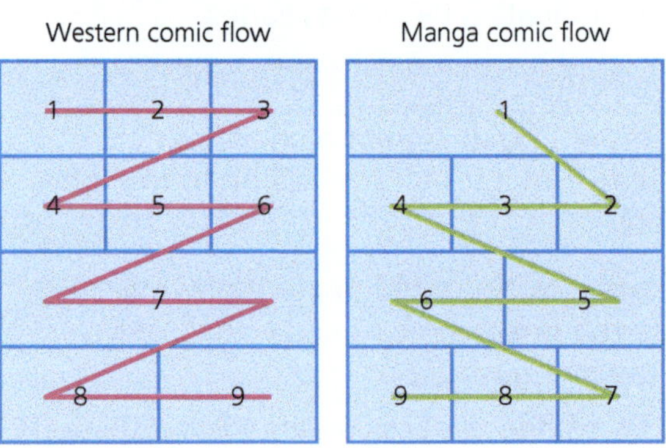

Figure 3.6 Examples of story flow in a Western-style and a Manga comic strip

Key terms

Story flow The path of the story from the beginning, to the middle, to the end.

Panel A container used to contain one scene in a comic strip.

Focal point The place in a panel where the creator wants the reader's eye to be focused.

Rule of thirds and panel staggering

The rule of thirds is a common technique used in many different forms of graphic and photographic construction and can be used equally well in comic design. It involves dividing the page into three equal chunks. For comics, this is usually done horizontally to create the rows of panels for the page.

This technique is often combined with something called panel staggering. Staggering is a method used to divide a comic row into a series of individual panels. This can be done by dividing the row up into two or three equal-sized panels, but this is not generally seen as the best approach. Instead, the size of the panels is dictated by the content that the panel needs to contain. So, one row may have two larger panels followed by a smaller panel on the end of the row, then the next row down may have two large panels which fill the row. This uneven pattern is why the technique is called staggering and is an effective way to guide the reader through the story as the creator intended.

If a comic has a regular pattern of panels similar to how a storyboard can be presented, the reader may interact with the panels in a way the creator didn't intend. For example, they may read down the panels rather than across, disrupting the flow of the story.

Panel shape and size

Panel shape and size can be used to indicate different actions in a comic strip. It can indicate the pace of the storyline and can be used to highlight important parts of the story. A common example of this is the use of a long panel spanning the width of the page to show either the passage of an extended period of time or distance, such as a character travelling down a long corridor.

Another use of panel design to influence story flow is in the size of the panels. Larger panels tend to slow down the pace of the story and a series of smaller panels speed it up. For example, a series of small panels in sequence might show the unfolding of a series of actions happening in quick succession. When creating a comic story, try to create some variety in the layout of the panels on the page and match this to the story flow, but remember the story flow of the panels shown in Figure 3.6.

Use a good variety of images in the panels to keep the audience's attention. If the same image is used in a range of scenes, consider making the storyline more concise to allow the imagery to change at a good pace.

Communication bubbles

As well as images, a number of text-based conventions are used to explain the story in comic strips. Speech or thought bubbles are used to show the speech or thoughts of characters. How these are used affects how emotion and expression are shown in comics.

Figure 3.7 Examples of speech and thought bubbles

Shape

The shape and style of the bubble indicates the type of communication it contains. Speech bubbles are usually rounded squares or circular in shape with a pointed tail off one corner pointing in the direction of the character who is speaking. The style of the bubble can also indicate the tone of the speech. For example, a spiky outlined bubble might suggest shouting or anger, whereas a bubble with a dotted outline might represent whispering or talking quietly. Communication bubbles representing speech from a radio, television or phone are shaped like lightning bolts or have the tail of the bubble in a lightning bolt shape.

Thought bubbles tend to be shaped as a cartoon-style cloud. There are usually two or three smaller circles leading off the cloud shape, which link the thought to the character.

Sequence and placement

The positioning of speech and thought bubbles in the panels is really important to the story flow. When creating speech in panels it is good practice to avoid crowding your panels with too many communication bubbles. In general, up to two or three per panel, depending on the panel size, is a good guide. Think carefully about where to place the bubbles – they should read left to right across the panel in the order you want the reader to read them. The bubbles also need to be positioned carefully so that they do not conceal any important part of the graphics, for example the facial expressions of the characters.

Narration and captions

Narrative and caption boxes are another convention used in comics to tell the story. These boxes usually contain a small amount of text which can be used to narrate the content of a panel or to clarify a change in the location or situation in the storyline. The boxes are usually placed in the top or bottom corner of the panel either to set the context for the panel or to link to the next part of the story. For example, they often contain text such as 'later that day' or 'to be continued ...'.

Figure 3.8 Examples of correct and incorrect positioning of a caption box within a panel

Onomatopoeia

Another key feature of communication in comic strips is the use of **onomatopoeia**. An onomatopoeia is a word that sounds like what it represents. They are often used to create emphasis for sounds and actions, for example, CRASH! or ZOOOOM! The spelling of these words reflect how it sounds and are usually combined with an exclamation mark.

> **Key term**
>
> **Onomatopoeia** A word that sounds like the thing it is describing. For example, 'Slurp'.

The style of text used in this type of communication is equally iconic. Onomatopoeias are designed to highlight key elements of sound, movement or communication and their design demonstrates this by standing out from the page. They use bold blocky fonts, which are oversized in order to create impact in the panel. They also usually have a bold, bright coloured outline in either one or a range of colours.

Figure 3.9 Examples of onomatopoeia

Creativity in characters and comics

Originality and imaginative design

We have talked a lot about design conventions and rules which can help you design your comic; it is easy to think that with all the rules to follow there isn't much room for originality, but this is not the case. It is important that your comic combines both comic creation convention that makes the comic accessible to the reader but also some really original and imaginative ideas to make the comic new and engaging.

Derivative design

With the huge range of existing comics and the ability to use templates to construct your comic it is very easy to create something that looks good and follows the conventions but is actually really generic. A comic which is based on another design is called a derivative. It is a fine balance to create a comic that is unique and creative whilst still following the conventions that make the comic easy as possible for the user to engage with. This is where your skill as a comic creator comes in. You need to be able to use the conventions of comic design effectively but combine them with creativity and originality to create a unique comic which is suitable for your target audience and meets the client brief.

Conventions of comic design and layout

There are many different elements to the design and make-up of comics which make them instantly recognisable as a comic.

Colour

Colour can often give you an idea of the genre or theme of the comic you are looking at. As a comic creator you can use this tool to indicate to your reader the genre of your comic. Here are some examples of colours which can be linked to comic genres.

Table 3.2 Colours linked to genres of comics

Colour	Genre
Red/pink	Romance
Red/green	Horror
Blue/grey	Science fiction

Typography and text styling

Typography is all about how we use letter style and fonts in our comics. There are some font styles which are very commonly linked to their use in comics, such as the fonts used for onomatopoeia. There are a number of different uses of text in comics and each one is visually identifiable by its style and layout. These include:

- narration or captions
- speech or thought bubbles
- onomatopoeia.

Narration, captions and speech bubbles

Narration, captions and speech bubbles have a distinctive but consistent form of styling in most comic styles. The style of text tends to be informal, often having the appearance of hand-written text. This reflects the informal comic style of storytelling, in contrast to the more formal style you would see in a conventional story book.

Focal points

Focal points allow the reader to follow the story from one panel to the next. The focal point is the main element in each panel that you want the reader to look at and depicts the key point of that panel and that part of the storyline. You would not expect there to be more than one focal point in a panel as this would confuse the reader. A reader needs the focal point in order to follow the sequence of the story.

Figure 3.10 Example of focal point

Environment and background

To ensure that the reader can fully understand the content of the comic, each panel will include an image behind the characters or other assets which tells the user where the scene in the panel is set. For example, this could be an image of a room, a street or a shop depending on where the action in the scene takes place. This will also support the use of minimal text in the comic panels as the scene is set by the background image.

Activity

In a small group, discuss how different colours can be used to show different feelings, genres and emotions in comic and character design. Select a colour and prepare some reasons why you think this colour is linked with particular genres, emotions and feelings. Share your reasons with the class. Provide some examples of how this colour could be used effectively in a comic.

1.3 Resources required to create characters and comics

Resources are the equipment that you need to make your comic strip. Planning of resources will allow you to make sure that you have everything you need to allow you to complete the project in the timescale that you have available. This will vary based on the method you choose to create your characters and comic. However, the basic computer hardware such as computer, keyboard, mouse and screen would be used for all methods of comic construction.

There are a range of peripheral devices that you might also consider using to create both your characters and your comic, such as:

- graphics tablet
- touchscreen
- stylus
- scanner
- digital camera.

When creating your characters, you may also consider using physical modelling materials, such as modelling clay. This may be the most suitable way to meet the requirements of the client brief and the target audience. To allow you to capture your characters and use them effectively in your comic you would still need to consider how you could digitise your characters – this is where you may need to use a peripheral such as a digital camera.

Activity

On your computer, explore what software you have that would be helpful when you are creating a comic or character. Look for some artwork software and something which you could use to create the structure of your comic. Try out the different software and tools and jot down any you like and how you could use them in your work.

The software you will need to use to create the comic also needs to be decided in the planning. You need to think about not just what software you may require for the construction of the comic strip but also what software you might need to create the characters you plan to use in the comic.

The software you choose for the creation of your characters will vary depending on what style and format your characters are going to take. Different software lends itself to different styles of character design, so your plans for your character design will influence your choice of creation software. For example, if you planned to create a cartoon-style comic character you may create a vector graphic which would lend itself to being created in software such as Adobe Illustrator, whereas if you are using photorealistic graphics in your comic, you would be more likely to choose a software such as Adobe Photoshop.

Here are some examples of software that could be used in the creation of your characters:

- Adobe Illustrator/Fireworks/Photoshop
- Serif DrawPlus/PhotoPlus
- Affinity
- Pixelmator
- GIMP.

There are a range of different software options that could be used to create a comic strip. Some are specific comic-creation software and some are more general software. Here are a few potential software choices:

- Microsoft Publisher
- Comic Life
- Pixton Comic
- iStudio.

1.4 Pre-production and planning documentation and techniques for characters and comics

Pre-production and planning for characters

Character design

When planning your character, you will need to plan the **aesthetics** of your character –basically how the character will look. There are a number of methods you can use to plan out the appearance of your character. To get the best effect you would probably combine more than one of these planning methods.

- Thumbnailing is the process of creating a series of small sketches of character design ideas. This is a good way of developing a design idea from the first thought, through any number of tweaks and changes, until the character idea is more developed and the key details decided. This can save time later if the character is fully developed before it is used in the comic.
- In some cases, character designs are created using fully detailed annotated sketches or hand drawn drafts (this can be called a visualisation diagram, as it allows the creator to visualise the details of the character). These allow the creator to plan out all the detail of the character design and include a range of views of the character, such as side, front and back. This technique can be used well after the thumbnailing process has been completed.
- Physical models of the potential character designs can also be created. This method may require a different set of skills to allow the creator to make a model which will reflect the design ideas. Modelling allows the creator to see how the different designs would appear in terms of scale and proportion and also allows the design to be viewed from all angles.
- It is also possible to create plans for characters digitally. There are a range of digital drawing software programmes which can be used to create digital drafts of the character. Software such as Microsoft Paint or similar software, or more complex drawing software from Adobe or Serif can all be used.

It is important to ensure that at the character planning stage the methods you use focus on planning the detail of the character, as this will help to support you in the creation of an effective character, rather than relying on the sophisticated tool you may use – this will come later.

Key term

Aesthetic How something looks, its appearance.

Character profiles

Often the design of a character is informed by the non-physical characteristics of the character, such as the character's personality and behaviour and their role within the comic. For example, are they the hero or the villain? This means that part of the planning process for creating a character is often creating a profile of the character. You can think of this like a mini biography of the character you intend to create.

To create a profile will need you to be able to plan out things such as:

- the character's personality
- the key design features of the character's appearance that might reflect that personality
- the backstory of the character, which may be included.

The backstory is a brief history of the character which explains how they came to be in the story. It usually explains the character's role within the story and the dynamic between them and other characters. For example, it would explain how a villain ended up in conflict with the hero character in a superhero comic.

It is likely that the physical appearance of the character would be influenced a lot by the non-physical characteristics. In comics, where the narrative and description is much shorter than in other forms of storytelling, details such as the appearance of the character are key to adding depth to the story that the reader can understand without it being explained in text.

Activity

You have been approached by a comic company who are looking to add a new character to their children's comic range. The range has an underwater theme and they are looking for a new character who is kind and patient and will teach the reader all about showing others these qualities.

Create a design for a character using one of the design styles discussed in this chapter, for example minimalist, geometric or doodle.

Pre-production and planning for comics

Plot structure

When planning your comic the best place to start is with the storyline. To do this you need to plan the plot structure. One way to think about this is to use a story arc. This involves plotting the key points of a story across axis, similar to drawing a graph. Time runs across the x-axis (the horizontal axis) and the key points of the story are plotted along this.

There are key parts of every storyline which you need to plan for.

- The beginning (exposition): This is where the scene is set, the characters are introduced and the main theme of the story begins. This is sometimes called the conflict, where the problem or issue to be resolved throughout the story is introduced.
- The middle: This is where the action in the story starts to increase as the story line moves forward. Towards the end of the middle section you will usually have the climax. This is the peak of the action that the plot has been leading to from the start.
- The end: This usually follows the climax of the story and shows a slow-down in the action as the story leads to the resolution.

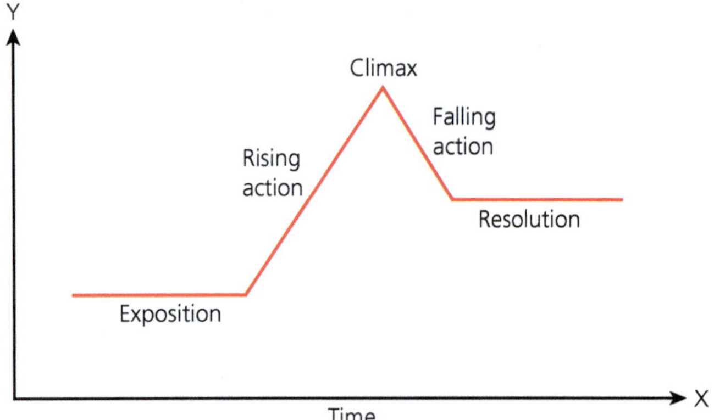

Figure 3.11 Story arc diagram

Script, storyline and storyboards

The script and the storyboard go hand in hand when planning your comic strip. You will know the basics of planning techniques from Unit R093. However, there are some guidelines for creating a script and storyboard for a comic strip.

The story flow through the comic is important as this is what will take your reader through the story. If the plot is confusing or difficult to follow the reader will not have a good experience of reading the comic and is unlikely to fully understand the purpose or meaning of the story.

There are three core stages to planning out the comic. The first is to draft out an outline for the story. This could be as simple as a series of bullet points which outline the key points in the story and create a clear story arc for the story following the method we looked at in the earlier section. Alternatively, it could be a fairly short paragraph of text which outlines the key points in the plot of the story.

The second is to create a script for the comic. This is not only for recording the character's speech and tone of voice (which might influence the facial expression of characters or the use of exclamations such as onomatopoeia), it can also be used to record information on captions, narrative and the staging of each panel and page. When the script is completed, it can be used to look at the flow of the story to decide where the page divides will fall and after this what the individual panels will contain. You can refer to R093 for the content and layout of a script.

The script can be used to inform the third planning stage, which is the creation of the storyboard. In comic creation the storyboard is an important planning document as it allows the other elements of the plans to come together and the creator to plan visually how the comic will look and consider any changes that are needed to allow the reader to have the best experience when reading the comic. The first stage would be to plan out the panels on the pages and sketch out the graphics for each scene, being sure to label the focal points of each panel so it is clear where the readers' eye should be directed. The speech, thought and narrative can be added at this stage, taking care to follow the left to right reading convention for the positioning of the bubbles and remembering that the bubbles need to be positioned so that the panel is not too crowded and that they do not obscure any important parts of the graphic. The

Storyline (part 1): Ryszard is talking to Sarah about going to the cinema using a smartphone messaging app on social media

```
SCRIPT
AT HOME IN LOUNGE, MESSAGING VIA SOCIAL MEDIA
on SMARTPHONE
               Ryszard
     How about going to see the new film that
     opens today?
               Sarah
     Yeah great, let me know what time?
               Ryszard
     Starts at 6.30 - meet outside at 6.00
               Sarah
STANDING OUTSIDE THE CINEMA
               Ryszard
     Hi Sarah - over here!
RYSZARD AND SARAH GO INSIDE
```

Figure 3.12 Example script for a comic

creation of the storyboard also allows the creator to review the story flow of the comic story line and make sure that it is clear and coherent. It is also a good time to reflect and make any changes to ensure that the brief is met and that the target audience requirements have been fulfilled, whilst changes can still easily be made.

Shot types

Planning the content of the panels is usually done at the storyboard stage of the planning process. One of the key parts of this is to plan the content of the panels, including the different shot types that could be used. Here are some types of shot that could be used in comic panels.

- Close-up and extreme close-up: These are used primarily to focus on the detail. The main image will fill the majority of the panel. In comics this shot is probably most useful to show the facial expressions of characters.
- Wide shot/establishing shot: This is a shot which looks to be taken from a distance, such as a street with a shop front showing the story setting. Wide shots are often used as an establishing shot at the start of a comic as they allow the user to identify the context of the story.
- Over the shoulder: This shot shows the scene from the point of view of one of the characters. This is done by positioning the view as if the camera is looking over the shoulder of the character. This can be used to show what the character is seeing at that point in time but is also often used to show the facial expression of another character in a conversation. For example, if a character is delivering bad news, then this shot captures the expression of the person receiving it.
- Medium shot: Sometimes known as a mid-shot. This is a shot where the camera is mid-way between a close-up and wide shot. From the shot you can see some detail but also the surroundings of the shot. You might use this to establish a scene to show where the character is in that panel.

Panel shape and styling

When the other planning documents are completed there is a final element of planning which is very specific to comic creation. That is the planning of the comic layout. As we saw in earlier sections of this unit, the panel shape and placement is key to the smooth flow of the story. Once the storyline and communication are planned out, you can complete the final planning document which is the plan for the layout of the panels. This does not need to be a full-size sketch of each page but can be a series of small sketches which show the pages and the layout and shape of the panels, much like creating thumbnail sketches for the character design. The script and storyboard should help with planning for the page breaks in the story.

Activity

Design a three-panel section for the comic where the character you created in the activity earlier in this section introduces themselves to another character in the underwater world. Consider the communication, panel content and shape in your plan.

Test your knowledge

1. What is the name of a box which contains the images in a comic?
2. What shape of speech bubble would you create to show anger?
3. What is a character trope?
4. What is the purpose of an onomatopoeia?
5. Which pre-production document allows the creator to visually review the story flow of the comic?

Synoptic links

You can find further information about this topic in Unit R093, Sections 2.1–2.3, 2.5 and 3.2–3.4.

Assignment practice

Task 1 – Plan a character

Time needed: 1–2 hours

You have been asked to devise a comic to help teach about odd and even numbers. The target audience for the comic will be children of Years 1 and 2 (5- to 7-year-olds).

Create a planning document to show your design for a character that could feature in this comic.

Topic area 2 Create characters and comics

Getting started

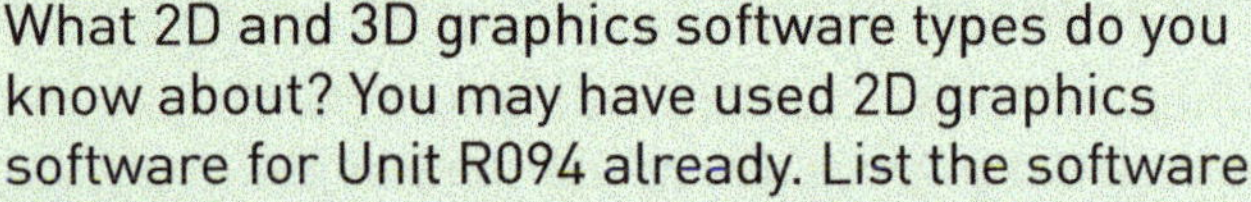

What 2D and 3D graphics software types do you know about? You may have used 2D graphics software for Unit R094 already. List the software which is available in your school that can be used to create characters.

2.1 Techniques to obtain and create components for use within comics

Technical skills to create characters for use as components within comic

There are a range of different tools and techniques that can be used to create characters that can be used in comics.

2D software for creating digital characters includes Photoshop, Fireworks, DrawPlus, PhotoPlus, Affinity, Pixelmator and GIMP.

Tools commonly found within these applications include closed shapes, geometric shapes, B-splines, layers, textures, fills and gradients, shadows, blending and grouping.

It is helpful to be able to use layers for different aspects of a digital character so that they can be edited separately. It is also useful to be able to use transparency to help 'trace' a visualisation diagram using closed shapes such as splines.

Wire frames

A wire frame uses lines and curves to represent a three-dimensional object. Key points or vertices are used to represent corners and these are joined by lines or edges. The individual lines can be manipulated to change the overall shape. The vertices are stored in the computer as coordinates. This means that the object once created can be rotated by calculating the relationship and distance between the vertices as the virtual camera or viewpoint moves or changes.

Polygons

In 3D modelling, objects can be created using a number of (usually triangular) polygons. The more complex and smooth the object, the more polygons are needed to display it and the larger the demand for storage space and processing power.

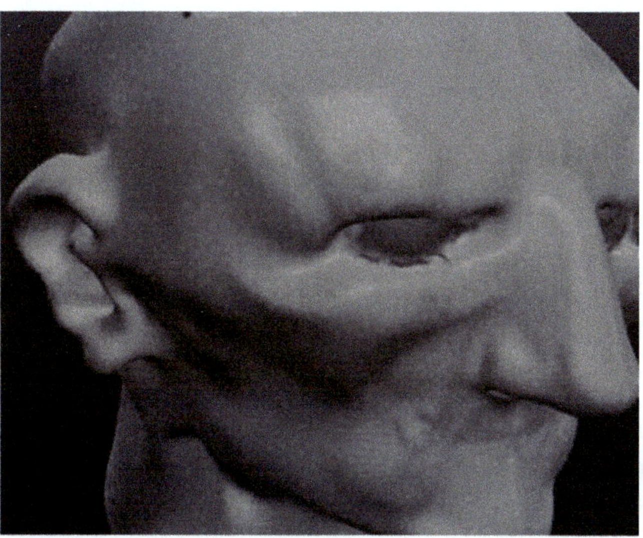

Figure 3.13 Example of polygon use in Pixologic Sculptris

Another way to use software to create a character is to import visualisation diagrams into 3D modelling software so the 2D or 3D model can be overlaid on the visualisation to achieve accurate scale and proportion. It is also possible to use layering and opacity to allow you to trace over elements of your visualisation diagram to enable you to recreate hand drawn assets in digital form. Assets such as textures and paints can also be imported to some 3D software, giving variety and originality to the character designs.

Elements of a digital character can also be created separately then combined within some 3D software applications, and you may find 3D template models available to use as the basis for a human, animal or object-based character rather than starting from a blank stage or canvas. Tools commonly found within 3D software applications include wire frame editing, extrude, pinch, crease, edge, create hole, bend, smooth, symmetry, texture and paint/fill.

Some 3D modelling software you could explore for this purpose are Sculptris, Seamless3D, Blender, Pixologic ZBrush and Wings 3D.

Key term

NURBS A method used to create curves in digital graphics.

NURBS

In 3D modelling, objects can also be created using Non Uniform Rational B-Splines or **NURBS**. These create curves using a series of control points (also known as control vertices or CVs for short). As you move the control points the shape of the curve changes.

NURBS were originally developed for use in the automotive design industry but are also now found in applications such as Maya and 3D Studio Max to create detailed characters for games, for example. You may recognise similar tools from 2D software such as Serif Drawplus, where splines and Bezier curves can be created.

Closed shapes

When using digital graphics software to create characters, it is important to use closed shapes. Otherwise, the various elements of the character cannot be filled because the software does not recognise that the areas are distinct. There are a range of different design types you could use in the creation of your characters which would lend itself to layering shapes to create the character design, such as geometric or minimalist. In Serif Drawplus, tools such as Bezier curves and splines are used, and there is also a bank of geometric and pre-formed shapes. In Photoshop, there is a range of custom shapes, geometric shapes and freeform closed shapes which can be used to generate parts of a character. Once created, the shapes may be edited by altering the position and number of nodes.

You can use layering and opacity settings in your chosen software to arrange a series of shapes in the layout you need to create your character shape and to allow certain parts of the shapes to be more prominent in the design to give the character its features. Once your layers and opacity are set as you need them to be, you can also then use grouping to fix these elements together. This allows you to take a series of different layers or shapes and combine them to make one full character – they are in effect stuck together from this point. This allows you to move the character as a whole to position it in the relevant panels. It can also allow you to resize the character so that it can fit the scale of the other assets in each panel, without having to worry about keeping the position and proportion of each individual element that makes up the character.

Model making

It is possible to use physical modelling to create characters to use as components in comics. You can do this by creating physical models using modelling materials such as modelling clay. You could then take photographs of those models to use in your comic. A consideration here is to think about all the different positions and expressions you may need from a character throughout the comic and the time and skill that would be needed to create a photograph of each of these. This method would also allow you to use a range of different textures and materials in the design of character which can add depth and detail to your design. Once you have created the models and captured the images you will then need to edit the images using image editing software to enable you to remove any background so that they can be effectively combined with other assets to create good quality panel content.

Techniques for creating assets for use as components within comics

Sourcing assets

There are various assets that need to be combined to create a high-quality comic. This element links directly to the planning element of this topic, as you will now source or create the assets you identified in Topic area 1. You will then organise and store the assets you need to create the comic strip.

Graphics

When identifying the assets, you need to consider whether you are going to create the asset or if you are going to try and source the asset. When sourcing an asset, you need to make sure that you comply with legislation regarding the asset, for example copyright law. You can use search engine settings to allow you to search for assets which are not subject to copyright, or you can follow the copyright legislation and use an image which will be subject to copyright. When searching for images that are not subject to copyright you can use a number of tools to help you. It is possible to search for royalty free images which often come from specific websites where images can be downloaded for free or for a small fee. It is also possible to use advanced search tools in a search engine to filter the results of an image search to allow you to search for images with certain permissions. For example, you can select usage rights such as images which are available under different Creative Commons licences and usage categories.

Typography

To create the style you want for your comic you might want to select a particular font to use throughout your comic to ensure that the text assets are in keeping with the overall look. There are usually a range of fonts available within the text tool of most graphics creation software, which you can use to create text assets directly in the software. However, if you wanted a style of font which is not available on your computer by default you can find a range of fonts online. These can be downloaded to your computer, and when downloaded and installed to the fonts folder you can access this font via the software, providing the fonts file type is compatible. One example of a large online source of fonts is Google Fonts.

Synoptic link

Copyright was discussed in R093, Topic area 3.

Editing assets

For assets that have been sourced from the internet you will need to edit these assets to make sure that they are visually and technically compatible with your comic.

When preparing an asset one key thing which you will often need to do is remove the background from an image. This allows you to use the item in the image that you need but removes any unwanted areas that will prevent the image from being effectively layered over another image.

Removing backgrounds can be done using a range of methods depending on the software you are using to create your assets. Here are some of the more common methods:

- Using the selection tool to:
  - select the parts of the image you need to keep
  - invert the selection to select everything else in the image
  - use the delete key to remove the now selected areas of the image.
- Using the magic wand or selection tool (such as the lasso tool) to:
  - select the areas you want to remove directly
  - use the delete key to remove these selected areas.

In most cases you will need to do some small-scale editing of the image to remove any small areas which cannot be removed using a large-scale selection method. You can usually do this using the eraser tool, set to a very small size.

As well as removing backgrounds from images, you may want to add filters or effects to create a certain mood or theme for a particular panel, or you may wish to add to all the panels in the comic to create a consistent theme throughout the story, such as by using a pop art effect. Most graphics editing software will allow you to add filters or effects to images, for example you may want to lighten or darken an image or blur or highlight a certain section to fit in with the storyline you are portraying. In most graphics editing software this option will be part of tool bar or the menus available when you are editing the image.

Figure 3.14 To layer assets to create the content for a panel you often need to remove background from images

Creating assets

You might want to create your own original assets for your comic yourself using graphic software. This option will allow you the creative freedom to design the assets exactly as you want them. When creating your assets, you need to think about what style of graphics you are planning to use throughout your comic. This is important as you need to make sure that your comic assets all fit well together and look professional, not mismatched.

A lot of comics use a vector style of graphic. These are the types of graphics you often associate with comics as they usually display bold blocks of colour and clear crisp lines, in contrast to bitmap images similar to those seen in a photograph which often appear to have more detail and shading in the images.

Synoptic link

You will have learned about the different graphic types in your work on R094.

To create vector assets there is a range of software available including Adobe Illustrator or Inkscape. For bitmap assets you could use Krita, GIMP or Photoshop as well as other options.

When starting to create your assets you need to think about how you set up your page. You need to consider the size of the asset you will need and how this will link to the size of the page you need to create. You also need to consider the file format you need to create your assets in (we will look at this more in Section 2.3).

Figure 3.15 Examples of effects and filters that can be applied to comic panel – pop art and newspaper comic strip styles

When creating your assets, you should be using the plans you have already made to help you, but you will still need to make a series of artistic decisions as you work. For example, you will need to think about what tools you will use to draw; this may sound simple but in most graphics creation software there is a wide range of tools that you can use – most imitate the effect created by different real-world artistic tools, such as paint brushes, pens, pencils and crayons. Each of these tools will provide a different appearance for the asset, so you need to think carefully about what you choose and then use the same tools throughout to create a consistent, professional style for your asset creation.

You also need to consider colour use in your assets – this is where your plans will help. Each asset is an important part of the storytelling in each panel, so it is important that you consider the colour choices to make your assets clear against the background. If an asset is intended to be a key feature of the scene, then the colours need to be carefully considered to ensure that the asset doesn't blend into the background or into another asset. If you are creating an asset that is used as the background or part of the background then these assets need to be able to blend together to form a coherent scene, without any elements standing out or looking out of place as this will draw the reader's eye away from the key storytelling features of the panel.

Using drawing tools and software to create effective assets is a skill that needs practice – make sure you do this before you try to create your final assets.

Activity

Using one of the tools you have seen in this section, create a clown style character facial design.

Synoptic links

You can find further information about this topic in R093, Sections 3.4 and 4.2.

2.2 Technical skills to create comics

Techniques for combining assets into comic panels

Panel layout and inserting assets

The layout of the panels in the comic strip is key to conveying the storyline to the reader. You need to think about the size of the panels to ensure that the assets you want to display and the communication you need to include can clearly be seen on each panel. You also need to think about how many panels will fit on the page and how this will impact on the story flow. For example, if you are planning a **cliff hanger** scene you would need to make sure this panel was the final panel on the page rather than the first so that the cliff hanger was upheld in the storyline. You also need to make sure that you don't have a page turn in the middle of a series of panels which are running in sequence to create the pace of the storyline. The shape of the panels also needs to be considered to ensure that you make the most impact on the reader. When inserting assets into the panels the assets need to be laid out effectively so that the key parts of the story depicted by each asset are clear to the reader.

A typical process to create a comic would be:

- create the panel layout for the page
- import the image assets and place in the panels
- crop/adjust/scale the panel content as required
- add speech bubbles and dialogue (use the script for reference)
- add any special effects
- proofread the comic page
- save the comic page.

Key term

Cliff hanger A story ending which leaves the reader in suspense.

Graphical assets

When placing your graphics into the panel you will need to think carefully about how you layer up your separate graphics to ensure that they appear in the best format to support the story. For example, if you are creating a background setting for the panel, think about where the objects are placed to ensure that they do not disrupt the main storytelling graphics. Also, if you are placing characters, think about how they are positioned to ensure that they are supporting the story; for example, if there is a conversation in the panel ensure the characters are clearly facing each other, or if some characters are further away in the scene have them appear smaller than those in the foreground. All these small things are important to ensure that the graphics help to tell the story effectively.

Focal points

As you will know from Section 1.2 of this unit, focal points allow the reader to follow the story from one panel to the next. The focal point is the main element in each panel where you want to the reader to look – this will depict the key point of that panel and that part of the storyline. As you place the assets in each panel think carefully about where the action is in the panel and where you want the readers eye to focus. You need to have a clear focal point in each panel and not a series of consuming images that will cause the reader to have to pause in their path through the storyline. Focal points should also help the reader to follow the flow of the story through the panels, so that the reader is encouraged to read the panels in the correct order. One way to do this is to think about how you create the focal point using graphics, for example this could be done by zooming in on a particular item or character in the scene, adding auto shapes or using a text exclamation such as an onomatopoeia.

Typographical styles

Comics are identifiable by another more subtle piece of styling – the choice of text style used for the written content such as speech bubbles and narration/caption boxes. It may seem like a small thing, but it really helps to make your comic look authentic and professional. The text styles used by comic creators are usually a little less formal, often those that appear hand-written with a pen or a marker are used. Most comic creation software or desktop publishing software will have a range of fonts for you to choose from, so you should be able to find a suitable font for your comic. Fonts can be categorised into two types: serif and sans serif.

- Serif fonts are fonts which have extended stems on the ends of the lines which make up the letters, like the fonts used on a typewriter. These fonts tent to be more formal than those used in a comic. Times New Roman is an example of a serif font.
- Sans serif fonts do not have the extra pieces of their lines and tend to look a little cleaner and simpler. Calibri is an example of a sans serif font, as is the text used in this book.

The fonts used in comics tend to be informal serif style. They also often use only uppercase letters, which is a style choice that is quite unique to comics. Try to remember to be consistent throughout your comic with your use of fonts – using a consistent font style throughout ensures your comic looks professional.

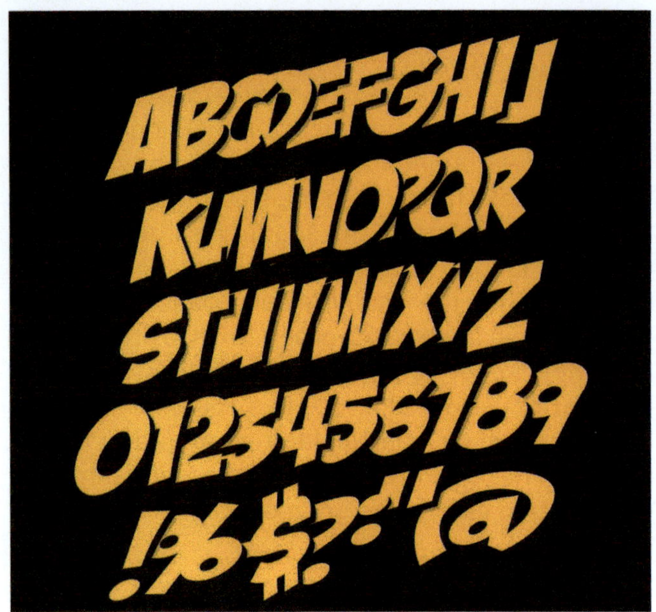

Figure 3.16 Example of comic style font

Techniques and skills to transfer a script, storyline or storyboard into a comic strip

Integrating the script

Integrating the script into the comic strip is an important part of creating and maintaining the story flow throughout the comic. When placing the communication items, you need to ensure that the communication does not obstruct the view of the focal points in the comic panels.

One of the more prominent items for the script that are a significant visual part of the comic and the storyline are the onomatopoeias. On a script they are likely to be represented as exclamations or in most cases as sound effects such as 'Bang!'.

Dialogue between characters and details of the script that include characters' thoughts or daydreams are likely to become thought or speech bubbles in your comic panels. You will need to look carefully at the layout and content of the panels to ensure that the panel is not too crowded but also that the sequence of the bubbles reflects the order of the intended communication – remember the reader reads the text across the panel from left to right.

Stage directions on a script tend to be shown in one of two ways.

- Text elements will be used as the actual images that make up the panel content. For example, the stage direction 'Joe walked into a coffee shop' might be partly represented by the background images of the panel showing a coffee shop.
- Captions or narration boxes are used to add detail to the setting. They are often used to state a change in either location or time, using the stage direction such as 'Later that day…', for example. These boxes tend to be short, with up to a sentence of text included. They are not boxes in which to add large sections of narrative; in a comic the main storytelling tools are the images and speech bubbles. Tools such as narration and caption boxes are complementary to these.

Figure 3.17 Example of caption/narration box

Some stage directions may also be shown by movement lines, for example a stage direction could say 'Sam runs down the field' – this could be shown with lines behind the character to show the movement and speed.

Activity

Using a software of your choice, create your own typographical elements for these onomatopoeias:

- Splosh
- Crackle
- Whoosh

Synoptic links

You can find further information about this topic in R093, Sections 3.4 and 4.2.

2.3 Techniques to save and publish characters and comics

Techniques used to save and publish characters in suitable formats

It is important to think about how you store your assets as you need to be able to locate them when you create the comic. You may also need to edit the assets to ensure that they are suitable for the requirements of the product brief. If you edit your assets, it is good practice to use version control to store the assets in a logical way so you can chart the changes you make and make sure that you use the correct version in the project. Version control means saving a different version of your asset each time you make changes and storing them chronologically by labelling them with either a number or the date so that you can easily tell which is the most recent, but also find older versions if you need to.

Whilst you are working on the creation of your assets you need to save them in the native format, that is the format that the creation software uses. This means that you have saved a version which can continue to be edited until you have completed your creation but also at any point in the future, so take care to keep these copies.

You will also need to make sure that any assets that you save as a final version will be in a file format that is suitable for use in the software you plan to make your comic in. Image file formats such as those discussed in R093 would be most suitable. Make sure you check the software you will be creating your comic in to find out what are the most suitable file formats for you to use when putting assets into your comic. It is also worth remembering that the PNG file format supports transparency in images which may be useful if you need to layer a number of assets in a panel to create a scene, where you do not want blank areas of the drawing space to obscure parts of other graphics. When saving your graphics consider how your comic will be used, so that the properties such as resolution are correct for either print or web use as you learned about in R093, Section 4.2.

Technical skills to save and export or publish comics

Your comic is a very important product for this unit, so, in a similar way to assets, ensure you take care to save it regularly and use version control and sensible file naming conventions so that you can always find your work and have copies from earlier in the creation process if needed. You also need to save these versions of the comic in the native file format for the creation software you are using so that you can edit these versions if you need to. Even your final version should be saved in the native format first, as you never know when you might need to make changes or additions to your final product.

The requirements of the brief are key to the exporting of the comic strip, so having the brief to hand is really important. This will allow you to ensure that the exported comic strip is suitable for the client needs. Considering, for example, how the comic will be distributed and viewed. As you will have seen from your work in R093, the file type selected for the comic has a significant influence on the properties of the comic. Some of the things you need to consider when choosing the file format are:

- File size: Does the comic strip need to be emailed or shared on the internet?
- Image quality: Does the comic strip need to be high quality or low quality?
- Product format: Does the comic strip need to be in print or electronic format?

When selecting a file format, ensure that the file you have chosen will be suitable for your client to view if they are receiving the work electronically and that the version they can view looks exactly as you intended. With some file formats there may be differences in appearance that you would not expect. For example, if you have downloaded a new font, as we discussed earlier in the unit, some file formats will only display this font if the user also has the font downloaded. If they do not, the software will select another font to display instead that may not fit the style and design of your comic. A file format to consider if you do need to protect layout and font features such as these is a format such as PDF, which is highly compatible with most computers, but also secures the format of the comic so that what you see in your final version will likely be the same for everyone viewing. It should be noted that this format is not editable, however, so the information above about saving in a native format is very important when choosing to use this file type.

Synoptic links

You can find further information about this topic in R093, Sections 3.4, 4.1 and 4.2.

Assignment practice

Task 2 – Create a comic strip

Time needed: 1–2 hours

You are working for a snack company who are releasing a new fruit-based snack bar called Bite. They have asked you to create a comic to advertise the new product which they hope will appeal to primary school children. The comic will be in the form of a short four-to six- panel comic strip for the supermarket magazine.

Activities

You have been approached by a comic company who are looking to add a new character to their children's comic range. The range has an underwater theme and they are looking for a new character who is kind and patient and will teach the reader all about showing others kindness and patience.

Following on from the activity from the last section, take another look at your children's comic character that is kind and patient.

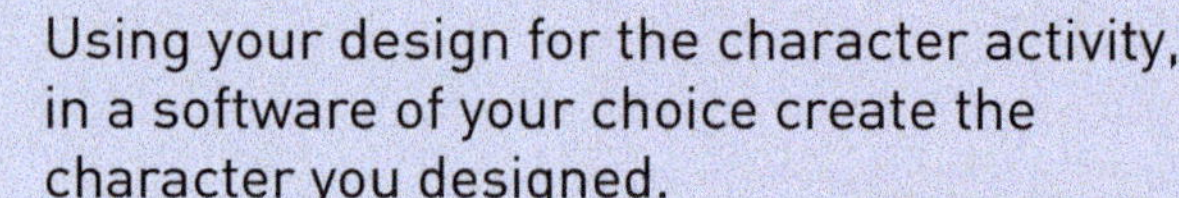

1 Using your design for the character activity, in a software of your choice create the character you designed.
2 Save and export your character in a suitable format to allow you to add it to the panels in a comic.

Topic area 3 Review characters and comics

Getting started

Think back to the two topic areas we have completed so far. Create a table with two columns and record the key things you think make a good character and a good comic. These ideas will help you with your reflection throughout this topic area. Use the column headings:

- What makes a good character?
- What makes a good comic?

3.1 Techniques to check and review characters and comics

At the end of your project it is important to look back over your product and think about how successful it has been. There are a number of ways you can do this, which we are going to explore in this section.

Techniques to check the technical properties of characters and comics

The technical property requirements of your characters and comic will vary depending on the brief you are given by the client. One way to check the properties is to create a checklist. You could write a list of the technical properties your comic needs to have and review the properties against that list. Your checklist does not need to be a complicated document – it could be as simple as a list of features with a tick box and a notes section so that you can jot down any changes you want to make to any items which don't meet the requirements.

Elements to check

Asset resolution

To ensure that your comic has a professional appearance and satisfies the client need you should check that the assets you have used in the comic are of a suitable resolution for the medium you have been asked to display the comic in. For example, if you have been asked to create a comic which can be used in a print format, the assets should all be of a high enough resolution to not appear pixelated when printed. This would compromise the quality of your final comic.

Character characteristics

The characters are key to the storytelling in the comic. To ensure the success of your final comic you need to check that these characters display as you wish them to. The test is more of a qualitative test, rather than a quantitative one such as the resolution of an asset. You need to make a judgement on whether your character meets the needs of your client brief.

- Character sizes: You could consider the size of your character in relation to things around them, such as the background or other characters. If some things are in the foreground and others further away, you may need to think about whether the sizes of the elements accurately reflect this.
- Character position: As we have seen earlier in the chapter the positioning of characters is key to storytelling. You need to be able to look critically at the characters and check that their positioning supports the storyline. For example, if characters are communicating, think about their position. It should show clearly who they are communicating with.
- Colours and shapes: You will have planned how to reflect the theme and genre of your comic. You may need to consider how well you think the use of colours and shapes in your final product reflects those plans and the intended theme or genre.
- Facial, physical and non-physical characteristics: Believable characters combine all types of characteristics to tell the story. You need to remember what the character is trying to portray in your work and think about how you can check that this is shown in the different characteristics of your character.

Figure 3.18 This panel would be highlighted in the review as the speech bubble is covering the character's face

Comic conventions

As we learned earlier in the unit there are a number of conventions which are used in the design and layout of comics. Part of your checks should be to review these conventions and check that they are being correctly used in your final comic. One way to do this is to read your comic (maybe even out loud) and try to put yourself in the shoes of a new reader and think about how they would interact with the comic. Would they get the experience of the story that you intended when you made your plan?

- Panel size, shape and layout: These elements are key to story flow, you can consider how these elements have been used to reflect the pace and content of different parts of the storyline.
- Placement of speech and thought bubbles: The order of bubbles should make it easy for the reader to understand the sequence of communication in the panels.
- Content of bubbles: You need to consider the content of the speech bubbles. The text needs to fit the bubbles and be clear and easy to read, so it does not not interrupt the flow of the story.

- Narration and caption boxes: These elements should complement all your other assets in supporting the storyline, and not be in the way of any other key parts of the panel.
- Onomatopoeias: You might want to consider the use of onomatopoeias in your review. They can be a very effective tool to support your storyline, but they can also get in the way if used poorly.

Comic resolution

We have talked about resolution in reference to the quality of individual assets, the same considerations apply to the resolution of the final comic product. As you saw in R094 there are different resolution requirements for different client requirements. This could refer to the medium required for the final comic but also the method of distribution. For example, you need to check that if you are making a comic for web use and distribution by email that the resolution is suitable for screen viewing but also that the final file size is sufficiently small to allow the document to be sent by email.

Techniques to review characters and comics

Suitability for client requirements

This part of the reviewing process considers the comic's suitability for the client brief and the target audience. There are a number of different checks that you would need to do to fully ensure that the final comic you have made is the best it can be.

As a general overview of suitability, you could create a document which compares the strengths and weaknesses of the characters you created and the overall comic product. To start to reflect in a more focused way, you could also create a comparison between the points of the client brief or of the success criteria for the project if you created criteria as part of your planning process. As with documenting the checks for technical compatibility, this does not need to be a complex process and could be a checklist or simple table to store your thoughts. The final area you need to consider is whether the comic is fit for the purpose the client intended, for example if the comic needs to advertise something to the reader or to teach them about a new skill, does the comic and its storyline do this effectively?

Suitability for target audience

Making your comic suitable for your target audience is a really important part of creating a successful final comic. There are lots of things that you can consider when thinking about how your comic meets your target audience. You could consider elements such as:

- The content of the story: It should be relevant and relatable to the target audience.
- The topic and the main themes of the story: The topics should be suitable for the audience of your comic.
- The language and vocabulary used in the comic: You should use words and phrases that your reader will understand and that are appropriate for their age.

Visual quality and reader engagement

The final reviews you need to complete on your final comic are to consider the visual appeal and aesthetics. This means reviewing how your final comic looks. This doesn't just involve whether it looks good to you as the creator but putting yourself in the shoes of the reader and thinking about whether the look and feel of the comic will engage them and draw their interest to the comic. The same thing needs to be considered when you review the comic storyline. You could consider things such as:

- The quality of the storyline: It should be engaging and exciting to the intended reader; you want them to keep reading.
- The structure of the storyline: The storyline should be clear and easy to follow, and you would expect it to lead the reader easily through the story.
- You need to be able to be critical of your work, thinking carefully about whether you engaged your reader enough to make them return and select another of your comics to read.

Activity

Find an example of a comic and label the positive and negative elements of the comic design. Think about what you have learned about comic and character properties and design conventions.

Synoptic links

You can find further information about this topic in R093, Sections 2.1, 2.4, 3.4 and 4.2.

3.2 Improvements and further developments

When you have reviewed your work, the final section in this topic area is to think about what may have constrained your characters and comic, how you could potentially improve the current comic and characters and what scope there is for further development.

Constraints which limit the effectiveness of characters and comics

A constraint is something that restricts or limits the way a task can be carried out. There are usually a range of different constraints which can impact a project. Here are some things you may have come across which might have limited your project or that are useful to be aware of for future projects.

- Time: The amount of time you had to complete the project may have been a constraint, but your skills in time management and how you used your time within the project will also have impacted.
- Resources: This could relate to any item you need to do your project that was perhaps unavailable or in short supply, which may have impacted the quality of your final characters or comic.
- Hardware: As with resources, the availability of hardware that you would have liked to use or perhaps a choice of hardware which did not work out as you hoped will have impacted your final work.
- Software: Again, this may have been the choices of software you had available to you and how well they allowed you to carry out your plan or how the software you chose impacted on your comic and character creation.
- Skills: Some of the skills you needed for the project may have been more of a challenge than you originally thought, or you may have been limited in the time needed to master the skills required – both of which could have impacted on the final comic and characters.

When thinking about the constraints of your project it is important to consider not just what the constraints may have been but also what their impact was, for example did they prevent you from adding a feature to your comic or character, or did they limit the quality of a certain element so that it does not reflect your plans? Reflecting carefully on the impact of any constraints of a project will help you consider the next part of this topic area, improvements.

Character and comic improvements

When considering the potential improvements you could make to your characters and comics, the key thing to think about is: what would be the impact of making this improvement? There are two core areas where you would expect meaningful improvements to have an impact. These are meeting the client brief and meeting the needs of the target audience.

Meeting the client brief

Your brief should be the first place to look when you consider potential improvements. Consider each element of the brief you were asked to meet and review how well you have met them. You can use your reflection from the earlier part of this topic area to help inform these improvements. Suggesting an improvement might mean discussing how you might improve your product to meet an area of the brief that you didn't achieve, but it may also mean looking at an area where you partially met the brief but, on reflection, you now think you could improve.

Meeting the needs of the target audience

Reviewing the needs of the target audience as you did in the first part of the topic area will be your second point for considering any improvements you might suggest to your work. You could look at things such as how well you think your comic and characters would engage the audience. For example, does the style and form of communication fit the age of the reader?

Are the characters and graphics designed in a way that will fit with the reader's interests and the genre of the comic you created?

Another important consideration when you are thinking about the target audience is accessibility. This is where you think about if the reader is able to access the story in the comic. This involves thinking about a number of areas such as:

- Readability: You need to think about how well any reader can access the story you have written. Target audience is key here: you need to think about the words and sentences they can easily engage with. This includes looking at the language you have used but also the amount of text you have used. It can also include the styling of the text, such as the font. There are such a wide range of fonts available, you have to think about the size and style of fonts to ensure that they are easy for the reader to access.
- Colour use: Another consideration for your improvements could be accessibility related to colour use. You should review your comic and look for any potential improvements in the way you have used colour. This could involve looking at the contrast between the text colour and the background colour, for example avoiding the use of green text on a red background – you should try and use high contrast colours to ensure that the text can be read easily. You could also look at your imagery and review whether your focal points are using colours that allow them to be picked out easily on the background, to ensure that the main points of the story are fully accessible to the reader, as we know this is important as comic storytelling is often largely done using the images in the panel.

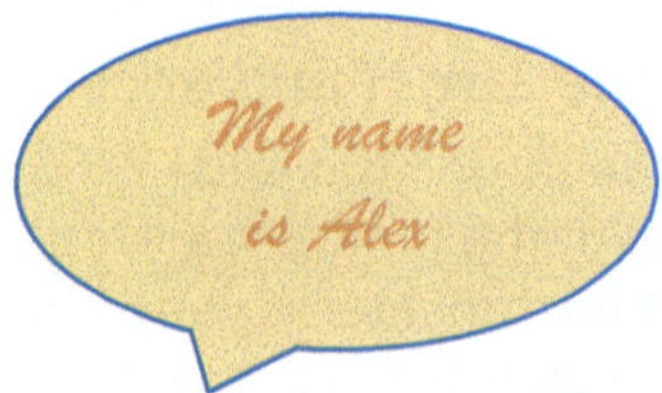

Figure 3.19 The poor contrast in colours between the background and the text in this bubble and the choice of font would make this an example of a potential improvement to this comic to help with readability

Your consideration of the impact of the constraints on your final characters and comic can also help to inform your improvements, as considering how to reduce the constraints might help you to make further improvements to your work.

Further development opportunities for characters and comics

The final part of this topic area is to consider what opportunities you might have to develop the characters and comic further. There are lots of exciting opportunities to explore.

Sequel or themed editions

If the first edition of your comic is a success you might be asked to create the next stage of the story for the client. This could come in a number of formats; one might be to create a sequel. A sequel is the next part of the story that develops on the original storyline, for example the characters have a different adventure in the sequel. It may also be that you are asked to create a second edition of the comic which uses the same characters and setting but is based around a theme, for example a seasonal theme or a theme in which the story is designed to hold a particular message for the audience, such as friendship.

Serialisation

This is when the storyline for the comic is split over a series of different instalments with each individual comic holding the next part of the story – you may recognise this from television where stories are often serialised. The key to serialisation is ensuring that the reader is gripped by the story so that they purchase the rest of the collection of comics to continue the story. This is where a cliff-hanger ending can be used effectively. A cliff hanger is a technique used to end one part of the series at a moment of high suspense or leaving the reader with an unanswered question that will not be resolved or revealed until the next part of the story. This technique helps to entice readers to move to the next comic in the series to discover what happens next.

Character development

This involves looking at how characters within the original comic could be developed further. For example, follow-on editions of the comic could each take one character and look at their place in the story, allowing the reader to learn a little more about each character in turn and adding more depth (and backstory) to the character than you would be able to do in a single comic edition. This might also be an area where the client might want to draw out a particular element of the original comic which proved popular with the target audience or that helps meet the purpose of the comic, and you can best do this by using a particular character to take up that part of the storyline.

Spin off products

There are a lot of opportunities for different spin off products if your comic were to be successful. Here are some areas to think about when considering how spin off products may be part of the further development for your comic.

- TV or film: A very common spin off from a successful comic is a move to TV or film, with the characters and setting transferred to either animation or live action media which combines the characters with movement and sound to tell the story. There are a great many examples of this form of spin off from a comic which are hugely successful such as Batman or Teenage Mutant Ninja Turtles.
- Books or graphic novels: Another common spin off is to create a book or graphic novel that uses the main themes and characters of the comic but develops a particular part of the storyline or a particular character into an extended story that cannot be captured easily in the limited page span of a comic.
- Merchandise: This can include a huge range of items that can be created and sold as part of a range of products with links to the comic and its characters. These may vary based on the brief for the comic and the target audience your comic is aimed at. For example, if your comic is aimed at a younger age range you could consider developing a toy range, whereas if your comic is aimed at an older audience you may need to consider other items such as clothing or household items such as mugs or notebooks. This is an area where you can be really imaginative and think in depth about what your target audience might like and why.

Activity

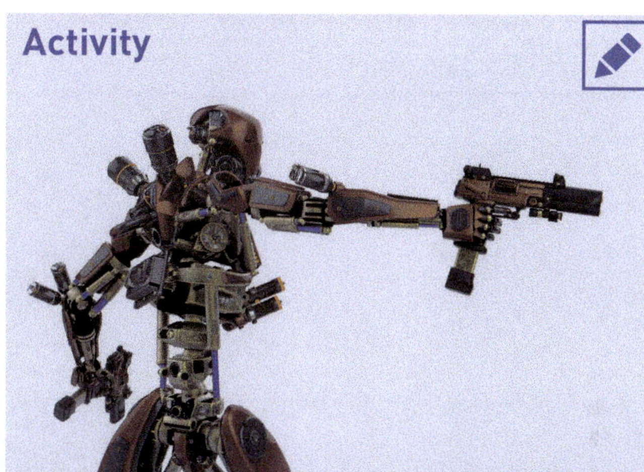

This character is designed to be a villain in a comic about future worlds for older primary school age children. What aspects could be improved?

Synoptic link

You can find further information about this topic in R093, Section 4.1.

Assignment practice

Task 3 – Plan how you might review a comic

Time needed: 1–2 hours

1. Create a document that you might use to review a comic. The document should allow you to review and record your thoughts on:
   - suitability for the client brief
   - suitability for target audience
   - aesthetics, visual appeal and reader engagement.
2. Use your document from Q1 to complete a review of the comic strip created for Task 2.

Unit R096

Animation with audio

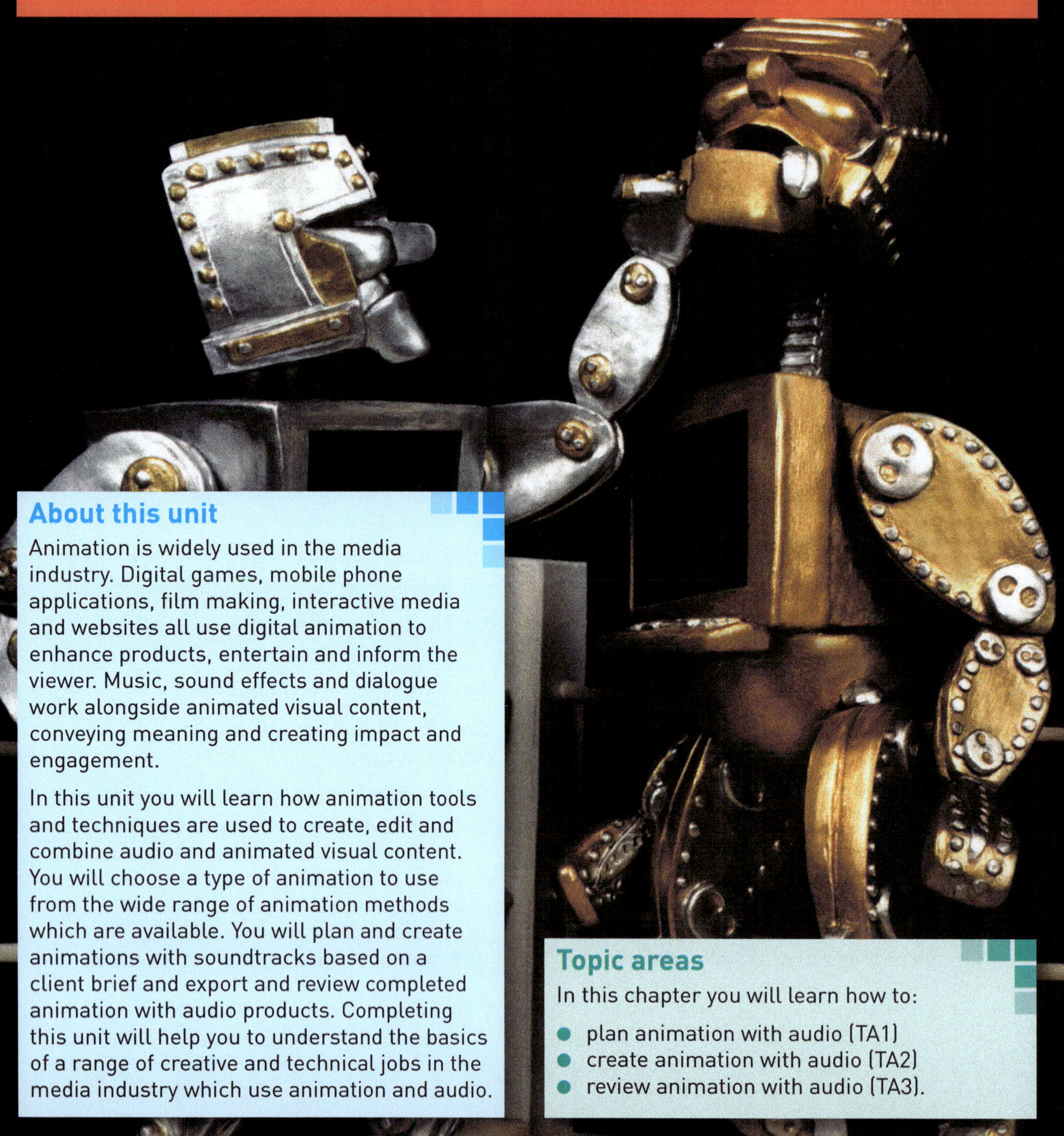

About this unit

Animation is widely used in the media industry. Digital games, mobile phone applications, film making, interactive media and websites all use digital animation to enhance products, entertain and inform the viewer. Music, sound effects and dialogue work alongside animated visual content, conveying meaning and creating impact and engagement.

In this unit you will learn how animation tools and techniques are used to create, edit and combine audio and animated visual content. You will choose a type of animation to use from the wide range of animation methods which are available. You will plan and create animations with soundtracks based on a client brief and export and review completed animation with audio products. Completing this unit will help you to understand the basics of a range of creative and technical jobs in the media industry which use animation and audio.

Topic areas

In this chapter you will learn how to:

- plan animation with audio (TA1)
- create animation with audio (TA2)
- review animation with audio (TA3).

Resources for this unit

Hardware capable of:

- capturing still images for animation purposes (digital camera, web cam or scanner)
- capturing audio for recording (microphone).

Software capable of:

- creating and editing animation. This could be static graphics editing software or software designed to animate movement digitally. Free to use examples include Gimp, Paint 3D, Photopea, Krita and Synfig
- creating and editing audio tracks. Free to use examples include Audacity and Garageband
- combining and exporting animation with audio. Examples include Synfig Studio, Adobe Character Animator, WickEditor, Cartoon Animator 4, Animaker and Moovly.

How will I be assessed?

You will complete an assignment that is set by OCR. This will be completed independently by yourself, without using any additional resources or teacher assistance to help you. The assignment will have a scenario or client brief that defines what you will need to create. You will work through a series of tasks that cover the three topic areas to plan, create and review an animation with audio product. Your portfolio of evidence will be marked by your teacher using the OCR marking criteria. It will then be externally checked/moderated by OCR to confirm your achievement.

Topic area 1 Plan animation with audio

Getting started

1. Open a web browser and load **www.canva.com/create/gif-maker**.
2. Choose 'Make a free GIF'.
3. Click 'Elements' on the left-hand toolbar.
4. Drag one of the graphics from the left-hand menu onto the canvas.
5. Click the thumbnail (little image) at the bottom of the page.
6. Change the time at the top left of the page to 0.2s.
7. Click the breadcrumb menu (...) on the thumbnail at the bottom of the page and choose 'Duplicate'.
8. Alter the graphic by moving, rotating or scaling the image.
9. Repeat steps 7 and 8 until you have 10 thumbnails. They should all be slightly different.
10. Click the 'Play' button at the top right-hand side of the page which says 2.0s.
11. Click 'Download' at the top right-hand side of the page and choose GIF (not PNG) as the file format.
12. Click 'Download' again and save your GIF.

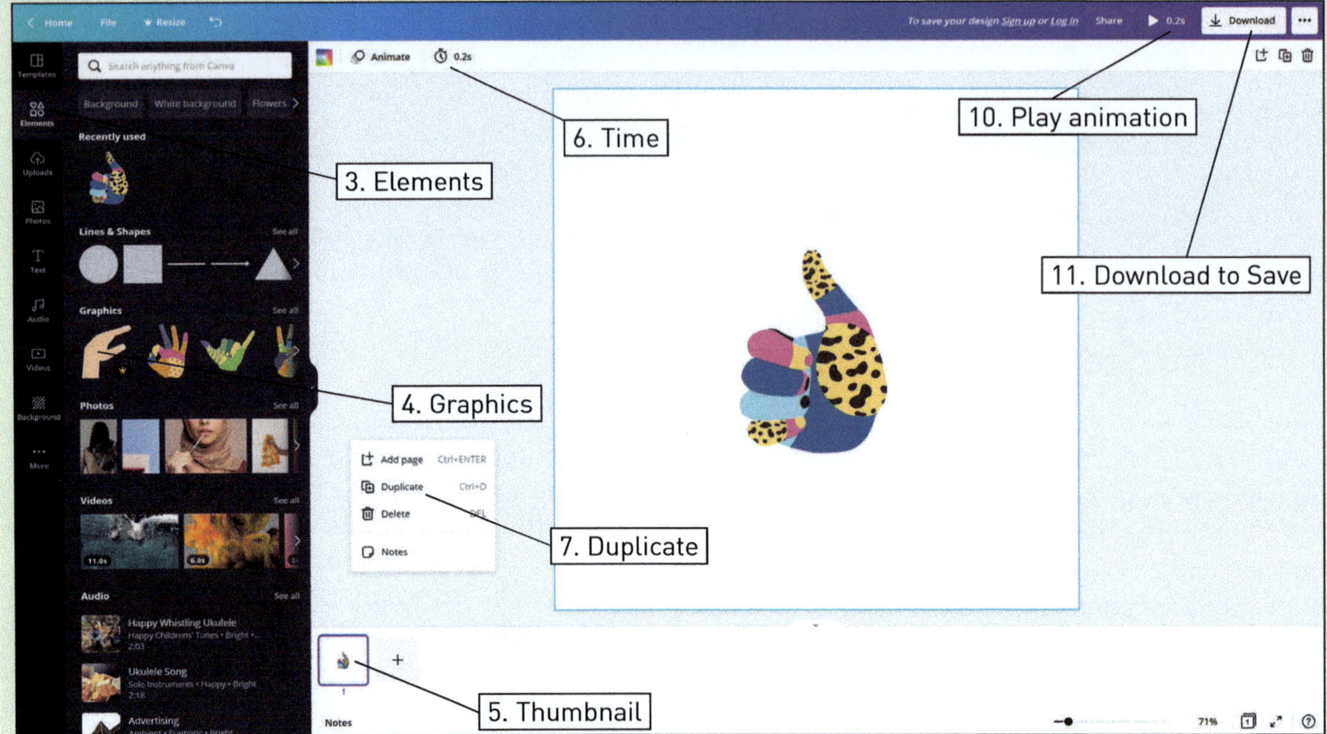

Figure 4.1 Canva workspace for creating animated GIFs

Compare the single static graphic you started with and the animated GIF you have made. Which catches your attention most? Why?

(You can do all the above without signing up for a Canva account, but if you want to save your design and change it later, you need to create an account and log in.)

1.1 Features and conventions of animation and audio

Types and methods of animation and their distinguishing features

The history of animation

The illusion of moving images to create life or 'animation' in static images was first achieved using devices such as the zoescope where images were viewed through a narrow slot as they span on a cylinder. All animation techniques work in the same way; by showing a series of static images in quick succession, the eye is fooled into seeing the images as moving. As a rough guide, anything more than 10–12 images per second will be seen by the human eye as moving rather than separate static images. Animation methods have evolved considerably over the past century, from the simplest flipbooks to complex Computer-Generated Imagery (CGI). Each type of animation has its own distinctive features, advantages and disadvantages.

Activity

Research 'the 12 principles of animation' as refined by Disney's Nine Old Men (Creative Bloq's summary would be a good starting point).

- Which principles do you think are most useful for your animation work?
- Which are the easiest to achieve?

The evolution of animation methods

Flipbook

Also known as kineograph animation, this is a simple technique, where a series of pictures is drawn on each page of a small book, starting at the back and working towards the front. When the pages are 'flicked' through quickly, the changing pictures give the impression of movement. If you want to try this for yourself, sticky notes are an ideal size and shape to use, and they have the advantage that they will stick together along one side. Flipbooks are easy to make and don't require complicated software, but they are not automated and it is not practical to create more than 100 or so 'frames' or images using this method, so only short sequences are suitable.

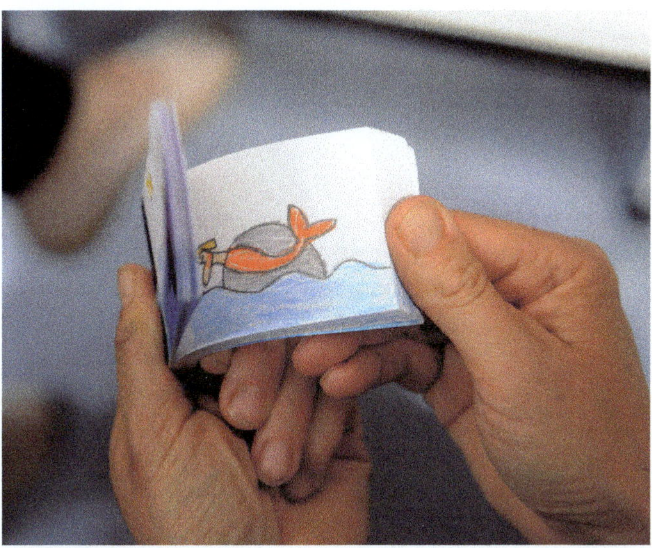

Figure 4.2 A flipbook

Activity

Using sticky notes, create a flipbook to show a short sequence of action such as a stick figure doing star jumps.

Cut out

This animation type uses paper, card or other flat materials. Shapes are cut out and arranged to make a scene or picture which is photographed from above. The cut out images are moved slightly and photographed again, and the resulting series of photographs is then digitised and shown in quick succession to give the impression of movement. This technique was most famously used by Oliver Postgate and Peter Firmin to create the children's television series *Ivor the Engine*, between 1959 and 1977. Cut out animation is quicker to create than cel animation, because the cut out images are repositioned rather than redrawn for each frame. When the images are digitised, audio can be added to create narration and sound effects which enhance the final product.

Figure 4.3 Cut out animation

Stop motion/Claymation and time-lapse

These animation types work in a similar way to cut out animation techniques. Here, the subjects of the animation are three-dimensional rather than flat and models, puppets and real objects can be used instead of or as well as drawings. Each frame of the animation is captured using a camera, which is usually mounted on a tripod or other device to ensure it does not move between shots. Stills cameras, smartphone cameras and in-built webcams can all be used for this purpose which makes these animation techniques widely accessible and reasonably cheap to produce. Some devices can be programmed to take photographs at a set interval, which makes time-lapse animation of natural imagery like sunsets or flowers opening easy to achieve.

The smaller the changes between each shot or frame, and the more images which are captured, the smoother the movement will be. Many examples of stop motion animation can be found in British children's television programmes from the 1960s to 2000. Try looking for episodes of *Paddington Bear* (which combined cut out and stop motion techniques) or the early work of Nick Park's Aardman Animations creation Morph, which appeared in *Take Hart*. The BBC series *Life* and *Blue Planet* made wide use of time-lapse to show the changing seasons or growth of plants over long periods, up to two years.

Figure 4.4 Stop motion animation

Figure 4.5 A cel animator's workstation

Activity

Research the parallax scrolling effect used in animation and film.

Make three cels (you could use cut-up poly pockets, laminator pouches or OHT transparencies) and generate three layers which could be used as a parallax background to action in an animation (for example, background hills, middle ground trees, foreground rocks etc).

Cel animation

This is created by drawing images on transparent film cels (originally made from celluloid which is where the name comes from). The cels can be stacked in layers and photographed, moving each cel or layer slightly between frames to generate movement when the images are played back at speed. The first feature-length animated film, Walt Disney's *Snow White and the Seven Dwarfs* (1937) was created using cel animation. Disney remained the most famous and successful animation studio for many years, and the methods used to create the illusion of movement, exaggeration and weight by the core group of Disney animators known as the 'nine old men' are considered the key principles of the medium to this day.

Computer generated (CG)

These animation techniques were developed from the traditional cel animation methods during the second half of the twentieth century, when a simple computerised animation sequence was used in the opening title sequence for Alfred Hitchcock's film *The Birds* (1963). The use of software-driven animation to fill in and render movements 'in between' key poses and points in the action – known as motion or shape tweening – was first used to create a feature-length animated film in 1995 with Pixar's *Toy Story*.

In CG animation, the computer creates some of the images and textures, so that not everything has to be drawn by hand. Algorithms work out how materials such as hair and fabric move through space and are affected by gravity. This has the advantage of reducing the need for artistic drawing skills, but can be very expensive, time-consuming and resource heavy. For example, Pixar used 117 computers running 24 hours a day to render *Toy Story*, a process which required some 800,000 machine hours to complete; and the film was created at roughly three minutes of finished animation per week.

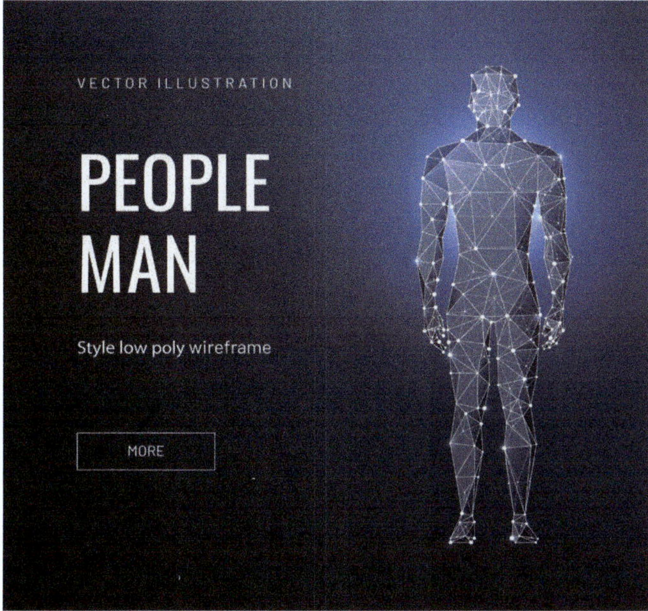

Figure 4.6 A wire frame image for CGI animation

Motion capture (often shortened to 'MoCap')

This is a process which uses computer software to translate movement from sensors on an actor onto a virtual skeleton or 'rig'. The virtual skeleton can then be overlaid with textures and shapes to generate a character which looks quite different from the original human actor but moves in a very realistic and believable way. This is also referred to as performance capture, since the actors can convey emotions and moods through their movements and poses which might be hard to create using drawing skills alone.

MoCap has become more widely used in recent years and can be found in children's TV series such as *Sid the Science Kid* as well as movies and avatars for web-based communication and video conferencing applications. Lip-synch tools can be used to add dialogue or vocalisations to visual animation of performance capture, which is an advantage of this animation method.

Motion capture is a growing sector of the British media industry, with companies such as The Imaginarium specialising in performance capture and universities offering degree level courses in motion capture.

Figure 4.7 An actor performing motion capture

Test your knowledge

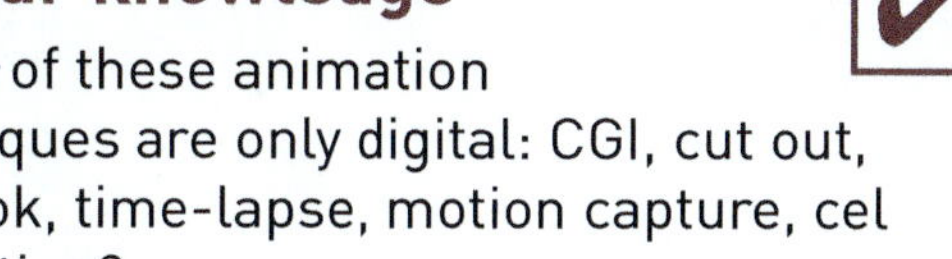

1. Which of these animation techniques are only digital: CGI, cut out, flipbook, time-lapse, motion capture, cel animation?

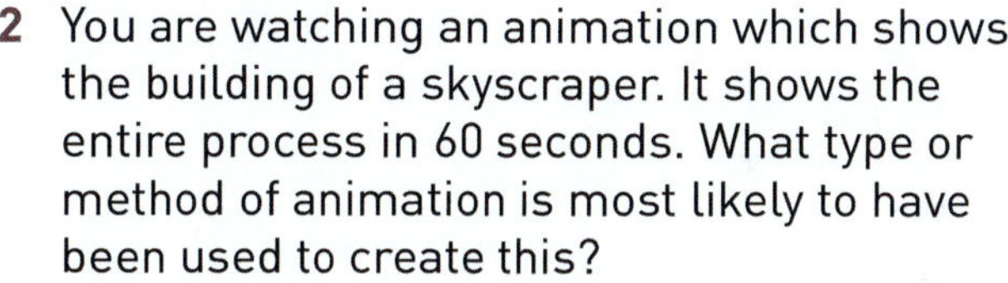

2. You are watching an animation which shows the building of a skyscraper. It shows the entire process in 60 seconds. What type or method of animation is most likely to have been used to create this?
3. Which animation method would you choose to create a short story featuring model action figures?
4. You have a series of digital vector images showing key points of action in a sequence. What animation method could you use to generate the final animation?

The properties and features of audio

Anything which can be heard is counted as audio. Audio in animations is either diegetic or non-diegetic.

- Diegetic sounds can be heard by characters within a scene.
- Non-diegetic sounds are generally added during post-production to enhance the mood and atmosphere.

Diegetic sounds

- Dialogue is the term used to describe speech between characters in a scene. As well as speech, dialogue also includes monologues (where one character speaks aloud) and vocalisations such as screams, gasps and giggles which convey emotion.
- Background or ambient sounds such as wind or waves, traffic, footsteps and so on which are not made by characters in shot but add to the atmosphere, creating a more realistic scene.
- Foley is the term used to describe sound effects (often shortened to SFX) which are created in a studio or inserted from pre-recorded libraries to enhance the main audio content of a sequence.

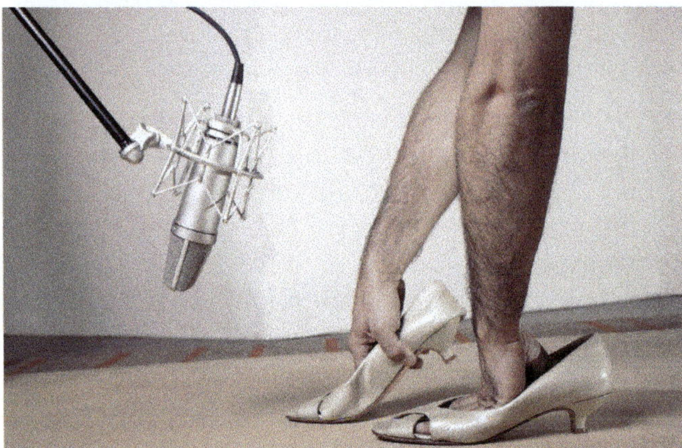

Figure 4.8 A Foley artist creating sound effects

Non-diegetic sounds

- Music (either instrumental or with lyrics). This can enhance the visuals of an animation or be the main focus, for example where the visuals 'act out' a song in a music video.
- Narration/voiceover, where commentary describing or supporting the visual content of a sequence is added, but the speaker is not seen on screen.

The properties of digital audio

Any sounds which are recorded live using a microphone will need to be saved using electronic storage in order to be used in an animation with audio. An understanding of the properties of digital audio will be helpful when digitising sounds.

- Bit depth refers to the number of 'bits' of information in every sample of audio. CD audio and music streaming services use 16 bit, whereas DVD audio supports up to 24 bit. For most animation work, 16 bit will be sufficient. However, if you were making a music video your client may prefer the larger dynamic range (and therefore better audio quality) which 24 bit allows.
- Sample rate is the number of times per second the audio is 'sampled' or captured. Higher sample rates generally mean better quality sound, but there is a trade-off between sample rate and file size, and generally a sample rate of 44.1kHz (Kilohertz) is enough. You may find that the audio recording software you use defaults to 16 bit and 44.1kHz and this will be acceptable in the majority of cases.
- **Gain** is the term used to describe how loud sounds are when they are captured or recorded and refers to the input levels and tone of a captured sound. It is often used to mean volume, but volume is more accurately used to describe the loudness of sounds when they are output. If sounds are distorted when recording, decreasing the gain can often help.
- Mono/stereo describes whether sounds are recorded and played back on a single audio channel or two audio channels. Mono tracks will output the same sounds through left and right speakers, whereas stereo sounds can split or pan (spread out) the sounds to send different audio to the left and right. Stereo (or binaural) audio sounds more realistic than mono and recording audio in stereo gives greater flexibility when editing and mixing tracks, as effects can be applied to left and right channels separately.

The purpose and conventions of animations

Animations are used for a variety of purposes, including to advertise, promote, entertain and inform. We recognise these purposes because of certain conventions that are used for each.

Key term

Gain The input level or tone of a sound.

- Animations for entertainment will often use narrative structures such as a three-part storyline and be focused on characters. When characters interact with each other, the 180-degree rule or convention means that the **virtual camera** shows them from the same side regardless of how tight or wide the shot is. This helps the viewer understand the content of a scene.
- Advertisements will commonly state and repeat the name of the product and include slogans and **stings** to try and make the product memorable.
- Informative animations such as tutorials and 'explainers' may be structured to show a sequence of actions. They may include voiceover rather than onscreen characters and unobtrusive background music, so the viewer focuses on the subject being explained. Text content may include annotated diagrams and captions and the subject matter tends to be non-fiction rather than narrative.

Key terms

Virtual camera A function of software which works out how objects will appear if captured from a specific angle or viewpoint within the scene or 'stage'.

Sting A short music clip used to introduce, link or end sections in an audio or audio-visual production such as a TV programme or radio commercial.

Synoptic link

There are other conventions for the use of particular shot types and transitions. You can read more about these in Unit R098.

You can read more about product branding and brand recognition in Unit R094, Visual identity and digital graphics.

Conventions used in audio to meet a purpose

Audio is used on its own for entertainment. Many different emotions and moods can be created in music, depending on the choice of genre, style and instrumentation. Plays and stories are created using a mixture of voices (dialogue), foley and background or mood music. Audio is also used for a wider range of purposes. News reports, documentaries and adverts can all be created using audio alone, to inform, promote or persuade. Broadcast radio, podcasts, internet radio stations and streaming services all use audio to meet a purpose. There are a number of conventions which help audiences to understand the audio they are listening to.

- Mood and emotion: These can be conveyed using particular types of music, for example low, sustained notes on strings suggest an ominous or serious mood. Music is often used in advertising and promotion to appeal to a particular target audience by using tracks which were current at the time the audience were teenagers.
- Scene setting: Audio can set the scene by using a combination of music, sound effects and non-diegetic or ambient sounds to prepare the audience for whatever dialogue is to follow. This makes the dialogue more effective and engaging than the spoken words alone would be.
- Structure of audio products: Certain audio products have a distinctive structure to help attract an audience's attention. For example, a travel or news bulletin on broadcast radio typically begins with an announcement and often a musical phrase introducing what is to come next. Similarly, a news reporter typically will generally 'sign off' at the end of a report with a recognisable phrase such as 'This is Jo Bloggs for Radio Nine, reporting from London'. In this way the listener knows that a particular section of an audio broadcast has ended. Chart music tracks often follow a recognisable structure or pattern (such as verse-chorus-verse-solo-chorus) and this predictability can help make a tune catchy and memorable. You can also find conventions in dialogue, for example the structure of a 'knock-knock' joke.

- Timing and **synchronisation** with visuals: Audio is widely used in combination with visual content to enhance meaning. Audio supports the visual content and helps convey character and action. Cartoons are greatly enhanced by adding foley; for example, the 'smash' sound when an expensive vase is broken by a clumsy character. You could test the effectiveness of this by finding some cartoon clips and watching them with the sound muted. The pitch, tone, pace and accent of a voice can also help generate engaging animated characters by matching their physical appearance. Think how different some well-known animated characters would be with a slower, deeper voice, a different accent or a faster pace. This can sometimes be used deliberately for comedic effect, as in *The Boss Baby* or *Family Guy*'s Stewie Griffin.
- Narration or voiceover: This is used to describe and comment on the visual elements of an animation with audio. Conventions mean we understand that a narrative or voiceover does not have to be associated with a character on screen and that the characters in a scene cannot hear the voiceover. Stings and jingles are musical shortcuts used in advertising to help make a product or slogan more memorable. For example, the opera singer character Gio Compario's musical phrase in the GoCompare adverts, or the whistled tune which accompanies McDonald's adverts in place of the slogan 'I'm lovin' it'.

Key term

Synchronisation Adjusting or aligning the timing of more than one thing so they match.

Activity

How many jingles or stings can you think of? Ask someone from a different age group what commercials they remember from their childhood. How many of those are memorable because of a jingle or sting?

Creativity in animation with audio

You have learned about the history and origins of animation and you now know about the conventions used, but you still need to be creative. So how do you balance using conventions and established techniques with originality? It's about using your imagination and your own ideas to come up with something different from what has been done before.

Even if you are creating a product for a client who already has an established brand or identity, you won't engage audiences if they think they have seen the concept before. There are a few things you can do to start:

- You can adapt existing designs, perhaps putting a recognisable character into a new situation or story.
- You could advertise a product by concentrating attention on what is new or different whilst creating engagement by using a familiar, established slogan or animation type.
- You can use the conventions of animation, storytelling or character design to help the audience understand characters' motivations. For example, you could use big eyes and large heads to create empathy and suggest cuteness in your characters.

What you can't do is re-use an existing character, plotline or scenario without making significant changes. A square-shaped cartoon character made from sponge who happens to be green and called Bill is not acceptable! Where ideas

Activity

Find examples of Christmas adverts which use animation. Suitable starting points could be John Lewis, Aldi, Sainsbury's or Disney Christmas adverts from previous years.

Discuss with a partner or group:

- What makes animation a suitable choice for these adverts?
- What types of animation have been used?
- How does the choice of music add to the effectiveness of each advert?
- What moods or emotions are conjured up through the adverts and how is this achieved?

are too similar to existing products, they are said to be derivative – that is, they are derived from something else and not original. You should avoid derivative work in your assignment portfolio because it suggests that your ideas are not original and creative. However, you can draw inspiration from existing designs and make them your own.

1.2 Resources required to create animation with audio

Resources used in animation

Hardware and peripherals

Animation requires different hardware and peripherals depending on the type and techniques used. Traditional methods such as cel animation, stop motion, Claymation and flip books rely on physical resources including cameras, tripods, paper, celluloid or other transparent media and drawing and colouring materials. Animation cels often have holes at the bottom edge so they can be placed on a 'peg bar' which keeps them lined up precisely. This stops the animation becoming jerky and prevents the backgrounds moving when they are meant to be static. A special tripod and camera combination called a **rostrum camera** is also used to make sure each shot or image is captured from exactly the same angle. When using a rostrum camera set-up, the camera only zooms in and out. Pans are created by moving the cels or backgrounds slightly over a series of frames. You can make your own rostrum and peg bar accessories to help produce good quality animation.

Claymation and modelling techniques use **rigging** or **armatures**. These are rigid, jointed 'skeletons' which the clay is modelled onto. This gives models stability and prevents them collapsing or sagging under their own weight, whilst allowing poses to be changed as required. You can make your own rigging using wire or pipe cleaners.

The terms rigging and armature are also used in digital animation, to describe digital skeletons and joints which help to constrain or define the range of movement of digital characters.

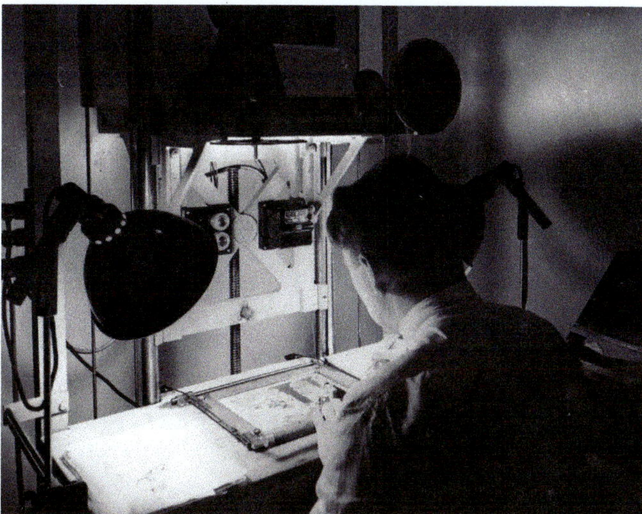

Figure 4.9 A rostrum camera set-up

Activity

Research examples of stop motion and Claymation online. A suitable starting point might be the work of Tim Burton or Nick Park, but you can also find many adverts and campaigns such as the NHS 'Five a Day', which uses stop motion animation.

Use what you have seen to inspire your own creation: make a plasticine model character with armature or swappable body or mouth parts.

Animations can also be generated using a combination of digital and non-digital techniques. Rotoscoping uses live action models which are filmed or photographed frame by frame. Each frame is then printed to allow the action to be traced as drawings and additional animation to be overlaid. Very accurate and realistic character

Key terms

Rostrum camera A camera which is mounted or fixed in position to a bench or platform (a rostrum) to enable continuity between frames in hand drawn and stopmotion animation.

Rigging A virtual skeleton used to create shapes for characters and objects in 3D animation

Armature Another name for the skeleton or support structure for a real or computer-generated model used in animation.

movements can be created in this way, without losing the sense of drawings rather than live action. Cel shading is used to digitally 'colour in' 3D computer-generated graphics to give the impression of a traditional, cel-animated approach. This can be seen in many computer games as well as in Japanese animated films.

The choice of which method or type of animation to use may depend on what resources and peripherals are available. Non-digital animation methods generally look more original and hand-crafted than digital animation and this can be useful if the final animation with audio needs to have a retro, familiar or cosy feel.

- Claymation in particular is useful for UK target audience appeal since the method is so widely associated with Aardman, which has its origins in the UK. However, Claymation is very time-consuming to create, especially if realistic movements from animals and human characters are required.
- Cel animation is capable of producing beautiful artwork. It has the advantage that cels for backgrounds and objects can be re-used instead of having to redraw them each frame, and this can make for smooth animations with good continuity. However, cel animation demands greater artistic skills and requires a larger amount of equipment than other methods.

Figure 4.10 A The armature model used for King Kong in the 1933 film

Finally, all non-digital animation methods need some kind of physical studio space which can be set up and left in position for as long as it takes to capture and digitise each frame. If such a space is not available, then digital animation methods where all visual content is created within a software application may be preferable.

Activity

Search online for examples of cut out animation techniques. A suitable starting point might be the work of Oliver Postgate and 'Smallfilms'.

Use what you have seen to inspire your own creation: make a character with movable body/facial features using cut outs from paper or thin card. You could draw or print images. Your character does not need to be human; it can be animal, vegetable, mineral, alien or fantasy-based.

Animation software

Animation can also be created using purely digital methods, by drawing content or importing ready-made assets directly into graphics editing or animation software. Animation software typically works by stacking or overlaying layers of visual content along a timeline. Key points within the action are marked using key frames to enable sounds and visual elements to be aligned or

Key terms

Onion skinning Overlaying frames so that the previous frame's positioning can be seen as a 'ghost' image. This allows the animator to line up objects precisely when setting up the next frame.

Tween Short for 'in betweening', the process of filling in frames to generate movement in between key frames.

synchronised. Dedicated animation tools include **onion skinning** (a way of viewing two frames on top of each other to see changes over time) and **tweening** (movement created automatically by the software). Tweening is very useful and saves time when animating simple movements but can also remove some of the hand-crafted feel to an animation, since it takes over some of the control of the animation process.

When choosing software to use for animation, the availability of tools such as layers, tweening, key frames and onion skinning will be important factors to consider. Whether the software supports armatures, rigging and lighting effects will also possibly influence the choice of software, depending on the style of animation which is to be created. There are free software applications which provide the full range of animation tools, but it can take time and practice to master such software and depending on the type of animation which is planned it may be quicker and easier to use more simple software.

There are also applications which are designed specifically to create 'explainer' animations. These have pre-loaded visual assets such as characters, objects and backgrounds. If originality in the visual elements is less important than creating a clear message, software like this might be chosen to compile an animation rather than building it from scratch including creating all the assets. A key consideration when selecting software for this part of your course will be whether or not it supports audio tracks.

Resources used to capture audio

Hardware and peripherals

There are two basic types of audio which can be added to animation: sourced and captured.

- Sourced audio includes pre-recorded music tracks and sound effects obtained from libraries and saved files.
- Captured audio is obtained by recording sounds and saving them.

Sourced audio is likely to be in the form of digital files which will already be in a suitable format for editing in audio software or inserting into animation software. For captured audio, the basic requirements are:

- a microphone
- recording and storage devices
- software capable of recording the sounds (unless the audio is being recorded in analogue form onto tape).

It is helpful to have a basic understanding of the wide variety of hardware, software and peripherals for capturing and storing audio, so that you can choose the most suitable resources when required.

Microphones

These are either built into recording devices or separate peripherals.

Inbuilt microphones do not offer choice over the way sounds are recorded but they will connect easily with the recording software and be compatible with the recording device. They tend to be set to capture a wide range of frequencies but with a bias towards recording speech. This makes them suitable for purposes such as podcasting, telephone conferencing and video calls. Smartphones, Dictaphones, laptops and tablets commonly have inbuilt microphones. Headsets and earphones also often include a microphone which is suitable for recording speech from one person at a time, though their limited range makes them unsuitable for dialogue. Inbuilt microphones are not particularly directional, meaning they pick up sounds from all directions around the device. This can result in unwanted sounds being captured along with the desired speech, music or sound effects. Removing these unwanted sounds during the editing process can be time-consuming, so audio technicians often choose to use an external microphone instead.

External microphones can be connected to recording devices through wired, wireless or Bluetooth connections. They are a good choice when you need to record particular frequencies or capture sounds from a specific direction. External microphones are categorised by type depending on directionality (the area from which a microphone collects most sound). Knowing which type of microphone to use can make a big difference to the quality of the sound which is recorded.

The different microphone types and their directionality is shown in Table 4.1.

Table 4.1 Different types of microphone

Microphone type	Description	Used for	Audio recording range pattern
Omni-directional	Picks up sounds from in front of and behind the microphone	Capturing ambient sounds to help set a scene	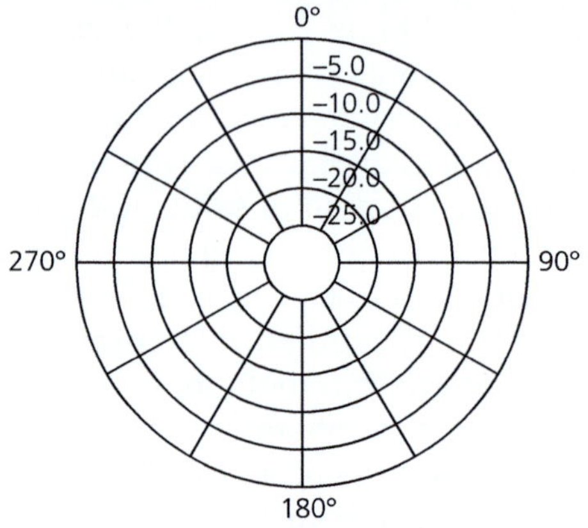 0° –5.0 –10.0 –15.0 –20.0 –25.0 270° 90° 180°
Cardioid	Picks up sounds from directly in front of the microphone with almost no sensitivity to sounds from behind	Capturing speech when conducting a face-to-face interview	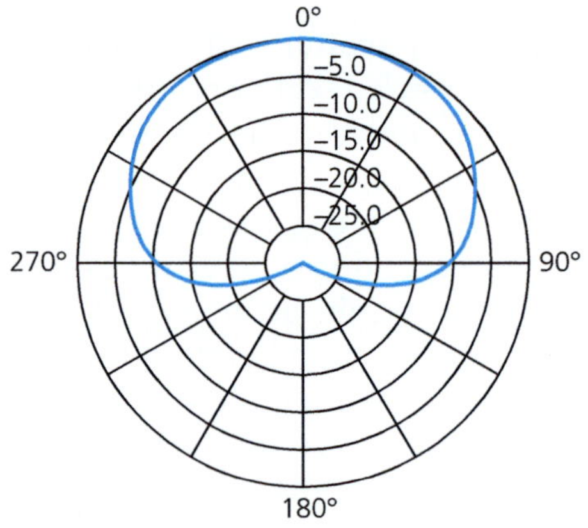 0° –5.0 –10.0 –15.0 –20.0 –25.0 270° 90° 180°
Super-cardioid	Has a narrow area of sensitivity at a longer range than cardioid microphones	Capturing wildlife sounds or sounds from a stage some distance away	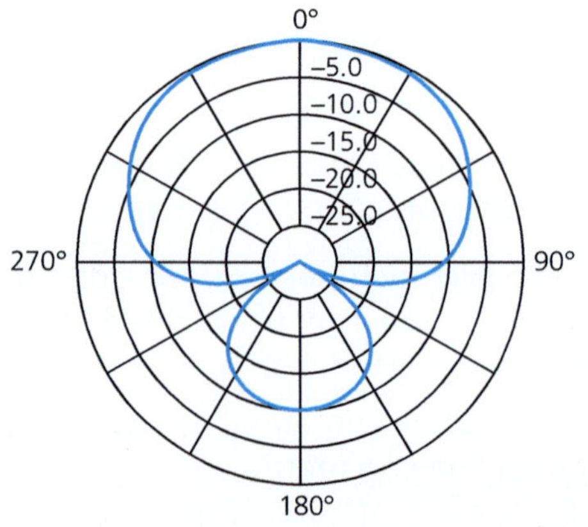 0° –5.0 –10.0 –15.0 –20.0 –25.0 270° 90° 180°

Wired external microphones connect to recording devices using USB or 3.5 mm jack connection (usually colour coded green), and dedicated microphones also commonly connect to mixing desks and recording devices using XLR connection. USB microphones are useful as they are generally 'plug and play', meaning they contain a built-in interface which is compatible with a wide range of devices. They are generally quite cheap to buy and are a reasonable choice for recording most sound types. However, USB microphones bypass the computer's sound card and this can result in 'latency' – a short delay between the sound being made and being recorded in the software. This makes it difficult to synchronise vocals with a music soundtrack unless the USB microphone also has a headphone output for direct monitoring. Microphones which plug into the line sockets on the sound card do not have this problem, but not all devices have line input sockets.

Figure 4.11 XLR, USB and 3.5 mm line 'jack' audio connectors

Audio capture software

Many music producers use a Digital Audio Workstation (DAW) to record, edit and mix audio tracks prior to storing the final products. This can be a physical device with its own storage capacity such as a mixing desk or a software application. The most commonly used free DAW applications are Audacity, Cakewalk and Waveform Free.

An advantage of using a software-based DAW is that all the tracks can be viewed on screen during the capture and mixing process, whereas some mixing desks only display outputs via physical dials and faders. But if sounds from a large number of inputs are being captured at the same time, a mixing desk will usually support more simultaneous inputs than a PC or tablet device.

Other peripherals and equipment

There is a wide choice of additional equipment to improve the quality of recorded audio. For example:

- Boom poles allow a microphone to be placed closer to a speaker without being visible in shot, making it easier to capture speech clearly.
- Wind deflectors made of foam or synthetic fur can be placed over a microphone to prevent unwanted noise from wind being captured along with the desired sounds.
- Microphones are often placed on a tripod stand to avoid picking up sounds from a person's hands if holding the microphone, and to leave the speaker's hands free.
- Radio mics are useful if the person speaking needs to be able to move around without getting tangled in microphone cables.
- Shock mounts are used in studios to stop microphones picking up unwanted vibration noise.
- Pop guards or shields are often placed between a microphone and the person speaking, to avoid capturing pops and other 'plosive' sounds which can impair the sound quality and be difficult to edit out.
- Audio technicians check the quality of the audio whilst it is being recorded using headphones, earphones or headsets. These are plugged in or connected wirelessly to the recording device, which can range from a mixing desk or DAW to a Dictaphone, digital audio recorder, smartphone or tablet.

Figure 4.12 Vocal audio recording equipment

The choice of which microphone, recording device and mixing software to use will depend on the type of audio being recorded, the location required and how the audio will be used. For example, if you needed to capture the ambient sounds of a city street to add distant background noise to a scene then it would be perfectly acceptable to use a smartphone and its inbuilt microphone. But if you were recording a podcast, the clarity of the dialogue is very important and there may be minimal or no visual content in the final product. In this case, you would want to use an indoor studio set-up using a mixing desk, cardioid XLR microphones with pop guards and shock mounts. You might also choose to record straight to an application-based DAW software on a PC.

Activity

Use a smartphone or recording device to record ambient sounds in different locations, for example, interior, exterior, nature, urban, human, machine. Listen to the recordings you have made.

- How clear are the sounds?
- How suitable is the audio quality?
- How might the quality be improved?

Test your knowledge

5 What resources (equipment, hardware, software and peripherals) would you use to minimise unwanted background noise whilst recording a conversation between two people outdoors?

1.3 Pre-production and planning documentation and techniques for animation with audio

Planning techniques for animation with audio

In the media industry, animation projects are often completed by teams of people rather than by just one person. The larger the project, the more people are likely to be involved. So it is important to make sure that planning documentation for an animation with audio is detailed and clear enough for different people to understand and work from. When planning for animations including audio, the visuals, sounds and how they fit together must be shown.

Pre-production documentation

There are several kinds of pre-production document which allow this.

- Timelines are helpful when planning how the visual and audio elements are combined and synchronised. They can use separate layers for elements such as music, action and dialogue and show which things happen at the same time.
- Scripts are able to detail the sounds heard during an animation and can include foley and music in the stage directions as well as setting out any dialogue or voiceover. However, scripts are less successful for planning the visual elements because they rely on a description of what is happening in each scene rather than showing it using sketches.
- Storyboards show the visual element clearly and arrows and annotations can be used to describe movement of objects in a scene as well as camera movements and shot types. Storyboards do not show audio as clearly, but speech bubbles, captions and annotations can all be used to indicate the sounds which accompany each shot or frame.
- Graphic scores are used to indicate not only which sounds overlap with each other, but also how loud different sounds are. This is done by using a layer for each sound type and increasing the height of the layer or sound to show louder sounds or higher gain.

It is likely that more than one type of pre-production document will be used when planning an animation with audio, unless the visuals or audio are very simple.

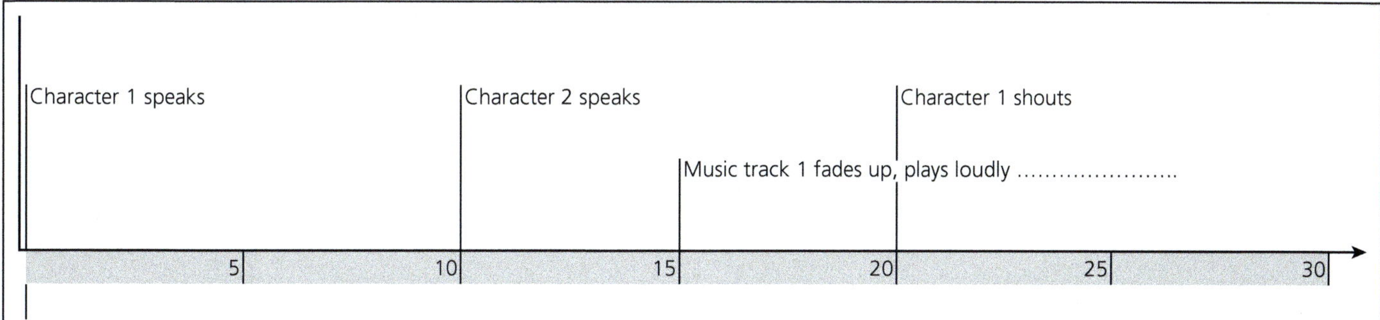

Figure 4.13 Example of a timeline used to plan animation and audio

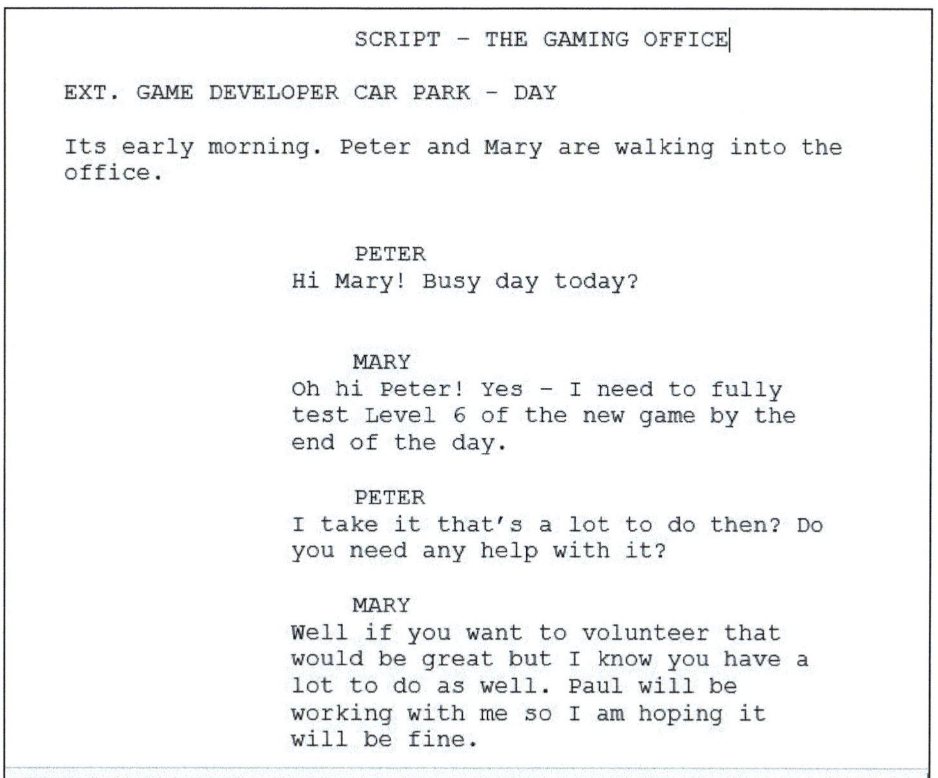

```
SCRIPT - THE GAMING OFFICE

EXT. GAME DEVELOPER CAR PARK - DAY

Its early morning. Peter and Mary are walking into the
office.

                PETER
            Hi Mary! Busy day today?

                MARY
            Oh hi Peter! Yes - I need to fully
            test Level 6 of the new game by the
            end of the day.

                PETER
            I take it that's a lot to do then? Do
            you need any help with it?

                MARY
            Well if you want to volunteer that
            would be great but I know you have a
            lot to do as well. Paul will be
            working with me so I am hoping it
            will be fine.
```

Figure 4.14 Example of a script used to plan animation and audio

Synoptic link

You can read more about how storyboards and scripts are constructed in Unit R093.

Planning for style

The final part of planning and pre-production is to make sure the style chosen meets the client's requirements and matches the target audience the product is aimed at. This can include making sure characters in the animation are inclusive and representative of a wide selection of the target audience. An animation which only appeals to part of the target audience is not fit for purpose. It can also mean choosing a style of animation which the audience will find engaging. Manga-style artwork may be used to appeal to a young demographic, whilst Claymation will have a wider appeal, including an older audience who enjoyed watching animations such as *Morph* or *Wallace and Gromit*.

Style is also important when choosing the audio to enhance animation. What accent or dialect should be used for dialogue and voiceovers? What language? Children's television characters like the *Teletubbies*,

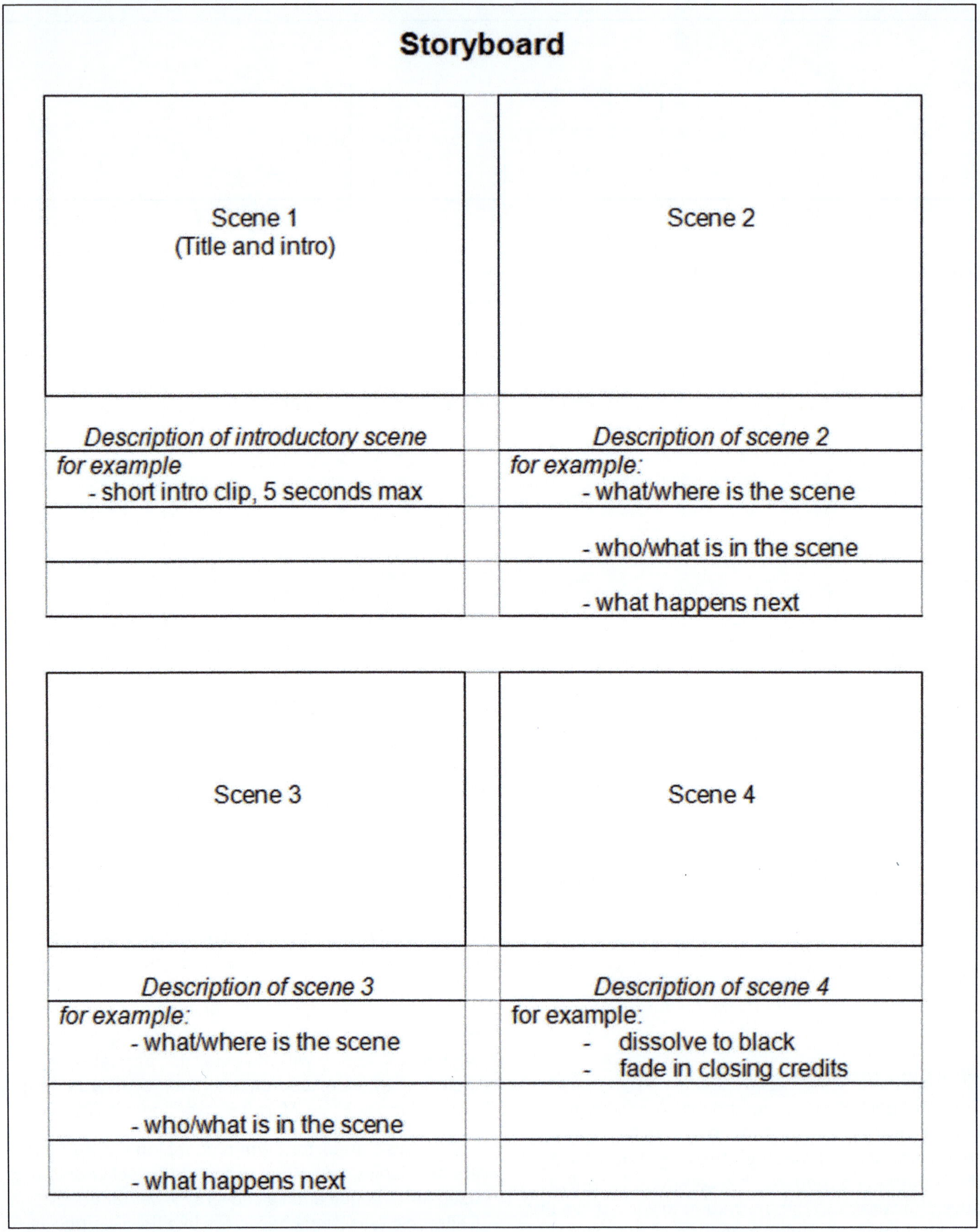

Storyboard

Scene 1 (Title and intro)	Scene 2
Description of introductory scene	*Description of scene 2*
for example - short intro clip, 5 seconds max	*for example:* - what/where is the scene
	- who/what is in the scene
	- what happens next

Scene 3	Scene 4
Description of scene 3	*Description of scene 4*
for example: - what/where is the scene	for example: - dissolve to black - fade in closing credits
- who/what is in the scene	
- what happens next	

Figure 4.15 Example of a storyboard used to plan animation and audio

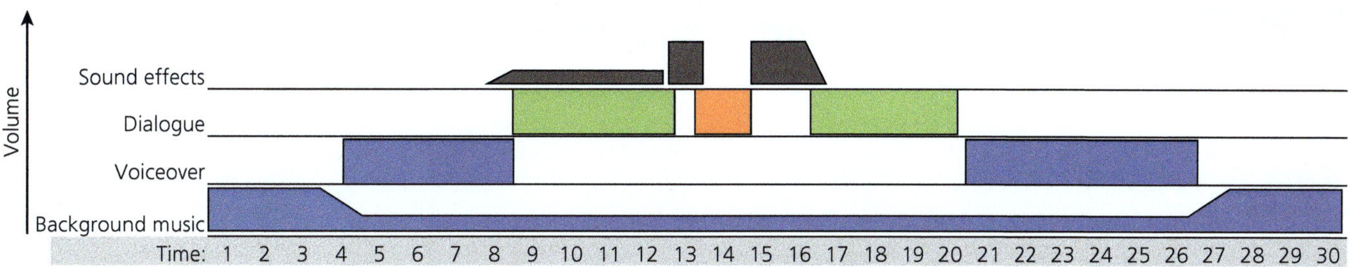

Figure 4.16 Example of a graphic score used to plan audio

Bill and Ben or the *Clangers* use made-up language which allows them to appeal to a wide audience. An animation which is linked to a particular place may need to use regional accents or dialects from the local area. There is lots of choice in the style, tempo, instrumentation, mood and genre of the background music you could choose to accompany an animation. The style you choose should match the visual content, but also the target audience. It's no use choosing something which appeals to you as the animator, if the target audience won't listen to it. Legislation also needs to be considered, since the use of chart music is likely to be expensive and you will need to consider copyright.

Activities

Figure 4.14 shows a script set outside a Gaming Office.

1. Make a list of the sound effects (SFX) and audio needed to accompany the dialogue in this script. You could include both diegetic and non-diegetic sounds.
2. Create a timeline to show how the SFX and other audio fit with the dialogue in the script. Which elements overlap? Which parts are loud, and which are quiet?

Test your knowledge

6. Stop motion using Lego™ would best appeal to what kinds of audiences?
7. What would be the disadvantages of using this kind of animation when advertising a product other than Lego™?
8. What would be the advantages of using this kind of animation?

Assignment practice

Task 1: Plan animation with audio

Time needed: approx. 1 hour

You have been asked to design a five-second animation with audio which will be used as a banner on the homepage of a website promoting a new gluten-free bread product. Statistics show more women than men buy gluten-free foods. The product costs about 30 per cent more than ordinary bread.

1. Create a mind map to help you interpret the client brief.
2. Create a digital mood board to show your initial ideas and planning for the animation with audio. This can include:
   - text
   - fonts
   - colour palette
   - sounds
   - examples of animations
   - examples of the type of animation you think would be most suitable.
3. Write a summary of your ideas, explaining how and why your choice of animation and audio styles and types are suitable.

Topic area 2 Create animation with audio

Getting started

Using only your own vocal skills and any items about your person or within easy reach, create a live rendition of the following foley-based script.

```
            SCENE 1:
            INT. A DESERTED HOUSE. 3AM. IT IS PITCH BLACK.
      SFX: Wind whistles faintly through the gap under the front door.
      SFX: Newspapers rustle softly on the floor.
      SFX: A mouse squeaks, scampers across the stair.
      SFX: Clock chimes 3 times.
      SFX: Slow, dragging footsteps shuffle along the hall.
      SFX: Key squeals as the front door is unlocked.
      SFX: Front door creaks open slowly.
      (Pause: silence for 2 seconds)
ELDERLY VOICE: (Evil laugh) Mwuahahaaaaaaaaa!
```

(Bonus activity: if you had to record this now without leaving the room, what equipment could you use?)

2.1 Techniques to obtain, create and manage assets

Visual animation assets

Once the visual content for an animation has been planned, assets must be created and prepared for use. Assets can be seen as the building blocks or components of the visual content – the backgrounds, scenery, objects, props and characters to be used in an animation. Anything which needs to move independently in an animation will generally be saved as a separate asset.

Asset creation can be done in a number of ways, but the first consideration is whether to use ready-made assets or create your own. Creating your own original assets is arguably more creative and your client may prefer something which has not been used before. But starting with a blank canvas and designing assets for every aspect of an animation can be a time-consuming and costly process. As a compromise, you could take existing assets and edit them to make them more unique and ensure they match the client's requirements. If your animation uses Claymation or stop motion techniques you might use models, props and objects which you have collected together and prepare them by creating costumes or set dressing. If you are using digital animation techniques, then you may want to make use of asset libraries.

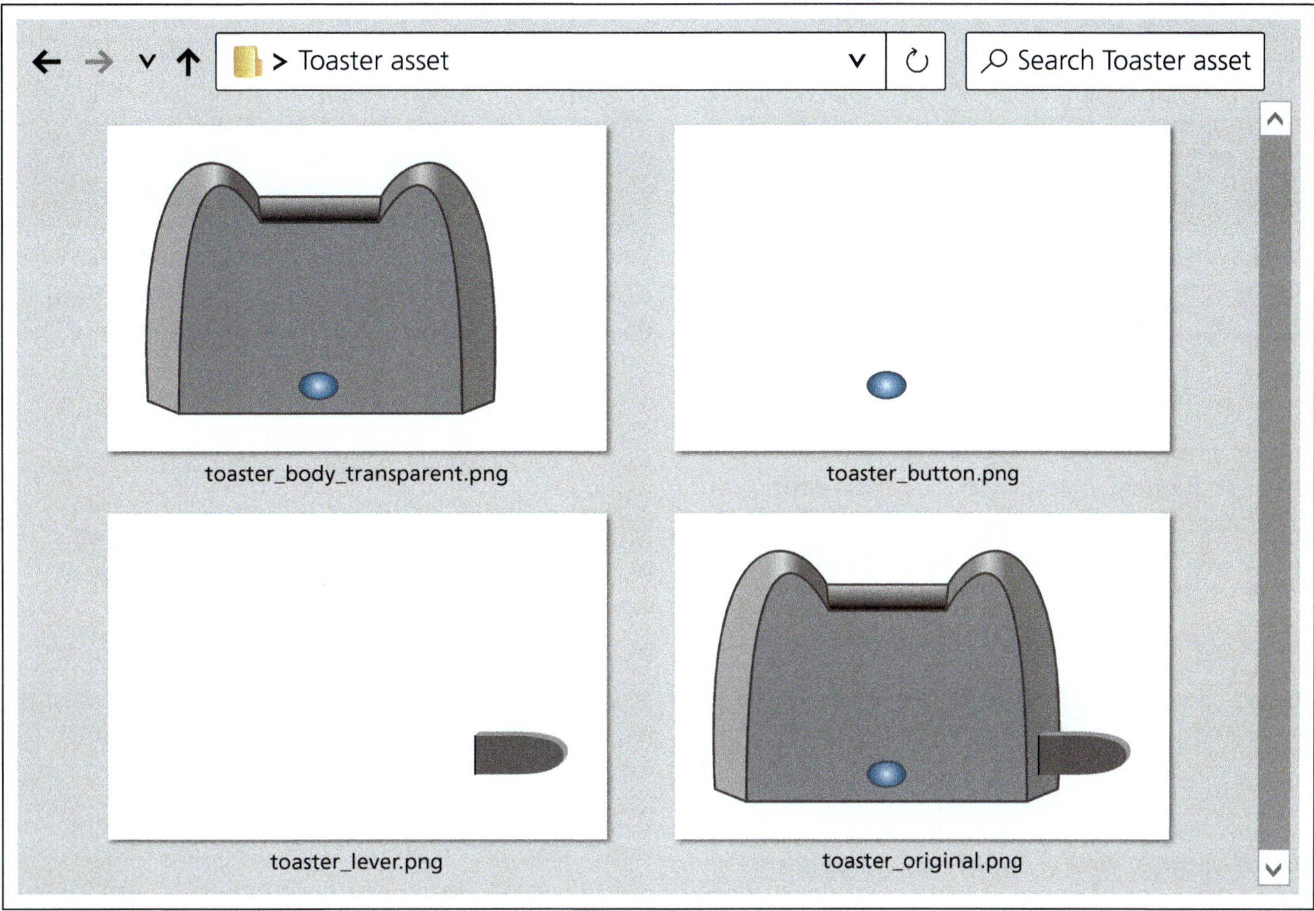

Figure 4.17 An example of folder management for animation assets

Asset libraries

Many animation software packages come pre-loaded with inbuilt libraries of assets. Others may host a library of assets online which you can access when you install the software. If your animation does not need to have original content, asset libraries can be a quick and convenient choice. Even if original images are required, for example for characters, other objects, textures and backgrounds from libraries may still be useful. Another advantage of inbuilt library assets is that they will be compatible with the software.

There are also many online 'stock' libraries of graphics and static images which can be used to save time when animating. Any legal requirements such as copyright, Creative Commons or licensing should be checked carefully before using such assets, and it is possible to use advanced search options to locate only images which are free to use.

Preparing digital assets

If you are using digital animation and working with static image files then the file format, resolution, file size, compression, transparency and whether it is a raster or vector image will all need to be checked to ensure any assets are suitable for use. This may mean converting, editing or resaving assets before they are added to the animation. This can be done using image editing software and tools, though some animation software will also contain simple graphics editing tools. Preparing assets by editing might include cropping or recolouring parts of an image or combining layers and objects together. Creating visual animation assets involves using drawing and graphics software tools to make shapes and lines and combining them to create closed shapes which can be filled with colour, shading or texture. If you plan to animate part of an image (for example, a character might move its legs to walk) then the image can be split into separate layers or different files. This makes them easier to animate later, but you should be careful to name and save these assets in a logical way so they can be found when needed.

It is good practice to name and save all the assets in a dedicated folder, either inside the animation software or separately. This ensures they can be re-used in further projects later if the client requests new content.

Synoptic links

You can read more about techniques to prepare and save image assets in Units R094, R095 and R098.

Preparing and digitising physical assets

If the chosen animation method uses physical assets such as models, cut outs, cels or stop-motion, they will need to be digitised so that they can be used within the animation software. This can be done by scanning or photographing each cel, shot or image and saving it in an electronic file format. The same choices of file format, resolution and so on also apply when digitising physical assets, but there are some additional considerations.

When using a digital camera to digitise assets, the camera must be kept in exactly the same position and care should also be taken to light the subject in the same way and from the same direction.

- Tripods and inbuilt camera flash can be used to achieve a consistent angle of shot.
- Holes can be punched in the corners of cels to fit onto a frame of pegs so they line up in exactly the same position each time.
- If models and sets are used with additional lighting, these can be taped in position to ensure **continuity**.

It is a good idea to capture entire shots (the content of one storyboard panel) in one session if possible, because changes to lighting are less obvious when the camera angle or shot also change. Some digital cameras can be set to capture images at set intervals of two or three seconds. This can be very useful if creating stop motion or Claymation animation, since the camera does not have to be touched each time an image is captured, so there is less chance of accidentally changing the camera's position. The animator can then concentrate on moving the models, cut outs or objects on the set or cels. Alternatively, wireless or Bluetooth remote shutter release devices are available for very little cost and can be used with cameras and smartphones to prevent moving the camera whilst capturing images.

When using the interval timer mode, the series of photographs is stored on the camera's storage card and can be transferred to the animation software at the same time.

It is important to consider the resolution and dimensions of the final animation when using photographs, as very large image files can take a long time to process within the animation software and make editing the animation time-consuming. If lower resolution images look acceptable in quality, they would be a good choice. Alternatively, image editing tools can be used to perform **batch conversions** and quickly alter the compression, resolution and size of multiple photographs as a single process.

Some animation software applications use the device's camera or webcam to automatically capture images at a set interval and import then directly into the software for animation. This can save time uploading and converting images if you plan to use stop motion or Claymation methods.

Key terms

Continuity Consistency from shot to shot and from scene to scene.

Batch conversion Altering properties such as compression settings of several image files at the same time.

Asset management

You should take care to choose suitable file names and folder structures when saving digitised physical asset files. Numbering each file consecutively is a good way to make sure the images remain in the correct order, and it is also good practice to use separate folders to store different characters, objects and backgrounds.

Audio animation assets

Techniques used to record and source audio assets

Recording techniques

Once the recording equipment, devices and software or DAW have been selected and set up, it is important to test the quality of the audio which is being captured. Microphone input levels can usually be adjusted using a traffic light coding system showing red where the sound level is too high. It is worth carrying out a few practice recordings to check input levels, to avoid having to spend time editing and re-recording tracks later. Once the sounds have been recorded, they can be saved using the 'native' or proprietary file format of the recording and mixing software or exported as compatible audio file formats if captured using a separate device such as a smartphone. They can then be edited before exporting the final audio files for use with the animation visuals.

Libraries

If there is no dedicated script or original sound planned for an animation product, it can be quicker and more convenient to source audio assets from libraries of pre-recorded sound effects and music, rather than recording them yourself. There are several online libraries which offer free sound files as well as royalty-free and copyright-free audio. It is important to realise that these are not the same, and more information about copyright can be found in Unit R093. Whether your assets come from free or paid for libraries, you should always keep a record of the source of these files in the form of an asset log. There are strict rules governing the use of current and recent chart music in particular, and a client is very unlikely to be granted permission to use such music free of charge.

Saving and asset management

All sourced audio assets should be saved in a file format which is compatible with the chosen audio editing software, and it is worth considering the balance between file size, compression and audio quality. Uncompressed file formats such as WAV will take up more storage space but may contain a higher quality of sound. Compressed formats such as MP3 files will take up less space, and the loss in sound quality may not be detectable to the human ear. This is especially the case where synthesised music is concerned. It is helpful to save all the audio assets together in a single folder so they are easy to locate once you begin to build the audio project. Naming them to reflect their content is also helpful, especially if they have been downloaded from libraries which assign long or random names.

Activity

One of the characters in Aardman's famous stop-motion animated film *A Grand Day Out* is a strange robotic gas cooker on wheels. Using any materials you like (including cut out), create a physical animation asset based on an appliance or device. It must:

- be no larger than 8 cm high
- have a way of showing emotions or mood
- be capable of moving.

2.2 Techniques used to create animation with audio

Techniques used to create and edit animation

Most animation software is laid out in a similar way with:

- a 'stage' showing the visual content one frame at a time
- a timeline which splits the animation into a set number of frames per second
- layers to separate visual components such as backgrounds, characters and text from the audio layer or soundtrack (if supported).

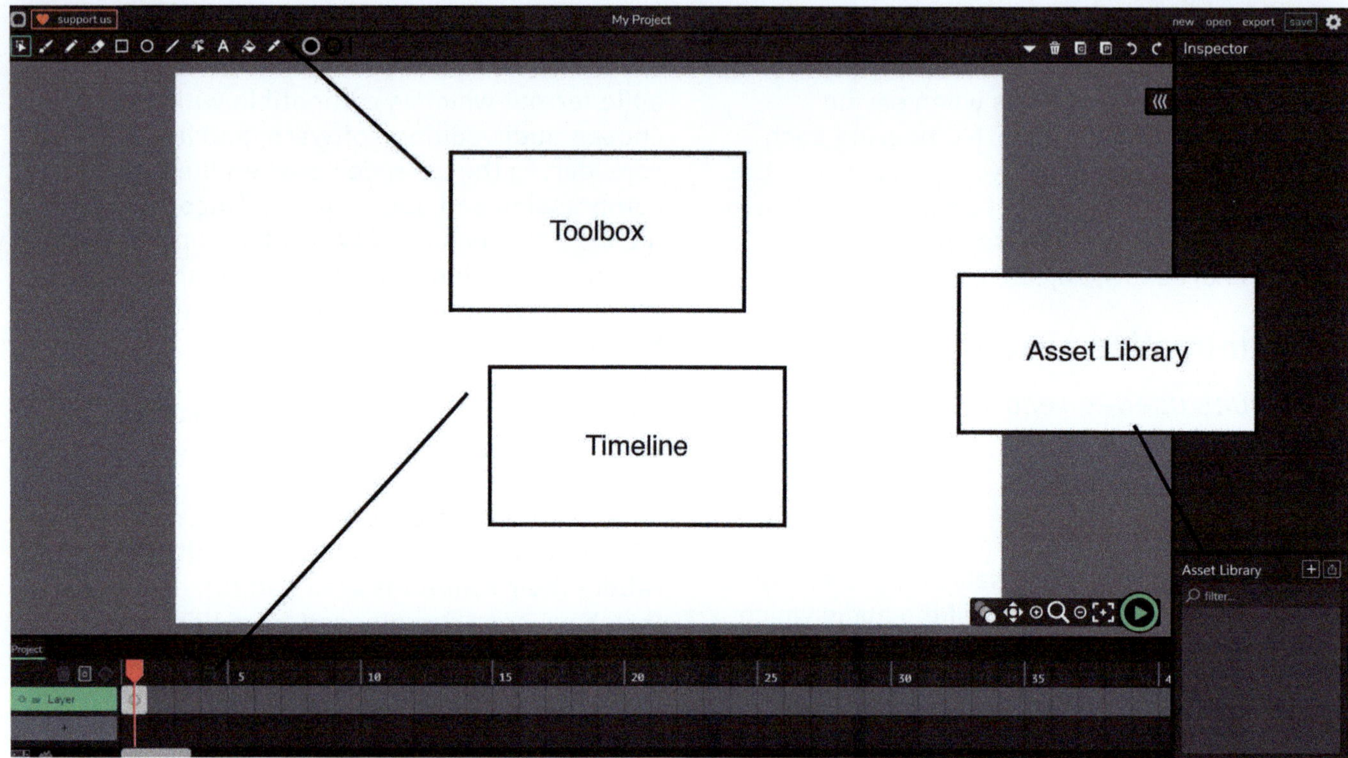

Figure 4.18 An animation stage within a software application

There will also generally be toolbars or toolboxes to allow editing of the components, and often a library where inbuilt assets and imported assets can be stored or linked ready for use. The software will usually include playback tools so that the animation can be previewed and checked during production.

The first step when creating an animation will be to decide on the dimensions of the stage (the height and width of the animation screen/scene) and the frame rate for the animation. Animation software will usually have default settings for these, but they may not be suitable depending on how and where your animation will be used. Changing the frame rate and dimensions later on is very difficult, so make sure you don't leave out this step!

Stage dimensions

The stage dimensions will be influenced by the platform where the final animation will be shown and the type of animation being created. An animated logo for a website might be created at 800 × 800 pixels and a frame rate of 12fps (frames per second). Animated movies such as *Toy Story 4* would use 24fps and generate content in 2K resolution (or more) with an aspect ratio of 2.39:1. The larger the dimensions of the stage and the higher the frame rate, the longer the animation will take to create and render and the larger the final file size will be.

Frame rate

Traditional animation contained 12 frames per second, because this is approximately the speed at which the human eye can no longer detect separate static images and instead sees them as moving. Greater detail and smoother movement are achieved by using 24fps, but this takes longer to create, especially when using stop motion and hand drawn animation techniques.

Timelines

Once the animation stage and frame rate have been set up, you are ready to begin animating. Timelines are generally marked in frames rather than seconds and show one division per frame.

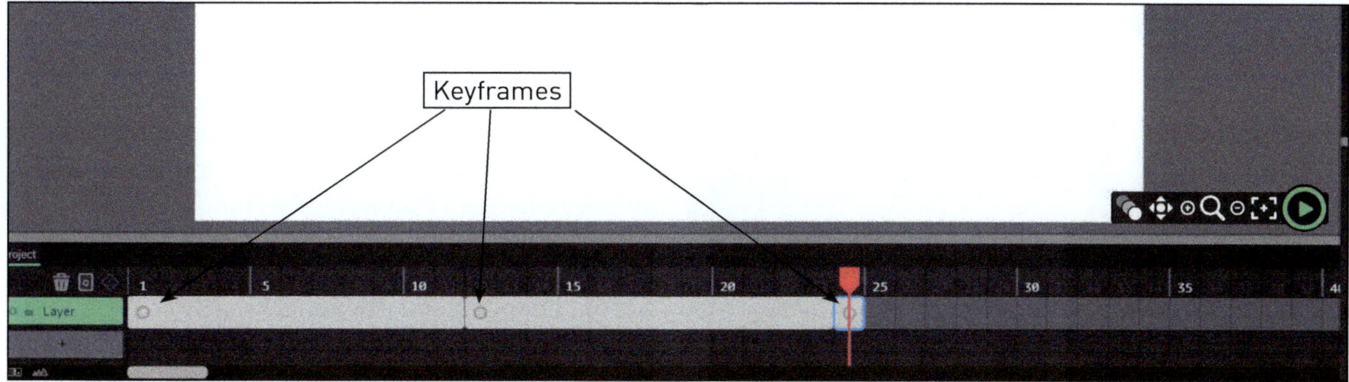

Figure 4.19 Timeline with keyframes at frames 1, 12 and 24

Keyframes

The start and end points for any action in animation are described as keyframes. As a rule, the images which would be drawn in a storyboard will be the most important 'shots' to capture and these will become the keyframes in the animation. For example, if panel 3 of a storyboard shows what the animation looks like 10 seconds into an animation running at 12fps, a keyframe would be created at frame 120 to show the contents of panel 3. Most animation software will allow the insertion of keyframes and will indicate these on the timeline with a marker.

Tweening

Historically when using cel animation, keyframes were created by lead animators and the task of drawing the frames 'in between' keyframes was carried out by junior animators in a process which became known as 'tweening'. As digital animation techniques were developed, computers took over the task of tweening. Animation software can take two key frames, the start and end of a movement, and calculate how to fill in the frames or steps in between automatically, saving the need for animators to create every frame. Most animation software will typically be able to generate tweens to move objects from one place to another on the stage (motion tweening). Some applications can also calculate how to change one shape into another gradually (shape tweening).

The process of creating a tween is similar in most animation software:

1 Create the first keyframe and add the assets into the stage.

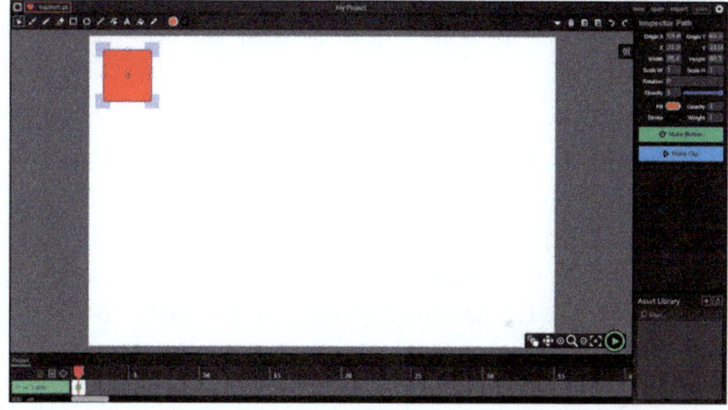

2 Then create an ending keyframe for the tween and move the assets into their final position or change their appearance.
3 Finally, use the tween tool to fill in the frames in between the keyframes. This is usually indicated with an arrow or line on the timeline.

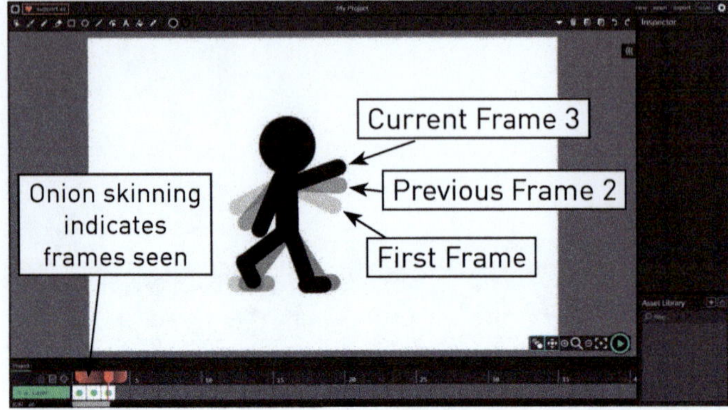

Figure 4.20 Three frames shown at once using onion skinning

Onion skinning

Animation software will often support onion skinning, where the previous frame can be viewed rather like a ghost or shadow underneath the current frame which is made slightly transparent like the layers of an onion. This allows assets to be lined up and altered precisely, creating smooth movement in the final animation.

Layering

Sometimes, parts of an animation are static whilst others move in different directions and at varying speeds. For example, the image of a character ice-skating across a frozen lake might be static in the middle of a frame, but the background needs to 'scroll' from right to left to give the impression of movement. This is much easier to achieve if the background has its own layer. Unless the parts of an animation need to interact with each other, it is a good idea to give each element (for instance, backgrounds, objects, characters) its own layer, especially if you plan to use tweening techniques.

Techniques to enhance movement

Creating animation by inserting assets and moving them either frame by frame or using tweening will generate a basic animation. This is fine for products such as explainer videos and some advertisements where the audio may be more important than the visual content. However, if an animation requires high quality, precise and convincing movements, then techniques can be used to enhance and improve the quality of movement.

Animation by ones or twos

If each frame of an animation is slightly different from the previous frame, smooth movements can be created. This is called 'animation by ones'. However, this is very time-consuming and not all animations need this level of detail. In order to save time (and money) when creating movement, animators may choose to duplicate each frame so that changes and movements only occur every other frame. This is called 'animation by twos'. Animation by twos produces movement which is slightly lower in quality and smoothness, but this is generally not noticeable to the human eye. If the loss in quality is not noticeable to the viewer it is an acceptable shortcut. Animators may choose to use animation by ones and twos for different shots in the same animation, depending on how much detail is required in a particular scene.

Holding frames

If everything on the screen moves constantly it can detract from the main focal point of a shot. To allow the viewer to concentrate on the focal point, other elements in the scene (characters, objects, backgrounds) may 'hold' still for a specific number of frames. This is easy to achieve if each element is in its own layer, because only the layer with the focal point (for example, a character who is speaking) is animated.

A single frame is duplicated in the other layers for as many frames as required. This is cost effective because fewer different frames have to be drawn or created, but it tends to result in lower quality animations overall. You can see this difference in quality when comparing animated children's TV programmes with the animated movies produced by studios such as Pixar and DreamWorks.

Resting frames

'Rests' are used to create stillness in a character between actions, by duplicating a single frame for a period of a fraction of a second up to one or two seconds. There are some basic 'rest' rules for animating faces; for example, a blink of a character's eye usually lasts a quarter of a second. That would be represented by three frames showing closed eyes if animating on ones at 12fps.

Rigging

Rigging is the process of creating a virtual skeleton or 'armature' for a character. By telling the computer where bones and joints are located, the animation software can generate realistic movements. The surface texture or skin is then overlaid on the armature to move the character or object like a puppet. Some software allows the animator to import a drawing or 3D modelled character and then create a rig, whereas other applications have a library of rig templates for animators to add textures and surfaces to. These rigs may also have movements pre-programmed, for example a human walking or a cheetah running. Blender, Maya and Synfig Studio are examples of software with rigging capability.

Techniques used to combine and edit digital audio to create soundtrack

Using audio editing software to edit and combine sounds

Once the assets are collected, edited if required and stored ready to mix, they can be imported into the audio editing software. Most software displays tracks as stacked layers along a horizontal timeline, often with a waveform representing the loudness of different parts of the tracks. It is good practice to name each track to avoid confusion when editing. Tracks can be moved up or down the stack, to increase or decrease their importance, and tools such as Autoducking (available in Audacity) can be used to decrease the level of background tracks when important sounds such as a voiceover are being played.

Captured sounds can be 'cleaned up' by using tools such as noise removal, compression, envelope and filter to remove unwanted or poor-quality sounds. Tracks can also be split, cut or trimmed to reduce their length or insert silence so that other sounds can be heard in between. Overall levels can be adjusted so that the correct balance of volume of the different sounds is achieved.

As well as balancing and mixing 'cleaned up' sounds, audio editing software has a wide range of tools and effects for editing and enhancing sounds. Some commonly used tools are described in Table 4.2.

Table 4.2 Common audio editing software tools

Tool	Use
Fade	Ensures sounds do not begin or end abruptly and can be overlaid or 'crossfaded'
Pitch adjustment	Makes a sound higher or lower without changing its speed
Speed adjustment	Makes a sound faster or slower without changing its pitch
Noise removal	Takes away unwanted background noises such as hiss, hum or wind noise
Compressor	Decreases the contrast between loud and quiet sounds (the dynamic range) in a track, allowing the overall volume to be increased without distorting
Envelope	Changes the volume of a track smoothly over time by creating control points
Filter	Reduces low frequency noise such as hum
Split	Cuts a track into parts so that silence or other sounds can be inserted in between
Trim	Cuts the start or end of a track to remove unwanted audio or silence
Level adjustment	Balances the volume of different sounds so that no single track or sound is overpowering

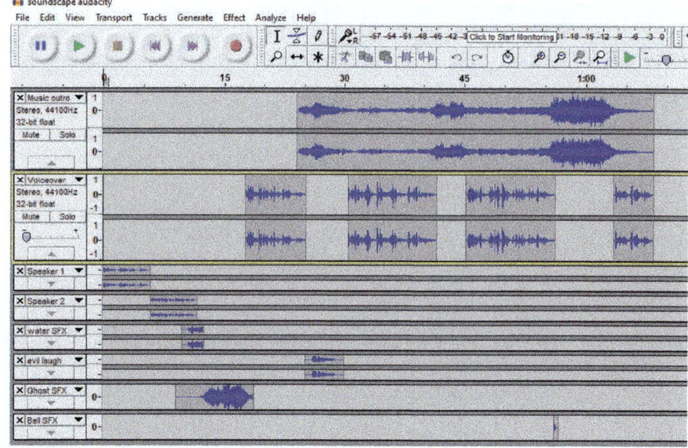

Figure 4.21 Multiple tracks can be edited and mixed in Audacity

Saving audio files

It is advisable to save the audio 'project' or work in progress regularly during the editing and mixing stage using the native file format. Applying version control also means that unsuccessful changes can be undone if required. Once the audio is complete, the master file in its native format should be saved and archived in case the client requests further changes and so that the project can be re-used if needed.

Exporting audio files

The finished audio must be exported using a file format which is compatible with the software being used to combine the animation and audio together. Most animation software will have a tutorial or help section which can be searched to find out which audio file formats are compatible. As well as compatibility, file size and audio quality will also contribute to the choice of file format. Most audio editing software will include codecs which compress and optimise the audio as it is saved. Codecs can be updated or installed if required, since not all codecs support all file formats.

File compression and final audio file size will be affected by several factors, as shown in Table 4.3.

Table 4.3 Factors affecting sound quality and file compression

Factor	Effect on sound quality	Effect on file compression
Sample rate	The more samples per second the higher the quality of the sound	Higher sample rates result in a larger file size
Noise/hiss	Background noise reduces the quality of the audio file overall	Reduces the compression, resulting in a larger file size
Stereo/mono	Stereo will improve the effectiveness of audio if directional sound is needed, but it doesn't improve the actual audio quality	The more channels used, the larger the file size

Techniques used to integrate animation and audio components within animation software

Combining and synchronising animation with audio

Once the visual and audio elements have been added to the animation software as separate layers, the sounds and visual content can be matched up or synchronised. This can be done by 'time shifting' – moving the elements by dragging them across the timeline, or by inserting extra empty frames to generate silence between sounds. If the animation requires multiple sound effects, these can be put into their own foley layer. This allows the visual content to be created first and the sound effects to be synchronised afterwards. If the soundtrack is completed first, then it is helpful to insert keyframes on the audio layer at moments when visual content needs to synchronise, before creating the visual elements.

Some software will allow you to change the volume of parts of the audio, whereas other applications will only set the volume for a whole track. It is important to make sure dialogue can be heard clearly and that all audio content is a suitable volume.

Stereo can be used to good effect if available, by changing the balance of audio elements to the left or right channel in order to match the position of the source of the sound in the visual content.

Synchronising speech with audio (lip-synching) is one of the most time-consuming and difficult effects used in animation. Some useful time-saving tips include:

- using a wider angle shot to avoid the need for precise mouth movements
- using voiceover or narration instead of onscreen dialogue
- using music and/or sound effects instead of speech
- choosing characters carefully – humans have a wide range of mouth movements. Would your animation work with a non-human character speaking?

- simplifying mouth movements rather than aiming for realistic **visemes**. Examples of this technique can be seen in animations such as *South Park* and the *Peanuts* movie.

Activity

Using audio software, create an audio file to introduce an artist to the stage of an arena or large concert venue. You could find ideas for effects, music, script and tone of voice by looking online for examples of darts, snooker or boxing match walk-ons.

2.3 Techniques to save and export animation with audio

Techniques used to save and export audio

If you are working on a complicated, multi-track audio soundtrack for your animation product, you will probably want to create and edit it in the audio software. Most audio editing software will save files using its own file format and file extension and this is known as the native or proprietary format. For example, Audacity saves project files as '.AUP' files and also generates folders called '_data'. Saving your audio soundtrack in this way means that you can re-open, edit and change it until it is finished. You can also '**roll back**' the changes to restore the file to an earlier state. This is where version control comes in. Before you make any significant changes to your audio soundtrack, choose 'Save As' or its equivalent, and rename the file or project. You can use numbers or dates in the file name to help you organise the versions or you can change the file name to describe the changes made. For example, Soundtrack v1.0, Soundtrack v 1.2, or Soundtrack _March, Soundtrack _April, or Soundtrack _Voiceover_ Added, Soundtrack _Foley_Added and so on. In a vocational or real-world context, a designer or animator may be working on more than one project at once, so using folders to separate different clients' work is important.

When your audio or soundtrack is complete, you need to be able to combine it with the animated visuals. To do this, your audio must be exported by saving it in a compatible file format, for example MP3 or WAV. You will want to check that the properties are suitable to meet your brief, for example, does the audio need to be stereo? What bit rate or sample rate do you need to use for the quality you want?

Key terms

Viseme The visual shape made by the mouth, lips and tongue when creating a speech sound (phoneme) such as 'Sh' or 'B'.

Roll back Undo changes by returning a file to an earlier state or previous version.

Technical skills to save and export animation with audio

In the same way, whilst working on your animation you will use the native file format for the software you have chosen and use version control to allow you to roll back any changes. When your animation and audio have been combined and edited, you should save a final master file using the native file format. That way, if your client chooses to commission further work you have access to the assets and source files you used. You would not give the master file to the client in most cases.

You will then export the final animation with audio using a file format which is compatible with the client's chosen device or platform. For example, if your client wants the animation to play on a smartphone or tablet, you might choose MP4 or MOV. If the animation is to be uploaded to a streaming service or online platform such as YouTube or Vimeo, then you should check which formats are compatible. Some platforms also require the use of encoders such as H.264 so it is a good idea to check the requirements of the client brief, to make sure your final product will be fit for purpose.

Synoptic link

This content links with R093, Section 4.2.

Assignment practice

Task 2: Creating an animation with audio

Time needed: 1–2 hours

You have been asked to create a short animation to help promote a new bread product. Your client has given you this storyboard to work from:

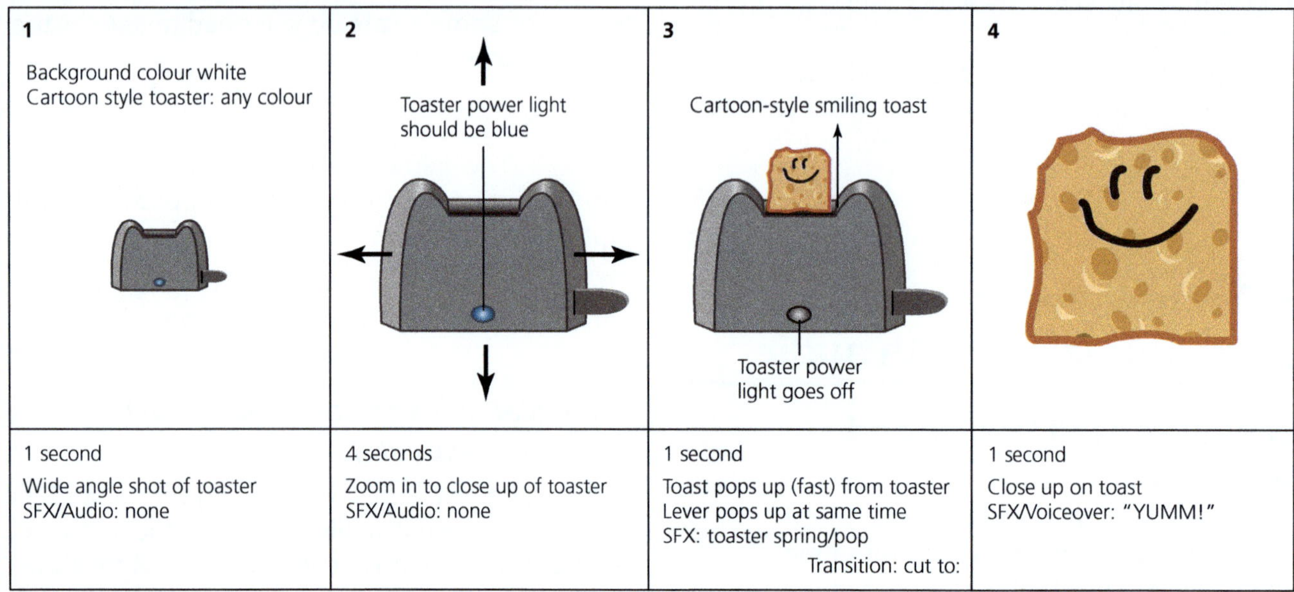

Create a first version of the animation with audio, save it and export it in a suitable file format for the client to view.

The client would check this version to see whether any changes or improvements are required. It should be complete enough to see and hear the content and make sure it matches the storyboard. Do not worry if it is not perfect but try and make sure the most important parts are completed.

Whilst you are working on this task, ask yourself which parts of the task are slowing you down, taking too long or proving hard to complete? These are the skills you might need to improve before you are ready to attempt the final assignment.

Activity

Find out the native file format used by any animation and audio software available to you at school and at home. Find out how to export a completed animation with audio, and make a note of which file formats you can select during this process.

Which platforms or devices can load and play these animations? Record this information for use when you design your own animation with audio products.

Topic area 3 Review animation with audio

Getting started

An animation with audio 'explainer' has been produced to tell customers how to connect and use a new video doorbell. It will play in the video doorbell app which customers download on their smartphones. The video doorbell's target audience is adults of all ages.

Write a list of success criteria which could be used when checking the animation with audio 'explainer's fitness for purpose.

For example:

1 The animation must include audio.

3.1 Techniques to test/check and review animation with audio

Testing and checking an animation with audio can be broken down into two main parts:

- testing functionality
- checking how successfully the product meets the client requirements.

Techniques to test/check the technical properties of animation with audio

Methods of testing and checking

It is a good idea to test functionality at regular points during the creation and editing process. This is called iterative testing and it means that bugs and glitches can be resolved as you go along. If you make many changes before testing and something doesn't work as expected, you won't know which change caused the problem. If you also use version control to give a different name to the project each time a significant change is made, you can easily undo or 'roll back' any changes which were unsuccessful.

Functionality testing can be recorded using a test plan. This lists each aspect being tested, how it is tested, the expected and actual results and provides space to record whether changes or fixes are required, along with somewhere to record the results of retests. Test plans don't need to include large amounts of text unless fixes are to be carried out by someone other than the tester. Examples of functionality tests would include whether:

- the animation with audio loads correctly
- the animation starts as required (automatically or when triggered) and plays smoothly without freezing or buffering
- the animation is an appropriate frame rate and overall length
- the animated movements are effective, convincing or appropriate
- visuals are clear and the expected size
- the visual and audio elements are synchronised correctly
- sounds are played as expected
- different sounds can be heard clearly and are at a suitable volume to mix and combine audio tracks effectively
- the file format is compatible and suitable for its intended platform, device or distribution channel.

Techniques to review the fitness for purpose of completed animation with audio

Reviewing how fit for purpose an animation with audio is primarily involves checking. This is a more subjective, less technical aspect of the review process than functionality testing, and test plans are not entirely suitable for this purpose. Checklists and success criteria are more commonly used for this task. These are created by breaking down the client requirements or design brief and listing the components the client would expect to receive in the finished animation with audio.

Some checks for fitness for purpose relate to the client and product, for example the client's name must be spelled correctly, prices on an advertisement must be accurate and the client may have a house style or visual identity which the animation would be expected to fit with. Other elements would relate to the distribution platform, for example if an animation is to be broadcast, the format and length will be important.

The final consideration would be whether the animation is suitable to appeal to or engage the intended target audience. This will involve considering the suitability of the chosen style, content, balance of text, audio and images and design conventions used. In order to be completely suitable, the finished animation with audio should be accessible to the audience, both practically (can the audience locate, open and view/hear the animation?) and aesthetically (will the chosen style and approach appeal to the target audience?).

Activity

Watch Pixar's 'remix' of *Up* as Manga (you can find this on Pixar's YouTube channel). Compare the remix and original animation, and identify the differences in style and conventions of animation and audio.

You could also search for Pixar's 'WALL-E in 16-Bit' game-style graphics, and identify the key features of the visuals and audio which fit retro game-graphics conventions.

3.2 Improvements and further developments

Constraints which limit the effectiveness of animation with audio

Once the animation with audio is finished, it will be checked and reviewed to work out whether improvements and further developments are needed. This will involve looking at the overall style, quality and content of the product and comparing it with the client requirements. Not only should it look and sound good, but it should also convey the message the client wanted, whether this is to advertise, promote, explain or entertain. It should also appeal to the correct target audience. However, there will be constraints which mean that the final animation with audio may not be able to be perfected:

- Time: An animator or sound editor may want to make changes to the soundtrack or visuals, but almost all products will have a deadline for overall completion. If a project runs over time, the client may miss a window for launching a product which means it will not sell as many units as anticipated. For this reason, there are often financial penalties for the project team if they fail to deliver the finished product by the agreed deadline.
- Resources: There may be improvements which could be made if different or better resources were available. For example, Claymation models are more stable and produce a more professional animated visual if they are made using rigging or armatures. If these are unavailable the animation may look less polished and of a poorer quality. The client might ask for a particular piece of music to be included in the animation's soundtrack, but the owner of the work may refuse to allow its use or there may not be enough money in the budget to pay for the necessary licences or permissions.
- Hardware: Improvement to the visual content might depend on using a better quality camera, tripod and lighting to capture still images; or a pressure-sensitive graphics tablet to create digital image assets of a higher standard. If none of these are available, the level of finish may not be as high as the client and designers hoped. The quality of audio recordings may be reduced if a limited range of microphone types is available or if all audio has to be recorded using the inbuilt microphone on a smartphone or tablet.

- Software: The overall quality of the audio and animation components will depend to an extent on the software chosen to combine and export the final product. Some software applications produce better visuals than audio, whereas for others the reverse is true. The animator or sound editor may suggest improvements which are not possible without better software which can generate high quality visuals and audio. In certain circumstances the software used can become obsolete (no longer working), as was the case when Flash Player was discontinued in 2020. An alternative export format would therefore be needed in order for the final product to continue to meet the client requirements.
- Skills: Some improvements to the animated visuals or audio content may rely on specialist skills, for example those of mocap studios or music composers. If an animator or sound editor wants to use such elements as original musical compositions, mocap or 3D animation in a product, additional team members will need to be employed to work on the project. This may be too time-consuming, too expensive or both.

The ability to make improvements can be affected by several constraints at once. For example, an animation may have been created using stock or library assets. Generating original assets would mean the client has a product which is new and different from anything the audience has seen before. But asset creation takes time, costs money and requires suitable software if it is to be done to a high standard. So, if originality is less important to the client (for example, in an explainer video or promotion) there is a reasonable trade-off in not using expensive, time-consuming original assets. On the other hand, if the animation's purpose is to advertise but the product is not shown accurately or clearly, then improvements are essential. Similarly, a voiceover which is drowned out by background music is no use in an advertisement and must be changed.

Animation with audio improvements

When deciding which improvements should be made, the animator or designer will have to consider which improvements are desirable but not essential. For instance, adding in extra shots or sounds to make the animation more interesting or engaging is less important than fixing spelling errors in the visuals. Some improvements would be expensive, especially if they will take a long time or require permissions to use copyrighted materials. The review process therefore often includes a discussion between the designer, campaign manager or production manager and the client, where the most important and desirable improvements are agreed, along with any budget and timescales needed.

Further development opportunities for animation with audio

The final part of reviewing a completed animation with audio involves considering further developments which could be made. This is where a designer, animator or freelance creative would look for future commissions from the client. There might be elements which a client initially wanted but which could not be put into place in the present product. A conversation with the client at the time of handing over the final product might cover what could be included as a follow-up if different resources, software or budget are made available. For example, if an animator has created a stop motion animation by animating 'on twos', the final product will have a lower level of smoothness but be achievable in a shorter timescale. A larger budget might allow animation on ones, creating a higher quality, smoother final product. The available budget might also influence the quality and originality of the soundtrack. Commissioning a musician to write a custom soundtrack will lead to a more original final product tailored to the client's exact needs, rather than relying on stock music tracks which may have been used elsewhere.

Developments to products can also be identified where spin offs or separate products naturally lead off from the original product. These can depend on:

- Length: For example, advertisements are often shortened once the audience has seen the full version a few times. This saves money when showing the adverts on broadcast television channels which generally charge a fee per minute. The advert would be shortened by cutting the least important parts and retaining the product placement, slogan and maybe the pricing information, relying on the audience's ability to remember the parts which have been cut out (because they were suitably engaging first time around).
- Product type and placement: An animation with audio may be uploaded in full on a company's YouTube or Vimeo channel but be included as a shortened 'taster' version on a website, along with a link. Clients may also consider placing their products on multiple channels and platforms where they can be seen by the intended target audience. For instance, a product which advertises fast food might be broadcast first on terrestrial TV channels in the evenings where it will mainly be seen by adults, and also later added to streaming and social media platforms where it will be seen at a similar time by teenagers to maximise its effectiveness.
- Story/narrative content: Animations created for the purpose of entertainment also often have spin offs from the original; think of Pixar's *Toy Story* and Illumination's *Despicable Me/Minions* franchises. Part of the task of identifying further developments could include writing a short synopsis or plot summary for a future spin off.
- Re-using components: Spin offs, franchises and brands (where the same set of characters appears in multiple stories or a series of adverts) would use the same characters, setting and digital artwork or assets. This is another important reason for keeping control of the stored assets and master version of the product. Without these, the client is unable to create a spin off or subsequent product easily, so is more likely to commission the same designer or animator for future projects. Another option is for the animator or designer to sell the assets or rights to use them to the client.
- Cross platform media: Animation products can also be developed further by using or distributing them on different platforms. An advertisement on terrestrial or broadcast television might typically be 30 seconds long. It could be shortened to five seconds in length in order to be used on YouTube. Explainer videos which use animation might be shown in their full length on a company's website, but provided in shorter chapters, instalments or sections on a company's Instagram feed. Television opening title sequences might be shortened to two-second 'stings' to re-introduce the programme after an advert break. Identifying how these developments could be made adds further value to the product when delivering it to the client and increases the chances of securing further work for the designer or animator.

Activity

Look for examples of adverts which have been cut to different lengths when broadcast on terrestrial TV channels, YouTube or social media. Try to work out what parts of the original have been cut – is it whole shots or scenes or has the editing process simply cut very short parts out of the length of a shot here and there? If you struggle to find adverts which have been shortened, try looking for trailers for animated films using a site such as IMDB as a starting point.

Assignment practice

Task 3: Review animation with audio

An independent computer game developer has asked you to create an animation with audio for a computer game cut scene. The game is a simple retro arcade-style shooter game which will be sold through the GameMaker marketplace. The client provided you with this list of requirements:

- The cut scene could be realistic like an actual movie with explosions in the background.
- The main character is going to be exactly the same as Optimus Prime but with a red body and yellow feet instead.
- The background music in the cut scene should be relatable.

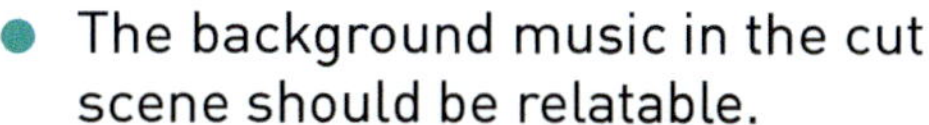

- I want to have the song 'Back to Life' that was in the *Bumblebee* movie.
- The cut scene needs to be finished in two weeks.
- There is a very small budget available for the cut scene.

You are about to send the client the completed animation with audio. Explain to the client why the final product may not have fully met the requirements. Your explanation should cover the constraints which would affect the content and style of the cut scene.

Unit R097

Interactive digital media

About this unit

In the creative media industry there are a huge variety of technical and creative job roles involving interactive digital media. This unit is all about creating digital interactive media. You will learn how to design and create media assets which will engage your target audience. You will also learn how to use your assets to create an effective interactive media product.

Topic areas

In this chapter you will learn how to:

- plan interactive digital media (TA1)
- create interactive digital media (TA2)
- review interactive digital media (TA3).

Resources for this unit

Hardware/equipment: Alongside standard computer hardware, you could use the following if they are available to you – digital cameras, scanner, stylus, graphics tablet, microphone.

Software:

- Interactive digital media creation software such as Adobe Dreamweaver; Serif Webplus X8, Google Web Designer, Microsoft PowerPoint; Thunkable, Appypie, Appinventor; Editor X; Rocketcake.
- Image editing software such as Adobe Photoshop, Adobe Fireworks, Adobe Illustrator, GIMP, Corel Draw, Serif Affinity Designer.
- Audio editing software such as Audacity, Garage Band.
- Moving image editing software such as Free to use Gimp, Paint 3D, Photopea, Krita and Synfig.
- Photo editing and video editing applications such as Adobe Photoshop, Lightroom, Luminar, Affinity Photo or Apple Photos. At the time of writing, open-source free applications include Rawtherapee, Darktable, Irfanview, Photpea and Gimp.
- Video editing software such as Adobe Premiere, Final Cut, Apple iMovie with open source applications Shotcut and OpenShot.

How will I be assessed?

You will complete an assignment that is set by OCR. This will be completed independently by yourself, without using any additional resources or teacher assistance to help you. The assignment will have a scenario or client brief that defines what you will need to create.

You will work through a series of tasks that cover the three topic areas to plan, create and review interactive digital media. Your evidence will then be marked by your teacher using the OCR marking criteria, which will then be externally checked/moderated OCR to confirm your achievement.

Topic area 1 Plan interactive digital media

Getting started

What is digital interactive media?
Create a mind map to show all the different types of interactive media you can think of. For example, food ordering kiosks.

1.1 Types of interactive digital media, content and associated hardware

What is interactive media?

Interactive media is media which allows the user to be involved in the process of watching or listening. This could involve user input such as clicking, typing or speaking to interact with the media.

The format types of interactive digital media

- Websites are a very common form of interactive media; they are a key part of everyday life. Websites serve a range of different purposes such as paying bills, passport applications, shopping and entertainment.
- Information points are a type of interactive media often seen in public places such as shopping centres or museums. They are often in the form of an onscreen map or image that the user can touch using a touch screen to access information.
- Mobile apps are a type of interactive media that is designed to be used on mobile phones. There are a huge range of apps that fulfil a range of functions.

- E-learning products are a form of interactive product that enable users to access interactive education content to learn new knowledge and skills.
- Digital maps are interactive maps which allow the user to interact with the content, for both navigation and geographical knowledge.
- Games are a form of interactive media which allow the user to play electronic games on a range of different devices. There are many forms of interactive games that allow the user to interact in a number of ways, such as by touch, movement or sound.

Influences on the format of interactive digital media design

The target audience and purpose of the interactive digital media is important for deciding the format that the product will take. For example, games designed for a young audience are likely to be in a format that is suitable for that age group, so they may include bold icons or buttons and potentially audio interaction rather than text-based interaction. Whereas a shopping centre interactive map would be in a format suitable for an information point – available to be accessed by a wide range of people but most likely adults, likely a text-based interaction that can be used in a noisy environment so unlikely to be suitable for audio interaction.

One of the most significant factors that will impact on the format of interactive digital media is the device that will be used to access it. This is particularly important as the interaction with the user changes based on the type of device being used. There are a range of ways that devices can allow interaction and incorporating these will impact the format and design of the media significantly. Interaction methods that different devices may provide include:

- mouse click
- track pad
- physical button press
- touch screen
- voice controls.

Content used in interactive digital media

The range of content that can be used in interactive digital media is huge. Table 5.1 explains some of the different types of content that could be used and what they might be used for.

Table 5.1 Examples of content used in interactive digital media

Content	How it could be used in interactive digital media and what it could be used for
Images	Images could be used in a number of ways to provide a visual representation of something within the interactive media, for example in an interactive map, illustrations of places could be the main way of identifying locations. Images could also be used to illustrate something which is explained using text or audio in interactive media, for example a diagram could accompany a written set of instructions to complete a task in an education interactive media product
Audio	Audio use in interactive digital media can take a number of forms. Audio could be one of the main ways of interacting with the user, for example through a voiceover or narration as part of an interactive map or storybook. It can also be used as a sound effect to accompany a movement or action, for example in a game or e-learning product. Audio content can also be used as an accompaniment to enhance the user's experience or to set the tone for the content, provide background music or sound effects to accompany actions
Video	Video is probably the type of content you most associate with digital media. Video is a way of displaying moving images, often along with sound. In the context of interactive digital media, video can be used in a number of ways, for example video is often used on websites to share information about a place or to provide an introduction to a person or product. Video can also be used as part of mobile apps to add moving image content, allowing the user to view something along with an explanation or narration
Animation	In a similar way to video, animation can be used to show moving images or graphics. Animations can be used in interactive digital media to entertain, for example as part of a game or mobile app. They can also be used very effectively to demonstrate something, for example in an education product to demonstrate a skill, showing a step-by-step animation of how each part of the skill is put together to complete the process

Content	How it could be used in interactive digital media and what it could be used for
Text	Text can be used in many ways in interactive digital media and the way it is used will depend on the product and also the audience. Text is used as one of the main ways of providing information in some forms of interactive media, such as websites and information points like those found in a museum that enable the user to use interactivity to access information on the exhibits. In other formats such as games or digital maps, text could be used as headings or to label key areas of the product which the user might need such as the menu, but in these cases the text is often accompanied by other forms of content such as sound and images to help engage the user in the content
Tables	Tables are a great way to give structure to information that your user might need to access. They can be used in an information point to display opening times of the attraction or to show a set of dates and information about that time in history in a museum. It is a good way of breaking large piece of text into chunks, so they are easier for the user to access. In some interactive media such as websites, tables can also be used to structure the pages into blocks so that the content of the page is evenly spread out in a structure that is clear
List	In a similar way to tables, lists can be used to summarise information or put it into a sequence. This might be something that is used in an e-learning product for a series of instructions or set of equipment. Lists can also be used as a format for a menu to allow users to see what options or pages they can select from in the process of moving around an interactive media product
Forms	Forms are an excellent way of allowing the user to interact with the digital media product. A form can be constructed to allow the user to add their own information and submit it. This could be used to give feedback, make a booking or place an order, or to complete a task such as a test. Forms can contain boxes to add text or tools to make selection from a number of fixed options such as answering a multiple-choice question or giving something a rating of 1 to 5. They are commonly used in interactive digital media products such as websites, mobile apps and e-learning products
Navigation buttons	Navigation buttons are often used in interactive digital media and are a way of allowing the user to interact with the content. They are commonly seen on websites and apps so that users can move from page to page as they choose, but can also be seen on games, maps and e-learning content to allow users to make choices and selections as they work through the content
Maps	Maps can be used in a number of different forms on interactive digital media, such as on websites to provide the location of the place advertised. They allow interactivity as the user can often move the map around to the place in relation to their viewing location. They can also be used in games – there is often a map function available to allow the user to orientate themselves in the fictional world
Quizzes	Quizzes can be used in a similar way to forms to help the user interact with the product or the content. They can be used to pose questions to the user which they can answer using functions within the product. This could be to gain feedback on a product or service offered or advertised via the interactive digital media. Quizzes could also be used to check knowledge or learning as part of information points, websites or e-learning products
Layers	Though not typically described as content, it is layers that are often used to display the content in digital interactive products. A simple example would be using text layered over an image when displaying content on a website or using text or sound over a video or animation to add detail to the content being displayed. There are lots of different content types you can use in creating digital interactive media products, and often that will involve using more than one content type at once

Using assets to create content

You can use all the types of content discussed in Table 5.1 to create the assets for an interactive digital media product. To make an effective interactive digital product you will need to combine different types of content in order to meet the purpose of the product and suit the target audience. For example, when creating a product with navigation buttons, such as an app, for a good user experience you would expect to combine a navigation button asset with audio assets, such as a sound effect, to emphasise the action. Or when displaying a video montage on a website, it would be more engaging to the audience to accompany this with sound or possibly a text layer to label the images.

Form and structure affected by the audience and purpose

In this topic area we have seen lots of examples of different formats that the content of an interactive multimedia product can take. The purpose and audience of the product can have a significant impact on the type of format that is use.

Purpose

Interactive digital media products can be created to serve a range of different purposes such as to:

- advertise or sell
- inform or educate
- entertain.

If you are trying to advertise or sell a product, it is likely that you will want to give the user information about the product and allow them to see what it looks like. This may mean that your product contains content such as good quality images or photographs and text which will describe the product and its features. You may also include demonstrations or recommendation videos to enhance the information.

When looking to inform or educate the audience you may need to draw on a wider range of content to achieve this aim. For example, you may use some text to explain a concept or theory and some images to illustrate this in visual form. But you may also use an animation to show the theory in context and a table to show some examples.

Products that entertain may also use a wide range of content formats. When designing a game or an app which is designed to entertain an audience, you are likely to want to use some form of moving image such as animation, but this also tends to be combined with sound and text. This type of interactive product is less likely to have large blocks of text but may use audio such as narration to provide information and fill in the storyline.

Target audience

The target audience is also a major influence on the structure of an interactive digital media product. The intended audience of the product should be considered at each stage of creation and you need to ensure that their needs are being met.

Layout

When planning the layout of your product you need to think about the needs of your audience to ensure that the user experience is the best it can be. For example, if you are planning a game or mobile app for young children you need to consider how they will access the content – they might need a clear, bold layout which allows them to see any buttons on links they need to click. You may also consider large buttons for links to ensure that they are easily clickable for children who may not have the fine hand control needed to click on a smaller button or one which is close to another item they may accidentally click.

In contrast, if you were designing an information point or website for an adult audience, you would probably consider how you could be the most efficient with the layout to ensure that there is not a lot of unnecessary scrolling or page changes when delivering information. You may have more content and buttons in a condensed area to minimise wasted time and space, whilst also ensuring the screen is not too cluttered. Designing a layout is often a bit of a balancing act to ensure it meets the needs of the user and the intended purpose.

Content affected by the audience and purpose

The content of an interactive digital media product should also change to suit the intended audience of the product. There are a number of different features of the target audience demographic (you looked at these in R093, Section 2.3) that you should consider.

The age of the audience will impact on the choice of content, for example when designing a product for an adult audience the choice of content could include a wide range of different formats which rely on the use of words such as text, tables, lists and forms. This may be less suitable for a younger age range where you may not be able to assume that the audience has a certain level of reading skill. For a younger audience you may consider more visual content such as icons, images or diagrams and videos as they are likely to be accessible to younger users as well as adults.

The location of the audience can influence the content chosen for the interactive multimedia product, particularly if the aim of the product is to advertise or sell a product or service. In these cases, you would likely select content which is linked to the geographical area where the product or service is available. For example, a product displaying information about shopping in a town would feature adverts for local shops.

The lifestyle and interests of the audience should also be considered when creating or selecting content for an interactive digital media product. This may be particularly relevant if you are creating a product which is designed to entertain or engage the user such as a game or a mobile app. You would need to consider what type of content would encourage the user to want to interact with the product and continue to do so.

Activity

Find an app, game or website that you use regularly. Copy and complete the table below about your chosen product.

Product name	
Product format (e.g. website)	
Product purpose	
Product target audience	
Describe the types of content used in the product	
Explain how well you think the product uses content to suit the audience and purpose of the product	

Hardware devices used to access interactive digital media

There are an ever-increasing range of devices that can be used to access interactive digital media products and they fall into a number of different categories.

Laptops and personal computers

A popular device used to access interactive digital media products is a personal computer. 'Desktop' versions are made up of a range of component parts with a monitor, keyboard and mouse. Interactive digital media products viewed on a desktop PC will be seen in a large scale so the content will be easily seen. There are a range of settings that can be changed such as screen resolution, text size and colour contrast to allow people to view the interactive digital media product in its most accessible format.

Laptops have some similar features to the desktop PC but the different components are combined into a smaller package with display screen, keyboard, mouse (or trackpad) in addition to the computer motherboard. The screen is usually fairly large, sometimes detachable and the settings adjustable to allow for optimum viewing. The main difference compared to a desktop is that a laptop is designed to be portable so they are smaller and can be folded away and they have a battery so they can run without the use of mains power for a certain amount of time.

Tablets

Tablets provide all their functions and tools in one small hand-held device. Unlike a laptop they are made of one piece that is a fixed shape and size. In order to make the device more robust and compact the tablet does not have a separate screen and keyboard but uses a touch screen to access the functions on the device. Whilst tablets are made to view interactive digital media products they tend to behave and be viewed in a different way to a laptop or desktop PC. This is known as the 'mobile' version instead of the full sized 'desktop' version.

Mobile devices and smartphones

Mobile devices and smartphones are very similar in make up to a tablet, though obviously they tend to have a smaller screen on which to view the website (in some cases not much smaller!) One consideration is that the orientation of the page when being viewed on a mobile device is the opposite of a desktop PC or laptop screen, so it appears to be more portrait than landscape. This is something to consider when creating the settings for your web page design.

Game consoles and smart TV

Game consoles and digital TVs can also be used to access interactive digital media products. In terms of how these would display these it is likely that both would look very similar as they would both use a TV screen to display the product. This will behave a lot like it would on a desktop PC or laptop but in some cases the screen size will be much bigger. However, the functionality of the access to the product may be a bit different on a TV and a console. A TV-based interactive digital media product is often controlled by your TV remote control and the console by the controller provided with your console. Both of these are not as flexible in terms of navigating and controlling as they would be if you were using a mouse or trackpad.

Figure 5.1 Kiosks are used in many different places

Kiosks

Kiosks can be used to access interactive digital media products and are sometimes found in places such as shopping centres, cinemas and museums. They often include a large screen seated in a base and the main control is often a touch screen. They tend to use imagery and large icons to help with control using a touch screen.

Devices link to target audience and purpose

The devices that are used to access the interactive digital media product will be influenced by the audience and purpose of the intended product. Some examples include:

- A device used to display a restaurant's mobile app used to take orders would need to be small and portable, as such the interactive digital media are likely to be designed for a tablet or phone and be accessed using a touch screen.
- Games are often designed to be used on a specific device, for example a console. This means the game needs to be suitable for that device and the devices needed to control the game and provide the interactivity such as controllers, headsets and keyboards.

Activity

You have been asked to plan an interactive digital media product to teach teenagers about cooking and healthy recipes.

What product would you make and what device would you make it for?

Why did you make these choices?

Adapting content to suit access methods

In the same way that the target audience and purpose influence devices used to access content, when it comes to selecting or creating content, this is also influenced by the access method. How the user is intended to interact with the content will affect the content chosen and also the design and layout of that content. For example, when creating a mobile app which could be used as a museum guide for visitors, the device it will be used on will likely need to be mobile for users to carry. This may make reading content or viewing images a challenge on a small screen, so the content is often delivered using audio.

Methods of user interaction within interactive digital media

The methods used to create the interaction within a product are key to creating the interactivity that makes the product different from conventional digital media in which the user is a passive participant in the user experience.

Here are some of the interaction methods that could be used:

- Touch screen/stylus: This method allows the user to interact directly with the content on the screen either by touching it with a finger or using a stylus which is a small pen link object which can be used to touch the screen.
- Voice controls; Voice controls allow the user to speak to the device to control the product. This requires the use of a microphone in the device.
- Camera input: Cameras on devices can be used to control aspects of interaction, for example some games used on a game console use a camera to detect the movement of the player in order to control the game.
- Keyboard/buttons: A lot of interactive multimedia products use buttons to allow users to engage with the content. These could be in the form of buttons within a touch screen or buttons on a separate keyboard or controller.
- Mouse/joystick control: Interaction can also be controlled by using a mouse to control a cursor on the screen, used to select or click on items. A joystick can be used to control the movement of an object such as a character within a product by moving the stick to change the direction or angle of movement.

Figure 5.2 A joystick is sometimes used when playing computer games

Test your knowledge

1. Identify three scenarios where you might see a kiosk-based interactive multimedia product in real life.
2. Select three types of content you might include in an interactive digital media product and describe a scenario where this would be the best type of content to use.
3. Identify three types of device used to interact with interactive digital media products. For each one, explain one way that it could be used.

Synoptic link

You can find further information about this topic in Unit R093, Section 2.3.

1.2 Features and conventions of interactive digital media

GUI (graphical user interface) design

The graphical user interface is the design and layout of the content that allows the user to interact with the product. When creating the design for GUI there are a number of things you need to consider.

Consistent use of layout

Consistent layout is a key feature of good user interface design. This allows users to become familiar with the layout which allows them to interact easily with the product, which is what any designer intends for users to be able to do.

There are some conventions which are usually followed that allow the user interaction to follow a familiar pattern with ease.

- Navigation: Often the buttons used for interaction with the user are placed around the edges of the screen. This is generally across the top and down the left of the page, with secondary options sometimes placed along the bottom of the page.
- Headings: Headings for the pages tend to run across the top of the page or section.
- Main content: The primary content for the page will be in the centre of the page.

House style

The house style is a set of rules which explain how products should be presented. A product is made up of a number of different elements which contribute to house style.

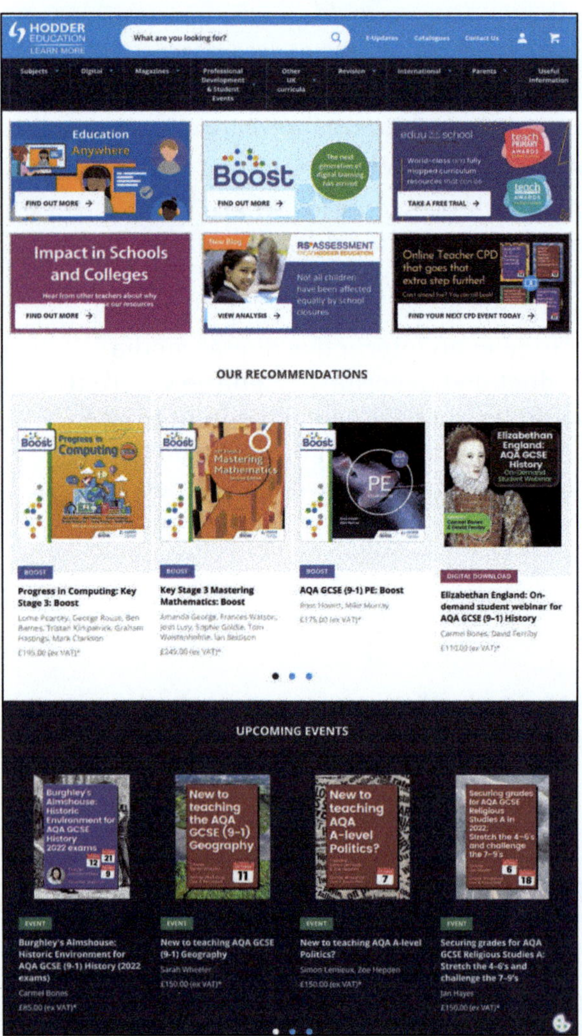

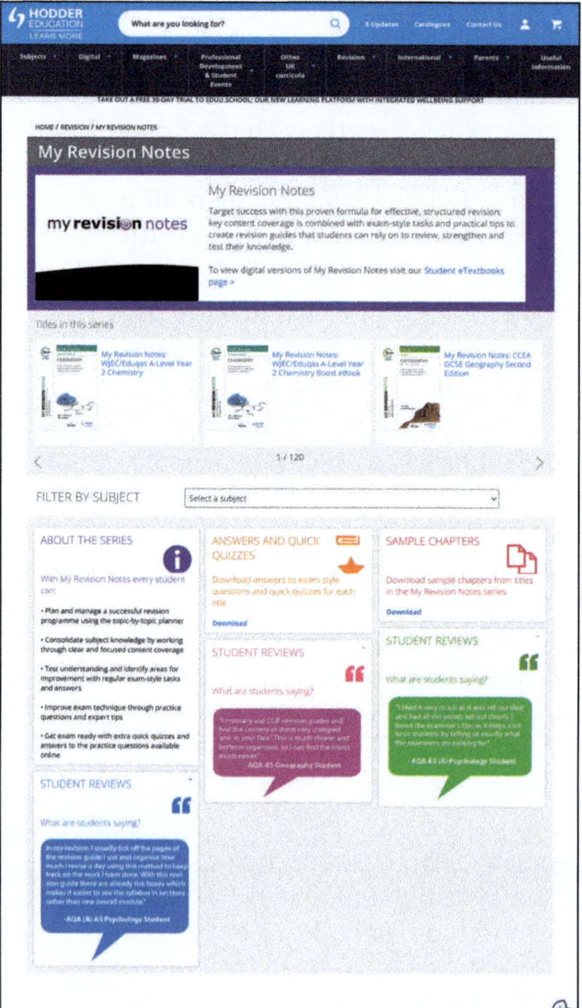

Figure 5.3 Some examples of house style used across a website. You can see how the layout, typography and use of colours demonstrates a house style throughout the site

Colour scheme

The colours used on an interactive product are key to the design appeal and usability of the interactive multimedia product. When creating a product, the colour scheme helps the product be instantly recognisable to the user and also allows the designer to use colours consistently to help the user interact with the product. For example, always using particular colours for a button or icon so that it is easy to spot. The colours in a house style are usually limited to approximately three colours – sometimes these link to an existing brand, such as the colours used in the logo for the product or brand. There are often two main colours with a third colour used for highlighting key elements or to allow the colours to be reversed to make a page appear different to the rest of the set but still part of the main house style.

Typography

Typography is how words and letters are displayed on the page. The key to good typography is ensuring that the text is easy for the reader to access. This can include making sure it is easy to read but also that it makes the reader want to view the text. Typography includes the selection of fonts which are suitable and accessible to the reader. Fonts can be categorised into two types – serif and sans serif. Serif fonts are fonts which have extended stems on the ends of the lines which make up the letters, for example like the fonts used on a typewriter. These fonts tent to be more formal. Times New Roman is an example of a serif font. Sans serif fonts do not have the extra pieces of their lines and tend to look a little cleaner and simpler. Calibri is an example of a serif font, as is the text used in this book.

The choice of font style used in your house style can indicate to the reader the type of content which is on the page. For example, a less formal font such as a sans serif style may show the reader that this is a more informal type of product or perhaps one designed for younger users, who will find the simple font easier to read. A serif font tends to make the text look more business-like and this will be the impression given to the reader. As well as font, text styles such as bold, italics and capital letters should also be considered when deciding on typography. You need to decide how and where such text styles will be used to help the reader access and engage with the written words in your product.

White space

Despite its name, white space does not in fact mean space which is white. It refers to the use of empty space in your interface design. Despite how it may look, this space is included deliberately in interface design to allow the user interaction to flow well and to allow the key parts of the page to stand out and not be swamped by other items which are less relevant or important to the user experience.

Remember, consistency is key to creating and using an effective house style.

Activity

Think of a famous brand. Copy and complete the table below with all the features of the brand's house style that make it recognisable.

Brand	
Colour scheme	
Typography	
Layout and white space	

Interface and interaction styles

In this section we are going to look at the different ways that a user can interact with an interactive digital media product. Selecting the most effective interaction methods for the purpose of the product and the audience will be key to the success of the product.

Table 5.2 The different ways that a user can interact with an interactive digital media product

Interaction style	Description and uses	Advantages	Limitations
Click	This type of interaction is usually actioned using a mouse or trackpad to allow the user to select an item, object or link and click to select it	Most users will be familiar with this type of control as it is common across desktop and laptop computers. This method provides a good level of control for selecting or clicking on smaller items	This type of interaction is facilitated by a mouse of trackpad. If you are designing a product for a different type of device which does not have this hardware option then click control may not be suitable
Touch/gesture	Users either touch on the screen or gesture across the screen to interact with the product	This type of interaction can allow for the use of touch screen devices or those with track pads to be used to access an interactive multimedia product. This can also be good for younger users who may find controlling a mouse or trackpad difficult	This type of interaction is largely limited to touch screen hardware. It also relies on the effectiveness of the hardware to respond to the touch screen interactions and the ability of the user to be familiar with the required interactions to enable the product to respond effectively
Voice control	Voice control allows the user to interact with the product by speaking. This could be responding to output from the product or giving instructions to the product which it will respond to in some way	This method of interaction is accessible to a wide user audience and can be used on a range of access devices from desktop computers to smartphones and consoles	To enable voice control, the device that is used to access the interactive multimedia product, will need to either have an inbuilt microphone, such as in a smartphone, or the device should have the capacity to attach hardware to enable audio input, such as via a microphone or headset
Motion/ movement	Some devices will allow you to interact with a product using motion or movement. This can involve using parts of your body to interact with assets on the screen	This type of interaction is useful for some types of product, for example game-style products where whole-body activities are an addition to the interactivity	This type of interactivity would not suit the purpose of some types of interactive digital media product. It would also require specialist hardware such as cameras or devices with motion sensors to enable this type of interaction to take place
Drag/drop	Drag and drop can be used to interact with a product in a number of ways, for example using a touch screen or a mouse or trackpad. This interaction is where the user interacts by dragging assets around the screen to certain locations to trigger an action in the product	This is a simple form of interaction that can be used on a range of different host devices. It can be quite easy to use, particularly on a touch screen device and generally would not require any other hardware	One limitation is that it relies on the user being able to move icons around the screen, so a high-quality reactive touch screen is needed for a good user experience. Drag and drop on a small-screen device such as a smartphone can be very challenging as there may not be enough screen space to pick things up and move them easily
Feedback/ closure	This type of interaction is often combined with those mentioned earlier in this table. Often when interaction takes place there will be a form of feedback to the user, this could be a sound, a visual cue or a motion such as vibration. Closure is when interaction is used to close an element on the product such as a pop-up box	These are often additional interactions to those listed above but they add an extra dimension to interactions and give the user a greater sense of control in their experience	Depending on the form of feedback used, there is often the need for other output methods, such as sound or vibration to accompany these methods. These types of interaction also need to be used with care to ensure that they do not take away from the user experience by being an annoyance or overloading the user with multiple elements of feedback/ interaction at the same time

Selecting interface and interaction styles

When planning and selecting the interface and interaction for your product you need to think carefully about a number of different questions and consider what functions your product needs to create the best user experience.

- What it the main purpose of the product?
- Who are the target audience?
- What type of interaction does the audience need to have with the product?
- What device do you intend the product to be accessed using?

Accessibility

When designing an interactive multimedia product, ensuring that the product is accessible to as wide an audience as possible is important and there are a number of tools to help make your product accessible. When designing, selecting and creating the features for your product you need to think carefully about the needs of your intended audience and how best to cater for those needs.

- Alternate text: When using visual content, it is good practice to set alternate text (often known as 'alt text'). This is where content is labelled with a brief description of what is shown. This can be used to show what is there if a page doesn't load correctly and can also be used when someone is using a screen reader. This allows a computer program to read out the text description of the content for a user who is unable to view the screen content themselves.
- Text readability: This is concerned with making the text as easy for the users to read as possible. It is based on a lot of different features – one is the choice of words used and how easy they are to understand. Other things to consider are the length of any pieces of text and the layout to make sure it is as clear as possible to the reader.
- Captions: Captions can be used to explain the content of images to help visually impaired users to access the content. Captions or subtitles can also be used on audio or video content to allow the audio content to be displayed in text alongside the sound.

Figure 5.4 An example of an interactive digital media product which has been optimised for computer and mobile device use

- Contrasting colours: When designing an interactive digital media product, you need to carefully consider the use of colour to ensure that the colour combinations do not make the content inaccessible to the users. For example, some people are colour blind which means they have difficulty seeing colour or identifying differences in colour – a common example is seeing the difference between red and green. This needs to be considered when choosing the colours for your product. It is also good practice to make sure that the key features of your product such as links, buttons or highlighting should not be shown solely with the use of colour as this could make the interactivity unclear to some users.
- Resizable text: This feature allows users to reduce or increase the font size of text on the page to allow them to read it at a size comfortable to them. This is usually accessed by a button on the home screen/page.
- Flexible input: One of the key features on an interactive product is to allow the user to input information to the product. To make sure that product is as accessible as possible it is important to allow flexibility in how information can be inputted into the product, for example it could be typed, written with a stylus or inputted verbally by using a microphone.
- Mobile device accessibility: To make sure that you have the largest widest potential audience for your product you need to allow for users to access the product on a range of different devices, such as tablets or mobile phones. To ensure this is possible, when creating your product you need to think about how you can allow users to access all the information and interactive features in different ways based on the device they are using. An example of this would be having a mobile/tablet version of the product or having a setting which allows the user to switch to mobile view.
- Screen size and orientation adjustments: In a similar way to mobile device accessibility, there needs to be flexibility to allow users to maximise their experience of the product for the hardware they are using. This could involve designing the product so that it will respond correctly if a user puts a device in landscape mode or designing the product so that it adjusts effectively to different screen sizes.

Activity

A team is working on an app for users to share seasonal craft ideas aimed at people age 40 plus. What three pieces of advice could you give to the team about how they could make their app accessible?

Conventions of interactive digital media

Non-linear navigation

When viewing an electronic page, a user's eye tends to follow one of two patterns.

- When reading text, the user tends to read across the page from the left to the right in a zig-zag pattern down the page.
- Those viewing a page as a whole are more likely to follow a circular motion from the top left in a clockwise direction around the page.

These viewing patterns are something to consider when designing the layout of the page. Users rarely view pages or sets of pages in a linear way, which means from top to bottom or left to right. For example, users are unlikely to start at the home page of the product and work their way systematically though each page. The benefit of non-linear navigation is that users are able to be much more fluid in their interactions with content. They view content in an order than appeals to them, often jumping from place to place and in many cases missing out some content altogether. This is why it is not good practice to create a product where the user can only take one route through the product; they will soon become disengaged if made to view content that is not relevant to them.

User friendly intuitive interfaces

The interface of an interactive digital multimedia product is vital in making sure that the user can access and engage with the content. When planning the layout of your product you need to think carefully about how easy your interface is to use. There are some rules that you can build into your design that will help the user be comfortable within your product and make the interface more intuitive to use.

- Use visual cues, for example the button design and location should help indicate what will happen if the user presses it.
- Buttons/menu items need to be big enough to click on (either with a finger, mouse or stylus depending on your design) – if a user has to repeatedly try to access content by clicking on a button, they will soon become disengaged with the product.
- If you use a button for a function, the style, placement and design of this button should be used consistently through the product so that it becomes recognisable to the user.
- When designing the layout, take into account the user viewing patterns referred to in the previous section and ensure you lay out items in order of priority along that path. For example, items you want the user to access first should not be in the bottom right of the screen.
- Remember white space – don't clutter the space so the user cannot see the important features or information easily.

Suitability for target audiences

When designing digital interactive media products, the target audience will influence the design of the interface. For example, when designing for a younger audience you are likely to rely on visual cues from graphics to support the interaction within the product, whereas for an older audience you have the option to use more text-based references. That does not mean that products for an older audience will have no graphical elements; graphics often make interactions easier to identify than text-based indicators for all audience groups. Colour schemes may also be influenced by the target audience (though often by purpose too). Convention tends to be that a range of bold colours will be used to make a product seem exciting and fun to a younger audience, whereas a more limited colour scheme with less colours is likely to be used to attract a more mature audience.

Creativity in interactive digital media

Originality and imaginative design

We have talked a lot about the design conventions and rules which can help you design your product – with all these rules to follow it may be easy to think that there is little room for originality, but this is not the case. With a market packed with products for people to choose to engage with, it is important that your design combines both effective easy-to-use functions, but also original and imaginative ideas to make it stand out. Sometimes creators take an existing design and change it a little bit to make it fit the needs of a different audience or client. This is called making adaptions and happens when the core content is the same but small changes are made.

Derivative design

With the huge range of existing products and the ability to use templates to construct your product it is very easy to create something that looks like a solid design which follows all the rules but is actually really generic. A design which is based on another design or product is called a derivative. It is a very fine balance to create a design that is unique and creative whilst still following the conventions and rules that make the product effective for a user to interact with. This is where your skills as a designer come in and where you need to demonstrate a good understanding of the purpose of your product and the needs of your target audience so that you can shape your design into something that is designed to meet the client brief.

Test your knowledge

4 Describe four things relating to accessibility that you need to consider when creating your product.
5 What is white space and how might you use it to create a good page/screen design in a product?
6 What is non-linear navigation and why is it so important in the design of interactive digital media products?

Synoptic links

You can find further information about this topic in Unit R093, Sections 2.1 and 2.5.

1.3 Resources required to create an interactive digital media product

Hardware used to create interactive digital media

A variety of hardware is used in the creation of interactive digital media. A selection is described in Table 5.3.

Choosing hardware

Often hardware choices are influenced by what is available to you. However, in a real work context you may be able to have more choices of the tools you use. The brief and task you are completing will influence the hardware you are using. For example, if you are creating digital artwork you may choose to use a graphics tablet; however, if you were building the structure of your product, a computer and mouse would allow you to use different software tools easily. Using hardware that isn't completely suitable for the task may mean that you have to compromise on quality or use more time to get the same result as you would get with a more suitable hardware choice.

Table 5.3 Hardware used in the creation of interactive digital media

Hardware	Description
Computer	A computer is the main device on which you will use the software and hardware required to create your interactive digital media product
Mouse/ trackpad	The mouse or the trackpad can be used for a range of functions when creating your product, from using the tools within software, to moving elements of the product or editing and adjusting parts of the product content
Stylus	A stylus can be used like a pen to write or draw. This could be used to create a hand drawn graphic to be used within a digital interactive media product
Monitor	A monitor is another word for the screen used to view the interactive product creation
Graphics tablet	A graphics tablet allows the user to draw using a stylus in a similar way to how you might draw on a piece of paper. You can use a tablet to make graphics or illustrations as part of the content for your product
Touch screen	A touch screen allows you to interact with the content on the screen by touching the screen itself and may form part of your computer or graphics tablet. This would be used for creating or editing either the product or content for the product
Microphone	A microphone can be used to record any narration, sound effects or audio content required
Digital camera	A digital camera can be used to create digital photographs and sometimes video content that you wish to include in your product

Software used to create interactive digital media products

As with hardware, there is a variety of different software available for creating interactive digital media products.

Table 5.4 Software used in the creation of interactive digital media

Software	Description
Web authoring software	Web authoring software are the programs that allow you to create the structure and navigation for a website and then build in a range of different content into the website pages
App creation software	In a similar way to website authoring software, app creation software enables you to create a structure for your app, to build in any navigation or interaction and then add the content to the product
Authoring tools	This is software for making all types of digital content for your product, ranging from word processing software for creating text-based content, through to audio or graphics creation software to create sound effects or artwork for your product
Kiosk interface software	Kiosk software is specifically designed to create a product that will work on a kiosk-style device, so it will be based around creating interactions with the content which suit this type of device. For example, kiosks are often used to display content on a large screen where the interaction is via a touch screen mechanism

Choosing software

The choice of software to create your product is reliant on the type of product you need to create and the requirements of the client and the target audience. It is possible to create different products in software that was not designed for that purpose, for example creating a website in presentation software. Similarly, it is often possible to create content in software that is designed to create the product itself, the compromise being that you will most likely be limited in the quality and range of tools available to create or edit content as this not the primary purpose of the software. Whilst it is possible do work this way, it is not good practice and would not be a good choice for making an effective digital media product. Try to ensure that you use the best software for your task and combine the assets in the product creation software as part of the construction stage. You will then have the flexibility to create good assets and an excellent structure and level of interaction for your product.

> **Test your knowledge**
>
> **7** Identify three items of hardware that you have in school that you could use to access a digital interactive multimedia product. Describe what multimedia assets could be accessed effectively by this item of hardware.

1.4 Pre-production and planning documentation and techniques for interactive digital media

Pre-production documentation for interface planning

When planning interactive digital media, you need to plan all aspects of the product. To do this there are a range of different documents that can be used to ensure that the layout and content is correctly arranged. You need to make sure that you make plans for the following features:

- screen designs
- colour schemes
- layout
- text
- navigation features
- graphical user interface (menus, buttons, links)
- media elements interaction.

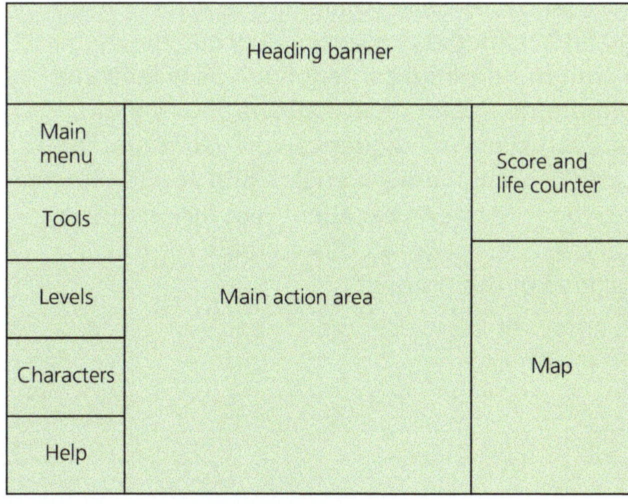

Figure 5.5 An example of a wire frame diagram

Wire frames

A key planning document for an interactive multimedia product is often a wire frame diagram (Figure 5.5). This is a diagram which takes the basic layout of the pages/screens used in the product and shows the position of all the key elements of the pages, both interactive and static elements. This is likely to include placeholders for content such as videos, images and interaction elements such as buttons, links, and so on. This is not generally a detailed plan but rather an outline that focuses on the layout and design of the page or screen. This enables creators to visualise the product and ensure that it has a good flow and a consistent design.

Visualisation diagrams

When planning the contents of pages you may want to use a visualisation diagram. This is essentially an annotated draft of the pages or screens of the product. These plans include sketches of the content of the pages such as navigation, graphics, text, images and media content.

Synoptic links

Visualisation diagrams are covered in detail in R093, Section 3.3 and R094, Section 2.3.

Storyboards

Storyboards are a key planning tool for interactive media products. They can be used to plan multimedia content such as videos and animations. A storyboard allows you to plan out each scene in sequence, including timings, scene content, camera angles and sound effects. Storyboards are an excellent tool for ensuring that the content created is suitable for the purpose of the product.

Figure 5.6 Example of a hand drawn storyboard

Pre-production documentation and planning for content

Master pages/page template design

We have discussed earlier in this chapter how important it is to have a clear and consistent design to the pages of your product so that users can navigate and access the content of the pages easily. A master page (sometimes called a page template) is like a template for a page. It allows you to create a page design with all the places for content planned out, which can be applied to all the pages on the product. Sometimes there may be multiple templates that can be applied to different types of page, for example you may have a template for a home screen but a different template for the pages within the product. This is a good way of combining consistency and engaging design.

Assets to form content

The planning of the assets in a product is really important. As there are a number of pages and the product is interactive there are likely to be a significant number and variety of assets needed to complete your product such as backgrounds, banners, buttons, shapes, text and different fonts. You can include multimedia assets in your plan such as:

- images
- videos
- sound
- animations.

For the interactive digital media product, you will also need to plan assets such as text and fonts to display information and assets such as navigation buttons which the user will need to move around and interact with your product. For each asset you plan you need to be able to demonstrate that you know why you will need that asset for your project. As well as understanding the purpose it is important to plan out the location of each asset so that it can be used effectively and is easy for the user to locate.

Properties of assets linked to purpose

When planning assets, it is important that you consider how the asset will meet the purpose of the product and how the properties of the asset will impact this.

- Age appropriateness: You need to think carefully about the design and content of your assets, for example is the style of the assets suitable for the age of your audience and does the content use language that is accessible to the audience you are aiming the product towards?
- Quality: The quality of an asset impacts the quality of your product. You want the user to see a professional finished product which gives them confidence in the information you are sharing. This can be quality in terms of having the correct resolution of content (discussed in the next section) but also quality in terms of ensuring that all the text has been proofread for errors and that the assets display as intended.
- Size on screen: The size of the assets on the page should be balanced and well thought-out. Size also indicates the importance of the asset; an asset designed to be the main function of a page should be large and clear to the user. Extra assets designed to complement the main feature should be smaller to reflect their importance on that page.

Technical compatibility of assets

The technical properties of assets will also need to be considered at the planning stage to ensure that the assets are suitable for the purpose and audience of the product.

- File size: The file size of an asset needs to be considered in the context of the purpose and use of your interactive digital media product. If you need your product to be accessed on a mobile device, potentially using mobile data or via Wi-Fi, you need to consider how large a file is and how long/how much data it will take to access this asset from a mobile device.
- File type: The file type will impact on the compatibility of the asset with the device the user is accessing the product on. When selecting assets, you need to be really clear about how the product will be accessed and what impact this has in terms of the files you might be able to use.
- Resolution: Resolution in still and moving images can alter the quality and file size of an asset. The higher the resolution the better the quality of a graphical asset but also the higher the file size, so you need to think carefully about the purpose of your product and decide what quality of asset you need in terms of resolution. You can read more about resolution in R093, Section 4.2.

One of the best ways to plan out assets is to create an asset table. This is a table that allows you to list the assets that you intend to use in a structured way. Things that you need to include for each asset are:

- Name: Saving your assets with a sensible name so you know what it is and where it is, will help when you create your product.
- Purpose: Why do you need this asset in your product?
- Properties: What size, length, resolution does the asset need to be?
- The intended location: Where will the asset be placed within your product?

Activity

Find an app or website you use a lot.
Select a page or screen from that product.
Complete an example asset table using the template below for the page or screen you have chosen.

Name of asset	Purpose of asset	Asset properties	Location/ use

Pre-production documentation

Navigation diagram

This planning element is an important part of interactive multimedia product design. It allows you to clearly see all the pages of the product and how they will link together using navigation features. It allows you to plan the user's route between the pages/screens. It is also a good opportunity to see if the website structure is practical. The arrow shows the direction of movement users can take between pages/screens. There are several ways to create a navigation diagram, such as by hand with a pen and paper or on a computer.

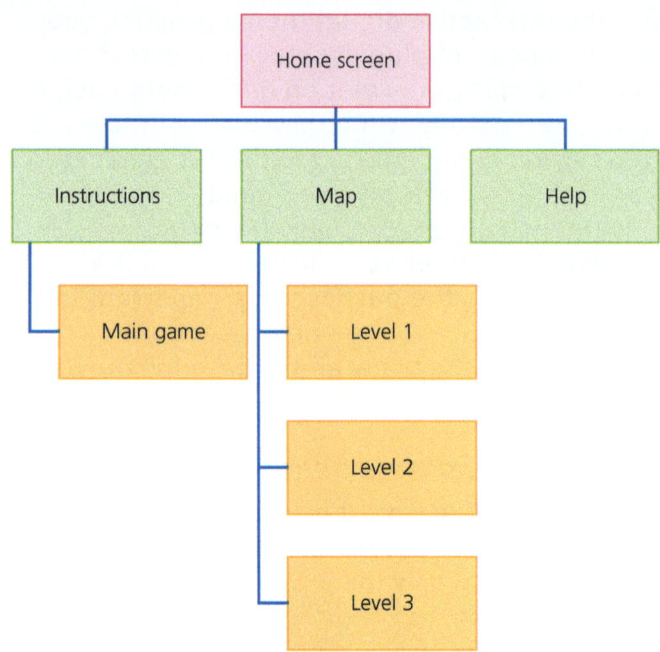

Figure 5.8 Example of a hierarchy diagram

Hierarchy diagrams/flow charts

The structure of the pages or screens can also be planned in a hierarchy diagram which allows you to plan out the layers of content in your product. This does not usually include the arrows for user movement between pages but does show which pages are on the same level.

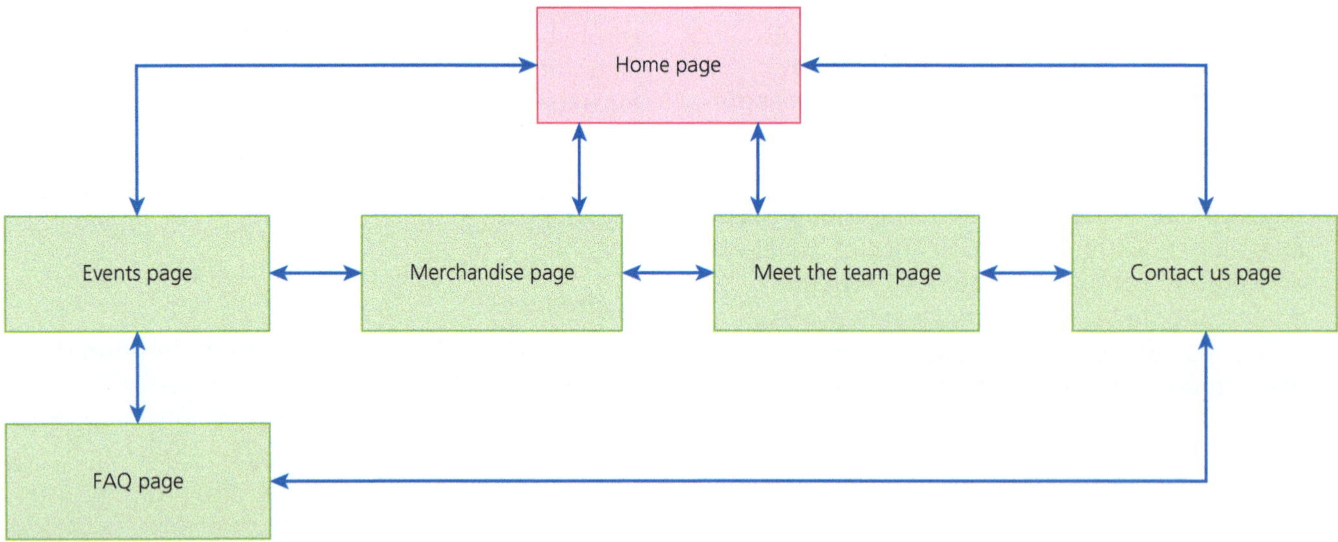

Figure 5.7 Example of a navigation diagram

Planning for user interaction

To accompany the diagrams in Figures 5.7 and 5.8, you also need to plan out the interactions the user may have when using the product. For example, what will happen when you click on buttons, or links or submit a form. Will it make a sound, close the window or take you to a separate page? A good way to display this information is to create a table for each page and as you plan the layout and content you can create a row for the planned interaction for that element.

Test your knowledge

8 Why is the quality of an asset in an interactive digital media product so important?
9 You are creating an interactive digital media product for use on mobile devices. What do you need to consider when thinking about the file size of your assets?

Synoptic links

You can find further information about this topic in Unit R093, Sections 2.1–2.3, 2.5 and 3.2–3.4.

Assignment practice

Task 1

Time needed: 1–2 hours

You are working for a snack company who are releasing a new fruit-based snack bar called 'Bite'. They hope the new product will appeal to primary school children. They would like to create an interactive multimedia product which teaches young children about different fruits.

Create a wire frame diagram to show the home page/screen of this app.

Topic area 2 Create interactive digital media

2.1 Technical skills to create and/or edit and manage assets for use within interactive digital media products

Getting started

Think about the planning we looked at in Topic area 1. Create a mind map of the different software you could use to make an interactive digital media product.

Techniques for sourcing suitable assets

When searching for assets there are a range of tools that you can use to make sure that the assets you source are the best fit for your product.

Advanced searching

In most search engines it is possible to add more detail to the search criteria using advanced search tools to narrow down the search results to the most suitable results.

- Search by feature/property: You can set the search criteria to search by various features such as file type, colours, size or aspect ratio.
- Search by licence: You can also set the search criteria to find assets based on their licence. This means the permissions that are attached to that asset which will allow or restrict your use of the assets in different scenarios. You can read more about different licences which can be applied to assets in R093, Section 3.4.

- Libraries: There are also large collections of assets stored libraries. These are searchable stores of assets which you can search and filter to locate any assets with the properties you need. You can read more about libraries and sources of images in R094, Section 2.2.

Creation and editing of different asset types

Making your assets technically suitable for their purpose

This next section looks at how to create and edit a range of different assets to make sure that they are suitable for the client brief and the audience needs. This can include editing the content of the assets, such as changing the length of a video clip. It can also mean changing technical properties such as the file size of an asset to make sure that it can be used effectively in the context of the brief, for example if it is to be used on mobile devices or online.

Static image assets

To ensure that static image assets are suitable, you will need to be able to make the correct choice between vector and bitmap images to suit the context of your product (see R094, Section 2.2). You also need to be able to edit images to make them more suitable to the audience and purpose of your product. There are a range of skills in image editing that you could use to edit and repurpose your image assets, such as:

- adjusting brightness, contrast and colour
- adjusting image and canvas size
- using filters and transformations
- retouching images.

Synoptic links

You can learn about digital graphics skills in Unit R094, Section 3.1.

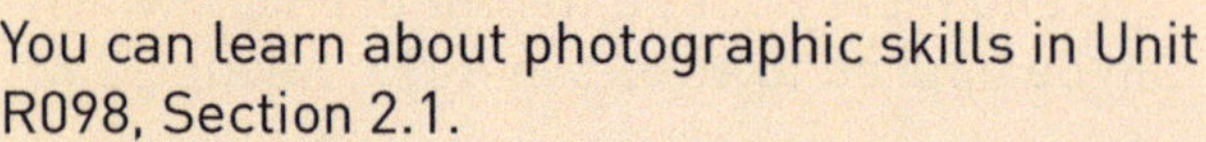

You can learn about photographic skills in Unit R098, Section 2.1.

Audio assets

There are a number of different types of audio asset that might be used in an interactive digital media product. Audio assets can be part of the main content of the product, for example as a music track or a video which includes sound or narration. Audio assets can also be additions to accompany interactions within the product, such as sound effects to indicate clicks or selections, or to accompany a character action or a page turn.

As well as understanding the different types of audio assets available, you also need to be able to use a range of tools and techniques to be able to create and repurpose audio assets. There are a range of core skills you need to be able to use to create audio assets, including:

- cut
- split
- trim
- extend
- file size/format optimising
- enhancing sounds
- volume editing.

Synoptic link

You can learn about these skills in Unit R096, Section 2.1.

Moving image assets

Moving image assets come in a range of forms such as animation or video. To make sure that the assets suit the audience and purpose of your product you will often need to edit or repurpose your assets to make them suitable. There are range of skills you might need to use to do this including:

- cut
- split
- trim
- extend
- speed/pitch tempo
- file size/format optimising.

Synoptic links

You can learn about these animation skills in Unit R096, Section 3.2.

You can learn about these video skills in Unit R094, Section 3.

Interactive assets

As well as assets to make up content on the interactive digital media product, there are a range of important assets that create the interactivity needed to make the product function and to engage the user.

- Diagrams: Diagrams are really useful when creating interactive digital media products, particularly when creating a product for purposes such as education or to provide information. It may show how something works or demonstrate how to do something – a diagram which the user can navigate is a great visual way to show this.
- Maps: In a similar way to diagrams, maps are a really useful way of providing information to the user. There are many apps that use an interactive map feature to guide the user to where they need to be. This is also a common feature in kiosk-style interactive products, to show the user where they are and where other places are in relation to the kiosk.
- Buttons and rollover buttons: A button is a key form of interaction within interactive digital media products. Buttons indicate actions to the user, such as to select items they want to use and to navigate their own path through the product.
- A rollover image is an image that changes to display a different image when the mouse is moved over the image. Sometimes these images are also used as a hyperlink or a button. An example would be a button which changes colour when the mouse is hovered over it.
- Banners: Banners are a great way of gaining the attention of the user. They tend to be large and eye-catching, using images, bold text or colours to stand out. They are mainly found at the top of pages or screens but are sometimes used to the sides or bottom of the page as well. They provide interactivity as they are usually a clickable asset that directs the user elsewhere in the product or to an external link.
- Navigation bars: The navigation of an interactive digital media product is vital. Without a functioning navigation system that allows the user to access all the content, you will not be able to achieve the requirements of the client brief. There are a range of different ways of linking the elements of the content together. Navigation bars and buttons are one of the most common forms of navigation. They allow users to click on buttons to select the page they want to go to.
- Forms: As part of your design you might want to use a form so that you can collect information from your users, such as comments, questions or bookings. A form would usually be embedded into a section on the product for the user to select responses or type answers to allow the product to collect data or the user to contact those behind the product.

Activity

Go to **https://www.bbc.co.uk/cbbc**

Select three pages you can access from this web address. Write a list of different types of interactive assets you can see on these pages.

Can you explain why these assets have been used in the way they have?

Synoptic links

You can find further information about this topic in Unit R093, Sections 3.4 and 4.1.

2.2 Technical skills to create interactive digital media

Product folder management

Effective folder management is key to creating any good product but is really important when creating an interactive digital media product. This is because you are likely to be working over a number of different pages and combining a huge range of assets and interactive elements to complete your product. This means you need to be clear and organised in the way you set up your work.

Structure of the product folder

The use of folder structure is important when creating an interactive digital media product. You need to ensure that you create folders to store the assets you need such as images, media content (videos and sound), design style elements and interactive elements, as well as the pages/screens themselves. You must ensure that they are stored in a clear and consistent location to enable you to effectively link the elements together. Your authoring files must also be separate to the published product files. Most of these must be managed through careful use of the software to make sure you do not end up with broken links to assets.

File naming conventions

When you are working with lots of different files to create a product it is important that all your elements are carefully named to avoid confusion when you are combining your assets to make the product. The first thing to remember is to give your file a sensible name which clearly states what it is, for example 'Homepage_intro_video' is much clearer than 'Vid1'.

The second thing to consider is version control. It is good practice to save a different version of a file each time you make changes to it. This ensures that you always have back-up versions if an error occurs or if you decide changes you have made do not improve the final product.

There are a number of different conventions you can use to apply version control to your files. Two common methods are:

- Date: Add the date to the end of your file name so you can chronologically see the order of your files, for example 'Homepage_intro_video_050621'.
- Version: You can label each new version of your file with a version number, for example 'Homepage_intro_video_V1'.

Techniques to create a consistently designed product

There are a range of different techniques you can use to create a consistently designed product which looks professional.

Master page/template elements

We have already discussed using master pages and page templates in our planning section; here we will look at what you would include when setting these up in product creation software. To make your pages, you need to think carefully about what you need on each page and where you want it to go.

Here are some key elements you need to consider when setting up your master page or page template. Remember you can have more than one page design for your product, but to make your product design consistent you should use only two or three designs which will be closely linked in appearance.

Fixed and editable content

When looking at your product plans, you need to consider what content is going to stay the same on each page/screen and what is going to change. The content of each page such as any text or media elements will be different on each page/screen, so you would not build this into your master page or template. These things would be included in what is called the editable region of the page (that is, where things can be changed). The things you are looking to include on a template or master page are those things that will be consistent across your pages. This will include any branding or logos, the main navigation of the product and the use of the house style.

House style

The house style is another important thing created on your master page or template. You can use the master page or template to set up elements of your house style such as:

- fonts and font sizes – you can set fonts and sizes for different parts of your text, for example headings, sub-headings and main text
- font colour – you can set the colours of fonts to different types of text
- colour schemes – you can create a style to use the house colours you have chosen throughout the product.

Navigation system

Your navigation system will be one of the main things that your master page or template will hold. This is a key part of the product which will need to be consistent for the user so creating one version that can be used across all the pages of your product is important.

The navigation on an interactive digital media product is often in the form of a navigation bar. This is where all the links are presented to the user in one place on the page. The main navigation bar will often have additional navigation options that appear as a dropdown or pop-out menu. The rollover technique is often applied to the navigation bar, meaning that when you hover over or click on a button or link it changes in appearance (often by colour) to show this action.

You can also add other navigation elements to the master page or template, such as hot spots. This is an area of the page that when clicked will take you to another page or part of the product. These are often used to link the logo of a product to the home page/screen.

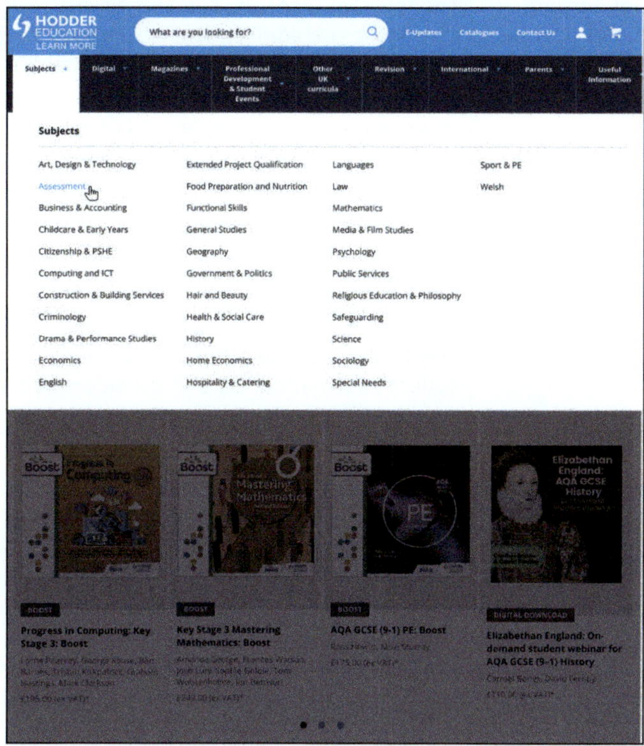

Figure 5.9 Example of a navigation bar with a dropdown sub-menu and rollover colour change

Activity

Select a website you use often. Look though the site and then try and create a sketch of their master page.

Table 5.5 Adding content to a product

Type of content	Description
Text	In most product creation software, you will need to create a frame for your text. This allows you to write within a box then move the text box to place it where it needs to be. This also allows you to arrange items easily and break up large pieces of text with other media to make the content more engaging
Images	In most software you will have an insert option that allows you to select the image file that you want to include on the page. You will need to have saved the file to a suitable format and location in advance. You will often need to set the dimensions of the image in the menu or create a frame to insert your image into which will dictate the size and position. In this insert process you will also be able to add a caption or alternative text
Tables	Tables are an effective way of adding structure to your content. You will need to know the number of columns and rows needed to store the information on the page, but the option to add a table can generally be found in the Insert menu

Type of content	Description
Lists	Lists are another way of clearly displaying information on your page. In some software there may be an option to add a bulleted or numbered list, in others you may need to use a text box as discussed above, then format the text to display as a list
Sounds and audio	The tools for inserting sound may vary from one software to another but it will generally be located within an 'Insert → Media' option, or a media menu. As with other items such as images, you will need to save the file to a suitable format and location in advance, to allow you to insert the file correctly
Video	The tools for inserting video may vary between software but it will generally be located within an 'Insert → Media' option, or a media menu. As with other items such as images, you will need to save the file to a suitable format and location in advance, to allow you to insert the file correctly
Maps	Maps can usually be added to a product as an object or as an embedded link to another site. When adding a map, you need to think about how you want it to appear on the page and make sure you set up the orientation correctly. For example, if the map is showing the location of a place or venue, it should be focused on this area, not a wider area
Forms	A lot of product creation software contains the facility to add a form to your product. This allows you to create an area where the user can input information, by selecting an option or writing in text boxes to collect information. Careful consideration needs to be given to the layout and format of forms to make sure that is easy for the user to provide the information you need

Product content

We have looked earlier at how to create, edit and repurpose content for your interactive digital media product. Now we will look at how you might add this to your product.

Playback controls

Due to the interactive nature of the product, there will be a number of controls relating to the use of media and interactive elements that you will need to set up.

If your product contains assets such as video or music you will need to configure the playback settings. This means deciding and setting whether the media asset starts as the user reaches the page it is on, whether the user has play and pause controls on the screen or whether the asset/controls can be viewed in a separate window.

Triggers and behaviours

Another key feature will be the triggers and behaviours within your product. There are a number of features here that you may build into your product.

- Pop-up message/dialogue boxes: You may want to add some messages to your user that pop up when certain actions take place, such as 'Are you sure you want to close this screen?'
- Drag and drop functions: You could include interaction such as games or tasks which require the user to select items and move them around the screen.
- Scoring: If your product has a game or task element you may need your product to record and show a score.
- User input: When you need input from the user such as a click, written text or a control device movement, the system needs to be told how to request and respond to this input.
- Customised screen messages: In some cases you may want a message to appear on the screen that is related to the user and their actions, for example, 'Well done Alex, that is your fastest time!'
- Feedback and closure: Feedback to the user can appear in a number of forms; a sound that goes off when something happens on the screen or a tick appearing at the side of a correct answer. Closure interactions are where the user is required to close something, such as a pop-up window.

Synoptic links

You can find further information about this topic in Unit R093, Sections 3.4 and 4.1.

2.3 Techniques to export/publish interactive digital media

Saving interactive digital media products during creation

Interactive digital media products native file formats

When you are saving your product during the creation process you need to make sure that your work is saved in the native file format. This is the file format that the software you are using saves in automatically. This means that when you re-open your project you can continue editing in that software easily.

Version control

We have looked at version control in Section 2.2. When saving in the native file format during the creation of your project you need to apply what you have learned about version control and save your work appropriately to enable the roll back of features during testing.

Exporting/publishing finished interactive digital media products

Techniques for exporting/publishing

When you have created a finished version of your interactive digital media product you will need to think about what file format you need the final product to be in to ensure that it works in the context of your project. This is likely to not be the native file format of the software. To get the product in a file format that is not the native format you will need to either export or publish your product as the file type you need to correctly display the content and allow access from the device used in your project.

Platform independent file formats

To allow your product to be accessed on a range of devices, it is helpful to have your product in a format that is not linked to a specific platform to avoid restricting the use of your product. Examples of platform independent file formats include HTML files for web-based content or a PPS file format, which is created from a PowerPoint file.

Synoptic links

You can find further information about this topic in Unit R093, Sections 3.4, 4.1 and 4.2.

Assignment practice

Task 2

Time needed: 1–2 hours

You have made an interactive multimedia product which takes the form of a three-page website about a bakery business which is launching their new gluten-free loaf product. The website has a range of multimedia elements, such as an animation about how the bread is made, videos of interviews about the benefits of gluten-free products and interviews with satisfied customers, as well as image and text content. The product has a range of navigation features such as buttons, hotpots and a navigation bar.

Create or source three multimedia assets for this product (they can be those listed above or others of your choice). Think carefully about the technical properties you will need for the assets to work well in the context of this brief.

Topic area 3 Review interactive digital media

Getting started

Think about an interactive digital media product you have used. Write a list of the top three most important elements to you regarding how that products works.

3.1 Techniques to test/check and review interactive digital media

Methods of testing and checking

Test plans

As you are creating your interactive digital media product there are a range of different elements that need to work fully to produce a successful product. To ensure that the product functions effectively you need to be able to test your work. To do this thoroughly you need to create a plan for the tests that you can use to structure your work.

One of the best ways to plan your testing is to create a test table. This allows you to not only record the tests you plan to do but also creates a space for you to record the result of the test, any remedial action you might take and the results of any retests. You would retest if the initial test was unsuccessful and if you had made changes to fix the problems.

Checklist

Another way of reviewing your work is to use a checklist. To do this you could create a list of all the elements from the brief that you think your product should include. You can then work through your product and check them off.

Success criteria

As part of the planning process, it is common to create success criteria. This is a set of things that your product needs to be or do to meet the client brief and the needs of the target audience. To check the product, you could use these criteria to check on the effectiveness of your final product at meeting the needs of the brief.

Iterative testing

This is testing which takes place throughout the creation of your product, not just at the final stage. This allows you to check different elements of your product as you create them, so that you can make changes as you progress and your final product will be more likely to be a success as the elements will already have been checked.

Elements of interactive media to test/check

Testing input or behaviours

- Trying to break inputs: One way to test the functionality of your product is to try and break elements of the product by putting in a range of different inputs and seeing how the product responds. For example, this could involve trying to add input to a form by entering an unsuitable response and seeing how the product responds.
- Following (or not following) navigation paths: Another way to test your product would be to try out all the routes of navigation that you have created. You can test the routes as you intended them to be used. However, as users are able to navigate the product in any way they chose, it is important to also check all the routes the user could follow, not just those they are expected to use.

Functionality tests

Functionality testing involves testing the functions of the product, essentially looking at if the product works as intended. It does not include the quality of content or how the product looks, just 'does it work'?

- Navigation: A core function of the product is the navigation. It is important to check that the user can access all areas of the product, in any pattern they choose and that wherever they navigate to within your product they can also get back to the home page/screen.
- Interactivity: Another function to test is the interactivity your product provides. This could be anything from button presses, to quizzes, to moving around a map. It is important that the user can have a hassle-free experience when interacting with the product and that the product behaves as both you and the user expect. To make sure this is the case, you need to test every feature, ensuring that you try any eventuality that the user might use.
- Inputs and outputs: The interactivity of your product depends upon input from the user and the product's ability to provide outputs in response to this. You need to ensure you test the product's ability to receive input and provide outputs. You could consider:
  - the user's ability to understand that they need to create some form of input and the clarity of the information that tells them what they need to put and where
  - the product's ability to allow a user to input data
  - the product's ability to create a response that makes sense in relation to the input the user provided.

Suitability of file formats

An important check to make will be to look at the file formats of the content and of the final product. The product may work well on the device used for creation, but you need to also consider the following:

- When the user accesses the product and the content, it needs to be able to work in the same way on their platform or device as the way you intended when you created it.
- When you need to distribute the product, the content and product need to be able to be shared effectively with no impact on the product or the final user experience.

Performance of multimedia assets

Testing multimedia functions

Multimedia assets are likely to be a large part of your finished product and how they work will have a significant impact on the success of your product. Table 5.6 includes some examples of things you might want to think about when testing your media assets.

Table 5.6 Testing multimedia functions

Testing playback and appearance	The appearance of the asset. The size of the asset. The functionality of any asset play, pause and stop functions.
Testing volume and quality	The volume and volume controls for audio assets. The quality of audio and visual assets and the impact of using them on different devices.
Testing user controls	The ease with which the user can identify the controls needed to interact with the product. The functionality of the controls to ensure the product behaves as intended.

Activity

Write a list of things you would look for when planning **functionality** testing for an electronic food ordering app.

Techniques to review the fitness for purpose of completed interactive digital media

Suitability for client requirements

When creating an interactive digital media product, there will always be a set of client requirements that you are trying to meet to make sure your product is a success. As part of your testing you need to carefully consider how well you have met these requirements, including whether your product is fit for purpose. If you wrote a list of success criteria, this would be an excellent time to use them as the key points to test against. You could also look at drawing up a list of strengths and weaknesses for your product and use these as a structure for this part of your testing.

Suitability for target audience

How suitable your product is for your target audience is also a consideration when testing. As well as usability you will also need to consider things such as:

- Suitability of content: You need to consider the characteristics of your target audience and think about whether the content of the product you have made meets the needs of the user.
- Accessibility: To be a success your product needs to be available to as many users as possible. You need to think about how people with different accessibility requirements might be able to access your product.

Review of audio-visual quality, aesthetics, appeal, interaction and engagement

The final consideration when testing is to look at the product as a whole. Now that you have looked at all the component parts you need to consider whether they work together and achieve the aim of the product. You could consider areas such as:

- Purpose
- Visual appeal
- Interactivity
- User engagement.

Synoptic links

You can find further information about this topic in Unit R093, Sections 2.1, 2.5, 3.4 and 4.2.

3.2 Improvements and further developments

When you have reviewed your work, the final section in this topic area is to think about what may have constrained your interactive digital media, how you could potentially improve the interactive digital media and what scope there is for further development.

Constraints which limit the effectiveness of interactive digital media

A constraint is something that restricts or limits the way a task can be carried out. There are usually a range of different constraints which can impact a project such as the ones you will carry out for this unit. Here are some things you may have come across which might have limited your project or that are useful to be aware of for future projects.

- Time: The amount of time you had to complete the project may have been a constraint, but your skills in time management and how you used your time within the project will also have impacted.
- Resources: This could relate to any item you need to do your project that was perhaps unavailable or in short supply, which may have impacted the quality of your final interactive digital media product. This could also include elements such as the budget for your product creation and any restrictions this could put on your product creation.
- Hardware: As with resources, the availability of hardware that you would have liked to use or perhaps a choice of hardware which did not work out as you hoped will have impacted your final work.
- Software: Again, this may have been the choices of software you had available to you and how well they allowed you to carry out your plan or how the software you chose impacted on your final product.
- Skills: Some of the skills you needed for the project may have been more of a challenge than you originally thought or you may have been limited in the time needed to master the skills required – both of which could have impacted on the final interactive digital media product.

When thinking about the constraints of your project it is important to consider not just what the constraints may have been but also what their impact was, for example did they prevent you from adding a particular asset to your product, change the way you implemented interactivity or limited the quality of a certain element so your plans were not reflected? Reflecting carefully on the impact of any constraints of a project will help you consider the next part of this topic area – improvements.

Activity

Think of a task you have carried out in a lesson recently. With a partner, discuss what constraints you experienced that may have impacted on how well you completed this task. Can you think of any ways that you could overcome those constraints in the future?

Interactive digital media improvements

Looking at the results of your testing and constraints of the project will help a lot when it comes to consideing how you might improve your product if you have the opportunity to do so. There are a lot of things you could consider for improvements, such as:

- Quality: This could relate to the overall quality of the product but also to individual elements such as layout, visual appearance or the functions of the product itself.
- Content and concept: You could think about potential improvements to the main concept of your product but also think about individual pieces of content and how they could be improved to add to the finished product.
- Overall style and design: This could include looking at consistency but also considering the needs of your target audience and how the style and design might be improved to better suit their needs.
- Animation/video/audio: You could also consider the performance and content of multimedia elements. There could be potential considerations in terms of the controls used and the quality and suitability of the assets for use in the product.

For all your changes it is really important to justify how the improvements improve the end product – whether this means that the product better meets the client brief or is more engaging to the target audience, your improvements should all be made with the aim of increasing the success of the product.

Further development opportunities for digital media

As well as any improvements you might make to a product, if a product is successful there is often the opportunity to make further developments or to create additional products which expand on the original concept, sometimes with a different aim or audience in mind. A successful product may also lead to a request from your client to do some further work for them, either building on the original product or on a different project. Consider what you could do if you had different resources or a different budget, for example.

- Scope: If a success then there could be the opportunity to expand the scope of the original product. If the product were a game this might mean creating a sequel or spin off game. If the product provided information about a museum exhibit, it might mean creating different products to run in other exhibit kiosks, for example.
- Additional multimedia elements: Once the product has been used for a while, you might consider adding different elements to the product to increase the range of multimedia assets it uses. For example, you might have used animation in the original version and may have the opportunity to add some recorded video footage to increase the range of content in the product.

Figure 5.10 Cinema ticketing uses a range of different interactive products for use on different devices

- More or different interactivity: When you conduct your testing and look at any constraints on your project it is likely that you will have find areas for development in terms of interactivity. You might want to add some interactive elements to areas that are more static or change a fairly simple level of interaction to something more complex, such as voice activation.
- Altering the product type: One way that you may develop a product further is to think about how you might alter the design to work on different devices. For example, if you have a kiosk-based product could you adapt this to work as an app for a mobile device to target a different audience? You might also expand your product range to include accompanying documents and product such as a website to accompany an app or game, or a magazine or comic which builds on the content of your product – the range of options is huge!

Synoptic link

You can find further information about this topic in Unit R093, Section 4.1.

Assignment practice

Task 3

Time needed: 1–2 hours

Using the brief for Task 2, create a plan for reviewing the technical effectiveness of the interactive product and its component parts.

Unit R098

Visual imaging

About this unit

Photographs and video are widely used in the media industry for different purposes. In this unit you will develop your skills in taking photographs, recording video and editing these to create portfolios of images and video sequences.

Nearly all digital cameras can capture both high quality photographs and HD or 4K video. Although smartphones are commonly used as a camera, a professional photographer/videographer can use advanced settings and apply different techniques. They will be able to control the subject, scene and lighting to produce something extra special in both photographs and video, using a DSLR or CSC/mirrorless cameras. You will learn about the technical and visual concepts that help create high quality images and video sequences.

Topic areas

In this chapter you will learn how to:

- plan visual imaging portfolios (TA1)
- create visual imaging portfolios (TA2)
- review visual imaging portfolios (TA3).

Resources for this unit

Hardware/equipment: Digital cameras, for example mirrorless CSC, DSLR and compact (not just smartphones), capable of recording both photographs and digital video.

Software: Photo editing and video editing applications are needed, for example Adobe Photoshop, Lightroom, Luminar, Affinity Photo, Photopea or Apple Photos. At the time of writing, open-source free applications include Rawtherapee, Darktable, Irfanview and Gimp. For video editing, examples include Adobe Premiere, Final Cut, Apple iMovie with open-source applications Shotcut and OpenShot.

How will I be assessed?

You will complete an assignment that is set by OCR. This will be completed independently by yourself, without using any additional resources or teacher assistance to help you. The assignment will have a scenario or client brief that defines what you will need to create. You will work through a series of tasks that cover the three topic areas to plan, create and review a visual imaging portfolio. Your evidence will then be marked by your teacher using the OCR marking criteria, which will be externally checked/moderated by OCR to confirm your achievement.

Topic area 1 Plan visual imaging portfolios

Getting started

Find out what image capture devices can do. If you have a digital camera or smartphone, what are the specifications for photographs and video? What resolutions and formats does it support? You should include any school equipment cameras in this activity. You could collect information or create a mind map or table of the main features and capabilities.

1.1 Features and conventions of photographic images and videos

Features and conventions of photographic images

Composition

Key term

Composition (photography) The way that a photograph is framed to be suitable and appealing for the viewer.

Taking a photograph in a work-based context is often about the intended purpose, which can be different to taking photographs for personal use. The first decision for the **composition** should consider how and where the photograph will be used. For example, if creating a photograph for the front cover of a magazine, you would turn the camera into a portrait/vertical orientation instead of landscape/horizontal.

Another example is when to include blank space for adding copy (a term used for the main body text on a magazine or book page). Thinking about the magazine front cover, you might need to include a clean background for the magazine title and so would have the top quarter of the image as a clear blue sky.

Figure 6.1 Alternative compositions – one of which is suitable for a magazine cover

Purposes and uses

The basic composition of photographic images will vary depending on what type of product or image the photograph will be used for. Some examples include:

- Specific products: Think about the orientation and shape. For example, magazine covers, calendars, greeting cards, CDs, billboards, product packaging.
- Abstract: This is where the image is not intended to be an accurate representation of what it actually is. Instead, the image is something that allows the viewer to imagine what it is, or what it means; possibly something unreal. One way to achieve this is with close ups since they don't give an overall or complete picture.
- Promotion: Advertising of a product is the main area to consider. That means the main product must be the focal point and stand out to the viewer (the rest of the picture could be blurred or out of focus).
- Documentary: In some ways, the opposite of abstract. A documentary photograph should show something exactly how it is. It could be a collection of photographs of an old building to produce a historical record.

Depending on the purpose of the photoshoot, you might need to compose the same scene in different ways. In practice, you might take a series of photographs with different compositions: portrait, landscape, with blank/white space at the top, bottom or side. You might then also be able to sell the photograph to different places for different purposes.

Activity

Search the internet using the term 'product photography'. You can categorise the results by 'images', rather than 'all'. Review two different types of result – one for how the photographs should be taken using a miniature studio on a tabletop and the second, the style of the actual photographs that are taken.

Make sure you find examples that are in both portrait and landscape orientation. You should also look at how and where the photographs are used e.g. in creating an advertisement with space for extra information.

Use and placement of props

A prop is an item that is placed in a photographic scene that gives meaning or purpose to the image. Props are not the main subject but add to or enhance an existing scene. Some examples include:

- A vase of flowers on a kitchen table for a house that is being advertised for sale, which suggests a homely environment.

- A drink on a table in a garden, to enhance a summer lifestyle shot.
- A picture or book on a shelf, where the content of the picture or title of the book is carefully chosen to give the intended meaning.
- A pair of muddy football boots at the side of somebody enjoying a cold drink, suggesting it is refreshing after a good game.

In general, the use of props can improve the visual impact and create meaning in a photograph because they can connect with the viewer in a particular way.

Synoptic link

See R093, Section 2.5 for how content and media codes work together to convey meaning, create impact and engage audiences.

Visual style

A large part of the visual style is decided when taking the photograph. This can be further enhanced in the editing, which you'll look at later.

The visual style of a peaceful scene will be different to one that is full of action. Altering the visual style can let you change a conventional, everyday kind of photo into something quite different, for example, including some movement in the foreground and using a low camera angle for dramatic effect. The visual style is linked to what message or meaning we want to get across. You can also think about what camera features and settings could be used. This includes:

- colour settings, for example vivid colour, monochrome
- lens angle of view, for example normal, wide angle, telephoto
- **shutter speed**, for example slow shutter speed, fast shutter speed
- camera angle, for example ground level, eye level for animals, impact on perspective

You will learn more about choosing equipment, settings and camera angles later in this unit.

Key term

Shutter speed The duration that the shutter is open for the photograph to be recorded.

We can characterise the visual style in a number of different ways:

- Conventional, for example a documentary style shot of the scene 'as-is'.
- Dramatic, for example close-up emotion, colour saturation (high or low), adding a colour cast, black and white (monochrome)
- Eerie, for example can be achieved with mist and fog.
- Serene, for example can be achieved with long exposure.
- Dynamic action, for example close-up scenes of sports such as running, cycling, skiing.

Test your knowledge

1 Imagine you have two different photographs of mountain biking. One is an action shot on a trail. The other shows a bike on the ground at sunset. Both are about bikes, but the content and visual impact is very different. How would you categorise the two different shots and what meaning does it suggest for the viewer?

Lighting effects

Many photographs can be improved by controlling or changing the lighting. One option is to add a bit of extra light such as using electronic flash. You might also block some natural light and create shadows (an example would be a slatted blind on a window with sunlight shining through). Some of the following techniques can be used with natural lighting to produce a different visual effect:

- Front lit (where the main light is behind the camera and directly onto the front of the subject).
- Back lit (where the main light is behind the subject and in front of the camera).
- Highlighted, for example use of electronic flash to highlight a particular area within the scene.

- Additional lighting with a specialised colour (for example, using red, blue or green coloured gels).
- Outdoor landscapes photographs in golden hour or blue hour (these have a special quality to the lighting).

Figure 6.2 A view of London during blue hour , shutter speed 1/30s, f5, ISO 1600

Activity

Use any camera that you have available. Choose one of the following themes and take photographs to show two different visual styles on the same theme.

- Transport
- School or home life
- Hobbies and interests

Features and conventions of video sequences

There are several areas to consider when recording video. The choices and options are often determined by what the video will be used for. For example, the needs of a news article will be different to a film trailer. To start, let's review the main features for recording video footage.

Camera work

The main two aspects are:

- camera shot
- camera movement.

Camera shots

This is about how much of the scene is included in the frame.

The impact and meaning of different camera shot types is summarised as follows. Note that these are the main examples and not a complete list of camera shots that are used in film making. Keep in mind that the impact and meaning is also defined by the content of the scene.

Extreme long shot XLS

Long shot LS

Mid shot MS

Medium closeup MCU

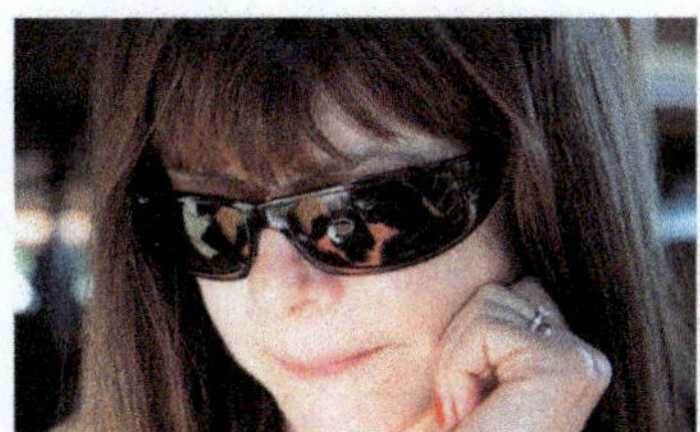

Closeup CU

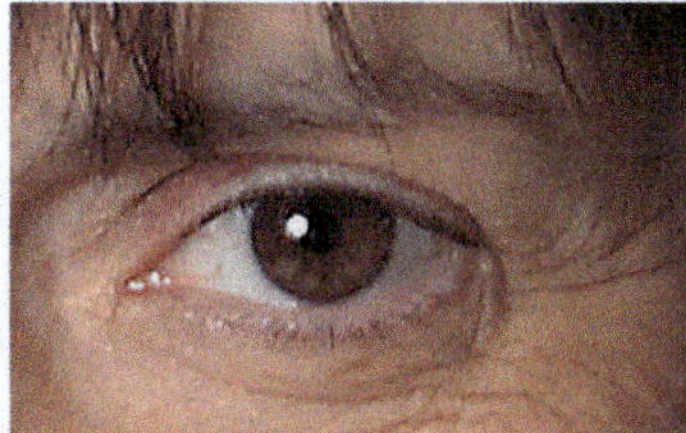

Extreme closeup XCU

Figure 6.3 Video camera shot types

Table 6.1 Types of video camera shots and their impact and meaning

Shot	Description	Impact	Meaning
Extreme long shot (XLS), establishing or wide shot	Taken from a distance and show the overall scene or setting	Give a context for the overall theme of the video or the environment for a particular scene	Displays the scale of a scene to show the viewer where the video or scene is set
Long shot (LS) or full shot	Slightly closer, shows some detail of what is happening. People are seen full length (from head to toe)	Introduces a scene so that the viewer develops an overview	Typically, the mood of the video, e.g. peaceful, calm or action based
Mid shot (MS) or medium shot	More detail in what is happening. People are seen with the upper half of the body	Viewer engages with what is happening and feels like they are part of the action	Can be defined by what else is in the scene (see mise-en-scene later). Viewer imagines what is just outside of the frame
Medium close-up (MCU)	Shows the head and shoulders of people, e.g. where two people are talking to each other	Engages the viewer by showing some detail and expressions	Expressed by the emotion and reaction seen in the people's faces and upper body posture
Close-up shot (CU)	Shows just the person's face. A more intimate shot, with more detail, emotion and expressions	Pulls the viewer into what is happening, whether they like it or not	Expressed by the emotion seen in the people's faces or detailed action (whether good or bad)
Extreme close-up shot (XCU)	Shows very small details such as a person's eyes, mouth, finger or a similar close-up of an object or prop	More informative for the viewer since they don't have the bigger picture	How things work, the mechanism, detail or process

Note that camera shot abbreviations can also be added to a storyboard to give a guide to what is wanted when recording and editing the video. Setting up the different shots is covered later in Section 2.3.

If you want the viewer to have an awareness of the content, long shots work well. If you want the viewer to learn, engage and be attentive with the content, mid shots are a good choice. If you want the viewer to have emotional reactions, close-up and extreme close-up shots can be both informative and powerful.

The terminology used for shot types is different for video and photography. For example, photographs of a person would normally be a portrait, whether full length or half-length, whereas in video shots, these would be described as a long shot (LS) and mid shot (MS) respectively. A macro shot in photography would be an XCU in video.

Camera angles

The main two options are high angle and low angle. These can be used to give meaning to the shot:

- High angle: Looking down on the subject or person, giving a feeling of superiority, for example.
- Low angle: Looking up at the subject or person, giving a feeling of being inferior, for example.

Camera movement

The second part of camera work is about any movement of the camera while recording video footage. These are typically done with the camera on a tripod although 'image stabilisation' (IS) makes this possible when hand holding.

There are different ways and directions to move the camera, many of which can be used even when the camera is on a tripod.

- Pan: Where the camera is slowly rotated from left to right (or right to left). Best used on a tripod to minimise any vertical movement. It is used to show distance between different people or objects and the scale of the scene.
- Tilt: Where the camera is slowly tilted vertically up or down. Also best used on a tripod to minimise any erratic movement. It can be used to show the size and scale of an object.
- Zoom: A feature of the lens is used to zoom in or out (getting closer or further away in the frame but without moving the camera).

Moving position includes any kind of motion to move the camera from one place to another while recording video. A simple example would be walking with the camera, although this tends to look poor as there is a lot of up/down movement due to walking characteristics. If you do try walking with the camera, aim to keep the camera as steady as possible in your hands.

A track and dolly is a separate piece of equipment to minimise the up/down walking motion. The camera is mounted on a dolly that has wheels and placed on a track (similar to a railway track but smaller). The dolly is then pushed along the track while recording the video. An example would be following a 100 m sprint at an athletics event to keep up with the runners. In terms of creating meaning, this helps to make the viewer part of the action as if they were there in person.

Another form of movement is commonly seen using GoPro and other action cameras, which can be mounted to a helmet for outdoor activities such as mountain biking or skiing. These are used as a first person shot in live action to give the viewer a feeling for what it would be like to be there. Most video shots otherwise are a third person, so more like a casual observer.

Camera orientation

This is a basic technique to ensure the orientation of the camera is suitable. When taking photographs, the camera can equally be in either a portrait/vertical or landscape/horizontal orientation. However, when recording video, the convention is still that it is landscape/horizontal. If recording video with a smartphone there is a natural instinct to record in a vertical/portrait orientation but that is of limited use when editing video footage and creating video products. Hence you should always try to record video in a landscape/horizontal orientation.

Lighting

This can be used to record something that is true to life or as a powerful tool to create a mood, theme, focus or alternative style to the video.

A long shot is more likely to include ambient (or natural) lighting. It records the scene as you would see it. Lighting can be used to create a mood or have more impact and engagement with the viewer. Extra lighting can be added to emphasise the main action so the camera exposure is correct for what the viewer should be looking at, with the rest of the scene darker. This is known as spot lighting – or lighting a particular spot that the viewer should be looking at for emphasis.

Use of in-camera audio

When preparing to record video, think about how important it will be to record the sound at the same time. Digital video cameras have built-in microphones, but you will need to check the audio recording levels to make sure the volume is high enough. An example would be an interview where the speech is an essential part of the recording. In many situations, recording audio at the same time can enhance the visual content to give it more impact and meaning. Some examples would be the sound of wind and rain, traffic, animals, rivers and waves. However, not all video recordings will need sound recorded at the same time as it can be added in post-production, such as a music track.

Post-production techniques

Post-production is defined as the video editing after the recording or production of the video footage. This allows the video editor to structure the video in an appropriate way for the type of product, enhancing the final sequence with titles, graphics and transitions as needed.

Structure

Different types of video product will have a different structure to the content and storytelling depending on the purpose. The structure, content and sequence are adapted to different types of video product, such as:

- Advertisements: Promoting products and services, seen on TV, social media, YouTube, Vimeo. Key information may include what it is, how much and where it can be bought from.
- Tutorials: Often a teaching resource, popular on YouTube. Key information is some sort of walkthrough on how to do something.
- Film trailers: Promoting the release of a new film, seen on TV, social media, YouTube, and dedicated websites related to the film. Key information will be a teaser for the film content plus film name, main actors and release date.

A commonly used approach for many videos is a basic three-part structure with a clear beginning, main content and ending. Some considerations would be:

- Beginning: Is there (and does it need) an introduction? In general, you should typically include a title to explain what the video is all about.
- Main content: This will link to the brief and what you want to show.
- Ending: Think about summarising the message of the video, using a punchline for example. This is also where the credits are shown.

The decision on the structure is related to the platform and medium. For example, if creating a news article, you probably want just the main content since the introduction will be covered by the news presenter. However, if creating a video for YouTube, you probably want to include both an introductory title and closing credits and links. In general, there are some conventions to follow for different types of video sequence, although like the rules of photography these can be broken at times. However, the breaking of rules has to be done in a careful and considered way.

Key characteristics of video products

Synoptic link

More information on the use of technical, symbolic and written codes is found in R093, Section 2.5. These should be chosen to match the type of product and target audience.

After deciding the structure for the video sequence, some thought can be given to what post-production techniques are needed for the type of product.

Additions to the main video and added when editing include:

- Titles: Can be used at the start of the video and sometimes at different points within the video.
- Graphics: Can be logos or the visual identity for the producer of the video, which can be static or motion graphics.

Table 6.2 Features and characteristics of video products

Type of video product	Features and characteristics
Journalism/news article	Factual representation, typically short, around 20–30 seconds, often with voiceover, no music or SFX, no title or credits, some consumer journalism clips, presenter direct to camera, on location, interviews using ots (over the shoulder) shots, cuts to build the story, strap lines with summary, publisher/news agency graphics to show who produced the material
Sports event coverage	May have full coverage of the entire event, multiple cameras, live broadcasts plus highlights as short features, sports commentator as voiceover
Documentary	Includes a range of shots – long, mid and close-up, commentary, often with titles, credits, possibly interviews, group meetings, following an investigative story, captions for facts, good lighting
Film genres	Examples would be sci fi, romantic, thriller/suspense, drama. Use of music, lighting effects (side and dark for suspense films), opening title, actor names, closing credits. Music genre to match the action and film genre

- Special effects: Can be added anywhere in the video sequence. Simple effects can be colour changes, lighting enhancements or sounds. More complex special effects are usually included as CGI.

Transitions

This is about how one scene transforms or changes into the next scene. They are applied in between the different video clips that were recorded. If no transition effect is applied, it would be seen as a jump cut. Examples of transition effects in the video editing software are:

- Mix/dissolve: Where one video clip transforms into the next over a short duration, without introducing a plain colour such as black. A mix/dissolve is usually completed in 1–2 seconds.
- Fade: Where the clip is changed to gradually fade into a plain colour, typically black or sometimes white. This can be used as a fade in, for example from black to the video or fade out to black, for example from the video clip to a completely black frame. Fades are also a fairly short duration (around 1–2 seconds) although a fade at the end of a video is sometimes maintained at black before the credits are scrolled up.
- Wipe: Typically a sideways movement of one clip to bring in the next but other directions of movement are included in this category.

A jump cut tends not to be intrusive as long as it isn't mid action so be careful where this is used. This is the most common type of transition. It can be used to create a more dramatic or shocking effect depending on the content of the next scene. An example would be a peaceful scene that then jumps to some dramatic close-up action. Fades, such as a fade to black, conveys meaning to the viewer that the scene is coming to an end. An example could be the end of one day and then fading into another scene for the following morning. A mix/dissolve is a gentler way of moving the attention of a viewer into the next scene, without any sudden changes to the mood or meaning.

Platform and medium related conventions

The conventions of these do vary, depending on the platform (what hardware) and the medium (what/where/how they are viewed). This is why you should think about the platform and distribution channel used by the audience to view the video. Some considerations include:

- platform used, for example TV screen, smartphone, tablet or computer
- distribution method, for example broadcast TV or streamed over the internet
- host platform, for example submitted to a YouTube, Vimeo or TikTok channel.

You should also consider the resolution of the platform (for example, 4K, HD, SD). It would be disappointing for the audience to have a low-resolution SD video if viewing it on a 4K screen and won't leave a good impression. On the other hand, a 4K video may not stream smoothly over some low bandwidth internet connections. Hence you would need to export the video at a suitable resolution for how it is going to be used.

Another consideration will be the orientation of the video. Convention is that video is always a landscape/horizontal format although some social media feeds are more tolerant of different orientations. An example here is Instagram, which displays portrait style video in the usual (vertical) orientation. However, remember that we are not looking to create personal content for social media – we will focus on what is used in the commercial or work-based world.

Synoptic links

More information on distribution platforms can be found in R093, Section 4.1.

More information on video file formats can be found in R093, Section 4.2.3.

Activity

Watch a series of video clips. These should include TV advertisements, film trailers and news clips. List the key features and characteristics for each one. Look for opening titles, captions, use of special effects and any transitions used in between scenes.

Creativity in photography and video

Originality

Original work means it is something new that isn't a copy of what somebody else has done before. It can be difficult to know if something is original without investigating what others have done. One option in this unit is to complete a web search with image and video results. Your search field could be the location or subject. Based on the results of that, originality would need something different.

In photography, it might be different viewpoints, lens choices, lighting or use of filters. In video, it might be different shots, viewpoints, camera movement, lighting, editing and storytelling.

Imaginative concepts

Originality can be achieved as a result of developing your own creative ideas. Positioning of props or people within a shot can transform a popular landscape shot into something that has a different impact and meaning. Lighting can also transform a shot, such as adding some fill-in flash to a specific subject or object in the frame. In video recordings, using different angles can also make the visual impact dramatically different. For example, this could be framing the shot from ground level rather than eye level when stood up.

With any imaginative concepts, you should always keep in mind the conventions of composition but experiment with your own creative ideas of when and where they can be changed. The more you specialise in one area of photography, the more imaginative ideas and concepts you will begin to develop for yourself.

Derivative ideas

These start with an existing idea and adapt it to some extent, meaning it will not be completely original but still a different style to what has been done before. For example, you might see a photo of a particular landscape at sunrise and take your own version. The weather and composition will be different, and the result could be seen as a derivative or extension of what has been done before. In video, you may be inspired by a sequence at a skate park or mountain biking trail. A derivative might be taken at a more local venue. To develop your own derivative ideas, you could research the work of other people first and then apply some ideas generation of your own.

Synoptic link

More information on developing ideas can be found in R093, Section 3.2 (using mood boards and mind maps).

1.2 Content used in visual imaging portfolios

Physical content of recorded video

This refers to the items that are used and typically seen within recorded video. In this unit, a video scene could be made using a combination of people, props and the set where they are placed.

This is slightly different and often more involved than taking a photograph even though some photographic projects would also aim to manage the entire scene in a similar way. When planning a video, the following considerations should be included:

- People: Who will be in the scene and what will they say and/or do? Actors will need a script to learn their lines. They will also need to know what action is needed – or what they do and where they move during the recording.
- Props: See earlier in this chapter – it is the placement of objects within the scene.
- Set: This is a place where the video is to be recorded. It might be a studio set with a background or alternatively, a place in an outdoor location. A set may be static and all the action carried out in front of it.
- Scenes: This covers the content of the video clip that is to be recorded. It might include a set but can be much broader to allow for movement of the camera and different shots for a specific part of the intended video.

Activity

Firstly, choose a suitable theme, such as your local town/city (your teacher will be able to suggest alternative themes). Create a mood board of photographic images using a web search. This gives a record of what has been done before. Secondly, in a small group create a mind map to generate new ideas to take different photographs, whether the same location with different light and composition, or somewhere new.

Assets

This refers to types of assets and where they are sourced.

- Audio and sounds: This includes the audio that was recorded along with the video together with any additional audio tracks and sounds in post-production. Examples would be sound effects, music and voiceovers.
- Motion graphics: Some video products will have an introduction, for example a film studio, which is typically created as a motion graphic. This is basically a graphic that can be animated to include movement of one more parts.
- Recorded footage: This is expected to be the main part of the video that is being created. It is what you physically record using a digital video camera.
- Sourced/stock footage: In addition to the recorded footage, some video products may be supported by stock footage that is sourced from the internet or other locations. This can be inserted into the main video sequence to clarify or explain an aspect of the content. An example would be some original footage of a historical event when producing a modern documentary.

Activity

In an earlier activity, you looked at the main features and characteristics of different video clips and how they are put together. Now watch a series of videos in different categories and make notes on the different content that is used. Examples are people, props, sets and other assets. In a small group, discuss why these could be very different depending on the type of video product.

1.3 Equipment for capturing images and video

Technical capabilities of camera equipment and accessories

Photographic image capture

The technical capabilities are set by the type of camera and the features/specification. To begin, let's look at the different types of digital camera.

CSC or mirrorless

Compact System Camera: A modern type of digital camera that uses an electronic viewfinder to display the output from the image sensor. Also has interchangeable lenses like a DSLR but is smaller, lighter and with a different lens mount. Has a wide range of photographic settings. Battery life is not as good as a DSLR, but they have more advanced systems for focusing in different situations and subjects.

DSLR

Digital Single Lens Reflex: The traditional digital camera for professional and keen amateur use. Has interchangeable lenses and a wide range of settings available. It uses an optical viewfinder (with mirrors and lenses to look through) and generally has an excellent battery life before needing to recharge. Quite large and heavy compared to other options.

Compact

A smaller digital camera, which tends to be an upgrade from a smartphone and yet fairly easy to carry around. Has a range of automatic modes plus manual selection of various settings but the lens cannot be changed. At a more advanced level, includes bridge or prosumer cameras that are a type of compact camera, with more settings and typically, a wide-ranging zoom lens. This category includes specialist cameras such as GoPro, drone and other rugged or waterproof cameras. Battery life tends to be quite short. A large part of this market has been taken over by smartphone cameras.

Figure 6.4 Top to bottom: mirrorless CSC, DSLR and camcorder digital cameras

Video camera

A dedicated video camera or camcorder will have a facility to capture still images. This might be a good option if you want to primarily capture video footage with the occasional still image. Video cameras may use an SD card to store digital video files or older models may use a MiniDV tape. However, DSLR or CSC have taken over a large part of this market, being able to record both high quality video and photographic images.

Smartphone

While very popular for everyday photography, these have minimal settings that can be adjusted (although some apps have modes that simulate similar effects). In general, these are quite basic for this unit but do have the ability to capture photographs and video using automatic settings. Small and lightweight, smartphones are nearly always carried, and results are good on modern versions when viewed on a small screen. However, as a point and shoot camera, their use is more appropriate as general knowledge for consumer use. For work-based photography and video recording you will need to learn in detail about equipment, settings and techniques for the higher levels of achievement.

Image quality

There are several factors that affect the image quality, covering the equipment and settings that are chosen.

Pixel count

This is typically expressed as a number of megapixels or 'Mp'. Some common examples would be 8Mp, 12Mp, 16Mp, 24Mp, 36Mp and 48Mp, with higher quality cameras having the larger pixel count. Using the example of a 24Mp camera, this may have an image sensor that is around 6000 pixels wide by 4000 pixels high (multiplying 6000 by 4000 gives you 24 million pixels). Using an optimal 300dpi for printing, a 24Mp image could be printed at 20" x 13.3". In reality it can be larger than this when taken on a good DSLR or CSC since the limiting factor in image quality might be the small sensor and/or lens if using other types of camera.

The main two equipment factors in addition to number of pixels are the physical size of the sensor and the quality of the lens. These vary depending on the type of camera and model.

Lenses for use with CSC and DSLR

Even DSLR lenses vary considerably in what resolution they can support and consumer grade lenses might limit the image quality on something like a 48Mp camera body.

Table 6.3 Sensor types and their characteristics

Sensor type	Characteristics
Full frame sensors: 36 mm x 24 mm (used with DSLR and CSC)	Enable higher quality images with less noise in poor lighting conditions
Crop sensors: DX or APS-C: around 24 mm x 16 mm (used with DSLR and CSC)	Offer good quality images and extend the focal length of the lens, multiplying it by around 1.5 (useful for wildlife and sports photography)
Smartphone sensors: varies but in the region of 7 x 4.5 mm	Being quite small, can have more noise in poor lighting although in-camera image processing has improved in recent years

Compact cameras and smartphones might be suitable for a small print or online use, but work-related or commercial use tends to need something better.

The focal length of the lens determines the angle of view (how much of the scene is in the photograph).

- Standard zoom: This might be something like an 18–55 mm on a crop sensor camera body or 28–85 mm on a full frame camera body. Both have the same field of view (a feature of the sensor in the camera rather than the focal length of the lens).
- Wide angle: This gives a much wider angle of view than the standard zoom range.
- Telephoto: This gives a very narrow field of view, so it appears that you have 'zoomed' in to magnify something in the scene.

Note that some cameras such as smartphones may have a digital zoom feature, which just enlarges the middle section of the image at the expense of resolution. This is not the same as a DSLR or CSC zoom lens.

Activity

Make a list of what cameras you have access to. Think about any you have plus those from family, friends and school. Include comments on what you know about the cameras and what features they have. List the main specifications in terms of image resolution, video formats, frame rates and lens focal length(s).

Figure 6.5 Angle of view using different focal lengths

Technical capabilities of accessories

Some of the different accessories you may use includes lenses, filters, tripods and flashguns.

- Lenses: On CSC and DSLR you have the option to change the lens. This could be for a different focal length, zoom range or potentially a macro lens. Apart from the focal length, the other key feature of the lens is the maximum **aperture** (the lowest f number that is possible). By having an f1.8 or f2.8 lens, you will be able to take photographs in lower light or have less **depth of field** than a lens with a maximum aperture of f4 or f6.3.
- Filters: These attach to the front of the lens, with a screw-in thread. Many effects can be added in post-production editing except for a polarising filter and long exposures with a neutral density filter.
- Tripods: With very slow shutter speeds, night photography and some landscapes, the use of a tripod can stabilise the camera to minimise camera movement and produce sharper photographs.

Key terms

Aperture The size of the opening in a lens that lets light pass through to the camera sensor.

Depth of field The range of distances from the camera that are in sharp focus.

- Flashguns: These usually attach to the top of the camera although can also be positioned off camera. They are frequently used in low light (indoors and outdoors) but also during brighter daylight as fill-in flash.

Types of additional/external lighting:

- Flash: Has a very short duration, used with photography.
- Continuous: Is constantly 'on' and used with video.

Video camera equipment for recording

When choosing your video camera, you should know its capabilities in terms of video formats, display resolution and aspect ratio.

Figure 6.6 Selecting the video properties in the camera menu

The video resolution and frame rate are typically linked as a choice within the camera menu.

Video format/resolution

Depending on the camera some of the formats Table 6.4 may be available.

When the format/resolution is described in numerical terms, such as 480p, 720p, 1080p or 2160p then these refer to the vertical resolution in pixels.

Figure 6.7 Comparing video resolution

Video frame rate

The most common options (which may be linked to the format/resolution) in a camera menu are likely to be:

- 25 fps
- 30 fps
- 50 fps
- 60 fps.

Fps is the number of 'frames per second'.

TV in the UK uses 25 fps. Recording video at 50 fps or 60 fps can be useful when there is a lot of rapid movement and you want it to look very smooth. This gives more scope for slow motion effects later on in the editing.

- Video aspect ratio: This is linked to the format/resolution. However, there is a pattern to them such as 4:3 or 16:9. In general, you don't need to be too concerned and are more likely to select a format/resolution rather than an aspect ratio.
- Video file format: When using a digital video camera, the recording options are likely to be either MOV or MP4.

Table 6.4 Video format/resolution

Format	Description
SD	Would be 480p (720 px wide x 480 px high). This is the standard resolution for DVD and an option for streaming services
HD	Would be 720p or 1080p. Using the example of full HD, this is 1920 px wide and 1080 px high. Blu-ray can use this resolution
4K/2160p	Is used in cinema as 4096 px wide x 2160 px high. In TV and display monitors, 4K is generally accepted as 3840 px wide x 2160 px high
8K/4320p	Is double the resolution of 4K, so for TV and monitors that would be 7680 px wide x 4320 high
3D/360	An option on specialised cameras that can record 3D footage or 360-degree panoramas

Both of these are compressed formats to balance out video quality and file size on the memory card. There are additional options when editing a video such as AVI and WMV, which you will learn about later in this unit.

Keep in mind that the recording capacity (and hence recording time) of the camera will be limited by the choice of format/resolution together with the storage capacity of the memory card. For example, a full HD video might be in the region of 150 MB–300 MB per minute. SD will be smaller, around 40–100 MB whereas 4K could be around 350–600 MB. Depending on the camera, file format and frame rate, the file size could be larger or smaller than these ranges, so it is worth checking the camera manual. At 4K resolution, an 8 GB card could easily be full with 15 minutes of video.

Most DSLR and CSC mirrorless cameras also tend to have a maximum recording time of 30 minutes. Video recording consumes significant power and can run a battery down very quickly. Make sure the battery is fully charged before heading out and try to take a spare battery if available.

1.4 Pre-production and planning documentation and techniques for photoshoots and video recordings

Pre-production documentation and planning techniques for photography and video recording

Before going straight out with your camera you will need to plan what you are going to do. This section is about planning the photoshoot so that you are clear about the purpose, together with the range of photographs and video that you want to get.

Hand drawn/written plans

Planning can take several different forms. An easy option is to summarise these on a piece of paper or notebook.

Your plan should cover:

- preparation including:
  - equipment choices
  - shot lists
  - storyboards
  - permissions and releases
  - weather forecasts
- travel to the photo location
- taking of the photographs
- recording of the video
- copying/transferring to a computer system
- workflow and editing of photographs and video
- export/publishing to a final portfolio
- checks on a final portfolio.

The theme of the photoshoot should be clearly defined. Examples would be for a wedding, landscape shoot, sport, nature, wildlife, portrait or urban architecture. One option is to use a mind map and put the theme of the photoshoot as the main activity. You should plan for the duration of the photoshoot, whether an hour or full day. Depending on weather and location you would then decide on what to wear and take with you. Your workflow will depend on the photograph file format (RAW or JPG), video format and what software you will use.

Synoptic link

Further information on permissions, model and property releases can be found in R093, Section 3.4.

Digitally created plans using software applications

In addition to hand drawn and written plans, some documents can be produced digitally using software applications. These include the use of:

- word processing, for example for scripts, shot lists, releases and permission forms
- spreadsheets, for example for workplans (but also an option for shot lists)
- storyboarding software applications for video pre-production.

Synoptic link

The use and content of scripts for a video can be found in R093, Section 3.3

The creation of a script and formatting it using layout conventions is best achieved using word processing software. Preparing a clearly formatted script for people to use in your video will make the process more straightforward and efficient.

Shot lists

You must be clear who wants the photograph and understand what it will be used for. The skill is to take a photograph that meets those requirements, which you can specify in a shot list.

One option is to identify any 'must get' photos and 'would like', for example a wedding will have a clear list of 'must get' shots. Other photoshoots will usually have a list of ideal shots such as the winner crossing the finishing line in a race or a natural smile in a portrait.

You may have a list of what you want to photograph but most shots and video footage might be based on what you actually see and have the opportunity to capture. These can produce good coverage of an event, but you should still have an idea of what you want in your shot lists before setting off. You can also annotate your shot list with camera settings and techniques, such as shutter speed, aperture and use of flash. A shot list can be basic or a form to fill in. An example of a form is shown here – you would add more rows as needed.

SHOT LIST		
Date/time:		
Location:		
Event/subject:		
	Photos	Video
1 Activity/people description		
2 Activity/people description		
3 Activity/people description		

Storyboard for video production

A storyboard should always be created for a video production before you go out and record your footage. It might be fairly basic but will still give a framework for what you need to record. Some video projects could be defined by a client, and you would normally produce a detailed storyboard for review and agreement. Once you have decided what the finished sequence will be like then you can fill in your video shot list.

A storyboard can be used for both the video recording and editing. You should consider what will be needed to tell the story of the event or activity. For example, this might have a three-part structure that starts with an establishing shot before including a range of shots and content and finishing with a static scene that fades to black with rolling credits.

Synoptic link

The content, layout and use of a storyboard for a video can be found in R093, Section 3.3.

Test your knowledge

2 You want to take photographs of a friend to use on a website to promote your photographic services. What document is needed to gain permission for this?

3 Make a list of what could go wrong if you are going to a wedding without any preparation or planning as the main photographer.

Pre-production documentation and planning for shots and video recording

Once you know what shots and video you will want, the next step is to plan how you will take/record them.

Location recce

For an outdoor location, you should try to visit the place where you will be taking photographs and recording video before the planned photoshoot. This allows you to complete a location recce, which is a way of recording key information.

Synoptic link

Further information on location recces is found in R093, Section 3.4.

Choice of viewpoint

The location recce should help you identify where the photos and video will be taken. From this you can start to develop ideas on what equipment you will need. For example, this might mean different lenses for a CSC or DSLR, possibly a tripod and/or flashgun. Sometimes your viewpoint will be decided by what equipment you have available. Hence, if you don't have telephoto lenses then you may have to get closer to the action.

Lighting considerations

In your planning you should also consider what the available lighting will be. You can do this by combining information from the location recce together with weather forecast information and the time of day when you will be taking your photographs and video. If the photoshoot will be near the start or end of the day, find out what sunrise and/or sunset times are. During these periods, the shadows will be longer with the sun low in the sky. Based on this information you can then decide whether any additional lighting could improve the image and video quality.

Table 6.5 Lighting considerations

Time/ location	Lighting consideration	Options for improvement
Sunrise/ sunset	Long shadows, poor lighting (fairly dim)	Additional lighting (flash or continuous video lights)
Bright sun (daytime)	Harsh shadows	Fill-in flash or use reflectors close to the subject
Indoors	Dark/poor lighting. Incandescent light sources (possible yellow cast)	Additional lighting, e.g. bounced flash, one or more video lights

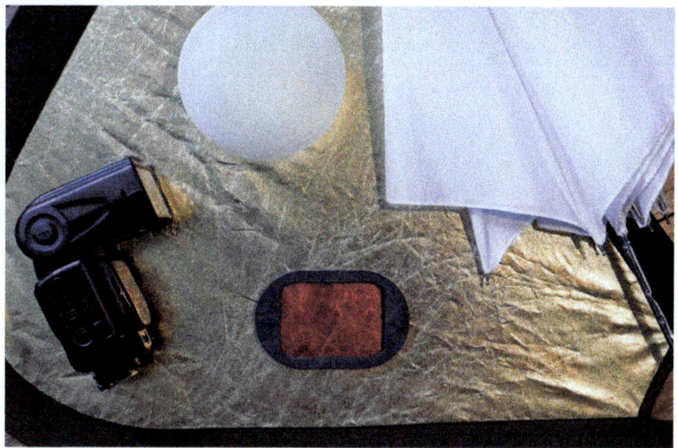

Figure 6.8 Additional light sources and reflectors

Pre-production documentation to assess and minimise hazards and risk

Risk assessment

Risk assessment can be completed for both indoor and outdoor locations. Examples would include a dedicated studio (indoors) or place where an event is being held. The risk assessment is typically completed after a location recce. Safe working practices may need to be identified so that the risks are minimised.

Synoptic link

Further information on risk assessments can be found in R093, Section 3.4.

Activity

Let's say that you have a task to take photographs promoting school sports. In small groups, discuss the following key points:

1. What will be the subject(s) in the photographs?
2. Where will the photographs be taken?
3. What features and settings of the camera will you want to use?

Topic area 2 Create visual imaging portfolios

Getting started

As a photographer, you might frequently take photographs at every opportunity that arises when you see something good. That is fine, but at other times you will need to plan a photoshoot. To start with, make a list of events and places that you will go to over the next week. Think about taking a camera to those places; make a list of what you might like to photograph and what video could be recorded.

2.1 Techniques and tools to take photographs

In this section you will start to learn about photographic concepts and how to get the best results from a digital camera. This does not mean leaving it on a fully automatic mode and using it as a point and shoot camera. By developing your understanding of camera features, you will know which would work well for different situations. By investigating the settings available, you will start to develop an understanding of what to use in different lighting situations.

Compositional choices for taking photographs

Think of these as guidelines rather than fixed rules since some people just can't wait to break the rules anyway. In reality, there are some established compositions that often work, and it is these basic concepts that we want to learn about. A selection of the basic 'rules', concepts and ideas are discussed here.

Rule of thirds

This is where you imagine the photograph to be divided by vertical and horizontal lines, which are at one third and two thirds distance apart, to create a grid with nine separate areas. The main points of interest can then be placed on the intersection of these lines inside the frame. A horizon can also be placed on the horizontal line that is on third from the top (or bottom) of the frame rather than straight across the middle. This is the most well-known 'rule' of photography but sometimes you can be a rebel and break the rule. The challenge is knowing when you can, or should, do that!

Figure 6.9 Using the rule of thirds

Leading lines

When composing the photograph, look for natural lines that draw the viewer into the frame, ideally starting at the lower left or right corner of the frame. These can be from a road, river, fence, path or similar object. Perspective is where lines converge such as a road or by standing underneath a bridge. A wide-angle lens often works well with this type of photograph.

Frames

This compositional technique is a way to focus the attention of the viewer so that there is less reason to think about the bigger picture and where the photograph was taken. The impact is to make the viewer look at what is within the frame, rather than wonder what is outside.

Orientation/viewpoint

There are two aspects to this. Firstly, the orientation of the camera as to whether it is horizontal or vertical. The second aspect is the viewpoint, whether high or low.

Figure 6.10 Leading lines and perspective

Figure 6.11 Using natural frames

Orientation will affect the potential use of the image, even though high-resolution cameras can be used by cropping the final image to be a portrait shape instead of the original horizontal shape.

Depending on who might use the photograph, try taking a photo in both orientations if possible. In between these is something called a Dutch angle or tilt, where the camera is held at an angle. Within a portfolio of images, try not to overdo the Dutch angle as a compositional approach – it can soon start to lose its appeal.

The viewpoint is where you take the photograph from. Most people take photos while standing up. Try getting low down to the floor or higher up than everybody else. This gives a different perspective that can make your photographs more eye catching and interesting.

Figure 6.12 Horizontal/portrait orientation

Composition for points of interest, anticipating movement

Points of interest can be either based on using the intersections in the rule of thirds or by encouraging the viewer's eye to be drawn to a specific point, for example by lines or frames. An example of some expected movement would be a person or animal running. When framing this type of shot, more space should be left in front of them than behind. What you don't want to do is have them positioned where they are just about to move out of the frame on one side.

Figure 6.13 Leaving space in front of the subject for them to move into

> **Activity**
>
> Search the web for more examples of compositional choices for taking photographs. The main ones are rule of thirds, using frames, leading lines but you will probably find other good examples using points of interest and different orientations. When you are ready, go out with a digital camera and try to apply each of the different compositional ideas. Store your photographs in your own personal folder for future reference.

Camera settings, techniques and choices for taking photographs

Exposure

An important technical part of taking photographs is getting the exposure correct. There are three factors which affect how bright or dark the photograph will be:

- shutter speed
- aperture
- **ISO**.

Exposure is basically a 'quantity' of light, which is determined by how long the shutter is open plus how large the aperture (hole) is in the lens to let the light through. Shutter speed and aperture are the core concepts, but the camera's ISO setting can shift these up or down.

Shutter speed

Shutter speed is the duration that the shutter is open to record the photograph. A fast shutter speed such as 1/1000s will 'freeze' most movement. Much slower than 1/60s becomes difficult to hold steady without camera shake with a standard focal length lens. The following list represents a difference of one exposure 'stop' in between each value. Notice that the time halves.

- 1/1000, 1/500, 1/250, 1/125, 1/60, 1/30, 1/15, 1/8, 1/4, 1/2, 1s

At higher focal lengths (telephoto) you will need a faster shutter speed to avoid camera shake, for example at 200 mm, you could use 1/250s. At wider focal lengths, you can use a slower shutter speed to avoid camera shake, for example at 28 mm, you could use 1/30th. Whatever the focal length, try to think of that as the minimum shutter speed (typically for a 12Mp resolution camera).

Nearly all modern digital cameras have some sort of built-in system to minimise movement of the camera at slow shutter speeds that would otherwise produce a blurred image because of camera shake. There are two main types of system to reduce this, which are referred to as vibration reduction (VR) and image stabilisation (IS). These are internal mechanisms in the camera or lens, which is a useful feature in dimly lit situations.

You should also consider whether your subject or scene is moving. If so, you may need a higher shutter speed to freeze the action. Examples would be people running, cycling, aircraft, animals, birds in flight. To avoid any blurred movement you might need 1/1000th or even 1/2000th second as the shutter speed. The quicker the subject is moving, the faster the shutter speed needed to freeze it.

Key term

ISO A camera setting that determines the sensitivity to light levels.

Figure 6.14 High shutter speed to freeze movement, 1/4000s, f4, ISO 1600

Aperture

Effectively this is the size of the hole or aperture in the lens that lets light through. A large aperture would be f1.4 and a small aperture f22.

- f1.4, f2, f2.8, f4, f5.6, f8, f11, f16, f22, f32

These are 1 exposure stop difference. Note that aperture number doubles every other value, for example f4 is 2 stops wider than f8.

Activity

This could be completed as a group activity or individually. If you haven't done so already, now is a good time to apply some of these settings and techniques. Using whatever camera you have available, take a set of photographs that has (a) moving subjects, for example cars on a road (b) stationary subjects, for example buildings. Try to include some close ups and wider (landscape) shots of the buildings with their different textures and features. You should aim to include the use of different shutter speeds, apertures ISO and lens focal length. Make any exposure adjustments where needed to make sure that you have taken a good shot.

The combination of shutter speed and aperture determines the exposure value. As an example, 1/250s at f8 gives the same exposure as 1/125s at f11 or 1/60s at f16.

The effect of the aperture will be on the depth of field. This is covered later in this chapter.

ISO

This is a camera setting that determines the sensitivity to different light levels. Higher ISO settings make the camera sensor more sensitive to light levels, which makes it possible to use faster shutter speeds or smaller apertures for greater depth of field. Changing the ISO will have two primary effects:

- It will change the exposure needed (the combination of shutter speed and aperture).
- At the higher end of the ISO range, the amount of noise in the photograph will increase. This is generally a bad thing and makes the photograph look a bit rough.

The performance of digital cameras at higher ISO has improved a lot over the last few years. It is now possible to get good results above an ISO value of 12,800 but that doesn't mean you should always go high, especially if wanting the best quality for large print use. The optimum ISO value will be the lowest value that allows you to use your preferred shutter speed and aperture, taking into account any movement and what depth of field is wanted.

Table 6.6 ISO

Photograph type	Subject	Possible ISO*
Sports	Fast action, movement	High: 1600–102,000
Low light	People, street scenes, buildings	Medium: 400–3200
Bright daylight	Landscapes	Low: 100–400

*Note that these are just examples and the optimum ISO might be very different.

How these are combined in exposure modes

Digital cameras have built-in light meters to measure how much light is in the scene. The light meter calculates what exposure is needed (exposure value or EV). The exposure mode affects the balance between shutter speed and aperture, sometimes setting one of these as the priority. Anything other than a very basic camera will have exposure modes as follows:

- P, S, A, M (used on Nikon, Sony and other cameras)
- Av, Tv (used on Canon cameras)
- Auto, scene.

See Table 6.7.

Auto ISO

This is a great feature in many situations but not all. You will need to know what the photograph will be used for. If social media, then fine to go up to a high ISO, otherwise for work based (print, commercial or stock use) then you should keep it to a low ISO. Otherwise, the quality may not be high enough and additional image processing may be needed to reduce luminance and colour noise. That is possible but outside the scope of this unit.

There will typically be extra features on CSC and some DSLR, but you should still understand the settings so you know when to select a feature and if it doesn't work, how to set up the shot yourself. The main technical aspects are the exposure and focus modes. After that, it's all about your composition.

With any camera, check the settings when picked up and before heading off for a photoshoot. This is still true for your own personal camera or one that is borrowed from somewhere else.

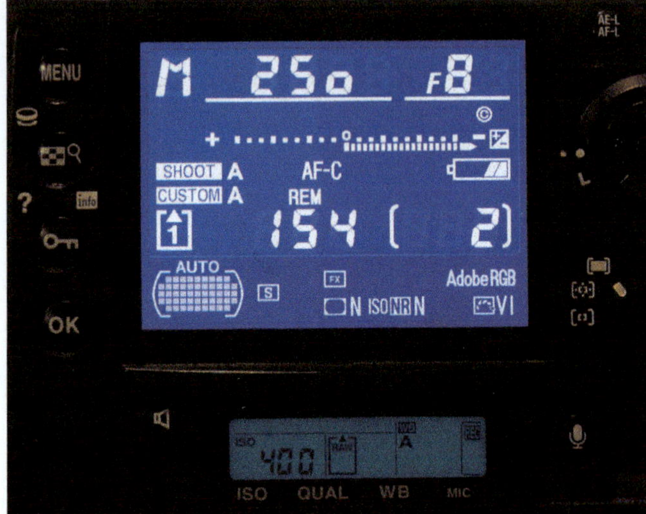

Figure 6.15 Camera settings 'info' display – check before taking photographs

Lens focal length

If you have a zoom lens attached to your camera, you will be able to change the magnification or angle of view. If you are some distance away, you might be able to 'zoom in' to the subject to take the photograph. Otherwise, you would have to move closer for a similar composition. If you wanted a wider angle of the scene, you could 'zoom out' with the lens or move further away. The zoom setting changes the focal length of the lens.

Table 6.7 Exposure modes

Mode	Type	Description
P or Auto	Fully automatic	This a programmed automatic mode where the camera selects both shutter speed and aperture. Generally suitable for point and shoot photography
S or Tv	Semi-automatic	Shutter priority mode. The photographer decides what shutter speed to use based on any speed of movement in the scene. The camera's metering system then selects a suitable aperture. Nikon and Sony use 'S' and Canon uses 'Tv'
A or Av	Semi-automatic	Aperture priority mode. The photographer decides what aperture to use based on what depth of field is wanted. The camera's metering system then selects a suitable shutter speed. Nikon and Sony use 'A' and Canon uses 'Av'
M	Manual	This is where you set both the shutter speed and aperture. Not often used in everyday photography but more practical in special situations such as creative lighting, studio, night scenes or special effects
Various symbols	Scene mode	These are a set of programmed automatic modes that optimise the settings for the type of photograph. Examples would be sports, portraits, landscape and night. Not all cameras have these, which tend to be found on some consumer models

Wide angle is lower numbers around 14–35 mm and telephoto the higher numbers from 70 mm to 300 m and higher. Examples of the composition and angle of view are found earlier in this unit.

Depth of field

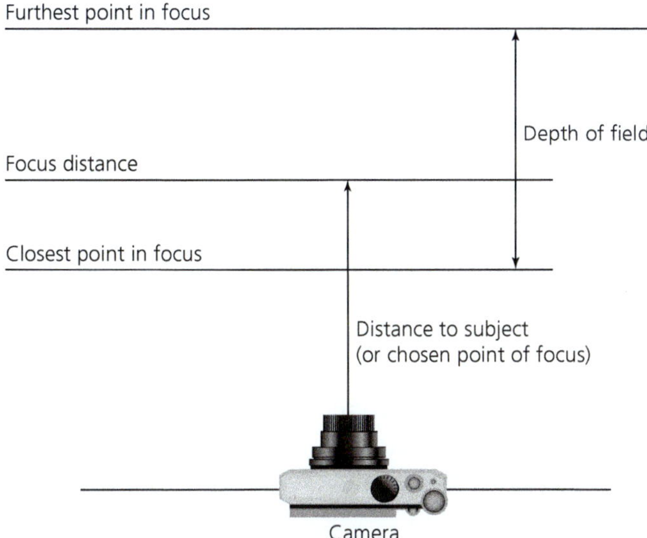

Figure 6.16 Depth of field

Figure 6.17 Effect of different apertures on depth of field

Depth of field is the range of distances from the camera that are in sharp focus. For example, if you are focused on your subject at 5 m away, the depth of field will be from 4 m to 6.5 m when using a 50 mm lens and f4 on a full frame DSLR or CSC. The depth of field is affected by the aperture, **lens focal length** and size of the camera sensor (smaller sensors will always have more depth of field).

Exposure compensation

A camera's built-in metering system can be confused by difficult or uneven lighting situations. Most cameras have a dial or menu that allows +/-2 stops. After taking a photograph, check the result on the LCD display and decide whether you need to take it again with exposure compensation.

Table 6.8 Effects of exposure adjustment

Exposure adjustment	Effect
Increase the exposure, e.g. +1 or +2 stops	The photograph will be brighter
Reduce the exposure, e.g. by -1 or -2 stops	The photograph will be darker

An adjustment of 1 stop in terms of exposure is either double (or half) the quantity of light that is received by the camera sensor. For example, this could be a shutter speed that is twice as long (1/250th second instead of 1/500th) when taken using the same aperture value.

Note that the effect of exposure compensation can be seen in the electronic viewfinder of a CSC but not a DSLR.

White balance

Digital cameras have a range of different settings for **white balance** (WB). There will also be an auto mode where the camera will set a value but be aware that this is not always accurate. This setting is more important when shooting JPG files since RAW files are easily adjusted when processing the images on the computer system. The typical range of options on the camera are:

- incandescent
- fluorescent
- daylight
- cloudy
- flash
- custom
- auto.

Key terms

Lens focal length A feature of the lens that determines the magnification or angle of view (how much of the scene is seen in the frame).

White balance A camera setting that compensates for different types of lighting to make sure the colours are correct.

If saving photographs as JPG files, make sure the white balance setting is suitable. Auto will work well in most situations but alternatively, choose a setting that is correct for what the lighting is actually like.

A note on using flash

Many digital cameras have a built-in flash, the exception being some professional models and mirrorless systems. External flashguns are attached using a 'hot shoe' on top of the camera body. Flash is not just used in darker conditions – it can also be used in bright daylight as 'fill-in' flash. If the faces of people are in the shade, for example with the sun behind them, then using flash will brighten their faces so you can see them properly.

If using flash to take photographs of people, especially at night-time, then an effect of the flash can be for eyes to be bright red. This can be reduced by using the 'red eye' flash setting, which outputs a pre-flash so that the eyes adjust to the bright light before the main photograph is taken.

Photographic image format

Most digital cameras will offer two different types of image file, which are RAW and JPG. A minority have a third option which is tiff and smartphones sometimes offer DNG, HEIF or Apple ProRAW. Basic cameras save photographs as JPG files that offer good quality and relatively small file sizes. RAW is popular for keen photographers and professionals who want more control over the processing of the images, but the file sizes are much larger and more specialised software is needed. With RAW files, the image information is stored straight from the sensor without any in-camera processing.

File extensions:

- JPG files: .jpg
- RAW files: the file extension is different depending on the make of camera, for example .crw (Canon) .nef (Nikon) or .arw (Sony)
- other high quality image options: .DNG, .HEIF/HEIC and Apple ProRAW.

Unless shooting in RAW, JPG provides a universal image format that can be used for just about anything. The image processing workflow is also simpler than if using RAW.

Within the camera there are typically some extra parameters that you can choose for JPG files and the image quality. These are the pixel dimensions and image storage/quality setting.

Firstly, the menu in a digital camera might provide options to change the image size, with a default setting at the maximum Mp for the sensor. If very high-resolution images are not needed this can be changed from say 24Mp, down to 12Mp or possibly 6Mp. This means more photographic images can be stored on the memory card, but you are not capturing the same detail. Most photographers leave this at the highest setting.

The second parameter is related to the image file type. If storing images as JPG, the menu might provide options for the amount of compression used when saving the file.

- Fine: Uses the least compression, creating high quality images and large files.
- Normal: Uses some compression, for a practical balance of image quality and file size.
- Basic: Uses a lot of compression, for images that are reasonably good but with a much smaller file size (not intended for larger prints).

Test your knowledge ✔

1 For a given photograph, which of the following exposures would produce the darker image – 1/60s at f11 or 1/500 at f8?

2 On a bright day, having checked the photographs on the LCD they all appear dark. What setting should be adjusted?

2.2 Techniques for processing photographic images

Basic image processing is all that is required by this unit. In this section we will review the main image processing techniques that you might want to include to optimise the photographs taken.

Synoptic link

You can refer to R094 Visual identity and digital graphics, Section 3.1 for the use of some tools and techniques in the processing of photographic images.

Adjustments to improve suitability

Checking image sharpness

This is not a processing technique but something that should be checked before going any further. Keep in mind that if the image is blurred through camera shake or poor focusing, you will not be able to fix it in the editing. This is why it is important to take a good photograph in the first place. Zoom in to 100 per cent in the imaging software and check that the photograph is still sharp.

Figure 6.18 Checking the image sharpness

Adjusting brightness/contrast

It is possible that a good number of images will benefit from a slight adjustment to the exposure. If using image editing software, the same type of adjustment can be done by changing the 'brightness and contrast' or 'Levels' in Photoshop. As long as your monitor displays correctly, you can make changes so that it looks good on the screen.

Adjusting colour/white balance

If the colours are not quite true to life, there is a good chance that the white balance was not set correctly when the photograph was taken. This can be adjusted in the image processing. Some image editing/processing software allows you to change the white balance on JPG files as well as RAW. Depending on the type of correction needed, you can either use image-adjust colour or change the white balance setting.

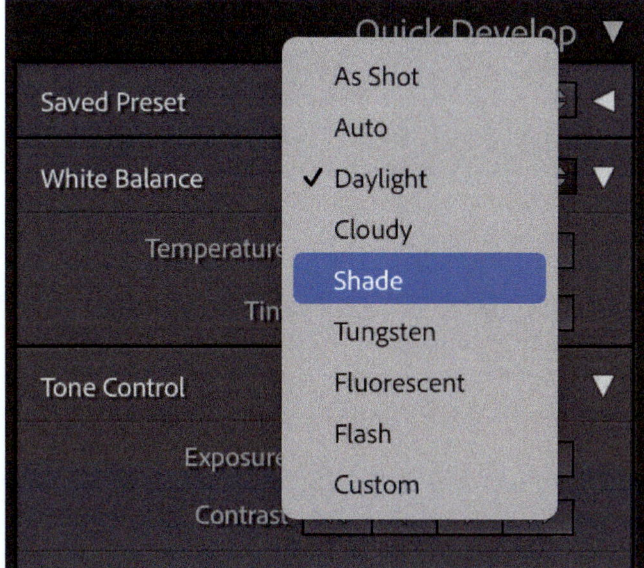

Figure 6.19 Adjusting the white balance

Adobe Lightroom allows you to change the white balance very easily on each image using a drop-down menu. Other software applications should have options to adjust the white balance or colour.

Cropping

An improvement to the framing of the subject can sometimes be achieved by cropping out the unwanted parts at the edges. Ideally you would have moved closer to the subject with the camera or used the zoom feature to effectively get a closer composition. If not, then within reason, the photographic image can be cropped in the image processing software application. Another reason to crop an image is to change the aspect ratio, for example from rectangular to square.

Figure 6.20 Cropping a photograph

Correction tools

Adobe Lightroom provides spot removal tools in the develop module. These can be used to remove blemishes, spots, sensor dust and small unwanted objects. Larger areas can be edited using different tools such as cloning, spot or patch tools in Adobe Photoshop or other image editing software. The cleaning up of any image should be considered a standard part of your workflow.

Selection of images based on technical suitability

Before deciding on the images for the final portfolio, an initial sort and check should identify any photographs that did not work, which can be deleted. Minor changes can be made to exposure through image processing so that wouldn't be a reason to reject a photograph at this stage.

The technical aspects for a photograph to check for would be:

- correct focus on main subject (lacks sharpness)
- camera shake or subject movement (lacks clarity)
- excess under exposure (too dark)
- excess over exposure (too bright).

Having rejected and deleted all the poor-quality photographs, what you have left will be a selection of technically suitable images. This is the first step towards choosing what will be used in your final portfolio.

Selection of images based on composition and aesthetic qualities

The second step in the selection process is to look at the composition of the photographs and think about their appeal and suitability. Ideally, your photographs should:

- demonstrate the effective use of rules of photography and composition
- demonstrate appropriate colour (for example, natural, vivid)
- include visual content that is suitable for the brief and/or intended purpose.

What you should have left is a selection of perhaps 10–12 images that are technically strong and compositionally good. If you don't have that many, it might be that you need to go back and take some more photographs (if possible).

Activity

Use the photographs that you took in the previous activity. Copy these to a computer system and check them for suitability in a final portfolio. Although they will not relate to a specific brief, you can still check the images for sharpness, exposure and composition. Pick the best photographs and make minor adjustments in the image processing to create a collection of your best images taken so far.

2.3 Techniques and tools to record video footage

Technical settings for video recording

This is about how you set up the video camera and what recording format will be used. Choices will mostly be made at the planning stage but here you will be applying those choices in the menu and controls of your digital camera.

Video format/resolution and frame rate

The selection depends on what you are recording the video for, so you should always think about how it may be used. Unless you are restricted by storage capacity of the memory card or the computer system and editing software, go with one of the higher resolutions that is available. You can always export the video at a lower resolution later but cannot increase it if the detail wasn't captured, for example you cannot increase SD to HD in your editing software.

The size of the video file will be determined by four factors:

- video format (for example, SD, HD, 4K)
- video frame rate (25/50/60 fps)
- length of recording (in seconds or minutes)
- file format and compression/quality.

Any video recording will automatically capture sound at the same time. This can be important, so check the audio recording settings in the camera. You may have an option to attach an external microphone which will improve the audio quality.

CSC and DSLR mirrorless cameras usually have two separate modes, one for stills and one for video. Make sure you are in video recording mode. To start recording video, there is usually a red button (separate to the shutter release for photographs).

Lighting scenes and subjects

On the day of recording, you may need to modify your plans slightly depending on weather, viewpoint and ambient lighting.

Figure 6.21 Setting up the video recording frame size and frame rate in the camera menu

The camera exposure system will adjust for the light level, but you can often improve this by careful positioning of your subject and scene. Some lighting should fall on the front of a person, such as on their face. If the sun is directly behind, their face could be in dark shadow so no detail can be seen. Here you can turn the person around and move to the other side so that the sun is behind you.

With any video shots, look carefully at what you are to record and move subjects around if needed. In difficult ambient light situations, you might need to add additional lights or reflectors to fill in the shadows.

Orientation

You learned about the convention of recording video in a horizontal/landscape orientation earlier in this unit. It is quite natural to use a DSLR, CSC or camcorder in this way but if recording footage using a smartphone, be careful not to use a vertical/portrait orientation.

Activity

Check your digital video camera menu for the video recording modes available. Look at and learn how to select a video format and frame rate for video recording. Go through the different options so that you are comfortable in selecting different modes.

Techniques for recording video footage

Framing

Before starting the recording you should frame the shot, taking into account any expected or planned movement (whether from the subject or camera). With video, it is a good idea to use a tripod where possible. This allows you to frame the shot in the viewfinder and lock the tripod head. Then you can organise the scene, check audio and when everything is ready – start recording.

Shot types

You learned about shot types earlier in this unit and here you are applying that knowledge. If your final video is to be engaging for the audience then a range of different shots should be obtained. For example, depending on the type of video you might plan to include an establishing shot for the beginning. That doesn't mean you have to record that shot first though – it could be at any convenient time in the day. You can arrange any of your video footage in the right place when editing the video in post-production. At this stage though, you should have a shot list so that you can mark them off when recorded. That is a way to check you have everything you want before leaving the scene.

Take a notebook or cue card with the different shots if you have either. These will be a reminder of how to frame the different shots, together with your storyboard and shot list.

Camera angles

Many people take photographs and video while stood up. However, this isn't always the best place for every shot. Try getting low to the ground – you can change perspective and use low angle shots.

Figure 6.22 Framing a low angle shot

Moving the camera

This introduces some extra challenges in keeping the motion steady. You will need to practice and ideally view the results on a computer to see what it looks like. Remember that a preview on a small camera LCD tends to look better than it really is.

- Panning: S L O W L Y move the camera from left to right (or right to left). Ideally use a tripod if you can.
- Tilt: S L O W L Y move the camera up/down.
- Zoom: Ideally on a tripod, frame the shot first and then slowly zoom in (or out) to the main subject or what you want the viewer to look at. Be very careful not to wobble the camera at the same time – at higher zoom magnification the movement of the camera is also magnified, and a very steady hand is needed. Some cameras might record the sound of the lens motor when zooming. Without an external microphone, there isn't much that can be done about this but be aware of it in post-production.
- Moving position: If walking with the camera, try to minimise the up-down motion of the camera. It can help to extend your arms and hold the camera away from the body. This is a good technique to practice. Alternatively, there are Gimbal stabilisers that dampen any camera motion, but this is a fairly specialised piece of equipment.

Activity

Take a video camera and record six different clips that use the different shot types: XLS, LS, MS, MCU, CU, XCU. Then record a series of clips that use camera movement including pan left/right, tilt up/down, zoom in/out and move/walk with the camera. When finished, transfer the video footage to your computer system for future reference. Don't worry about the content to meet a brief – at this point it is about using different shots and movement.

2.4 Techniques and tools for editing video footage

Tools and techniques for editing video (post-production)

Having recorded your video footage, the next step is to transfer it to a computer system. You can then open your video editing software application to create a video sequence. To transfer your video, either just copy the video clips using the computer hard disk or use a software application such as Adobe Bridge or Lightroom (these can transfer both photographs and video).

Once you have transferred your video clips, you can then select which clips will be used to create your video sequence. These will be your assets for the video.

Your video editing software will be needed to import these video assets into its own library before you can create your video sequence. Once imported, the usual process is to place them on a timeline before applying different editing tools and techniques. Keep in mind that having planned what you will be creating, you should have decided what the total duration or running time will be for the final video sequence. This will affect how many video assets are used and how you will edit them.

Cut/split

It is quite normal to trim a video clip or asset from its original length into something shorter. For example, you may have recorded 30 seconds of video, but it might only be a 10-second piece that you want to include, or you may wish to include 20 seconds of the footage at one point and 10 seconds elsewhere. This process is where you **cut** or **split** the video clip.

> **Key terms**
>
> **Cut** (video) To trim or remove a piece of video footage from the start or end of a clip.
>
> **Split** (video) To separate out a video clip into two different assets so that they can be used at different places on the timeline.

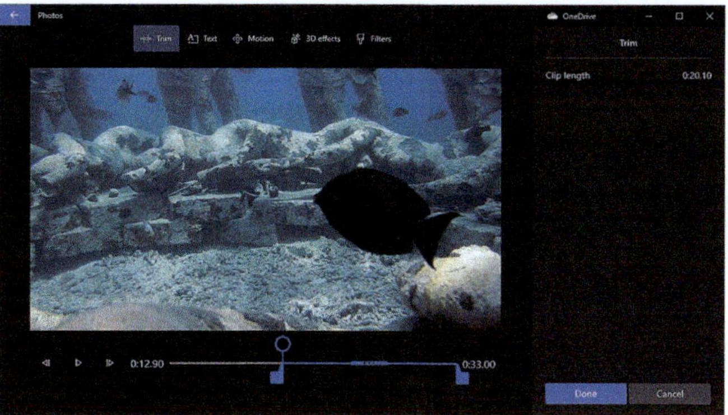

Figure 6.23 Using trim/cut tool in Microsoft video editor (Win 10)

Move/position on timeline

You can drag and drop video assets to different positions on the timeline. There will be a scale in seconds (and minutes when zoomed out) so that you can see the start and end time for each clip and the total sequence.

Adjustments

Any video editing software will have a range of options for making adjustments, corrections or changes to the video. Basic adjustments would be:

- brightness/contrast
- colour.

Adjustments can be made to each individual video clip. For example, if your video clip is slightly dark then you can brighten it or alternatively, if there is a colour cast it can be corrected.

Transition effects

The point of change from one video clip to the next is called a transition, which you learned about earlier in this unit. Video editing software has a range of different transition effects such as:

- dissolve
- fade to black (this works well at the end of the video).

Without an extra transition effect, it will be a jump cut (which might be fine). In general, you shouldn't use a mix of the transition effects that are available; you should pick a style that is suitable for the type of video and keep to it.

Applying effects

These would be seen as additions to the video rather than adjustments. Examples include:

- adding title text at the start
- adding captions during the video sequence as overlays, for example for explanations, commentary on the content or watermarks. This is one way to clarify the copyright on your work and the content
- adding credits at the end of the video, which may scroll from the bottom to the top.

Editing of audio track

Your video footage is likely to have recorded the audio at the same time. This will be automatically imported to the timeline on an audio track when placing the video. Depending on what software you are using, it is likely that you will have multiple audio and video tracks that you can use for different purposes.

Within the video editing software you can edit the audio in several ways. Firstly, you may want to increase or decrease the volume of the audio. Alternatively, you may want to delete it so that you can add a voiceover that is recorded and imported separately. Another option is to import a music track to play in the background, whether through part or all of the video sequence. When editing the audio, check that the volume is consistent across the entire video sequence. This is especially important with voices so that the listener can hear what is being said without having to change the playback volume.

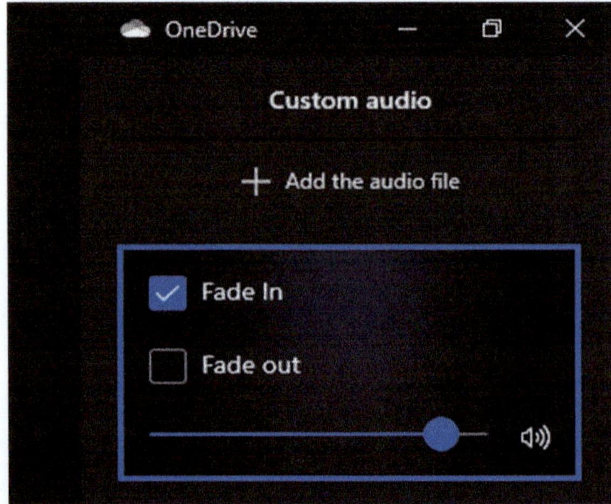

Figure 6.24 Changing the audio volume

Insertion of still images

Some video sequences can benefit from additional content in the form of still images (for example, photographs). Your video sequence shouldn't be made up entirely of these since that would make it more of a slide show. However, they can enhance certain types of video products. An example would be a documentary, where there is a static scene for around three seconds to display a still image. This could be something like a historical record, photograph, book or other object.

If wanting to insert still images, these first have to be imported into the video editing software. You can then place them onto a different track in the timeline. You will need to carefully combine the video clips and still images to make sure the final sequence displays what you want correctly.

Activity

Transfer your video footage from the previous activity if not already done. Now you can import the different clips into your video editing software application. Create a reference tutorial on the different shots and movement. Add text-based captions to state what camera shot or movement is being used. Save the video project when complete.

2.5 Techniques to save and publish/export portfolios of photographs and video sequences

Techniques for creating image portfolios in different media

In this unit, a visual imaging portfolio will typically be made up from:

- a collection of your best photographs, probably around 10–12
- a finished video sequence, probably between 20- and 60-seconds duration.

Format of the photographic portfolio

Different formats exist depending on what the portfolio is to be used for. In a work situation you would find out the format of the portfolio when negotiating with the client at the start of the project.

Contact sheets

These are for proofing purposes or as an index. They would not be the main portfolio on their own since they are generally a low resolution. One example would be a single sheet that shows your 10–12 images, such as four rows of three images.

Presentation

This could be a digital presentation using a display monitor. If requested by the client this could be supplied as a scrolling and looping display. These can be created using presentation software such as PowerPoint (PC/Mac) or Keynote (Mac). Here, the presentation would be similar to a slide show but using manual advance rather than automatic/timed.

Digital slide show

Photographs prepared at a specific resolution for display use and a slide show created using the computer system features. A slide show would have pre-defined timings for moving to the next image.

Exhibition

This format could be as a set of large, framed prints with photo mounts. Examples would be print sizes of 12" x 8" (approx. A4) or 16" x 12" (approx. A3). Ideally photographic prints will have a resolution of 300dpi so a 12 x 8-inch print will need a total of 3600 x 2400 pixels. However, some photo printers are optimised for slightly lower resolution, where 254dpi is not uncommon.

Folder of image files

A basic way of storing or supplying photographic images is by exporting or copying to a folder on your computer. If exporting your photographs from a software application, the image properties will need to be suitable for the intended use. You will have options for the file format, pixel dimensions and resolution. These portfolios or folders of images can be made available for your client or customer. For example, this could be using cloud or web-based storage, memory stick or CD/DVD. Another use is that of a storage archive. These would be your masters or digital negatives. They will be full resolution and stored securely for future use.

Digital portfolios

A photographic portfolio can be used to promote your own services as a photographer. These are likely to be printed although it is also possible to have this as a show reel on a tablet or other device. If placing these on the web you should consider adding a watermark to show that you own the copyright. An example would be: © 2022 [yourname] photography.

This can be placed in one of the corners or across the bottom of the image. Adobe Lightroom has a facility to add watermarks when exporting images. With other image editing software, you can add a text layer with your watermark.

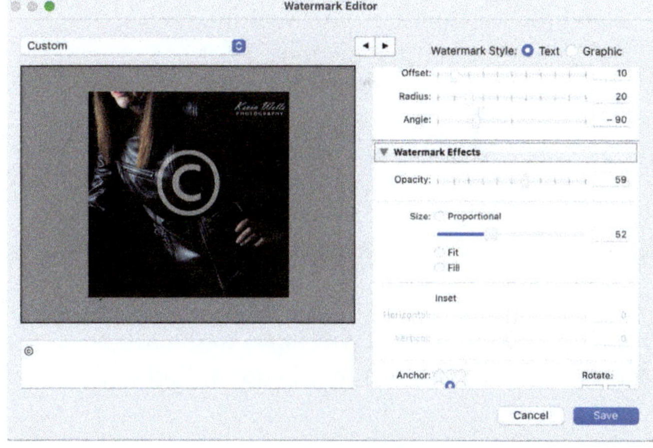

Figure 6.25 Setting up a watermark for the export process

Don't forget – backups. Copies should also be created using a different medium/location. Examples would include portable external drives and/or web-based storage. Only after this should you consider clearing the memory card from the camera, so that you always have two copies somewhere.

Processes to create a video file for playback

When the video editing is finished, you will then be exporting the video sequence in a suitable format and resolution. There are several processes and options to do this.

Rendering video

This is where final quality of the video sequence is generated by the editing software, by combining all the clips, transitions, effects and titles. Until this is done, all you see in the editing software is a low-quality preview.

Techniques for saving/exporting

Saving and exporting a video are two different things in video editing software.

- Saving: This generally saves a project file for use by the video editing software, but this does not contain any video footage. It is just an index for how the video is structured and sequenced. This will be a proprietary or native format of the video editing software.
- Exporting: This is where the video file is created so that it can be watched on a different computer system. Part of the export process is to first render the video, which creates the full resolution video that applies the effects and transitions. The final video file is then created and saved.

Video formats for different platforms

Depending on the platform that will be used for viewing the video, you will need to decide on a suitable file format. In most cases, this will be a MP4 or MOV file. Some of the potential platforms for viewing the video will be:

- social media such as YouTube, Vimeo, TikTok
- HD broadcast
- interactive media.

You should check the up-to-date requirements for uploading videos to social media. For example, YouTube used to be H.264 but changed to H.265 as a more efficient format for high quality with a lower file size. With any video, you can always export in a lower quality or resolution, but it cannot be improved. That means you cannot create a true 4K video quality from HD footage.

You should also think about version control when editing the video. When working in the video editing software ensure you occasionally save your project to the final system. This means that you always have a backup of where you were last. Each save should include a version number so that you have an incremental file for everything that you have done.

Synoptic link

File formats for video are covered in R093, Section 4.2.3.

Activity

Export the video project from the previous activities. You should choose a suitable filename and format, such as MP4, which will be a relatively small file size and still good quality. This may take several minutes to render and export depending on your computer, software and length and format of the video.

Topic area 3 Review visual imaging portfolios

Getting started

Hold a photographic competition in your class. Submit the best photograph that you have taken during the course and let the teacher be the competition judge. They may comment on the strengths of each submission before deciding on the overall best shot, explaining the reasons for their choice.

3.1 Techniques used to check and review visual imaging portfolios

In a visual imaging assignment, all of the following will be important to the client requirement. The content must be what the client wanted, the images and video should have some good visual appeal, be sharp (not blurred) and show good exposure and colour. If any one of these is not right, then it should not be included in a final portfolio. It is quite possible that a large number of photographs and/or video are rejected for one reason or another. You can speed up your decision-making by removing any images that did not work for any reason.

Techniques to check the technical properties of visual imaging portfolios

Methods of checking

Your planning will have identified what is needed for the client. Before submitting your final portfolio, you should check that it meets what the client or customer wanted. This can be achieved using a checklist, which can cover both technical and visual areas. The format of the checklist should include:

- Structure: A written record is the best approach, which works well as a table on an A4 page. That means you can file all your checklists away for each visual imaging commission or project that you complete.
- Content: Header information should identify the project, date, time, locations, client, output formats and so on. The checks will need to cover both the photographic portfolio and the video sequence. The types of checks should cover the technical requirements (size/resolution, sharpness, file format, quantity, duration) plus the visual aspects (composition, impact, suitability for the brief, storytelling).
- Use: This provides a documentary record of your checks for both the photographic images and the video sequence. It might even be supplied with the visual imaging portfolio to a client in some cases.

Elements of visual imaging portfolio to check

The technical areas to check are:

- File size: For both photographic images and the video sequence. To some extent, this will be defined by the choice of file format.
- Properties: File format, pixel dimensions, resolution, video format.
- Format: Playback testing for display size and media compatibility.

The concept of being able to critically look at your own photographs is an important skill to develop. The aim is that you learn how to look at the work you produce.

In your final portfolio, which may be around 10–12 photographs, you will probably have rejected many more from all those taken. Keep in mind that you need to know why you chose the final images and rejected many others. Reasons could be composition, image sharpness, exposure or lighting. You should record the decision-making process for this.

Key areas to cover in a photographic review

- Comparison of what was wanted and what was produced.
- Comments on the technical quality of the photographs.
- Comments on the composition used in the photographs.
- An explanation of the visual style, whether creative or conventional.
- What you believe are the strengths, positives, advantages and benefits.
- What you believe are the weaknesses, negatives, disadvantages and drawbacks.
- An explanation of the extent to which the portfolio is fit for purpose in your own personal opinion.
- Use technical language and terminology where possible.

Techniques to review the fitness for purpose of visual imaging portfolios

Suitability for client requirements

In terms of suitability for client requirements, the areas to consider would be:

- The content of each photograph in the final portfolio and how effectively they meet the brief
- The range of content and how many photographs are included
- Your interpretation of the original brief, which will have influenced your approach
- How easy it will be for the client to view the photographs and video on their own computer system
- Distribution methods and platforms that the client may want to use.

Try to consider these areas from a business perspective as if you are working in the commercial sector. One approach is to summarise the information in a checklist. If you can explain how and why you have done what was wanted then you have completed the first stage in confirming the fitness for purpose.

Suitability for target audience

The two main areas to consider are:

- Suitability of content: Try to imagine yourself as the target audience. That is one way to look at the photographs and video in a different way to that of the creator. When imagining yourself as the audience, keep in mind what characteristics would be appropriate - you can use your knowledge of audience demographics from R093 for this.
- Accessibility: A recommended approach is to consider how hearing or sight impaired audiences would access the products. You should be aware of any aspects of the portfolio that would or would not work for them.

Review of visual quality, aesthetic, appeal and engagement

To fully complete a detailed review there are four areas to consider. These are:

- Quality: For the photographs, consider the sharpness, exposure and colour. For video, consider the stability movement, exposure and lighting.
- Aesthetics: For both photography and video, consider the shot types, composition, framing and use of mise-en-scene. Make sure you understand whether your approach has been conventional or creative across the range of images and video.
- Appeal: For both photography and video, consider whether the visual content is likely to be attractive and interesting to the target audience.
- Engagement: For both photography and video, consider whether the visual content is likely to be engaging and inspiring for the target audience.

When compiling a checklist, try to include some or all of the information in the mind map in Figure 6.26. This identifies some of the key areas that should be considered. You can add to this as needed for additional factors in your review.

Activity

In the previous activities, you have created a video file for playback. This activity is to decide whether it meets a specific brief. Let's say the brief was to create a tutorial style video to show the use of camera shots and movement. Review how effectively your video would meet that brief. It is likely that there will be several areas for improvement and that it isn't a good match – but that is to be expected and needed in this exercise. Comment on what worked, what didn't and to what extent the video is fit for purpose.

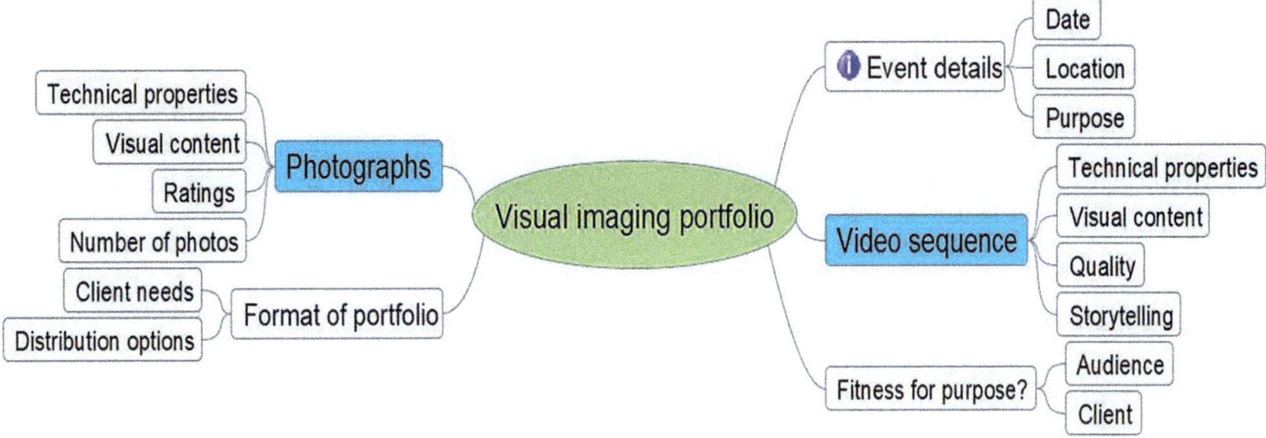

Figure 6.26 Consideration for a review of a portfolio

3.2 Improvements and further developments

Following on from your review and justifications, you may still be able identify some areas for further improvement.

Constraints which limit the effectiveness of visual imaging portfolios

Visual imaging portfolio constraints

The overall effectiveness of the visual imaging portfolio may be limited for various reasons. The main areas to consider would be:

- Time: Some assignments can have a time constraint whereas others are more flexible. An understanding of this can help with your planning of future visual imaging work.
- Resources: These will be primarily the digital camera and to some extent the computer system and software. The camera specification and availability of lenses plus other accessories can impact on what you are able to create. Considering this can help you identify what you might want in future visual imaging work.
- Hardware: This will be more about the computer system. Therefore, try to identify any restrictions or limitations of the computer performance that may affect the capability of editing 4K video footage and/or lower resolutions.
- Software: You are likely to have used a different software application for processing your photographs and editing the video. Consider the workflow and whether this was efficient or problematic.
- Budget: In a work-related context, this covers both your time and equipment. If on a fixed price commission, you will have a constraint of how much time you can spend and still make a profit. If you have to buy additional equipment to fulfil the brief, you will need to know that the extra equipment will help you achieve higher payments in future projects.
- Legislation: Your photography and video recording may have been constrained by legal requirements such as the completion of model and property releases, permissions, and the sight of any trademarks in your images and video. This can be a real problem, especially if wanting to submit your visual imaging portfolio to stock libraries for further income.
- Skills: These can be for both the use of the camera and the editing in post-production.

Visual imaging portfolio improvements

The next step is to consider what would be needed to improve one or more areas of the visual imaging portfolio. Some of these would mean retaking photographs, recording extra video footage and some could be improved with more time in post-production. Improvements should be considered in terms of how well they meet the client requirements and target audience engagement.

- Portfolio content: This is about how well the portfolio satisfies the brief and what parts of the content could be better. There is temptation to include your best photographs, but sometimes one or more might not be a good match for the brief. That is where you may be able to identify some improvements.
- Camera settings: This is mainly about the exposure settings that you used when taking the photographs. If photographs have any blurred movement, check what shutter speed was used and whether a faster setting would have frozen the movement for a sharper image. Depth of field is affected by the aperture value, so you could consider whether more or less would improve some of the photographs. The video footage can be considered separately. The camera settings would be mainly about the format/resolution and frame rate, so think about whether any changes to these would improve the final video. Note that improvements in these areas would mean having to retake the photographs and video.
- Lighting: Look at the subject in the photographs and video. Decide if the lighting was acceptable. If it needed some improvements in lighting direction and strength, it would mean re-recording, which would be a good learning exercise for the future. Some minor issues can be resolved in the image processing and video editing software, and you may be able to identify specific areas where this is possible,
- Composition: In the photographic portfolio, consider whether the original composition could be improved to give the images more appeal. Some adjustments can be made by cropping a photograph in your software, for example to create a rule of thirds composition from a wider angle. This usually needs a quite high-resolution photograph in the first place so that there are still a good number of pixels in what is to be used. In a similar way, consider whether the framing of a video shot could have been improved.
- Stability of video: This really only applies if you have some movement of the camera or if any footage was recorded at a high zoom magnification (which tends to amplify the slightest movement). If you were walking with the camera, you may see some significant camera shake when viewing the video on a large display. Earlier in this unit, you learned about different techniques that could improve this, for example using different accessories such as a tripod.
- Image processing: This applies to the photographic portfolio. Questions to ask here are whether there is any scope to improve the photographic images by different processing. Note this does not mean creative graphics which is a different unit.
- Video editing: There are several considerations on how a video edit could be improved.

When thinking about improvement, you must look at what you have created, recognise any issues and why they occurred. The next step is then to decide whether any of these areas could be improved in the image processing and video editing or if you would need to repeat the photoshoot and video recording. In a work-related situation, having to retake a photoshoot or video recording is not good for the budget, even if it is possible to do. However, if you produce some good work, on time and within a budget, further work and commissions from clients should be possible.

Further development opportunities for a visual imaging portfolio

Further development of a portfolio means being able to use the original work in different contexts or projects. Examples would be:

- stock library use
- part of further commissions from the client
- sales to other clients
- promotion of your own photographic and video skills.

Further development of the visual imaging portfolio could also be expanded for the existing client, in terms of:

- Portfolio content: Could additional photographs or video be added to the existing portfolio, whether from the original photoshoot or a new one?
- Length: Could the video sequence could be extended to have a longer duration, whether by adding more of the original footage or recording new footage?
- Product type and placement: If the portfolio is to promote a product, whether further development of the product placement and emphasis could be added.
- Story/narrative content: The main area to consider is the video although storytelling can be achieved through photography as well. Consider whether there is the potential to add or extend the storytelling in the initial visual imaging portfolio.
- Re-use of components: Suggesting further uses for the photographs and video material to your client could be a selling point for your work.
- Cross platform media: Consider how your photographs and video could be used and distributed in a different medium. This could mean that different versions are exported for uses with different platforms. This can have limitations such as how HD video cannot be effectively upgraded to 4K while maintaining quality.

Activity

Based on any issues that you identified in the previous activity, you can now describe what needs to be done if you are to improve the video product. It may need titles, captions, different footage and/or editing. Any or all of those are fine but here you need to explain why.

Assignment practice

You have been asked to produce a portfolio of visual imaging materials, on one of the following themes:

- Hobbies
- The garden

The content of the visual imaging materials should include a range of different shots, composition and framing. The purpose of the portfolio is to inspire others to get involved.

The final portfolio should include both a selection of 10–12 photographs and a short video around 30 seconds.

Unit R099

Digital games

About this unit

The digital games sector has a huge variety of technical and creative job roles. This unit will enable you to identify core features of digital games and understand the basics of planning, designing, creating and testing digital games.

In this unit you will learn to interpret client briefs to devise original digital game concepts. You will learn to plan digital games effectively and to use a Game Design Document to create engagement among developers and clients. You will learn how games software is used to create, edit, test and export playable digital games. Completing this unit will help you to understand the basics of a range of creative and technical jobs in the digital games sector of the media industry.

Topic areas

In this chapter you will learn how to:

- plan digital games (TA1)
- create digital games (TA2)
- review digital games (TA3).

Resources for this unit

Software: Software capable of creating a digital game with at least one level/room. Examples include GameMaker Studio, Construct, Clickteam Fusion, Scratch, Blender and Unity.

Resources to support planning a games concept: These include word processing and desktop publishing applications, artwork tools, applications for graphics editing and digitising equipment such as cameras and scanners.

How will I be assessed?

You will complete an assignment that is set by OCR. This will be completed independently by yourself, without using any additional resources or teacher assistance to help you. The assignment will have a scenario or client brief that defines what you will need to create. You will work through a series of tasks that cover the three topic areas to plan, create and review a digital game concept and playable digital game. Your portfolio of evidence will be marked by your teacher using the OCR marking criteria. It will then be externally checked/moderated by OCR to confirm your achievement. The assignment is worth 30 per cent of the total marks for the qualification.

Topic area 1 Plan digital games

Getting started

Think about any digital games you have enjoyed playing. Make a list of what you like about them. If you have listed several games, can you work out whether they have anything in common? If you can, share your list with others. Are any of your games the same? Can you work out why a particular game might be popular with lots of people?

1.1 Types, characteristics and conventions of digital games

Types of digital game and their characteristics

There are many thousands of different digital games and more are being added to the global game market all the time. They may look and feel unique and be played on different devices, but there are a few popular game types which have distinct characteristics. Before designing and creating digital games to meet a client brief, it is helpful to consider which game types appeal to particular target audiences and work best on specific platforms and devices.

Key terms

Massively multiplayer online (MMO) Games played over the internet by many players at once, either collaboratively or competing against each other. Often expanded to include MMORPG – Massively multiplayer online role-playing game.

Role playing game (RPG) Games where the player takes on a character. Most often based on fantasy worlds but can also be based on real life roles such as armed services, farming simulation.

Musical Instrument Digital Interface (MIDI) Synthesised music created using MIDI sequences has a distinctive 'computerised' sound as it tends to lack expression. But it can convey mood. Arcade-style games often use cheerful, fast-paced synthesised music.

Table 7. 1 Types of digital game and their characteristics

Game type	Characteristics	Platform/s used	Possible target audience
2D arcade	Simple, pixel-art graphics, 8-bit style, often 'retro' feeling with **MIDI**-type sound. Games can be maze or shooter type, often skills based	PC, early consoles, emulators	Older gamers who like nostalgic 'retro' games
3D **RPG**	Photorealistic graphics, open-world style, fantasy or war themes. Often based more around problem-solving, missions and quests than physical skills	Consoles, online games	Gamers who like an immersive experience and character-driven games
MMO	Often open-world, free ranging games. Battle, fantasy or post-apocalyptic themes. Often based around missions involving teamwork or cooperative gameplay	Online games, often console based or PC	Gamers who like collaborative play and social aspects of playing alongside others. Can appeal to competitive players who like to compare their skills with others
Simulation	Real-world career applications such as pilot/air traffic controller/ musician/farmer/business tycoon/ sports team manager. Real-life simulation. Often using keyboard or controller inputs to generate realistic actions	Traditionally PC-based, but now commonly console-based	Gamers who enjoy escapism and/or skill-based challenge to try difficult or dangerous tasks in a safe environment
Game-based learning	Includes critical thinking and problem-solving skills within game-type tasks, presents educational content through games, routes and progression can be tailored to the individual based on results	Wide range of platforms and devices, based on which platforms are popular with the intended (player) target audience	Often school-age gamers, but can also be aimed at adults in education or seeking to improve personal skills or aspects such as wellbeing
Augmented/virtual reality	Experiential, multi-sensory gameplay often involving physical movement, skill or exploration. 3D graphics and surround sound audio, **haptic** feedback often used alongside AR/VR headsets. May use realistic tools and controls rather than keyboard or console inputs. Variety of themes including both realism and fantasy as well as learning-based games	VR headsets linked with platforms such as Oculus or PlayStation. Also PC-based or smartphone-based with connected or tethered VR headsets	Dedicated gamers, professionals under training (mechanics, pilots, surgeons), players using VR and AR games to improve health or wellbeing by learning social skills in a safely managed environment

Conventions and styles of digital games

Games can be categorised by type, but they can also be defined by their genre, gameplay style and visual style. Huge variety can be achieved by mixing and matching genres, objectives and styles but there are some conventions or expectations which genres often follow.

Activity

Create a mood board showing examples of game art, characters, fonts, scenery and in-game props or objects for one of the following visual styles used in digital games: photorealism, 3D graphics, fantasy based, 8-bit, modelled on real world.

Table 7.2 Conventions and styles of digital games

Genre	Conventions	Gameplay style	Visual style
Action	• Multiplayer games based on defeating opponents (other players or **NPCs**) by working collaboratively • Violence of varying levels • Physical skills such as reaction speed and hand–eye coordination involved	First- or third-person selectable views	• Photorealism, 3D graphics • Game world may be modelled on real locations such as particular cities
Sports	• Single player games use NPCs to make up team numbers • Mimic the genuine sport rules and gameplay • Allow customisation of teams/players or 'manager' mode	Selectable views	• Photorealism, 3D graphics • Based around real world (often team) sports such as basketball and soccer • Game may be modelled on real teams, players and sports leagues
Role-playing game	• Player 'character' appearance, physical and non-physical characteristics can be customised • Teamwork or collaborative multiplayer gameplay • Large open-world or free-roaming game environments	First-person selectable views	• Fantasy-based or based on real-world jobs or simulation • Fantasy-based games may include cartoon/animated graphics • Real-world themed games frequently use photorealistic/3D/VR visual style
Quest	• Cooperative gameplay as MMO or with NPCs • Problem-solving, exploration and logic-based tasks	First-person selectable views, top-down views	• Fantasy-based • 3D graphics may be photorealistic or animated/drawn style
Strategy	• Real-life scenarios such as battle planning and logistics • Based on traditional non-computer/board games such as chess, card games, wargames	Top-down views for board-game based games Selectable views	• Gameplay often more important than visual style so high-end graphics may not be needed

Key terms

Haptic Relating to the sense of touch, for example as vibrations and force feedback in controllers and peripheral devices.

NPC (non-player character) A character which appears in the game but is not controlled by the player(s). NPCs can be opponents to work against, friendly characters which the gamer helps or used to advance the plot or storyline of a game.

Games will appeal to players for a variety of reasons. Some gamers prefer to play collaboratively and socially online, whilst others want to beat their own personal best or improve their own skills. Some gamers like 'retro' arcade-style games which are simpler and less resource-dependent, whilst others want to play the newest possible games using the latest hardware. Some games appeal to a player's need for escapism, whilst others allow gamers to try out dangerous or complex real-life challenges in a safe (and cost effective) way.

Most games take a lot of time, effort (and often money) to create. One challenge game developers face is how to keep players engaged in playing the game, so that it represents value for their investment. Games may therefore increase in difficulty or complexity, starting with simple challenges and building on these. Multiple levels, side-missions and spin offs can also be introduced to keep players interested. Upgrades with new features can be added to existing titles. These provide variety and are cheaper and quicker to produce than starting a completely new game. Upgrades also build on gamers' loyalty by re-using familiar and popular characters and game worlds. New versions of games may therefore keep the same visual style, genre and gameplay style, but introduce new objectives.

Game objectives

A game objective answers the question, 'What is the player trying to do or achieve?'

Table 7.3 Common game objectives

Objective	Key feature/s
Quest	• Often found in role-playing and MMO games • A series of tasks must be completed to earn a reward
Race	• Carry out an activity or action faster than other players or NPCs
Strategy or tactics of battle	• Use problem-solving, logic and planning to deploy resources and defeat an enemy • May mimic real-life warfare or be fantasy-based
Survive	• Navigate or act to avoid or defeat enemies, preserve lives or health and live as long as possible in the game world
Problem-solve	• Overcome challenges, solve puzzles or riddles • May be linked to cyphers and cryptography, real-life situations or fiction/fantasy
Beat the clock	• Complete an action or task within a time limit
Collect	• Find and gather as many points, resources or in-game rewards as possible
Shoot	• Combine physical skills such as aiming, hand–eye coordination or reaction times to shoot accurately and score points or defeat an enemy
Escape	• Use hand–eye coordination or problem-solving and strategy to move from a place of danger to one of safety within the game world
Build	• Construct physical in-game buildings, farms, industry or empires; or friendships and social groupings
Score	• Obtain as many points, lives, rewards as possible • Play against others to score more than other players or beat your own personal best • Often use high-score tables, leagues and other methods of comparing success

Games may involve one objective or many and even the most complicated games can be simplified to work out what their objective is. For example, a 3D game such as FIFA 21 is strategy or tactics-based and success is measured by scoring more than your opponents.

Most game objectives also answer the question 'How does the player tell when the game has been won or lost?' Even 'open-world', 'free roaming' games, which mimic real life and don't have a definite ending or winner, use objectives such as 'be successful', 'earn in-game rewards' or 'build a (better) habitat or social community'.

Activity

Using your own background knowledge, conduct an internet search or discuss with a partner and list at least one game title for each game objective in Table 7.3.

Objectives and platforms

Some game objectives are well suited to particular platforms. For instance, car racing games are immersive when played on a console with peripherals such as steering wheels and pedals. Simple 'click and score' and 'beat the clock' games that don't require many inputs work well on smartphones. On the other hand, team-based quests and multiplayer survival games which may take many days to complete are suited to a PC with a large monitor or screen, a fast reliable internet connection and a headset with a microphone for communicating with other players.

Objectives and target audiences

Ensuring a game has a clear objective is one way to increase its appeal to the target audience. It can be a mistake to dismiss a particular game objective by assuming it is not suitable for your target audience. A wide variety of gamer types enjoy different game objectives. But you may be able to increase the chances of success with a game design by choosing objectives and platforms or devices which that target audience commonly uses. For example, if you think that teenagers prefer consoles which support peripherals such as VR headsets and like competitive games, you might design a console-based VR game with a 'shoot' objective that players would find immersive and engaging.

Creativity in digital games

You have learned about the different types and characteristics of digital games and you now know about the conventions and objectives they use, but you still need to be creative. You need to consider how you balance using established conventions, genres, styles and objectives with originality.

This is about using your imagination and your own ideas to come up with something different from what has been done before. Even if you are creating a game for a client who has already published games and titles, your game won't engage audiences if they think they have seen it all before. You can adapt existing games by devising different challenges, scenarios or missions, or adding in new features and gameplay or pathways. You can create a different gameplay using the same genre or place new characters and players within an existing theme or game world.

What you can't do, however, is re-use an existing game design and only change a minor aspect, for example swapping the player character for one that looks different into an otherwise identical game. Where ideas are too similar to existing products, they are said to be 'derivative' – that is, they are derived from something else and not original. You should avoid derivative work in the game concept part of your assignment portfolio because it suggests that your ideas are not original and creative.

However, you can draw inspiration from existing designs and established conventions. You just need to be sure that your idea is different and original enough to be clearly your own. You will learn later in this chapter how you can make use of ready-made assets, sounds, backgrounds, tile sets and so on, and alter or edit them to make them more original. This can help to speed up the game creation process compared with the time taken to design and create entirely new assets.

1.2 Resources required to create digital games

Hardware and peripherals

The basic hardware needed to create a computer game can be as simple as a keyboard, mouse, monitor and computer with a text editor. This set-up allows developers to create games using text-based coding or scripting languages. It works well where there is a team of developers creating a new game, because the game will be tested by someone other than the game's creator, using the intended platform or console. However, the basic hardware of a desktop PC or laptop cannot fully test a game's functionality if the game outputs include sounds, haptic feedback (vibrations mimicking actions in the game) or virtual reality, or if the peripherals needed to play the game include controllers, touchscreens or microphones. As you will learn later in this chapter, testing is carried out during the creation process. A range of input and output devices, hardware and peripherals are therefore commonly used to test that a game works as expected.

Computer systems

These need fast enough processors to handle the game mechanics, a sound card capable of generating the game's soundtrack and suitable graphics capabilities to display gameplay without tearing or blurring.

Monitors

Fast screen refresh rates and high resolutions are needed for high-definition photorealistic game graphics. Serious gamers will use large dedicated monitors or TV screens which support the latest HD capability. This is not an issue when creating arcade-style 2D games and games designed to be played on smaller smartphone screens or devices such as the hand-held Nintendo Switch, but if a game is intended to be played using a small screen, then testing using a window of realistic size is important.

Figure 7.1 A gaming setup with HD monitor and headset

Speakers and headphones

Most games use a variety of sounds to enhance the gameplay experience and provide feedback, so speakers or headphones are important when creating and testing games. Capabilities such as stereo audio and surround sound may also be used to make gameplay more realistic. Online and multiplayer games often allow voice input for players to collaborate together, so a microphone is also important. Many gaming headsets combine earphones and a microphone and are designed to be comfortable during long periods of use. They may also be wireless to allow player movement, in the same way as VR (virtual reality) headsets.

Interface controls

Traditionally, computer games were played using keyboard inputs, but with the development of dedicated gaming platforms and consoles, many different interface controls and devices are now used. Game controllers are designed to fit players' hands and use only the buttons and controls needed for the game. Controllers can be attached to mobile phones to enhance the player experience. A variety of adaptive controllers are also available to make games accessible to players with different mobility requirements. Other interface controls also include mouse, joystick or joy-pad, wheels and pedals for driving games, eye-toys or cameras which sense player movement and translate it into action in VR gameplay, and physical tools and hand-held accessories such as Nintendo's Ring Fit.

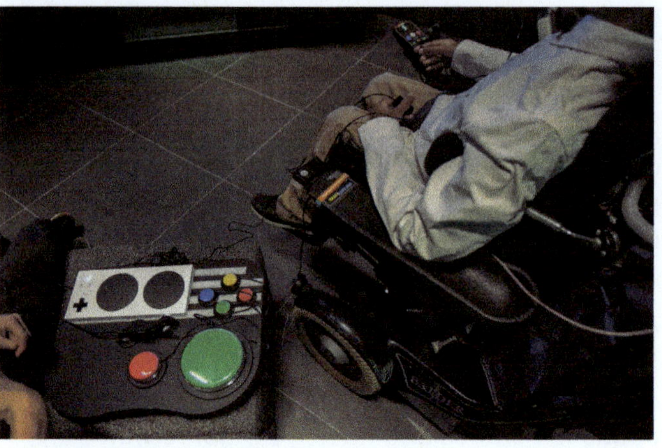

Figure 7.2 Adaptive gaming controllers

Hardware and peripherals best suited to particular game types, genres or platforms

Game hardware and peripherals have developed to improve the gameplay experience as digital games evolved. For example, in a fantasy-themed role-playing game (RPG), the player character often moves around the game world and interacts with a range of objects in order to complete quest-style objectives. The earliest text-based RPGs required players to type in instructions such as 'pick up sword', 'open door' and so on. This slowed down the game and limited the gameplay experience to those with reasonably good reading and writing skills. The same quest in a modern game might make use of a VR headset and sensors to detect the player's movements, so that reaching out to pick up an object will translate to the same action for a first-person player character in the game. This arguably makes the same game much more immersive and engaging to play.

Figure 7.3 Gaming controllers

Simple arcade-style games do not need the sophistication of VR and peripherals if the only inputs are selecting, clicking, shooting and so on. Such games are well suited to smartphone handsets where touchscreen input and motion sensors are sufficient. In these games, engagement comes instead from things like brightly coloured graphics, upbeat audio, fast-paced gameplay and often gambling or chance-based successes. As a general rule, the more complicated and realistic a game, the more sophisticated the hardware and peripherals need to be. This is one reason why many modern games are available via streaming and subscription-based services. The processing power and speed required to generate the gameplay is too much for the average gamer's PC or smartphone alone to handle. Choosing a suitable device or platform for a new game is also important because a mismatch might mean the game is targeted towards the wrong audience to be successful. Serious gamers will not want to play on a smartphone, and a casual gamer who plays to fill in a few minutes whilst waiting for a bus would not be interested in a game which requires an expensive console or streaming subscription.

A game developer may not have access to all the interface controls or devices which the final game will use, since this could be expensive and peripherals can be updated, which would cause problems. Instead, developers use test bed software to test games by mimicking how they look and behave, using a desktop computer. Test beds can be either simulators or emulators.

- Simulators: These mimic game environment features which are created in the software. They use all the game's intended variables and configurations, so the game's visuals and audio are similar to the intended final product. Simulators don't attempt to copy the hardware or physical controllers. Keyboard and mouse inputs are used instead of a controller, handset or physical peripherals. Games created using editors and game engines can be tested using simulators.
- Emulators: These also mimic the game's software variables and configurations but try to imitate the physical controls and appearance of the intended gaming platform or device as well. Emulators usually require the use of assembly language, which can be quite specialist and needs a high level of accuracy. This can make emulators too difficult for novice game developers who create games using the 'drag and drop' features associated with game editors rather than working with code.

Advantages and disadvantages of test beds

There are several advantages to using test beds:

- Simulators and emulators have the advantage of being widely available and in many cases free and/or open source. Google's Android Software Development Kit (SDK) includes an emulator, and several digital onscreen iOS are also available when developing games to be played on smartphones and mobile devices.
- Both simulators and emulators are available for playing retro-style games using modern computers and devices. This means that when you have created a game, you can try it out to find out whether the gameplay experience is successful and matches your plans.
- Using test beds is a good option for independent or freelance developers. Unlike a larger game publisher or distributor which would have a separate job role for testing games, independent developers carry out all aspects of the game design and creation themselves and might not have the budget to purchase the platform or console they are designing for.

However, there are disadvantages to testing games without using the intended final devices or platforms:

- Emulators can be hard to set up and configure and may not be available for the intended platform or device.
- Because simulators only mimic the software of a game, programming errors in the inputs may be difficult to detect, and player feedback through the game's outputs will not be presented realistically.
- Both emulators and simulators run slowly compared with the real devices and platforms which can make testing a game's smoothness difficult.

Activity

Carry out a search for online game emulators and see if you can play some classic retro games.

- Identify the features of the original platform or controls which are being emulated (mimicked). For example, 'the original game used a joystick. The emulator replaces this with arrow keys'.
- Are the games still engaging and enjoyable to play? If so, why? If not, why not?

Software

Designers and game developers have a range of options when it comes to choosing the software to be used to create a new game. The choice of software to create a game will depend on factors such as compatibility, price, level of programming skill and creativity and the amount and type of support available to the developer. Independent and freelance developers may choose software which is not platform specific. This gives their games the maximum flexibility and market appeal, which is useful if they do not yet have a buyer or client for their work. These are known as 'third party' developers. At the other end of the scale are 'first party' companies such as Microsoft, Sony and Nintendo. They make their own platforms for games (Xbox, PlayStation and Switch) and will employ game developers to create games 'in-house'. These games will be tailored for their precise needs and make use of the particular peripherals, controllers and interface of their platform or distribution channel. The software used to create games for first party companies is often specific to the platform which will be used to play the games. This means for example, that Sony's PlayStation game creation software won't be any use for making Nintendo Switch games, and so on.

Game engines

The term **game engine** first came about in the 1990s with the rise in 3D 'first person shooter' games. A game engine is a collection of tools including graphics rendering, audio, algorithms and physics engines. When used together they allow a wide range of new games to be built using pre-set code and algorithms. This means that the same engine can generate games to be played on different platforms, whereas in the early days of computer games, the source code had to be built from the 'bottom-up' by game developers working for specific game distributors such as Atari. Game engines can be written in any programming language and often include 'drag and drop' features or graphical user interface (GUI) versions where the code is generated in the background. Beginners with little coding experience can easily create games using these, although they may not be able to access all the tools unless they know how to customise the code. Game engines often have online forums where developers can support each other and share blocks or sections of code for particular game features. Examples of game engines include Blender, Unity, Clickteam Fusion and RPG Maker. GameMaker Studio and Unreal Engine's additional tools and features such as sprite editors and test or debug areas mean these game engines are more accurately described as **Integrated Development Environments** (IDE).

Key terms

Game engine An application or package containing a collection of tools and resources for making games.

Integrated Development Environment (IDE) A collection of tools such as a code editor, runtime environment, library and debugger used to create software.

> **Key term**
>
> **Game editor** A set of tools for use when modifying elements within a particular game.

Game editors

A **game editor** (also known as a level editor) allows players and developers to make customised levels for pre-released games. Examples of this include 3D games such as *Doom*, where players and fans can create their own levels. Racing games may include a level editor to allow players to create new tracks. Level editors can be developed and released by the original creator of a game or by fans who are interested enough to write their own level editor software. Disadvantages of level editors include the limited variety of changes that can be made and development costs. Game creators may prefer to release Software Development Kits instead.

App development software

Games can be created using software that allows publishing to a range of mobile platforms. Since not all mobile phone operating systems are the same, this is an important factor if you want to design a game to appeal to a wide target audience. Some app development software supports coding like HTML, whilst others work on a 'drag and drop' basis, using pre-set templates and code which can be customised to a greater or lesser extent. The advantages include compatibility across a range of mobile devices and operating systems, whilst disadvantages include a lack of independence for the designer and also costs to buy the app development software.

Software development kits (SDK)

Software development kits (or SDK) are a set of tools designed to allow customisation of games for a particular console or platform. Because they are produced by and specific to one type of platform or console, the possibilities for game development may be limited. This is designed to protect the intellectual property or brands of game designers or publishers. On the other hand, they provide a way for publishers to gain access to new titles and talent, so they may choose to provide a lot of support for budding game designers. Examples include the Xbox Development Kit (XDK), the Nintendo SDK (available through the Nintendo Developer Portal) and PlayStation Partners which includes access to an SDK tool known as Middleware.

> **Activity**
>
> Investigate the game creation software which is available to you in school and at home. Find out:
>
> - whether it is free, licensed or subscription-based
> - whether it is a game engine, IDE, game editor, app development software or SDK
> - what types or styles of games can be created using the software
> - whether there are inbuilt or online manuals or tutorials to help you learn to use the software.
>
> If you have a choice of software, which do you prefer and why?

When you design and create your own digital games you may have a choice of software available to you, or you may have to design your game concept around the software which is available. Even if your software makes some aspects of the game concept difficult or even impossible to achieve, these elements can still be included in the Game Design Document (GDD). They can also be listed and discussed as improvements and further developments at the review stage.

1.3 Pre-production and planning documentation and techniques for digital games

Game concepts

The process of planning a new digital game begins with devising a game concept or idea. The starting point for this could be a particular genre, objective, platform, style or theme. An independent game creator or programmer may have total freedom of choice but would need to 'sell' the concept to a client in order to secure funding to create the game. Someone who works for a game publisher or distributor is more likely to be given a client brief which outlines the intended platform, target audience and so on for the game.

Idea generation

In order for a new game to be successful without encountering problems of copyright, trademark and other legislation infringement, the concept (underlying idea) needs to be original. There are limitations to the number of truly original storylines which exist, but there is almost infinite variety in the settings, characters and combinations of story arcs and challenges which can be used to make a new game. Setting a player the same challenges and gameplay as an established game and only changing the appearance of the characters or settings is unlikely to make a successful game. Players will already know how to win or achieve the game's objectives and the creators of the original game may not be happy if you try to earn money through re-using their concept! You can find out more about intellectual property rights in Unit R093.

Re-using established characters and settings but providing new objectives or missions is described as derivative work. This often happens where a successful franchise or series of games has been created by a distributor or game developer. For example, *The Legend of Zelda* or FIFA games which are regularly updated. A publisher would be very unlikely to give permission for an independent developer to use valuable and successful game content. When developing your own game work, you should aim to be as original as possible.

> **Activity**
>
> Create a mind map to record initial ideas for a game based on learning to tell the time.
>
> You might start with nodes such as target audience, style, objectives and genre, but you should try to add other nodes based on this chapter and include sub nodes to provide detail and depth.

Pre-production documents to illustrate game concepts

Pre-production documents and planning documentation are created for two main audiences, the client and the programmer. These two audiences have different needs. The client would be interested in why players would choose the new game over all the other games which are available. The client will have questions such as: What sets the new game apart from others? Why is it better? Why is it worth investing money in developing this game? What will the game look like? How will it be engaging for the player? On the other hand, the game's programmer does not need to know any of these things. A programmer or developer would be interested in the game mechanics (how the code works and what it does). Technical aspects such as movement, scoring, interactions, controls, levels and so on all need to be planned, and a range of pre-production planning documents can be used to achieve this.

You may already have learned about some pre-production documents from Unit R093. In the very early stages of planning, a game designer might create a mind map or mood board. These allow lots of ideas to be recorded quickly in a single document and can easily be shared between interested parties such as the game programmer, client, developer and publisher. This is helpful if several people are working together to develop a new game idea. Mind maps can be used to generate many ideas from a central theme or genre. Narrative-based games could start with a storyboard, plot outline or backstory so that the characters are interesting and engaging before they are placed into the game scenario.

Mood boards can provide helpful insight into the visual style of games aimed at a particular target audience or made for a specific platform.

Key term

Concept art (game) Sketches, images or drawings showing exactly how characters, objects and terrain will look in a game.

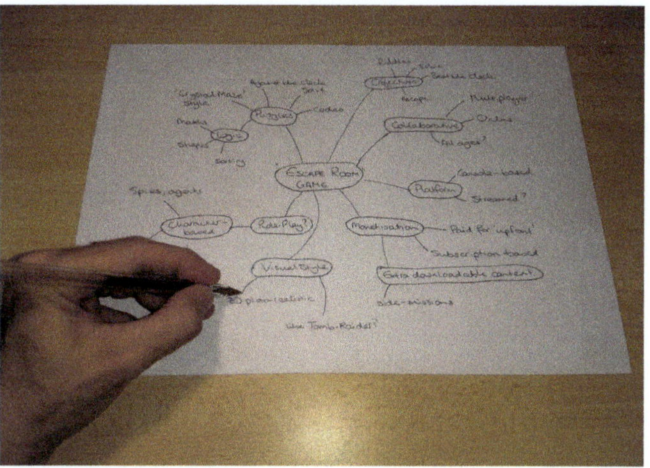

Figure 7.4 An example of a mind map

A mood board is a good starting point to collect reference art, which is content such as photos, images or colours in a similar style to that which will be used in the game. This helps the client to understand what the designer has in mind, so that changes can be discussed and agreed before **concept art** (accurate designs for the final characters, objects and terrain) is created.

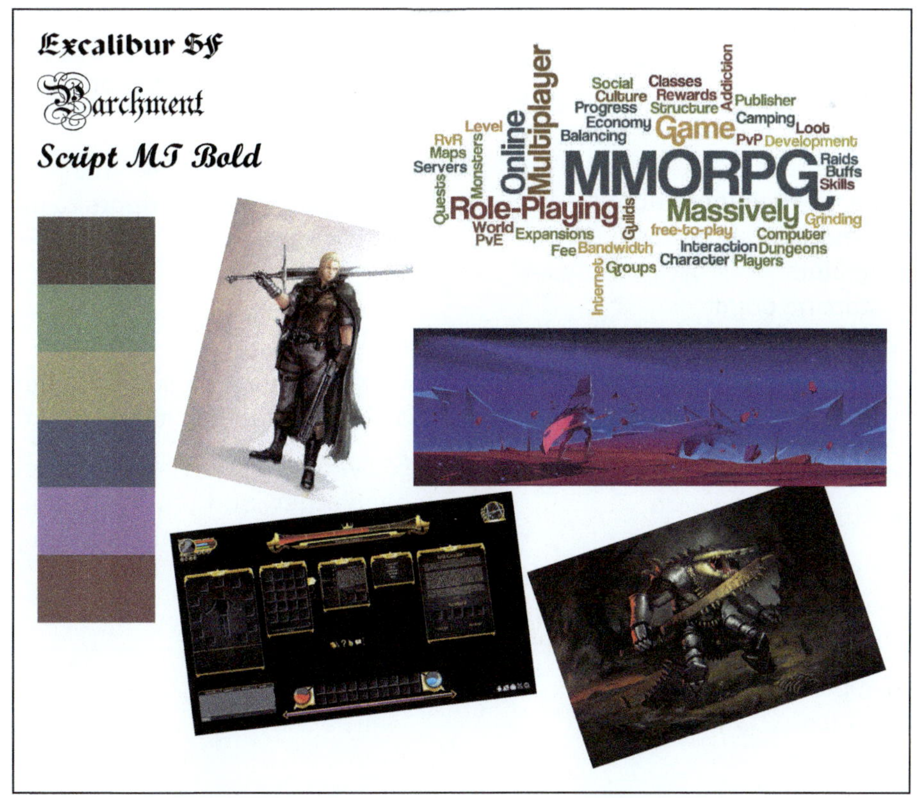

Figure 7.5 An example of a mood board

Initial idea generation and pre-production documents which are shared with the client should set out a suitably original idea for a new game and outline its most important basic elements; the **unique selling point** (USP), objectives and overall visual style of the game.

- The game's USP will set out what is different or new about the game. This is important because it has a large effect on the target audience and their decision to try a new game. The USP will often be written as a one or two sentence summary stating what is special or unique about the game. It will also usually be placed at the start of a Game Design Document.
- The game objectives are important because they set out what the player is trying to achieve whilst playing the game. Unless the game has clear objectives, it will not hold a player's attention for long.
- The visual style is important because it will have an impact on the length of time and the budget needed to create the game. 3D photorealistic game graphics take longer and require more resources to create than simple 2D graphics. The visual style may also determine which platform or device the game will be played on.

Activity

Use an internet search to find out about basic story lines. Searching for information on 'the seven basic plots' or 'story archetypes' would be a good starting point.

Which basic plot or story type best matches these stories?

- *Cinderella*
- *The Good Dinosaur*
- *The Lion King*

Synoptic link

You can read more about story arcs, plot lines and narrative planning in Unit R095, Characters and comics.

Game planning

Synoptic link

Pre-production planning, including some examples of the documents, is also covered in Unit R093, Section 3.

Pre-production documentation and planning

Mood boards, mind maps and **reference art** are used to generate initial ideas for a new game, but once the basic concept has been generated, more detailed and precise planning and pre-production documents are required. Some of these are used to inform a client about how the game will look and how it will be played, whilst others are used by the game's programmer to build and code the game itself.

Pre-production documents such as narrative pathways, concept art and story arcs are useful for clients, whereas more technical documents such as flowcharts and diagrams help developers when coding the game mechanics.

Key terms

Unique selling point (USP) What makes an item different from other products and therefore desirable.

Reference art (game) Images from existing games or other products to indicate what style or type of graphics will be used in a game.

Activity

Use a decision tree to map out the plot for a simple 'Choose your Own Adventure' game.

Show how decisions and consequences link to each other, and branches can join and cross (like a mesh) as well as taking their own plot line (like a star).

Table 7.4 Pre-production documentation

Pre-production document type	Description	Purpose/use
Concept art	Original drawn or digital artwork	Shows the visual style (cartoon, realistic, etc) and intended appearance of characters, NPCs, in-game objects, terrain and scenery of the game 'world'. Also used to show the style, layout and fonts used for menus, start screens and cut scenes
Flowchart	Diagram containing text boxes and arrows	Shows what events happen and in what order, where loops occur (e.g. new character is locked until score exceeds 50) and how the game begins and ends. Flowcharts also show how scoring mechanisms work and are displayed in the game to provide feedback to the player on progress and success (e.g. if enemy is hit, play 'destroy' sound effect and add 100 points to the score) This type of document is particularly helpful for programmers to use when coding a game
Decision tree	Branching diagram	Shows the structure of a game where many possible routes can be followed, making the game re-usable. Examples would be an open-world game genre where there is no particular start or end point
Narrative pathway	Diagram with a linear structure	Shows how a game with one set storyline is structured. For example, each mission must be completed in a particular order to progress to the next level/room
Story arc	Graphical representation of the key points in a storyline plotted using an X and y axis	To show how a narrative develops from the start, through points of challenge and resolution to the end. Also shows how different characters are key to the story at particular times
Input-output table	Diagram with input-output or if-then relationships	Shows triggers and events, for example: IF score→30 THEN Load next level

Minimum viable product

The idea of a **minimum viable product** or MVP is useful when designing and planning games. To find out the MVP of a game, reduce the game components and gameplay to their most basic level, taking out everything that can be removed and still allow the game to be played. For example, a science-fiction flight simulation game based on a film franchise may be at its basic level 'aim and shoot at those shapes to destroy them before they can destroy you'.

Testing those components to see how long the game holds the player's interest and attention will reveal if the core concept and gameplay are truly engaging. Even if the high-end graphics, audio and complex controls are missing and you just provide the player with simple geometric shapes and button presses, the game should still be engaging and hold the player's attention. Many modern console games use photorealistic graphics and yet have a very simple MVP such as 'avoid capture', 'beat the clock' or 'use reaction speed to shoot'.

Once you have identified the MVP for a new game, open-source game code or game kits such as the Unity Asset store can be used to build an MVP version quickly and efficiently. This frees up time to develop original artwork, soundscapes or characters in greater detail. Generating an MVP version first is also helpful because it allows functionality testing to be carried out to check whether the game works even if the artwork or audio are incomplete.

Key term

Minimum viable product (MVP) The minimum features a game needs to keep player's engagement and interest.

Activity

Read **https://fundayfactory.com/media/147699/age-appropriate-game-design-for-children.pdf** then create a mind map to show the most important things to keep in mind when designing games for particular age groups.

Test your knowledge

1 Which pre-production documents would be most suitable to plan the following:
   a the scoring system and how it is displayed to the player
   b the choices and possible routes through a problem-solving strategy game
   c the plot or storyline of a role-playing quest game?

2 Who would be the main audience for these planning documents:
   a a mood board showing visual style
   b an input-output table
   c reference art showing character ideas?

3 True or false: a game programmer needs to know about the game's concept and USP in order to create the game.

Assignment practice

Task 1: Plan a digital game

Time needed: approx. 1 hour

You have been asked to devise an educational game to help teach about odd and even numbers. The target audience for the game will be children of Years 1 and 2 age (5- to 7-year-olds). Your client wants a simple game which can be played on a desktop computer, laptop or tablet.

Create a Game Design Document for the above game idea. Your GDD should fit onto a single page.

Topic area 2 Create digital games

Getting started

A new game based on Ancient Egypt is planned. It requires a scarab beetle NPC. Use the internet to find and save a suitable image for this NPC. Award yourself points based on how many of the following you can achieve:

The image should be a top-down (bird's eye) view of the scarab	2 points
It should have large mandibles (jaws shaped like antlers)	2 points
It should be green in colour	2 points
It should be animated as if walking/moving	10 points
It should be saved as a GIF	2 points
It should be saved with the filename Scarab_Spr.gif	2 points
It should be 64 × 64 pixels in size	5 points
It should be complete, saved and ready for use in less than 10 minutes	5 points

2.1 Techniques to explain game concepts

Game Design Documents (GDDs)

The process of turning an idea for a new game into a finished product often depends on persuading a company or individual client to take up the idea and organise the development, coding, testing and marketing of the game. The main tool designers use for this is often a Game Design Document.

What is a Game Design Document?

A Game Design Document (GDD) is a pre-production planning resource which is written for a target audience that can include developers, clients, customers and investors. Its purpose is to inform and to promote. It explains all aspects of a new game clearly, so that developers know how the game should be coded and clients can be persuaded to invest in the creation of the game. Once the production phase begins, the GDD is used to keep the creation process on track, making sure nothing is missed and the main elements are created as planned.

Format and content of a Game Design Document

GDDs are typically set out as word processed documents, and these might be saved as PDF files so that they can be viewed on a wide variety of devices. They can be sent to the client or audience as hard copy (print-out) or as an electronic file, although video and presentations may also be used if the GDD is delivered to the client in a face-to-face or online meeting as a live 'pitch'. The document would be expected to be bookmarked or include a contents list so that it is easy to tell what content is where. It would also typically use a combination of text and images. If aimed at the client, the GDD would concentrate on the game concept (visual style, USP and objectives), but if the audience also includes the game programmer or developer then details of the game mechanics would also be included.

It is possible to find different templates for GDDs online, but they commonly include a combination of artwork, diagrams and text under clear headings such as:

- unique selling point (USP)
- genre
- platform
- target audience
- synopsis
- gameplay
- objectives
- art
- sound and music.

The layout should be logical and uncluttered, and you should make sure that any images (concept art, screen layout designs and so on) are large enough to be clearly seen. Page numbers are usually included and sections may also be numbered or labelled to help locate them during discussions between the client and designer.

If you choose to use a published GDD template, you should consider whether the font, layout, colour scheme and style are a suitable match for your game concept and the client. A client may well have brand guidelines which set out the colours, typography and so on which make up its visual identity. If your GDD matches these closely it helps align your ideas with the client's preferences or tastes. This could in turn make the client more likely to adopt your game idea and commission its creation.

Purpose of GDDs

Engaging and informing the client

To be successful, the GDD needs to engage the client. Positive language is therefore used to help persuade the client that a game concept is worth time and money.

The USP mentioned earlier in the chapter often appears at the start of the GDD. It sets out what is new and different about the game idea or concept in no more than one or two sentences.

Activity

Devise a USP for an elevator pitch for a game idea. (If you can't think of a new game idea, base your pitch on an existing game which you know well.) You have only 30 seconds at most to engage your audience's attention and interest to explain:

- what is special about the game
- how it is different from everything that has come before
- why you think it will be a successful game.

Other elements of the GDD which are aimed at the client include:

- Target audience for the game – does the client already have a ready-made audience waiting for a game that will appeal to them?
- In-game purchases or monetisation – will the game make a profit or provide publicity for the client? Or will the game serve a different purpose such as educating, promoting wellbeing or raising money for a charity?

Once the client's attention is captured, the GDD should describe what the game looks, sounds or feels like and exactly how it is played. This is achieved through artwork and diagrams such as concept art and flowcharts showing gameplay, or through narrative text telling the story of the game. The client needs to know:

- why someone would want to play the game
- how the game is played
- what the player is trying to achieve in playing the game
- how the player knows when the game is finished or has been won.

If a GDD is created digitally, then sounds and moving images, reference art and concept art can be included to help show the intended style and content of the game.

Informing the developer

A game developer or programmer would also use a GDD once the production phase begins. You do not have to promote the game concept to the people who will code and create it, because they are more interested in the technical details of the game. The following table shows some of the technical details which the game developer would need to know. These may appear in the GDD as diagrams, flowcharts and tables rather than being described in prose text.

Table 7.5 Informing the developer of technical details

Game aspect	Developers might ask
Game structures, progression, scoring, timing and levels	• How does the game progress from start to finish? • How are levels unlocked or completed? • What scoring system is used? Points? Lives? Health? • Is there a time limit for completing parts of the game?
User interface, interactivity and controls	• How does the player communicate with the game? • What input controls are used? • What sort of feedback is given to measure progress or success?
Game appearance, game objects, concept art	• What visual style is used? 2D? 3D? VR? Cartoon style? Bitmap/pixel art style photorealistic?
Geometric parameters, game mechanics and core loops	• Is there a set progression route through the game or is it a free-roaming open-world? Does the game reset?

Whether a GDD concentrates more on persuading the client or informing the developer depends on the type of game being described. Character-driven, quest-style games might require more narrative and concept art, whereas skills-based, arcade-style games may instead include more programming details for the developer.

Activity

Further research: Read about the game development process here: **https://www.cgspectrum.com/blog/game-development-process**.

Make a note of key points about GDDs and game creation which could help you later when you design and create your own games.

Are there job roles explained in this article that appeal to you? Which type of role appeals most:

- designing or creating?
- pre-production, production or post-production?

Extension: Research online game beta testing.

2.2 Technical skills to create and/or edit and manage assets for use within digital games

Preparation of assets for use

Most computer games will include a range of asset types in order to create player engagement. This can include those shown in Table 7.6.

Table 7.6 Different types of asset

Asset type	Used for ...
Static images	Backgrounds, terrain and textures and tile sets to generate walls, mazes and rooms
Moving images	Characters and in-game objects, or animation or video in the form of cut-scenes telling the game's backstory
Text	Explaining game objectives and controls and displaying score, health, lives and inventory
Sounds	As background music, dialogue or sound effects and player feedback

All assets must be stored using file formats which are compatible with the game creation software. If the assets are created outside the game software, they may need to be converted using graphics, video or sound editing software or through the use of an online file converter such as Zamzar.

If you cannot see an asset file which you have saved when you browse to import it, it is very likely that its format is not supported. Often a list of supported file formats can be found within the software's help files or manual.

Hand drawn artwork can be digitised using a scanner or camera. Image editing software tools can then be used to crop, resize and alter the resolution of sourced and created images before they are imported into the game creation software as assets to be used as backgrounds, characters, props and so on. Video, animation and audio editing software should be used to prepare different asset types for use in the game. Asset preparation can include:

- Changing the length of a video to create a short cut scene introducing the backstory of a character or mission.
- Shortening a piece of music to create a looping background music soundtrack or motif.
- Formatting text to use a font, size, colour and emphasis which matches the visual style of the game.
- Animating static images to create moving characters or objects, for instance a 'walking' character for an arcade-style maze game.
- Flipping images horizontally or vertically so that a player character can change to face the direction it is moving.
- Duplicating or editing the extreme edges of static images to enable their use as scrolling backgrounds.

Synoptic links

You can find out more about the techniques used to edit animation and audio in Unit R096, and static images and video in Unit R098.

Before

After

Figure 7.6 Editing an image to create a scrolling background

File size and compression should be considered along with compatibility. It is no use having a beautifully drawn character if the animation file used to generate its movement is too big and the game lags or freezes. Animated GIFs are a good choice for making moving objects, players and characters in simple 2D arcade-style games.

Game creation software will often include built-in asset libraries with compatible graphics, audio and video. These limit the game designer's creativity but save time and usually mean that compatibility does not have to be tested. Some games engines also include simple graphics editors so you can create images and animations within the software. This is helpful because the graphics will not need to be scaled, resampled or converted and will be stored in the game engine's library ready for use.

Asset management within game creation software

Once you have sourced or created the assets for use in your game, they should be saved in the game creation software ready for use. It is good practice to name the assets with a prefix indicating their intended use in the game. For example:

- Spr_ for sprites
- Obj_ for objects
- Snd_ for sounds, and so on.

Individual images used to make up an animated object should be named using consecutive numbers, for instance 'tiger_run01', 'tiger_run02' to indicate their position in an animation loop.

It is also a good idea to separate different types of assets into folders, so that background images are in one folder whilst characters are in another and so on. Objects in a game often change appearance when inputs are received. For example, when a bullet hits a balloon, the balloon object's sprite changes from 'Spr_balloon' to 'Spr_burst_balloon'. Naming your assets appropriately and saving them in folders helps when coding actions and events like these, because it makes it easy to locate the file you want.

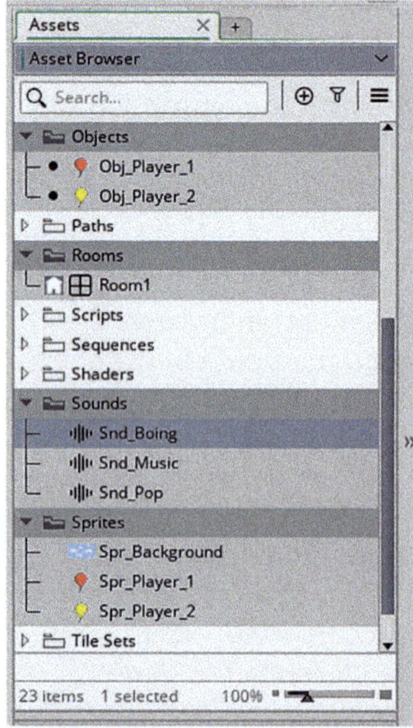

Figure 7.8 An example of asset management in game creation software

Activity

Using the example in Figure 7.7 as a guide, create an image of a city street which could be used as a scrolling background.

The style can be photorealistic or digitally drawn; and you could draw your own image or source or save a pre-existing one.

The left- and right-hand edges must match exactly in order for the scrolling background to be successful. You can test this by pasting three copies of the final image side by side.

Extension: Can you create a suitable scrolling background image for a vertically scrolling game?

2.3 Technical skills to create digital games

Techniques used to create digital games

The terminology used by different game creation applications can differ slightly. However, game creation follows roughly the same ten-step process, regardless of which game creation software you choose to use.

1 The game's 'world' (its room, stage, terrain or level) is created first and aspects like dimensions, boundaries and the speed or frame rate of the game are set up.

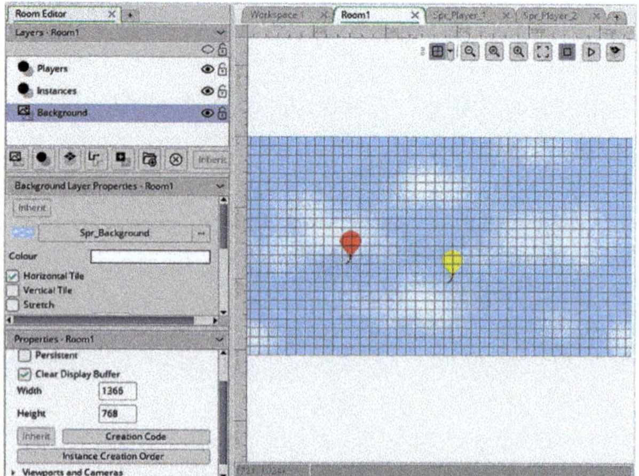

Figure 7.9 The game's 'world'

2 Geometric parameters such as gravity and scale are usually defined at the beginning of the creation process. This is important for platform-style games in particular but defining whether the background is static or scrolling is also important at this stage.

3 As each asset is added, parameters such as visibility and solidity are defined. For example, to create an invisible doorway at the end of a level which triggers unlocking the next part of the game, or to make boundaries solid so that characters cannot pass through them and exit the game area.

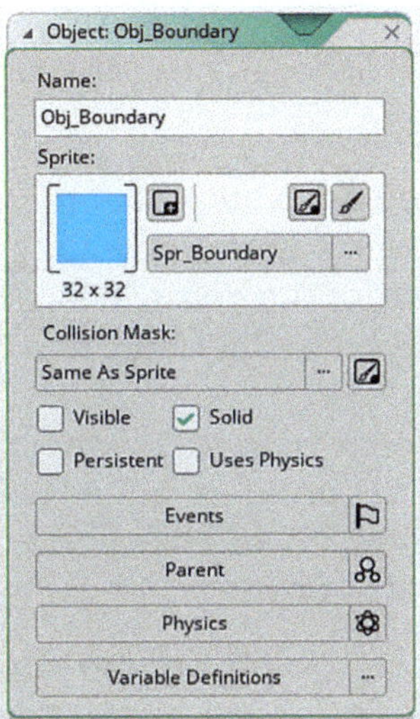

Figure 7.10 Defining asset parameters

4 Objects, NPCs and player characters are added and any automatic movements are set up. These are often defined in terms of input-output, cause and effect, or If-then relationships, and some software may refer to them as 'actions' and 'events'. For example, 'On creation/when spawned, start to move in direction X at a speed of Y'. Routines (sometimes called procedures, blocks or scripts) to detect collisions and control automatic actions and events are added. For example, 'If object A collides with the edge of the game area, then it will reverse direction and move away, and the sound Snd_bounce will play once'.

5 Routines to generate outputs based on player inputs or triggers are added. For example, when the left arrow is pressed, character Obj_player01 will move in direction X at a speed of Y.

6 Once the basic parameters and controls are set up, additional features such as scoring, timing, lives, health and so on can be added. Each feature should be tested on creation to ensure it works as expected before moving to the next addition. By the end of this stage of the process, the game will be playable and fully functioning, but it will lack some of the things which make it appeal to a target audience.

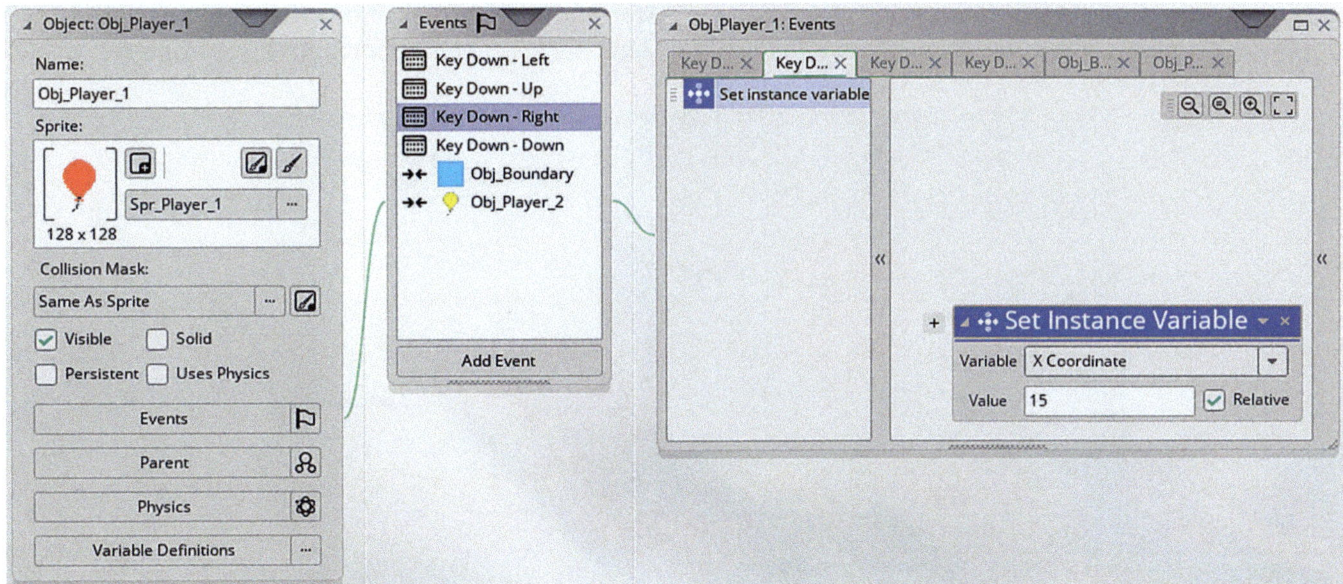

Figure 7.11 Routines to generate outputs

7 Elements which make the game more engaging are added. These include background music and sound effects. Swapping basic static character and object sprites for better-quality animated assets can be done at this stage if the game has so far been built as an MVP version.

Figure 7.12 Adding elements to make the game more engaging

8 When the gameplay coding is complete and working as expected, extra elements for the game start can be added. These may include the Game Start Splash Screen and Menu and customisation options, cut scenes, backstory and gameplay instructions.

9 The game ending can also be considered now. Features such as a high score table, Game Over/Restart screen, a cut scene leading into a new level or power-up options screens can all make a game more engaging to play and improve the target audience appeal.

10 Finally, if time allows, any elements of the game from the GDD which were desirable but not essential can be considered.

Tips for game creation

Iterative development

You should always remember to make changes to your game iteratively – that is, one at a time. Each significant change or addition should be the trigger to save the game with a new version name, and each significant change will be tested to make sure it works before moving on to the next phase of development. That way, any unsuccessful changes can be reverted by rolling back the game to a previous version.

Coding cheats and shortcuts

Game developers will often add shortcuts or cheats into their code, to allow them to jump straight to a particular part of the game. For example, if you are testing Level 3, you don't want to have to play all the way through Levels 1 and 2 to get to the part you need to test. Adding a short cut such as 'If Key N is pressed, go to Next level', or 'If 3 is pressed, add 300 relative points to the score' can save a lot of time.

In a real-world context, these cheats are obviously removed before the game is released, but for the purposes of making a game for your assignment, it is helpful to leave the cheats in place. Make sure your game documentation tells an assessor what actions the relevant shortcut keys complete.

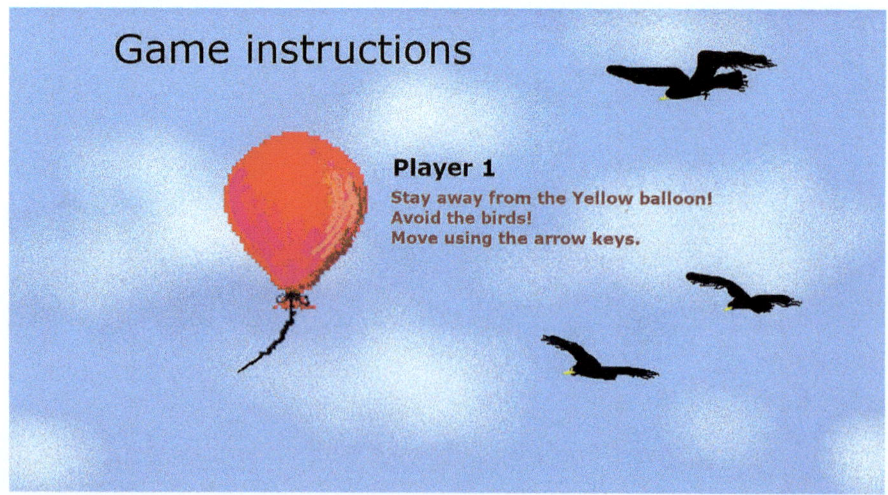

Figure 7.13 Adding extra elements for the game start

Activity

The MVP of Frogger is to move the player character from the bottom of the playing screen to the top whilst avoiding obstacles. Test this statement by trying out an early version here: **http://bbcmicro.co.uk/game.php?id=1934**.

Then create a simple game with the same MVP using game creation software of your choice.

2.4 Techniques to save and export digital games

Saving digital games during creation

Whilst you are creating your game, you will obviously need to save it. Most games creation software will save files using its own file format and file extension, for example UNITY3D, BLEND or YYP, and this is known as the native or proprietary format. Saving your game in this way means that you can re-open, edit and change the game until it is finished. But you will not be able to play the game outside the creation software as a standalone file, so it cannot be used for the final product.

If something goes wrong or you wish to amend your idea, you may need to be able to roll back the changes to restore the file to an earlier state. This is where version control is important. Before you make any significant changes to your game, choose 'Save As' or its equivalent, and rename the file. You can use numbers or dates in the file name to help you organise the versions, or you can change the file name to describe the changes made. For example, Game v1.0, Game v 1.2, or Game_March, Game_April, or Game_Level2_Added, Game_Score_Added and so on. The version naming system should make sense to the game developer. In a vocational or real-world context, a developer may be working on more than one game or project at once, so using folders to separate different clients' work is important. And choosing appropriate file names is vital; you don't want to offend your client by using names which are unsuitable!

Once you have made a significant change or addition to your game, you should test it before moving on to the next part of the work or rolling back the changes if they were unsuccessful. This is known as iterative working and it is a good idea because it means you test one thing at a time. If you leave all your testing until the game is finished, you won't know what causes a particular test to fail. It is much easier to fix each problem as it occurs, and this also means you should have a game which is always fully functioning, even if it does not yet include every part of the planned content. So, if you run out of time you can still deliver a playable game to your client.

Exporting finished digital games

When your game is finished, you should save a final master file using the native file format. This ensures you always have a game to return to and edit, in case your client decides to commission further work using the same project. You would not give the master file to the client in most cases, to protect your future income. In order for your client to try out or use the final game, you would export it, using a file type which is compatible with the type of device or platform the client requested.

Some games creation software will generate games as HTML or EXE files and these will not require any specialist software in order to run the game. Other applications may have a free-to-download reader which enables the game to be run without installing the full application or software package. For the purposes of your assignment portfolio, you will need to export your game using a suitable format. You could provide a simple explanation of how to load and open the game so someone else can play it, for example to assess it. This would be especially important if you choose to use an emulator.

Synoptic link

Properties and formats of media files is further discussed in Unit R093, Section 4.2.

Activity

Find out the native file format used by any game creation software available to you at school and at home. Find out how to export a completed game, and make a note of which file formats you can select during this process.

Which platforms or devices can load and play these games? Record this information for use when you design your own games.

Activity

How would you go about publishing a digital game on the Amazon or Google Play store for Android smartphones? Read about the process here: **https://help.yoyogames.com/hc/en-us/articles/115001624867-Android-Compiling-Your-App**.

- Why might developers choose to publish via the Google Play store?
- What are the disadvantages of doing this?
- What alternative publishing and distribution channels might an independent game developer choose?

Assignment practice

Task 2: Make a playable game

Time needed: approx. 1 hour

Create a Minimum Viable Product (MVP) version of the game set out in this Game Design Document:

Game Design Document

Objective: Escape/strategy. Player 1 chases Player 2, who tries to avoid being caught.

Game environment: A top-down, 2D maze which is an underground dungeon where the dragon's hoard is kept.

Concept art: Player 1 will be a Red Dragon. The MVP player is represented by a Red Square. Player 2 will be a Blue Wizard. The MVP player is represented as a Blue Circle. The MVP maze is made up of black walls on a yellow background.

Platform/peripherals: The game will be played on a desktop computer or laptop using a keyboard for input controls.

Gameplay: There are two players. Player 1 moves using WASD keys, Player 2 moves using arrow keys.

Timing: The game has a 30 second timer. If Player 2 avoids capture for 30 seconds, Player 2 wins. If Player 1 catches (makes contact with) Player 2, the game ends and Player 1 wins.

Score: One-hit death for Player 2.

Topic area 3 Review digital games

Getting started

Look at the job profile of a computer games tester here: **https://nationalcareers.service.gov.uk/job-profiles/computer-games-tester**

- Make a note of the skills and knowledge needed for the role.

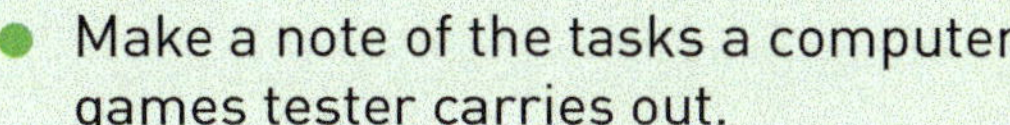

- Make a note of the tasks a computer games tester carries out.
- Would this job role interest you?
- What is the most attractive part of this job role to you? Why is this?
- What is the least attractive part? Why?

3.1 Techniques to test/check and review digital games

Techniques to test/check the technical properties of digital games

Testing and checking a digital game in this unit can be broken down into two main parts:

- testing functionality of the game
- checking how successfully the Game Design Document explains the concept of the game and meets the client requirements.

These two tasks are quite different, and it is helpful to keep them separate from each other.

It is a good idea to test functionality of the game at regular points during the creation process. This is called iterative testing, and it means that bugs and glitches can be resolved as you go along. If you make the entire game before testing and discovering something doesn't work as expected, you won't know which instruction or variable caused the problem. You should therefore use version control to give a different name to the game each time a significant change is made, so that you can easily undo or roll back any changes which were unsuccessful.

Methods of checking and testing

Test plan

Functionality testing can be recorded using a test plan (sometimes referred to as a test log). This is generally set out in a table and lists each aspect being tested, how it is tested, the expected and actual results and provides space to record whether changes or fixes are required, along with somewhere to record the results of retests. Test plans don't need to include large amounts of text or great detail unless any fixes are to be carried out by someone other than the tester.

Types of test data

Examples of functionality tests would include:

- **Normal tests**: These involve playing the game using the planned controls, rules and behaviours.
- **Extreme tests**: Behaviours and actions at the extreme limits of what the game allows are used. For example, checking that a 60 second timer allows you to play up to 59.9 seconds but not 61 seconds. Or testing whether all three lives work.

Key terms

Normal test data Data which should be accepted by a system or programme, for example 5 should be accepted if the range is 1–10.

Extreme test data Data which should be accepted by a system and is at the boundary of what is allowed, for example 10 would be extreme if the range is 1–10.

Exceptional test data Data which should not be accepted by a system but should trigger feedback to the user, for example 11 would be exceptional if the range is 1–10. Different data types would also be exceptional, for example A if the range is 1–10.

- **Exceptional tests**: These are inputs and actions inputs which the game should not allow. For example, using multiple jumps to overcome gravity or trying to make a player exit the boundaries of the game room/screen without consequence.

Activity

You can look for more in-depth information on types of testing used in software design and development using BBC Bitesize as a starting point.

Elements of digital games to test/check

Test input or behaviours

Game developers use game testers to work through all the inputs and actions in a game. Testers will try to cheat or break the game as well as testing that all the intended rules and parameters work as expected. This job role suits a methodical person with a good eye for detail, and it can be a great way for gamers to try out new games before they are made available to the public.

Tip: If you add cheats and shortcuts to your game whilst creating it, don't forget to remove or disable these before exporting the final game!

Functionality tests

In order to fully test a game's functionality, the tests in Table 7.7 must all be considered.

The functionality testing and input and behaviour testing will result in a list of problems, glitches or bugs. Some of these will need to be fixed straight away or the game will not be playable. It is a good idea to prioritise fixing errors and correcting programming (for example, a broken link to unlock the next level) over making changes which merely improve the visual impact or audio quality (for example, making a better quality cut scene or game splash screen). That way, if you run out of time, the most important errors will have been resolved and you will still have a functioning game to deliver to the client.

Table 7.7 Functionality tests

Functionality test	Examples of what is tested
Navigation features	• Can the player move in the expected directions? • Do the correct screens, levels, power-ups etc unlock as planned? • Does the game's splash or load screen make it clear how to enter the game and how to play?
Interactive features	• Is the player able to select, click on, type, manipulate and respond to in-game props and characters as planned? • In a multiplayer game, can players interact with each other to allow cooperative play?
Inputs and outputs	• Do all the keyboard, mouse, console, controller and VR inputs produce the correct outputs as planned? (For example, if I click space, does the player character jump?) • Do all outputs work as expected? (For example, when I shoot, does the bullet sound effect play and then stop? Does the bullet prop appear? Does it destroy itself and the object it collides with?)
Scoring, timing, game start and game end	• Does the game score increase and decrease depending on inputs and outputs as planned? • Does the game start work as expected? • Do timers work as planned? (For example, the level restarts after 30 seconds.) • Does the game end work as planned? (For example, the game reloads, or the high score table is shown, or a level up cut scene appears.)
Object movement	• Do all in-game objects including players move at the correct speed? • Do in-game objects move in the intended direction/s? • Do objects stop on collision with a solid object or game screen boundary? • Are static objects static?
Geometric parameters	• Do in-game objects obey the rules of speed and gravity as planned? • Does the global game/level work at the correct speed? (For example, 30 frames per second) • Do objects remain within the game screen boundaries? • Are visible objects shown? • Are solid objects solid?

Test your knowledge

1 Which of these items check a game against the client needs and which are functionality tests?
- Game ends after third hit.
- Colour scheme matches the client's visual identity.
- Game loads within three seconds of being opened.
- In-game micro purchases work as expected.
- Game's main character presents a positive role model for the target audience.

Techniques to review the fitness for purpose of a Game Design Document

The second part of the review process in this unit concerns checking whether the Game Design Document is fit for purpose.

The GDD's purpose is to explain and promote an idea for a game to the client. In order to do this successfully, it should:

- be set out clearly
- be easy to understand
- include suitably detailed artwork or description to show what the game will look and sound like
- outline all the key elements of the game: the genre, objectives, gameplay, and so on
- explain exactly how the game will be played
- explain how and why the game is original
- explain how and why the game will appeal to the target audience (the player).

It is likely that some of the above elements will have been created more successfully than others in the GDD. Understanding which parts lack fitness for purpose is important, because otherwise the client may reject the game idea altogether. It may help when checking the GDD to put yourself in the position of a Dragons' Den entrepreneur. Does the GDD stand out and capture attention? Does it seem original and different? If not, it requires improvements or further developments.

To review the GDD, take each section in turn and read it carefully as if you were seeing it for the first time. If you knew nothing about the game before you read the GDD, would you understand it? The review process will reveal strengths – if the GDD does the things in the bulleted list above, then it is fit for purpose. However, your review might reveal weaknesses such as:

- Parts of the overall concept which are under-developed, poorly described or missed out altogether.
- Poor choice of language to promote the game concept effectively for the client. If the game comes across as dull the client is unlikely to be impressed. You should describe the concept in an exciting and engaging way to persuade the client to commission the game.
- Typographical errors in the text which can appear unprofessional. Your GDD should suggest that you have thought of everything and leaving spelling and grammatical mistakes in the document creates a poor impression.
- Poor choice of design style for the GDD. As explained earlier in this chapter, if you already know who the client is, then using a colour palette, font and style which match the client's brand or visual identity can be helpful. If you don't know what the client's design style is then the GDD should avoid quirky fonts and extreme colour schemes which might be off-putting to the client.
- The concept itself may be weak. The final game is only as good as its idea – is the game concept original and creative, or derivative and cliched?
- The GDD might assume too much knowledge. If a freelance game designer uses the GDD to pitch an idea with the hope of getting it commissioned, then the GDD will be the first the potential client sees of the game concept. When reviewing the GDD you need to do so objectively, to make sure all the absolute basics of the concept, objectives and visual style are included.

The second audience or user for a GDD is the game's programmer or developer. When checking fitness for purpose, you should therefore consider whether the technical aspects of the game have been explained in enough detail for a developer to know how to code them.

Activity

Read through the GDD for a new version of Splatoon here: **https://www.artstation.com/artwork/k4PeYz.**

Discuss with a partner, or make notes to record the positive and negative aspects of this GDD:

- for the client
- for the game developer.

3.2 Improvements and further developments

Digital game constraints

The process of checking and testing a digital game will result in a list of things which are not yet quite right. But there will be constraints which mean that the final game may not be able to be perfected:

- Time: A game developer is likely to have a deadline to work to and may not have enough time to complete all the improvements.
- Resources: There may be some aspects of the game which need different resources, hardware or software. For example, the concept art may have specified detailed 3D graphics. To do this, an extensive range of resources including motion capture suits, performers, studio space with greenscreen facilities and the software to process and render the mocap footage would all be required. If such resources were unavailable, the game might have had to be created using 2D graphics instead.
- Legislation: Improvements might rely on using existing characters or content from other games, films or franchises. These would be covered by legislation such as copyright or trademark. The owner of the work may refuse permission for their use, or there may not be enough money in the budget to pay for the necessary licences or permissions.
- Skills: There may be parts of the game which could be improved but the developer does not have the skills to code them. Paying someone else to make these improvements could be too costly or time-consuming and result in missing the game's deadline for release.

Digital game improvements

Some of the improvements will be essential and it is worth setting aside a reasonable amount of time to fix these bugs and glitches. Generally, the types of errors high on a priority list for improvements would be those that improve:

- gameplay: this could include errors as important as the game not loading or not playing
- mechanics: this could include errors such as spawning a player on top of a trap which instantly ends the game
- geometric parameters: this could include errors such as a glitch which allows the player to leave the game screen.

Some aspects of the game are known as aesthetics. Aesthetics are important to the client because they help sell the game and represent the brand, title or publisher. For example, improving the visuals or the quality of the in-game audio would increase player engagement and make for a better gameplay experience. But there is no point in having a game which looks and sounds stunning, if it can't actually be played, so aesthetics tend to be lower down the list of priorities for improvements.

Finally, testing and checking the game may reveal the need for changes to the level of difficulty. If the game is too easy it is unlikely to hold the player's attention for long. But if it is too difficult, the player may not engage with the game at all. As a rough guide, make sure the game is accessible to the least-skilled type of player in the target audience group. But if it is too easy for the most skilled player type, consider ways that the difficulty can increase as the player progresses through the game. This might be through:

- multiple levels
- increasing the number of enemies or challenges
- decreasing the time allowed to complete part of the game, and so on.

Making the game easier is likely to be a higher priority than making it more challenging and will also take less time and resources. The GDD is a good place to explain possible improvements to the level of challenge or difficulty, if there is not enough time or insufficient resources to make the improvements.

Further development opportunities for digital games

Improvements are changes which fix problems and make what is already in the GDD or game better. Development opportunities are things which are not currently included but could be added in future to create a more successful product. Because this unit involves both designing and creating a game, there will be many opportunities for further developments to the Game Design Document, the game itself or both.

Developments to the Game Design Document

Because the design proposal and Game Design Document are used by both the client and the game creator, there are many aspects to consider when choosing developments. See Table 7.8.

Table 7.8 Developments to the Game Design Document

Developments for the client	Developments for the game creator/developer/programmer
Explain the narrative or character backstory in more depth	Add geometric parameters such as speed, gravity, room speed or frame rate
Include a variety of landscapes and settings for different levels to show the game world better	Add details of game flow such as how the next level is triggered or the sequence of levels or challenges
Show how the scoring system is displayed on screen	State how assets are used within the game, for example, changing an object's sprite when an event or action takes place

It is also worth considering the wider role of the GDD when planning developments. The GDD is a planning tool, but it is also used during the production phase to keep the game creation process on track. If the GDD is to be used as a development log during the production phase, you could see if there is scope to develop it by including space to record changes to the design or when each part has been created and tested. Numbering or labelling each section or element of the GDD can allow cross referencing against the test plan and a separate development log if needed.

Developments to the digital game

The finished game is also likely to have scope for further developments. For example:

- Narrative or objectives: It may be that only one level or mission has been created, so developments could involve making the rest of the planned elements of the game.
- Appearance and style: The game may have been generated using an MVP, meaning aspects such as the sprites, objects and game world or terrain need to be added to make the game look pleasing to the player.
- Player feedback/outputs: Audio elements such as feedback sounds and background music may not have been added but would enhance the game and make it more engaging.
- Cut scenes could be added to provide context to the gameplay.

Development ideas might be even more ambitious, if you had expanded resources, software, budget and skills. Potential developments might include:

- A slightly different version of the game, played using another platform, console or device, for example using VR or haptic feedback to enhance the player experience.
- A multiplayer or online version of the game as a logical improvement or development, building on the version which has already been created.
- Ways to monetise the game by including micro-purchases or creating downloadable content or expansion packs, making it more attractive and profitable for the client.
- A second game instalment, with new challenges or missions which would increase the difficulty and challenge of the game to keep players engaged.

Describing these developments to the client clearly and comprehensively is a good way to secure further work. If the client is happy with the results so far, then it is more likely that the same designer of developer will be commissioned to work on future developments. This is another important reason for keeping control of the stored assets and master version of the game. Without these, the client would find it difficult to develop the game further and again this makes it more likely that the same developer will be commissioned to work on developments. Another option is for the developer to sell the original assets (or sell or licence the rights to use them) and/or the entire game code to the client.

Activity

Suggest any improvements or further developments which could be made to the GDD for the new version of Splatoon **https://www.artstation.com/artwork/k4PeYz** to make it more useful to the game developer or more commercially attractive to the client or an investor.

Assignment practice

Task 3: Test/check and review

Part 1

Time needed: approx. 1 hour

An MVP version of the game in this Game Design Document has been created and tested.

Copy and complete the following test table by filling in the four empty columns.

- Work out which test results mean something needs to be changed or fixed.
- Prioritise the changes and fixes by numbering them in the order most to least important.
- Which failed tests are essential to correct and which are only desirable? Give reasons for your choice of priorities.

Test	Result	Are changes needed? Yes/No	Describe change required	Priority/ importance (number)	Reason for priority
Player 1 is a red square	Pass				
Player 2 is a blue circle	Player is a blue square				
Player 1 red square moves using WASD keys	Pass				
Player 2 blue circle moves using arrow keys	Up and down arrow are the wrong way around. Pressing up arrow moves player down, and pressing down arrow moved the player up				
Maze walls are black and solid	Walls are black. Player 2 goes through the walls though, and can disappear off the edge of the game screen				
Game has 30 second timer	Timer counts down but game does not end when it reaches 0, it just goes into minus numbers				
If Player 2 avoids capture for 30 seconds, Player 2 wins	If Player 2 avoids capture, nothing happens				
If Player 1 catches Player 2, the game ends and Player 1 wins	If Player 1 catches Player 2, the game restarts. Nothing happens to tell the players who won or why the game restarted				

Part 2

Time needed: approx. 1 hour

The following is the first draft of a Game Design Document. Read it through carefully, then:

- Explain how suitable this draft is to present to the client.
- Explain how suitable it is for the game developer/creator to use when making the game.
- Explain what you would add or change to improve this GDD (without changing the overall game concept) to make it more suitable for the client and game developer/creator.

Game Design Document

Objective: Escape/strategy. Player 1 chases Player 2, who tries to avoid being caught.

Game environment: A top-down, 2D maze which is an underground dungeon where the dragon's hoard is kept.

Concept art: Player 1 will be a Red Dragon. The MVP player is represented by a Red Square. Player 2 will be a Blue Wizard. The MVP player is represented as a Blue Circle. The MVP maze is made up of black walls on a yellow background.

Platform/peripherals: The game will be played on a desktop computer or laptop using a keyboard for input controls.

Gameplay: There are two players. Player 1 moves using WASD keys, Player 2 moves using arrow keys.

Timing: The game has a 30 second timer. If Player 2 avoids capture for 30 seconds, Player 2 wins. If Player 1 catches (makes contact with) Player 2, the game ends and Player 1 wins.

Score: One-hit death for Player 2.

Glossary

3D Three-dimensional video (most films are made in 2D).

4K/8K Very high-resolution video formats.

Aesthetic How something looks, its appearance.

Antagonist One of the main characters in a story, often the villain.

Anthropomorphism Applying human physical and non-physical characteristics to non-human items such as inanimate objects or animals.

Aperture The size of the opening in a lens that lets light pass through to the camera sensor.

Armature Another name for the skeleton or support structure for a real or computer generated model used in animation.

ASA Advertising Standards Authority.

Assets The different images collected that will be used to make the final product.

Batch conversion Altering properties such as compression settings of several image files at the same time.

Branch Line or arrow linking the central title, nodes and sub-nodes to show connections.

CGI Computer generated imagery.

Cliff hanger A story ending which leaves the reader in suspense.

Codec Software which compresses and optimises (audio) data when saving a file.

Composition (photography) The way that a photograph is framed to be suitable and appealing for the viewer.

Concept An idea for something which has not yet been created.

Concept art (game) Sketches, images or drawings showing exactly how characters, objects and terrain will look in a game.

Constraints Things that restrict the way a task can be carried out.

Continuity Consistency from shot to shot and from scene to scene.

Conventions Established ways of doing something within a type of product.

Copyright A form of protection for the originator of creative work, see Intellectual property.

Cut (video) To trim or remove a piece of video footage from the start or end of a clip.

Demographics Study of target audience characteristics.

Depth of field The range of distances from the camera that are in sharp focus.

Derivative Imitating or based on another source such as the work of another artist or designer or a product which already exists.

Dialogue The words spoken by a character, narrator or voiceover artist.

Diegetic (ambient) Sounds which are part of the action and can be heard by the characters in a scene. For example, dialogue and ambient noise.

Digital graphic A static image-based graphic that is created digitally using a software application.

DPI Dots per inch (where a print product needs typically 300 and a web graphic 72).

Ethos A set of ideals or characteristics that are followed by a group of people.

Exceptional test data Data which should not be accepted by a system but should trigger feedback to the user, for example 11 would be exceptional if the range is 1–10. Different data types would also be exceptional, for example A if the range is 1–10.

Export The process of changing the image properties and saving a file for use by the client in a suitable file format. This should be a format that is not specific to your image editing software. Examples would be JPG, PNG or PDF.

Extreme test data Data which should be accepted by a system and is at the boundary of what is allowed, for example 10 would be extreme if the range is 1–10.

Focal point The place in a panel where the creator wants the reader's eye to be focused.

Foley Named after sound-effects artist Jack Foley. The process of recording everyday sound effects to enhance audio quality and support visual actions.

Gain The input level or tone of a sound.

Game Design Document (GDD) A pre-production planning resource outlining all the details of the proposed game.

Game editor A set of tools for use when modifying elements within a particular game.

Game engine An application or package containing a collection of tools and resources for making games.

Gantt chart A type of horizontal bar chart used to plan a project schedule (what needs to be done and when). It is a good way to monitor whether a project is within its deadlines, what work has been completed and what is still to be done.

GDPR General Data Protection Regulation

Genre A way of describing the theme or style of creative work, for example horror or romance.

Haptic Relating to the sense of touch, for example as vibrations and force feedback in controllers and peripheral devices.

Hazard Something that could result in injury or harm to people or equipment.

Impact The effect or influence on the viewer.

Integrated Development Environment (IDE) A collection of tools such as a code editor, runtime environment, library and debugger used to create software.

Intellectual property Something unique that is created or developed in a person's mind, which can be an idea, story, game, artistic work, symbol or invention. This can be protected for the creative person's own benefit, through copyright, trademarks or patents.

Interactive Something which allows the user to be involved in the process of watching or listening. This could involve user input such as clicking, typing or speaking to interact with the media.

Interface The system that allows the user to interact with the product.

Intuitive Something that feels natural and instinctive to the user.

ISO A camera setting that determines the sensitivity to light levels.

Lens focal length A feature of the lens that determines the magnification or angle of view (how much of the scene is seen in the frame).

Logo A small graphical image that is used to represent an organisation or brand.

Location recce Short for reconnaissance. A visit to a location to check its suitability and requirements for producing media.

Massively multiplayer online (MMO) Games played over the internet by many players at once, either collaboratively or competing against each other. Often expanded to include MMORPG – Massively multiplayer online role-playing game.

Meaning What is being communicated indirectly.

Minimum viable product (MVP) The minimum features a game needs to keep player's engagement and interest.

Musical Instrument Digital Interface (MIDI) Synthesised music created using MIDI sequences has a distinctive 'computerised' sound as it tends to lack expression. But it can convey mood. Arcade-style games often use cheerful, fast-paced synthesised music.

Native file format The file format that the software saves into automatically.

Node Main idea leading off from the central title or theme 'hub' in a mind map.

Non-diegetic Sound that is outside the action captured on film and not heard by characters in a scene. For example, background music, narration and voiceover.

Non-player character (NPC) A character which appears in the game but is not controlled by the player/s. NPCs can be opponents to work against, friendly characters which the gamer helps or used to advance the plot or storyline of a game.

Normal test data Data which should be accepted by a system or programme, for example 5 should be accepted if the range is 1–10.

NURBS A method used to create curves in digital graphics.

Ofcom UK Regulator for communications services.

Onion skinning Overlaying frames so that the previous frame's positioning can be seen as a 'ghost' image. This allows the animator to line up objects precisely when setting up the next frame.

Onomatopoeia A word that sounds like the thing it is describing. For example, 'Slurp'

Optimisation Balancing compression, sample rate and file size to maintain the best possible quality audio.

Pan Camera movement from side to side.

Panel A container used to contain one scene in a comic strip.

Photography The art of how to capture light. It is made up from the direction, source, quality and strength.

Pixel The smallest part of a digital image, each with a unique colour.

Platform A method for sharing media content.

Podcast A digital audio file made available online. Often created as a series and involving spoken dialogue, interviews and conversation.

PPI Pixels per inch (technically the correct way to state the resolution of a digital graphic but otherwise the same as DPI).

Primary sources Those from which you obtain information 'first-hand' from an original source and are typically more reliable.

Protagonist One of the main characters in a story, often the hero.

Qualitative A measurement based on its quality, such as the quality of a drawing.

Quantitative A measurement based on a quantity, such as the number of sweets in a packet.

Recce See Location recce

Reference art (game) Images from existing games or other products to indicate what style or type of graphics will be used in a game.

Resolution A property of an image that states how many dots per inch are present. (Different to the resolution of a story.)

Rigging A virtual skeleton used to create shapes for characters and objects in 3D animation.

Risk The chance that the hazard will actually cause injury or harm.

Risk assessments The process of identifying what risks exist, documenting the results.

Role-playing game (RPG) Games where the player takes on a character. Most often based on fantasy worlds but can also be based on real life roles such as armed services, farming simulation.

Roll back Undo changes by returning a file to an earlier state or previous version.

Rostrum camera A camera which is mounted or fixed in position to a bench or platform (a rostrum) to enable continuity between frames in hand drawn and stop motion animation.

Safe working practices A way of working safely when a risk or hazard has been identified.

Save The process of storing your master file in the image editing software at high resolution in its proprietary format. In Adobe Photoshop, this will be a PSD file.

Secondary sources Those where the information is obtained 'second-hand' or where somebody else has already put their own interpretation on the original information. The accuracy of information might need to be checked when using secondary sources.

Segmentation Splitting a target audience into different categories.

SFX Special effects or sound effects.

Shutter speed The duration that the shutter is open for the photograph to be recorded.

Sourcing Locating items such as assets for your work, which you did not create.

Split (video) To separate out a video clip into two different assets so that they can be used at different places on the timeline.

Stage directions Descriptions of what happens in a scene and how dialogue is said (tone of voice).

Stereotypes An assumption made about people who are part of a particular demographic.

Sting A short music clip used to introduce, link or end sections in an audio or audio-visual production such as a TV programme or radio commercial.

Story flow The path of the story from the beginning, to the middle, to the end.

Sub-node More detailed idea linked to the content of a node.

Symbolic codes What something represents.

Synchronisation Adjusting or aligning the timing of more than one thing so they match.

Technical codes The use of equipment or techniques in specific ways.

Tilt Camera movement up and down.

Track/dolly When moving the camera position, with the camera attached to a moving dolly that is placed on a fixed track.

Trope A generalisation of how a character with a particular trait might look.

Tween Short for 'in betweening', the process of filling in frames to generate movement in between key frames.

Typography The style and arrangement of letters in a particular way to make sure that it can be read and fits the style of the document it is used in.

Unique selling point (USP) What makes an item different from other products and therefore desirable.

VFX Visual effects.

Virtual camera A function of software which works out how objects will appear if captured from a specific angle or viewpoint within the scene or 'stage'.

Viseme The visual shape made by the mouth, lips and tongue when creating a speech sound (phoneme) such as 'Sh' or 'B'.

Visual identity A combination of elements that summarise a business or organisation, which can be recognised within the market.

Volume The output level or loudness of a sound.

White balance A camera setting that compensates for different types of lighting to make sure the colours are correct.

Wire frame A plan using basic lines and shapes to show where items would be placed in a design.

Workflow The order that tasks and activities are completed in, including which activities must be finished before others can begin and which can be completed at the same time as each other. Good workflow means that a project runs smoothly and efficiently without wasting time.

Written codes The language that is used, whether printed or spoken.

Zoom in/out Camera change to a closer or longer distance shot.

Acknowledgements

Photo credits

R093 p. 1 © Vegefox.com/stock.adobe.com; **fig. 1.1** © Stuart Miles/stock.adobe.com; **fig. 1.2** © Drobot Dean/stock.adobe.com; **fig. 1.3** *l* © Irina Strelnikova/stock.adobe.com, *r* © Pagina/stock.adobe.com; **fig. 1.4** © Leszekglasner/stock.adobe.com; **fig. 1.5** © leungchopan/stock.adobe.com; **fig. 1.6** © Petr Vaclavek/stock.adobe.com; **fig. 1.7** © Wavebreak Media/stock.adobe.com; **fig. 1.10** © ojtisi/stock.adobe.com; **fig. 1.11** © Kevin Wells; **fig. 1.12** © Chaosamran_Studio/stock.adobe.com; **fig. 1.13** © Kevin Wells; **fig. 1.14** © Dmitry/stock.adobe.com; **fig. 1.16** © Kevin Wells; **fig. 1.17** © sakurra/stock.adobe.com; **R094 p. 50** © Pixel-Shot/stock.adobe.com; **fig. 2.2-2.8** © Kevin Wells; **fig. 2.11-2.12** © Kevin Wells; **fig. 2.22** © Kevin Wells; **fig. 2.24-2.26** © Kevin Wells; **R095 p 80** © James Thew/stock.adobe.com; **fig. 3.1** © Idey/stock.adobe.com; **fig. 3.2** © Elenabsl/stock.adobe.com; **fig. 3.3** Delesign.com; **fig. 3.4** © Jemastock/stock.adobe.com; **fig. 3.5** © Bitter/stock.adobe.com; **fig. 3.7** © K3Star/stock.adobe.com; **fig. 3.9** © Gstudio/stock.adobe.com; **fig. 3.10** © Polonio Video/stock.adobe.com; **fig. 3.15** *l* © Yayasya/stock.adobe.com, *r* © BNA Photographic/Alamy Stock Photo; **fig. 3.16** © Jirawatp/stock.adobe.com; **fig. 3.17** © Malchev/stock.adobe.com; **p. 107** © DM7/stock.adobe.com; **R096 p. 108** © Paul/stock.adobe.com; **fig. 4.2** © Stephan Rumpf/Süddeutsche Zeitung Photo/Alamy Stock Photo; **fig. 4.3** © Flauma/Shutterstock.com; **fig. 4.4** © Iryna Imago/Shutterstock.com; **fig 4.5** © Earl Theisen Collection/Archive Photos/Getty Images; **fig. 4.6** © Lagunov/stock.adobe.com; **fig. 4.7** © Gorodenkoff/stock.adobe.com; **fig. 4.8** © Luciana C. Funes D/stock.adobe.com; **fig. 4.9** © General Photographic Agency/Hulton Archive/Getty Images; **fig. 4.10** © Ben Stansall/AFP/Getty Images; **fig. 4.11** *l* © Roman Fernati/stock.adobe.com, *m* © Fototocam/stock.adobe.com, *r* © TheVectorminator/stock.adobe.com; **fig. 4.12** *l* © Chote26/stock.adobe.com, *m* © Kevin/stock.adobe.com, *r* © Dumitru/stock.adobe.com; **R097 p. 142** © Scharfsinn86/stock.adobe.com; **fig. 5.1** © Leka/stock.adobe.com; **fig. 5.2** © Jakub Krechowicz/stock.adobe.com; **fig. 5.6** © Smolaw11/stock.adobe.com; **fig. 5.10** *l* © Vichai viriyathanaporn/Alamy Stock Photo, *r* © Shuang Li/Shutterstock.com; **R098 p. 173** © Kevin Wells; **fig. 6.1-6.6** © Kevin Wells; **fig. 6.7** © Patryk Kosmider/stock.adobe.com; **fig. 6.8-6.15** © Kevin Wells; **fig. 6.17-6.18** © Kevin Wells; **fig. 6.20-6.23** © Kevin Wells; **R099 p. 210** © Cddesign.co/stock.adobe.com; **fig 7.1** © Gorodenkoff/stock.adobe.com; **fig. 7.2** © Chris J. Ratcliffe/Bloomberg/Getty Images; **fig. 7.3** *l* © Tarasov_vl/stock.adobe.com, *m* © Marco/stock.adobe.com, *r* © Mehaniq41/stock.adobe.com; **fig. 7.5** *wordcloud* © Eoseye/stock.adobe.com, *inventory* © Persetan/stock.adobe.com, *character* © J. Florencio/stock.adobe.com, *terrain* © Klyaksun/stock.adobe.com, *alligator* © 9'63 Creation/stock.adobe.com; **fig. 7.6** © Black Spring/stock.adobe.com

Index